THE FLESH OF THE MATTER

The Flesh of the Matter

A Critical Forum on *Hortense Spillers*

Edited by Margo Natalie Crawford
and C. Riley Snorton

VANDERBILT UNIVERSITY PRESS

Nashville, Tennessee

Copyright 2024 Vanderbilt University Press
All rights reserved
First printing 2024

Fred Moten's essay is a revised and expanded version of his essay "Feast for the Senses," which appeared in the publication *Frank Stewart's Nexus: An American Photographer's Journey 1960s to the Present*, published by Rizzoli Electa in 2023. Copyright © The Telfair Museums.

The archival fragments included in this volume are included courtesy of the Hortense J. Spillers papers, MS.2019.013, Pembroke Center Archives, John Hay Library, Brown University.

Library of Congress Cataloging-in-Publication Data

Names: Crawford, Margo Natalie, 1969- editor. | Snorton, C. Riley, editor.
Title: The flesh of the matter : a critical forum on Hortense Spillers / edited by Margo Natalie Crawford and C. Riley Snorton.
Description: Nashville, Tennessee : Vanderbilt University Press, 2024. | Includes bibliographical references and index.
Identifiers: LCCN 2024016845 (print) | LCCN 2024016846 (ebook) | ISBN 9780826507495 (paperback) | ISBN 9780826507501 (hardcover) | ISBN 9780826507518 (epub) | ISBN 9780826507525 (pdf)
Subjects: LCSH: Spillers, Hortense J.--Criticism and interpretation. | Spillers, Hortense J.--Influence.
Classification: LCC PN75.S64 F58 2024 (print) | LCC PN75.S64 (ebook) | DDC 801/.95092--dc23/eng/20240730
LC record available at https://lccn.loc.gov/2024016845
LC ebook record available at https://lccn.loc.gov/2024016846

Front cover image:
Simone Leigh, *Georgia Mae*, 2017
Salt-glazed stoneware, porcelain, and resin
34¼ × 14¾ × 15 inches (87 × 37.5 × 38.1 cm)
Solomon R. Guggenheim Museum, New York
Purchased with funds contributed by the International Director's Council, 2017
2017.73
© Simone Leigh, Courtesy Matthew Marks Gallery

For black feminists who are still conjuring.

Contents

Acknowledgments — ix

Introduction. On Gathering — 1
Margo Natalie Crawford and C. Riley Snorton

ARCHIVAL FRAGMENT 1: Calendar entry for The Scholar and the Feminist Conference — 10

1   On Thon, or, Thinking Gender in the Interstice — 11
    C. Riley Snorton

2   Oracular Fever Medicine: A Time Travel Oracle for Hortense Spillers — 31
    Alexis Pauline Gumbs

3   The Fineness of a Sentence, or, Hortense Spillers's Theoretical Acuity — 42
    Kevin Quashie

ARCHIVAL FRAGMENT 2: A letter from Toni Morrison to Hortense Spillers, 1984 — 72

4   When Hortense Spillers and Toni Morrison Meet in the Clearing: The Hieroglyphics of Marking and Unmarking — 73
    Margo Natalie Crawford

5   Performance and Preformance — 92
    Fred Moten

ARCHIVAL FRAGMENT 3: Journal Entry on Gwendolyn Brooks — 111

6   Black Reconstruction, or, Names for Love: Hortense Spillers as Reader — 112
    Anthony Reed

7   The Errant Protester: Tracing Black E/motion in the Visual Work of Hortense Spillers — 130
    Amaris Brown

8   "whatever marvels of my own inventiveness": Black Feminist Archival
    Tradition in the Notebooks of Hortense Spillers   148
    Kiana T. Murphy

9   All the Things You Could Be by Now If Hortense Spillers was Your Mentor   173
    Nicole A. Spigner

    ARCHIVAL FRAGMENT 4: Images of Hortense Spillers in her living room   194

10 The Black Living Room   195
    Shoniqua Roach

    ARCHIVAL FRAGMENT 5: Journal entry, 1970   223

11 Mama's Marvelous Tar Baby: Black Feminist Experiments
    in Spillersian Ecdysis   225
    Ra Malika Imhotep

    ARCHIVAL FRAGMENT 6: *Sparebone* Program   254

    ARCHIVAL FRAGMENT 7: Letter from Judith Butler to Hortense   255

12 Grammars and Impression Points: Appreciating Hortense Spillers   256
    Deborah E. McDowell

13 Bridging Figurations: Hortense J. Spillers, Essayist   268
    Thadious M. Davis

    ARCHIVAL FRAGMENT 8: "In the Flesh," handwritten talk   278

14 "All the Things You Could Be and All the Things You Are"   276
    Sharon P. Holland

    ARCHIVAL FRAGMENT 9: Handwritten album list in Spiller's journal   298

    Afterword   299
    Hortense J. Spillers

    Appendix: Transcriptions of Archival Documents   305
    Contributors   319

Acknowledgments

Hortense Spillers wrote the following in a journal entry dated March 10, 1973, "Saturday going into Sunday, 12:10 am": "A writer has words, the world, and his/her own soul. To get them running on one accord is the hoped-for thing." As co-editors, we thank Hortense Spillers for achieving this "hoped-for thing." Her profound scholarship expands the contours of black critical thought and black feminist theory. Spillers' work and words have opened up new worlds. This book is a testament to the ever-evolving dimensions of the Spillersian world of black feminist critical thought.

During every stage of our co-editorial work, Gianna Mosser, director of Vanderbilt University Press, was a dedicated guide and consultant. Her unwavering commitment to this book inspired us as co-editors. Our gratitude to Gianna Mosser is tremendous.

We thank Ann duCille, emerita professor of English at Wesleyan University, and Mary Murphy, Nancy L. Buc '65 Pembroke Center Archivist at Brown University, for their steady support as we brought the Spillers archive into this book.

We also thank Simone Leigh for giving us permission to include an image of her sculpture *Georgia Mae* (2017) on the book cover. In the essay "Simone Leigh and the Monumental," Spillers describes the power of Leigh's art as the "refusal of the eyeball." The art of Spillers' work as a theorist can also be described as the refusal of the eyeball (the refusal of the gazes that invade the opacity of black life, black aesthetics, and black genders).

We give our deepest thanks to the contributors in this volume who with great care have taken up the task of writing with and about Spillers.

INTRODUCTION

On Gathering

MARGO NATALIE CRAWFORD AND C. RILEY SNORTON

The idea for this collection emerged while planning a gathering in celebration of Hortense Spillers's work at Cornell University. In 2016, when we co-convened The Flesh of the Matter: A Hortense Spillers Symposium, we were Cornell professors trying, by any means necessary, to create an intellectual home in Ithaca, New York where Spillers wrote many of the essays that set her brilliance in motion. As co-conveners we hoped the symposium would serve as a homecoming of sorts. During Spillers's Cornell years, she became the wondrous theorist who was known for writing essays that have the scope and depth that most writers can only create in book-length form. Pivotal conferences honoring Spillers (at University of Pennsylvania in 2000 and at Johns Hopkins University in 2001) propelled her to collect the essays and create the tour de force *Black, White, and in Color*. Before the essays were collected in 2003 in *Black, White, and in Color*, a wide range of enraptured readers had already *collected* the essays and embraced them as transformative.

The Flesh of the Matter: A Critical Forum on Hortense Spillers is a gathering of readers caught in the "iconic folds" of her words. It, perhaps, goes without saying: Spillers's scholarship provides the opening and occasion for all that follows. Her commitments to thinking through and across silos of scholarly activity and political action indelibly shape the contours of this anthology. Gathering here is both method and mode. As Spillers writes in the preface of her formidable collection, "This essay

1

does not offer a solution, just as its 'relatives' in this volume, but, rather, finds and circumlocutes certain static in a field of force. Doing so may be preferable, after all, to the false certainty of solutions."[1] Her practice of "finding and circumlocuting certain static in a field of force" is the reason why she has gathered such a wide constellation of thinkers and dreamers. Spillers's circumlocutions are exquisite. She dodges the static and takes us elsewhere, as we gain new ways of thinking about matters such as the psychic hold of slavery, what we really mean when we refer to intersections of race, gender, sexuality, and class, and how the "borders" of American literature and African American literature are cut.

This book aims to resist any framing of Hortense Spillers's body of work. We hope the essays and archival fragments in this book will dislodge any frames that try to contain the "spill"—the profound excess in Spillers's body of work that we continue to *flesh* out. In the preface to her formidable collection, *Black, White, and in Color*, Spillers shares how, "The essays gathered here were motivated, then, by exactly such urgency, the awful need to respond in the moment, on point."[2] Referring to the post-1960s instantiation of "Black Studies" and "Women's Studies" in the US academy, Spillers explains how both fields were "called upon to hit the ground, already running."[3] Spillers's work prepared a generation of scholars to "hit the ground, *always* running," and the scholars gathered in this book flesh out Spillers's arresting, paradigm-shifting ideas about "the one," ungendering, pornotroping, flesh, vestibularity, and more.

Throughout her writing and in her public projects, Spillers makes evident the stakes of her work and the work before us. Spillers's analysis grounds us in the political realities of the present and asks us "whatcha gonna do?" The answer is never obvious but can be reposed as a question to sustain the opening, to sustain the ethical encounter. As she makes clear in *"The Crisis of the Negro Intellectual*: A Post-Date," now is a time to lean into suspicion, to sustain doubt in the face of the seemingly obvious or inevitable, as it is also to realize that there is no way to engage and come away clean. In a 2006 interview concerning the mission of Africana Studies, Spillers explains that she saw the work of writing at the dawn of the institutionalization of Black Studies in terms of "opening a long, whole corridor, a conversation, with all of the other disciplinary stakes."[4] From her description, we gain the sense that the gathering also requires an *intramural protocol* for thinking together—with difference—across any arbitrary and calcified boundaries between disciplines, or between politics and theory or culture.

There is an urgency, "an awful need" to find insurgent ground in the present. And in this, Spillers also offers us a model. The proliferation of crises from environmental collapse to the proliferation of global fascisms that gives the contemporary moment its particular texture provides an opening and an occasion to "play" with the "production process of the object of knowledge" toward a new system of value and a different schema for being and becoming.[5] But first we must learn how to read, which Spillers defines "as an elaboration and complication of competing, overlapping, and complimentary discourses." Far from transparent, we read ourselves into/and the situation. We get read. The gathering is an activation, initiating the reader into ways of reading and perceiving, identifying, and responding to the urgencies at hand.

She has gathered us. Radical black feminist theory continues to be a gathering of ideas that do not settle into disciplines and institutional grids. The essays gathered in this book do not coalesce. They are an open space where we can hear the intensity of the reverberations of Spillers's words. On the meta-level, Spillers created a new grammar, in black critical theory, that refuses what she describes as the *"theft of* the dynamic principle of the living that distinguishes the subject from his/her objectification."[6] When readers gather around Spillers's signature essay form, they begin to think about the most nuanced dimensions of Black life, gender, class, sexuality, and race. Her essays gather *and* release as she makes analysis inseparable from speculation.

The power of Spillers's essays is the voice of a theorist who discovered, while writing her dissertation on African American sermons, the flow, layers, and rupture that shape Black critical thought. This book aims to show the flow of Spillers's early work to her most recent writing on "Afropessimism and Its Others" and her public intellectual gathering work in *A-Line: A Journal of Progressive Thought*, an online journal founded by Spillers in 2017. Spillers hails her *A-Line* audience in the following manner: "Our audience is the informed reader or enlightened specialist desperate for timely critical intervention." In a 2019 *A-Line* essay entitled "Arts Now," Spillers analyzes a long tradition of leftist cultural workers aiming for a writing that would have both "political analysis and poetic vision." Spillers cites Olaf Hansen's use of these words in his introduction to the collection of Randolph Bourne's essays, but this idea of the bringing together of "political analysis and poetic vision" also illuminates what this introduction to *The Flesh of the Matter: A Critical Forum on Hortense Spillers* hopes to underscore.

Spillers stands out among theorists and critics as one of the visionary thinkers who makes political analysis become a poetic vision. All of the contributors in this book, and all of the fragments from the Hortense Spillers papers at the Feminist Theory Archive and the Black Feminist Theory Project, established and curated by the Pembroke Center for Teaching and Research on Women at Brown University, testify to the inseparability of Spiller's political analysis and poetic vision. At its etymological root, an anthology is a gathering of flowers. In the 1630s, *anthology* began to refer to a collection of poetry. We draw on these historical meanings to organize and offer this anthology of the poetics of Spillersian theory (the "furious flower" that Spillers's essays have become). Gwendolyn Brooks's resonant line (in "The Second Sermon on the Warpland") "The time / cracks into furious flower" captures the spirit of Spillers's transformative interventions in black feminist theory. Spillers's criticism on Brooks's poetry is as remarkable as her criticism on William Faulkner and Toni Morrison. In a journal note dated March 4, 1973, after Spillers recalls the first conversation she had with Brooks, she muses, "Who's afraid of Gwendolyn Brooks? I am." This sense of awe is what many readers of Spillers's work continue to feel. This anthology aims to honor the incredibly generative opacity of Spillers's writings.

In the late 1980s, as Spillers was travelling to many universities in order to deliver lectures on her work-in-progress "In the Flesh: A Situation for Feminist Inquiry," she wrote many outlines for the public talks. In one of the outlines, she crystallizes what was at stake as she, in the 1980s, tried to "gather" the conceptual pieces of a black feminist theoretical framework. She writes:

> 4. Before a field of cultural/social studies can be cleared for a systematic investigation of African-American women's community, the historic

subject must be purged of its thorough investments by and infection with the sense of the subject as an unalloyed moment of pure being. By attempting to look at this potentially rich field of cultural study under a new intellectual entitlement, we are attending to a conceptual crisis—to discover the terms of a <u>self-address</u> and to compel these strategies of a public and theoretical evocation that are appropriate to this period of consciousness.

5. Trying to speak at the site of an abandoned historic intersection.

Above these last words "at the site of an abandoned historic intersection," Spillers adds the words "—in theory—." In these lecture notes, we see how Spillers frames the "conceptual crisis" facing black feminist theory—how to "discover the terms of a self-address." All of Spillers's work, throughout the decades, has confronted this conceptual crisis and created more space for the practice of black critical theory that must be done at the "site of an abandoned historic intersection."

This work at the space of abandonment begins in the early stages of Spillers's theory and criticism. Demanding freedom from the standard ways of theorizing "the body" makes Spillers, as a young professor at Wellesley College, write a play entitled *Sparebone: A Drama in Three Acts with Music and Dance*. The program for the production of the play included the following language: "Sparebone is that part of the living body which no other part can do without. Though the term may not be found in any of the biological sciences, we needn't despair because every biologist himself has one." Early-style Spillers discourse was as theoretically playful as her later work. The idea of a sparebone that complicates what a biologist can know anticipates her signature theory of flesh that complicates "the body" and her reworking of the very word and idea of "interstices."

In "Interstices: A Small Drama of Words," Spillers opens with the poem, "Who Said It Was Simple?" by Audre Lorde. The typed remarks of her contribution to Barnard's Conference on Sexuality (1982) convey her edits and revisions, including markings to break the lines of verse and correct capitalization in the poetic epigraph. Lorde delivered "Coal" earlier that year at Barnard College. As meditations on liberation,

> **Who Said It Was Simple?**
>
> There are so many roots to the tree of anger/That sometimes the branches shatter/Before they bear.
>
> Sitting in Nedicks/The women rally before they march/Discussing the problematic girls/They hire to make them free./An almost white counterman passes/A waiting brother to serve them first/And the ladies neither notice nor reject/The slighter pleasures of their slavery./But I who am bound by my mirror/As well as my bed/See causes in Colour/As well as sex
>
> And sit here wondering/Which me will survive/All these liberations.
>
> Audre Lorde[1]
>
> When I told a friend of mine that I was going to address the issue of sexuality as discourse during a spring conference at Barnard, she laughed: "Is that what you talk about when you make love?" Silence. "Well?" Well, I hadn't thought of that, but now that she had broached the question, what about it? There probably

FIGURE I.1. Excerpt of the typed first page of a draft of "Interstices: A Small Drama of Words"

the fourth line of "Coal" reads, "There are many kinds of open," which syntactically and conceptually echoes the first line of "Who Said It Was Simple?"—"There are so many roots to the tree of anger." Lorde and thus Spillers begins with a question about plurality in roots and form, and while Spillers primarily focuses on nonfictional texts concerning Black women's sexuality in feminist and other forms of intellectual discourse, her call to action in the conclusion, "As I see it, the goal is not an articulating of sexuality so much as it is a global restoration and dispersal of power, in which act sexuality is rendered one of several active predicates. So much depends on it," picks up on Lorde's final lines, in which another rhetorical question takes the form of a response—"and sit here wondering / which me will survive / all these liberations."

"Interstices" takes a formal approach "to examine those rhetorical features of an intellectual/symbolic structure of ideas that purport to describe, illuminate, reveal, and valorize the *truth* about its subject."[7] In naming the absence of discourse on Black women's sexuality by Black women, Spillers also carefully elaborates the ways forward. Both Spillers's approach and response to the problem occur on aesthetic terms.

What does it mean "to supply the missing word?" In one sense, it is to proliferate the terms of engagement and to seek out models of Black women's creativity that offer points of entry to alternate symbolic worlds. In her typed remarks, Spillers turns to the possibility of shifting domination: "The fact of domination is alterable only to the extent that the dominated subject recognizes the potential power of its own double consciousness. The subject is certainly seen, but she/he also sees herself/himself." To which she adds, with emphasis: "<u>And Others</u>."[8] While her handwritten addendum does not appear in the printed essay in *Black, White, and in Color*, the implications permeate the text, sharpening the stakes of what it would mean for feminist discourse to successfully achieve its aims to establish a liberatory epistemic break from regimes of domination. "And Others" also provides another angle on an approach to the "global restoration and dispersal of power": namely, to hold and meaningfully contend with the idea that the object of other's interpretation is also an interpreter of words and worlds. Finally, "And Others" functions as a form of poetic intervention—

> The subject is certainly seen,
> But she/he also sees
> Herself/himself. <u>And Others.</u>

The rhythmic quality embedded in her syntax magnifies the repercussions of the many missing kinds of interpretation currently underthought, underwritten, or otherwise screened from view. Our survival, indeed, depends on it.

Spillers's poetic interventions set the rhythm of this anthology's flow. Like Charles Mingus's song, "All The Things You Could Be by Now If Sigmund Freud's Wife Was Your Mother," which Spillers draws on for the title of her noted essay on psychoanalysis and race, there is a sense of movement in this collection without an easy reliance on coherence. In one of her 1970s journals (in her archive at Brown University), Spillers muses, "We have shared the same wound." On the blank space of one journal page, she writes, "Oh! Grave is an adjective, not a noun." Spillers's resonant subtitle in her legendary 1987 essay "Mama's Baby, Papa's Maybe: An American Grammar Book"—gains new dimensions when we see the steady search for a new grammar in her unpublished writing. There is a constant attention to "grammar" in her archive. In lecture notes entitled "Psychoanalysis and Literature," she presents the idea of "transcending grammar." She writes, "Freud points out the absurdities of logic—Faulkner, Woolf, Joyce were not flaunting grammar; they were transcending it—stream of consciousness art."

Streams of consciousness shape this *Critical Forum on Hortense Spillers*. Fragments from her archive form the soundtrack of this book. They are not subheadings. While there are points of resonance between the archival fragments and some of the essays that precede or follow them, the fragments are provocations and opportunities to gather, encounter, and take in Spillers's thinking. In one of the unpublished creative pieces, Spillers writes, "Did you feel like shoutin', when you came, came out of the wilderness, came—came out the wilderness—came—came out the wilderness." The scholars included in this volume have been hailed by Spillers. We feel like shouting as we come into the Spillersian space for radical black critical thought. The Spillers archive gives one a deeper sense of the role of music in Spillers's search for a new grammar. "I go home in Roberta Flack," she writes in one journal entry. This book aims to make readers feel the musical moves of what Spillers calls her "theoretical apparatus." As coeditors, we have gathered scholars who "go home" (in many different directions) through deep engagement with the nuances of Spillers's theory and criticism.

Notes

1. Hortense J. Spillers, preface to *Black, White, and in Color: Essays on American Literature and Culture* (Chicago, IL: University of Chicago Press, 2003), xvi.
2. Spillers, preface to *Black, White, and in Color*, x.
3. Spillers, preface to *Black, White, and in Color*, x.
4. Keith D. Leonard and Hortense Spillers, "First Questions: The Mission of Africana Studies: An Interview with Hortense Spillers," *Callaloo* 30, no. 4 (Fall 2007): 1,057.
5. Hortense J. Spillers, "*The Crisis of the Negro Intellectual*: A Post-Date," in Spillers, *Black, White, and in Color*, 428–70, 451.
6. Hortense J. Spillers, "Notes on an Alternative Model—Neither/Nor," in Spillers, *Black, White, and in Color*, 301–18, 302.

7. Spillers, "Interstices: A Small Drama of Words," in Spillers, *Black, White, and in Color*, 152–75, 153.
8. Spillers, "Interstices," 153.

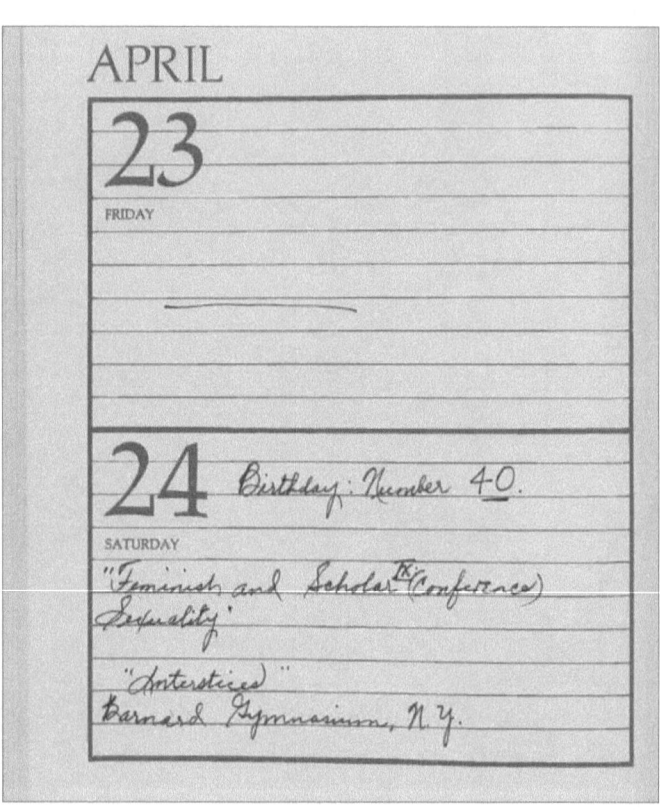

ARCHIVAL FRAGMENT 1: Calendar entry for The Scholar and the Feminist Conference

1 On Thon, or, Thinking Gender in the Interstice

C. RILEY SNORTON

> The collective and individual "I" lapses into a cul-de-sac, falls into the great black hole of meaning, wherein there are only "women," "minorities," "blacks," and "other." I wish to suggest that the lexical gaps I am describing here are manifest along a range of symbolic behavior in reference to black women and that the absence of sexuality as a structure of distinguishing terms is solidly grounded in the negative aspects of symbol-making. The latter, in turn, are wed to the abuses and uses of history, and how it is perceived. The missing word—the interstice—both as that which allows us to speak about and that which enables us to speak at all—shares, in this case, a common border with another country of symbols—the iconographic.
>
> —Hortense Spillers, "Interstices: A Small Drama of Words"

> What is missing in African-American cultural analysis is a concept of the "one."
>
> —Hortense Spillers, "'All the Things You Could Be by Now, If Sigmund Freud's Wife Was Your Mother': Psychoanalysis and Race"

Having taught in women, gender, and sexuality studies programs for the last decade, I often assign Hortense Spillers's noted essay, "Mama's Baby, Papa's Maybe: An American Grammar Book" and rarely without coupling it with "Interstices: A Small Drama of Words," which was first delivered as a talk at the 1982 Barnard Conference on Sexuality roughly five years before "Mama's Baby, Papa's Maybe" appeared in print. I organize my syllabus in this way to highlight how the material and the symbolic are transitive in "Spillersian" thought, that is, to draw attention to the implications of the psychic, visual, and ontological dimensions of Spillers's questions and approach. Across her oeuvre, she offers a way of seeing and reading sexuality and gender as intertwined racializing discursive projects wherein the question of blackness throws into stark relief how gender is not separable from sexuality but one of its conditions and effects. Even in "the absence of sexuality as a distinguishing term," as Spillers describes in the first epigraph of this essay, Black women are catalytic to the production of sexuality—that "locus of great drama—perhaps the fundamental one" complete with actors, "scripts, scenes, gestures, and reenactments, both enunciated and tacit."[1] To occupy the interstitial (or to be the missing word) then, might be like finding oneself in the breach between the subject of enunciation and the enunciated subject or sitting on the razor's edge where history and myth meet. It is living in (or perhaps, out) the reality of a "dominated political position" within the machinations of systems and tactics, including at least racial capitalism and misogyny.[2] With Nina Simone's "Four Women" playing on a loop in hushed tones in the background, my students and I attend to and contend with the implications of Spillers's work for the disciplines of women, gender, and sexuality studies. Surely, had her work not existed, it would have had to be invented.

Appearing in print ten years after "Interstices" was initially published, Evelyn Hammonds offers another illustration and syntactical rejoinder—black (w)holes—to express the complex relationship between the "visible" and the "not absent," as they constitute two sides of gender's racializing paradigmatic coin. In her essay, she describes Spillers's "Interstices" as "one of the earliest and most compelling discussions of black women's sexuality," as it informs Hammonds's theory of the import and impasse of discourses of black female sexuality on the proposed subjects/objects of queer theory.[3] For Hammonds and many Black feminists, Spillers's methodological model of reading for and across the elided, eclipsed, and other sites of negation toward the generativity of constructed and constructive silences is particularly instructive. As highlighted in the epigraphs, and in what I perceive to be an act of political and scholarly vigilance, Spillers homes in on the "lexical gaps" and missing words and concepts that characterize the dominant grammars of American life and comprise the elements of their resistance. As she relates in "Interstices," "We are, after all, talking about words, as we realize that by their efficacy we are damned or saved."[4]

This essay attends to the prescience and ongoing relevance of Spillersian thought for the field of transgender studies, which emerged alongside queer theory as its "not absent" twin in the early 1990s although it continues to be perceived as its much younger sibling. Working within the frames offered in her elucidation of the interstitial—the discursive, the historiographic, and the iconographic, this essay is organized into three parts. The first two sections examine the volatility and remediations of race/sex/gender during the Civil War and its aftermath, beginning with a discussion of the 1858 proposal of the genderless pronoun, "thon," a contraction of that one that also carries other meanings, as a contracted form of that yonder and as an alternate spelling of then. Across the late nineteenth century and until the mid-twentieth century, *thon* captivated philological audiences, inspiring much debate, and appearing in dictionaries, crossword puzzles, and newspapers. The second part extends the spatial and temporal dimensions of *thon* in a reading of a contemporaneous figure in military history, often described as the first Black woman to serve in the US military, but as archival sources bear out, was variably named and variably gendered. The third part is a meditation on revision, iconography, and method in a reading of the character Cuffee in *The Harder They Fall* (2021) and the interplay between thon, as "that one" and "the one" that Spillers describes as a missing concept in attending to black interiority. My aim here is to attend to the psychic, visual, and ontological dimensions of racialized sexuality as it pertains to conceptualizing transgender and thinking gender as a mutable category, and in doing so, to turn to, or perhaps persist within a great black (w)hole of meaning.

That One, That Yonder, and Then

Thon was not the first proposed genderless pronoun in English. Earlier examples include "ou," which was proposed by the Scottish economist

James Anderson in 1792, and "it," suggested by Samuel Taylor Coleridge in 1808.[5] According to Dennis Baron, "Between 1858 and 1912, coiners came up with 70 gender-neutral pronouns, some of them invented independently more than once."[6] The oldest and most extensively used pronoun is the third person singular "they," which has been continuously in use for the last six centuries and disparaged for its usage as such since the eighteenth.[7] The *Oxford English Dictionary* "traces singular they back to 1375, where it appears in the medieval romance *William and the Werewolf*."[8]

The first inclusion of "thon" appeared in *The Standard Dictionary of the English Language* (vol 4, 1897). The entry contained both description and rationale:

> **thon** [THON's, *poss.*; THON, *obj.*] That one; he, she, or it; a pronoun of the 3d person, common gender, a contracted and solidified form of *that one*, proposed in 1858 by Charles Crozat Converse, of Erie, Pennsylvania, as a substitute in cases where the use of a restrictive pronoun involves either inaccuracy or obscurity, or its non-employment necessitates awkward repetition. The following examples, first as ordinarily written and afterward with the substitution of the genderless pronoun, illustrate the grammatical deficiencies of the English language in this particular and the proposed method of removal: "If Harry or his wife comes, I will be on hand to meet *him or her* (or whichever appears)." "Each pupil must learn *his or her* own lesson." With the substitution of *thon*: "If Harry or his wife comes, I will be on hand to meet *thon* (i.e., *that one* who comes)." "Each pupil must learn *thon's* lesson (i.e., *his or her* own)."[9]

The word's creator, Charles Crozat Converse, specified the use of "thon" in the nominative and objective and "thons" in the possessive, mirroring the usage of the third person singular "it, its." The addition of an apostrophe in Funk and Wagnalls publication may indicate a difference in usage since the time of its proposal. Yet as a punctuation mark meant to indicate possession or an omission of letters and numbers, its addition may also correspond to thon as "a contracted and *solidified* form," overwriting the term's constitutive elision and redoubling its nominative properties. Relatedly, one might speculate about the various ways gender is expressed as "contracted and solidified"—bifurcated, referenceable, and naturalized, but thon was not developed to address the matter of gender and its lived expressions. The first example of thon's usage offered with the definition attempts to suture the term to heteronormativity.

Thon remained in Funk and Wagnalls' publications throughout most of the twentieth century and appeared in other sources, including in the Merriam-Webster 2nd International Dictionary with the more succinct definition: "A proposed genderless pronoun of the third person" (1934). Converse was a seeming jack of all trades: a philologist, an attorney, an inventor, and a composer, most notably setting to music Joseph Scriven's poem, "What a Friend We Have in Jesus." Born in 1832 in Warren, MA, Converse studied law and music in Leipzig, Germany and received his law degree from Albany Law School in 1861. Many of his musical compositions were published under anagrammatic pen names, C. O. Nevers, Karl Reden, and E. C. Revons. While Converse is credited for coining the term in the midst of the Civil War in 1858, he would formally propose consideration among the reading audience of *The Critic and Good Literature*, a New York-based magazine of literary criticism, in a letter to the editors published more than twenty-five years later in August of 1884.

Converse began his letter, "That a new pronoun, of the singular number and a common gender, is needed in the English language, is a fact patent to every English speaker and writer."[10] Yet it was the philological atmosphere, which he described as "full of winged words" that aim "to produce a minimum of word-body with a maximum of flying power" that Converse credits as encouragement for bringing "thon" forward as a term for wide adaptation.[11] The proposal prompted much discussion. Well-known philologist Francis A. March described thon as "a very happy suggestion," and expressed his hope "that it may be received favorably and in due time adopted."[12] Harvard professor of art, Charles Eliot Norton, wrote to Converse about thon:

> Such a pronoun would undoubtedly be a convenience, did it exist. The difficulty lies in its being yours. All forms of speech have grown, and I do not recall an instance of the use by a civilized race of any word, not a noun or a verb, deliberately invented by a philologer, however ingenious.[13]

Among its critics, some worried that thon would be confused with "thou," which was not in especially high circulation. One particularly adamant naysayer called Converse a "grammatical crank" and warned that thon "would drastically increase the cost of already overpriced schoolbooks: students would need new grammars, spellers, geographies, and arithmetics—even blank copy books would be affected."[14] One might hear in this critic's anxiogenic response at least one implication of gender as constitutive to a distinctively American grammar, offering evidence as to how grammar is also a set of hegemonic social and cultural techniques shaping and shaped by a national project.

It is important to keep in mind that thon, as Converse proposed, was not an attempt to address the problem of gender but a problem in language, offered up to reduce "awkward repetition." Its roughly one century of usage—from the Civil War era to 1961, when it was removed from English language dictionaries, prompts a question about its decline at a critical moment in racial and sexual justice movements in the United States, in which the word may have been put to use by politically fomented communities looking to create other enunciative possibilities and meanings. It was, after all, in 1965 that Dr. John Oliven was credited with coining the term "transgender," or more precisely entering the term "transgenderism" into sexological discourse, in his book *Sexual Hygiene and Pathology*.[15] This, of course, comes after public understandings of gender as mutable, conveyed through media coverage of famous trans people like Lucy Hicks Anderson and, especially, Christine Jorgensen.

Yet the critic's concern over the revolutionary potential of thon, as a catalyst for the rewriting of grammar and geography is in one sense not overstated. As previously mentioned, thon has other meanings, as a contraction of that yonder and as a variation of then. The spatial and temporal dimensions of thon's alternate definitions invite an understanding of pronouns—not as a descriptor of persons but in terms of a distant horizon, which may have occurred in the past or exist as a future potentiality. Put differently, thon suggests the not yet and as yet of gender. It brings forth other considerations about how one engages with others, as it holds as an open question the where and when of a person rather than the who or what of a person or thing. Kara Keeling explores these questions of temporality and personhood in her noted essay, "Looking for M__: Queer Temporality, Black Political Possibility, and Poetry from the Future" (2009). If thon implies a relational uncertainty, then it also serves a deictic function. And what if we regarded all pronouns in this way? That is, rather than approaching a pronoun as the referent to a given subject or object, what if we related to it as dependent on the context in which it is offered or used. Here in the obsolete uses of "thon," we might approach ourselves and others in terms of temporalities of emergence and clear some ground to undergo a process Spillers describes in "Mama's Baby, Papa's Maybe" for speaking "a truer word" to "await whatever marvels" of our "own inventiveness."[16]

To be clear, I have not chosen to share this brief history of thon to advocate for its recirculation. Rather I am interested in what thon could reveal, or at least repose, about gender and grammar, wherein gender is not binary or even proliferative but situational, relational, and context emergent. But allow me to approach this from a different angle by attending to the scant military records of Private William Cathay, whose roughly two years of military service has been the fodder for national memorialization and popular reimagining. In doing so, I hope to make clearer the implications of thinking about the potential of "nonbinary" to give expression to gender as an unfinished project of hegemony.

Thon and Then Some

On November 15, 1866, twenty-two-year-old William Cathay and two companions enlisted in the US Army in St. Louis, Missouri. Described by the recruiting officer as 5' 9" tall, with black eyes, hair, and complexion, William was assigned to Company A of the 38th Infantry, one of several battalions of Buffalo soldiers tasked with protecting settlers, controlling the Native population of the Plains, capturing cattle rustlers and thieves and guarding stagecoaches, wagon trains and railroad crews along the Western front. Like all new recruits, William was subject to a medical exam upon entry and declared by the examining surgeon to be "free from all bodily defects and mental infragility, which would, in any way, disqualify him from performing the duties of a soldier."[17] By all historical accounts, William Cathay's just less than two years of military service was unremarkable. His company never saw direct battle, and rheumatism and neuralgia caused William to spend several months in the infirmary. As a soldier, William was never signaled out for praise or punishment, but Cathay is invariably named in military histories as the first Black woman to serve in the US army.

In a first-hand account to the *St. Louis Daily Times* published in 1876, Cathay explained how illnesses framed her service beginning with contracting smallpox shortly after enlisting. "Finally," Cathay professed, "I got tired and wanted to get off. I played sick, complained of pains in my side, and rheumatism in my knees. The post surgeon found out I was a woman and I got my discharge. The men all wanted to get rid of me after they found out I was a woman. Some of them acted real bad to me."[18] On October 14,1868 William Cathay and two other privates were discharged at Fort Bayard on a surgeon's certificate of disability. William's certificate included statements from both the captain of the company and the post's assistant surgeon. The captain's statement read that William, since under his command "has been . . . feeble both physically and mentally, and much of the time quite unfit for duty. The origin of his infirmities is unknown to me."[19] The surgeon's statement claimed Cathay was of "a feeble habit. He is continually on sick report without benefit. He is unable to do military duty. . . . This condition dates prior to enlistment."[20]

It would appear that the scandal of William's assigned sex at birth was not documented in the official military and medical record, as both captain and surgeon's statements refer to an unknown prior cause or condition—a foreshadowing of Cathay's disparaged disability benefits claim, which brought their life into public view. As told to the *St. Louis Daily Times*, Cathay began military service as a girl when she was "carried off" to Little Rock, Arkansas, by Col. William Plummer Benton of the 13th army corps. Born near Independence, Missouri, to an enslaved mother and a freeman, Cathay was conscripted into service as a cook after her enslaver died at the beginning of the Civil War. On the circumstances of the first term of service, she shared: "I did not want to go."[21] Under Benton, Cathay traveled through various parts of Arkansas, Louisiana, and Georgia and was eventually sent to Washington City where she served as a cook and launderer for General Sheridan and his staff, with whom Cathay continued to travel through Virginia and Iowa until stationed in Jefferson Barracks (in St. Louis, MO) for some time. From enslavement to military conscription and service, the circumstances of Cathay's disabilities is indicative of the biopolitical logic of "will to not let die," wherein debility, or what Jasbir Puar has identified as "the right to maim" acts as a complimentary logic to the right to kill and nests within what Saidiya Hartman describes in terms of the violence constitutive to "female gender as the locus of both unredressed and negligible injury" in the application of US law to the enslaved.[22]

After being discharged, Cathay lived in New Mexico, travelled to Fort Union and later to Pueblo and Trinidad, Colorado, while working intermittently as a cook or launderer. At some point in late 1889 or early 1890, Cathay was hospitalized in Trinidad for nearly a year and a half. As DeAnne Blanton explains, "She was probably indigent when she left the hospital, so she filed in June 1891 for an invalid pension based upon her military service."[23] The original application gave Cathay's age as forty-one and made reference to military-service related deafness, rheumatism, and neuralgia. In July, Cathay submitted a supplemental affidavit, which mentioned the case of smallpox contracted at the beginning of their service.

On September 9, 1891, a medical doctor, acting on behalf of the Pension Bureau, described Cathay as 5'7", 160 pounds, large, stout, and forty-nine years of age. He reported that she could hear a conversation, and therefore was not deaf and that there were no physical changes in her joints, muscles, or tendons to indicate rheumatism or neuralgia.[24] The doctor also noted that the complainant walked with the aid of a cane, as all ten toes had been amputated. If he asked, the report did not indicate the cause of the amputations. And apparently, the doctor did not know that neuralgia was a problem of the nerves and not the muscles. The use of female pronouns in the doctor's report marks the first usage in reference to William Cathay's military service. It would recur in February 1892, when the Pension Bureau rejected Cathay's claim on the grounds that no disability existed.

At this point, we find ourselves neck deep in contradictions, produced by the gaps and silences in the archive, and yet the imperative here is not to get to the bottom of it but rather to hold and bear witness

FIGURE 1.1. Described as "the image of American female Buffalo Soldier Cathay Williams a.k.a. William Cathay (1844–1892)," although according to an article in the *Pueblo Chieftan*, the image is of Cathay's mother Martha, a matron of the Lincoln Colored Home and Orphanage.

to the complexities of an assemblage of materials meant to convey a singularity of person but who themselves seemed to demand consent to be a plural being. We know that Cathay went by William and also by Kate Williams and John Williams and James Cady, that Cathay was briefly married and separated, sending her husband to jail for stealing from their household, and that they seemed to always be on the move. The descriptions of what happened to Cathay following their denied claim vary widely. Some hypothesize that Cathay lived just one year past their denied claim. Others suggest that they established a school or boarding house in Trinidad, Colorado or Raton, New Mexico. Some Pueblo historians claim that the image that accompanies Cathay Williams's Wikipedia entry, of a figure in profile, wearing a bonnet, long skirt, starched collared shirt and workman's jacket is actually a photo of Cathay's mother, Martha in front of an orphanage and old folks' home for Black folks in Pueblo. In addition to the demands to materially provide for themselves and their loved ones, their movement was perhaps precipitated in part by a desire to find a location of irreducibility—to find a place where Cathay did not first have to be a thing for others. To exist in and as thon, which in this instance might feel like mysticism in the flesh, and what Fred Moten contends about blackness as "prior to ontology."[25]

Aside from the two-paragraph article on Cathay in the *St. Louis Daily Times*, there is no public record of what Cathay thought about things. In the National Park Service's online materials about the Fort Union National Monument, they are described both as an "oddity" and "a strange case."²⁶ Making use of language like "real gender," the National Park Service's treatment of Cathay's story underscores how trans identification and ways of being seem beyond normative historical interpretation.²⁷ And I am not suggesting that Cathay would have understood themselves to be trans or nonbinary, even as I feel a resonance, rather I have attempted to read Cathay's existing archival materials according to Spillers's ruminations in "Interstices," wherein "the threatened return of the metaphors of experience to their original ground of tangible and material meaning demonstrates the distance we must travel between the status of the protected and that of the unprotected, or the difference between sex and sexuality."²⁸ That is to say, Cathay may very well have been the first and only Buffalo Soldier who was assigned female at birth, but thon was that and *then some*.

The various ways Cathay has been revisited in monument, literature, and popular culture also indicate a relationship between the interstitial and the symptomatic, in which the impetus to remember them seems to reiteratively confer and confirm them in a gendered telos not borne out in the archive. Attempts to valorize the variably named Cathay include a bust of their imagined likeness at the Buffalo Soldier Monument in Leavenworth, Kansas. A third of a room is also dedicated to the story of their military service at the Buffalo Soldiers National Museum in Houston. There are biographies, numerous articles, and at least one novel, *A Daughter of a Daughter of a Queen* (2018), penned by Sarah Bird as a "tribute in fiction" to the inscrutable Cathay. In 2021, Cathay was also the source material for the transmasculine character, Cuffee in Netflix's *The Harder They Fall*.

The Bigger They Are . . .

The Harder They Fall (2021), drawn from the full idiomatic expression, "the bigger they are, the harder they fall," is the first feature-length film directed and co-written by London-based writer, director, and singer-songwriter Jeymes Samuel, also known as the Bullitts. Plot, setting, and characterization evince the kind of play permissible within the spaghetti western, as outlaws and lawmen outsmart and outmuscle each other in the ambiguous past of the US West. Before the film commences, a note reads: "While the events of this story are fictional . . . These. People. Existed," which was also made into the copy for an ad campaign including images of some of the film's biggest stars. As film critic A. O. Scott suggests, "This isn't about historical accuracy, or even realism; it's about genre."[29] He continues:

> The point is that the vivid assortment of gunslingers, chanteuses, saloon-keepers and train-robbers—all of them Black—who ride through picturesque mountain ranges and frontier towns have as authentic a claim on the mythology of the West as their white counterparts. They exist, in other words, as true archetypes in a primal story of revenge, greed, treachery and courage.[30]

Whether they existed, which is often the catalyzing truth of recuperative histories, is only one of many questions to address, as audiences are asked to imagine what kind of encounters might have taken place between famous and lesser-known Black historical figures.

Among the cast of characters reimagined for the film, the first Black deputy US marshal west of the Mississippi River, Bass Reeves (Delroy Lindo), Rufus Buck (Idris Elba), the notorious leader of an outlaw Native and Black gang, the formerly enslaved cowboy, Nat Love (Jonathan Majors), and Mary Fields (Zazie Beetz), also known as Stagecoach Mary and Black Mary, who was the first Black woman to serve as a star route mail carrier in the United States. Within the first fifteen minutes of the film, audiences are introduced to Cuffee (Danielle Deadwyler), as the bouncer at Stagecoach Mary's Saloon. Described in the screenplay as a "smooth-cheeked young bouncer in a sharp vest, hat, and crisp shirt" and as "soft-spoken" and "smoothly confident," audiences soon witness Cuffee's fighting skills, as Cuffee dispenses with two would-be patrons who have refused to remove their firearms before entering the saloon. The screenplay does not make any mention of the character's gender and uses he/him and she/her to refer to Cuffee at different moments in the script. However, Cuffee is also subject to a particularly long and pointed look from Nat Love, who seems both impressed and bemused by Cuffee's skills and stature. It is also through a series of furtive glances between Nat, Mary, and Cuffee that audiences begin to understand that a love triangle exists between them.

FIGURE 1.2. Danielle Deadwyler as "Cuffee" in *The Harder They Fall*.

FIGURE 1.3. Cuffee is dressed in a long red skirt after Nat Love asks them to take on "feminine" clothes as a disguise.

FIGURE 1.4. Cuffee as "Cathay" in the Maysville bank. Visually, the white people and white wall emphasize Cuffee's color contrast. Just before this scene, the film describes with overlaid verbal text that Mayville "is a white town."

While much of the pleasures of the film are found in witnessing Black Hollywood's A-list turn in superb performances as badass gangsters, charting their own paths across the then unchartered territory of the American west, the movie's plot pivots on the question of paternity. Samuel explains about the film, "On the surface, 'The Harder They Fall' is a revenge story, a man hunting down the killer of his parents. Beneath that, however, it's much deeper. It's a love story about two men caught in a never-ending cycle of violence because of their loss. It's a story where both the hunter and hunted are essentially the same person, only to have a final confrontation with tears."[31] As a love story between half-brothers, the film implores us to think again about the psycho-social plot and implications of "mama's baby, papa's maybe," a phrase, which Spillers discusses in her "Interstices" essay as a folk-saying from her childhood, that as it pertains to feminist discourse is suggestive of what it means "to know the seductions of the father and *who*, in fact, the father is" that "might also help the subject to know wherein she occasionally speaks when she is least suspecting."[32]

Cuffee is later "revealed" to be Cathay Williams through an uncomfortable scene of offscreen undress and the return to scene of Cuffee cross-dressed (in women's attire) and pressed to share their "real name." To the question, Cuffee responds: "Cuffee my real name. Name I was born with is Cathay Williams."[33] While film critics are firmly divided on whether the film is a "positive portrayal"—which precipitates the question—of what? Of the historical figure? Of transmasculinity? Gender fluidity? Queerness?—the film lays bare the difficulties of representing and interpreting the past. Cuffee-as-Cathay is feminized, which is in keeping with the impulses of popular historiography, in which they are represented as a Black woman with no apparent "gender trouble." As Kadji Amin has argued, "*no one is binary*"; "it is an idealized opposite [of nonbinary], not a lived state of being," and yet the reiterative representation of Cathay as femme prompts a question about how gender's dominant grammars construct the grounds of public memory.[34]

The scene of Cathay's reveal is also an instance of gender subjectification as deictic without being utopic. There is no easy way out of racialized gender's morass—no way to come clean, and representing Cuffee/Cathay's gender as situational does not disentangle it from the histories of slavery, indenture, and displacement. As Spillers relates in "Mama's Baby, Papa's Maybe: An American Grammar Book," as "this body whose flesh carries the female and the male to the *frontiers of survival* bears in person the marks of a current text whose inside has been turned outside."[35] Spillers's theorization of ungendering is a critical context for imagining gender as subject to rearrangement, wherein black gender-as-fungible produces a grammar of gender, both enunciated and tacit, as I have argued elsewhere.[36] One might read Cuffee's performance of Cathay as a kind of gender maneuvering made possible by their status as ungendered, for which there is evidence in the film's narrative and visuality. The red dress is donned, after all, so that Cathay can rob a bank in a white town, and Cuffee reappears in the costume audiences are first introduced to them in the following scene. At the end, and after they have witnessed the losses of many with whom they fought alongside, Cuffee shares a not quite chaste kiss with Stagecoach Mary before leaving with Bass Reeves, explaining "I kinda always wanted to be a sheriff, deputy, Marshal person."[37] Perhaps this conclusion is a nod to William Cathay's military service, and in keeping with the referent, audiences can imagine how law enforcement did not represent a sense of belonging or fidelity to the state or national project but rather a location from which to do more fugitive living.

But how to attend to the psychic life of fungibility? Even if one does find some room to maneuver within confinement. Here we must linger with the one, or what Spillers defines as the "individual-in-the mass and the mass-in-the-individual" that marks "an iconic thickness: a concerted function whose abiding centrality is embodied *in the flesh*."[38] We might begin to approach the one by considering the provocative ontological question posed here: being a plural being. And yet as Spillers also relates the one "is both conceded and not-oneself," which I take as correspondent to an iconic thickness that subtly reworks W. E. B. Du Bois's "double consciousness"—in an exponentializing conceptualization of seeing, speaking and being.[39] As Spillers contends:

> Before the "individual," properly speaking, with its overtones of property ownership and access, more or less complete, stands the "one," who is both a position in discourse-the spoken subject of *enonce* that figures a grammatical instance and a consciousness of positionality-the speaking subject of the *enonciation*, the one in the act of speaking as consciousness of position. As the former is mapped onto his/her world by social discursive practices, the latter comes into the realization that he/she is the "one" who "counts."[40]

Thus, rather than amending the historical record to reflect that Cuffee or Cathay is a multigendered historical figure, I am proposing that we regard them as a structure that brings into view how racialized gender is a violent, sometimes fatal game of having and being had. To exist at the frontier of gender, then, is to navigate a system of signs as if one's very life depends on it and for which one's personal experimentation with gender might also serve as a form of self-defense. And while thon, as Converse proposed, might eliminate the redundancies of gender pronouns in language, Spillers's the one, on another other hand, is concerned with a process of tapping into an interior intersubjectivity, which I regard as a decolonial praxis, even as she does not name it as such. To be clear, and as the brief history of thon bears out, to find a new word is not the same as finding the missing one, and to signal proliferative and proliferating gender as a sign of "progress" is tantamount to mistaking the map for the territory.

And so, it seems we are back where we began: at the interstice. And no word—as proposed or imaginatively reconceived—will rescue us from this breach. But we must continue to meaningfully contend with how diffuse modes of power—articulable as sexuality and gender and, of course, as race—produce a lived sense of being entangled, which may very well be a way of locating the one. Maybe then we might unsettle the grounding assumptions of the human subject who stands on sexuality's stage and turn to the question of a trans past—not with a measuring stick for accuracy, but with a poethical impulse to gain our political bearings in a past that continues to hurt and a future constituted by doubt.[41] Maybe then the trans kid, and the Indigenous child, and those that seek control over their reproductive capacities could be seen as enmeshed with one another in a common politico-discursive frame in this present moment of white nationalist natalism.

The juridical threat to trans people's and women's bodily autonomy is premised on a reductionist logic that insists that reproduction is a matter of ontologized capacity. This biopolitical mode of biocentric determinism shapes public discourse on all bodies, and Black and trans bodies acutely. Attending to these forms of vicious entanglement becomes the grounds for what Spillers describes in *"The Crisis of the Negro Intellectual*: A Post-Date" as the task for black creative intellectuals, namely "reformulating the object of the search" and "rethinking, as well, one's own involvement—where he/she is situated regarding the conceptual apparatus—in identifying what the object is."[42] To think with the capaciousness of Spillersian thought and the theoretical apparatuses she has offered is to see without conflating how distinct communities (themselves an ideological construct) share a cultural topography. Put differently, not all Black people are trans, and not all trans people are Black but, in another moment of compounding racial-gender violence, we are the one that counts. "We are all, after all, just talking about words," and now, a little more than forty years after Spillers delivered "Interstices," her concluding line bears repeating: "So much depends on it."[43]

Notes

This essay was initially published in *boundary 2* 51, no. 1 (2024), in a dossier on the work of Hortense J. Spillers.

Many thanks to Duke's Literature department, the organizers of "The Nicknames of Distortion" symposium held at the Pembroke Center at Brown University and Whit Pow and Nicole Fleetwood, organizers of the Trans Lineages symposium at NYU for their critical engagement with this essay at different stages of its development. Thank you also to Andrea Adomako for reading and listening to multiple iterations of this essay. And a term to fully express the gratitude I feel for Hortense Spillers and what she has set in motion is another missing word.

1. Spillers, *Black, White, and in Color*, 153.
2. Spillers, "All the Things You Could Be by Now," 82.
3. Hammonds, "Black (W)holes," 131.
4. Spillers, "Interstices," 159.
5. Baron, "Thon Was Word of the Year in 1884."
6. Baron, "The Oldest Genderless Pronouns."
7. Merriam-Webster Dictionary, "The History of 'Thon.'"
8. Baron, "Oldest Genderless Pronouns."
9. *Funk and Wagnalls New Standard Dictionary of the English Language*, vol 4 (1897), s.v. "thon."
10. Converse, "A New Pronoun," 55.
11. Converse, "A New Pronoun," 55.
12. Baron, "Oldest Genderless Pronouns."
13. Baron, "Oldest Genderless Pronouns."
14. Baron, "Oldest Genderless Pronouns."
15. Oliven, *Sexual Hygiene and Pathology*, 514.
16. Spillers, "Mama's Baby, Papa's Maybe," 203.

17. Blanton, "Cathay Williams."
18. "Cathay Williams Story," *St. Louis Daily Times*.
19. Blanton, "Cathay Williams."
20. Blanton, "Cathay Williams."
21. "Cathay Williams Story," *St. Louis Daily Times*.
22. Puar, *The Right to Maim*; Hartman, "Seduction and the Ruses of Power."
23. Blanton, "Cathay Williams."
24. "Cathay Williams: The First African-American Woman to Enlist in the Army and the Only Female Member of the Buffalo Soldiers," National Association of Black Military Women, accessed Sept. 12, 2024, https://www.nabmw.org/cathay-williams.
25. Moten, "Blackness and Nothingness," 739.
26. "The Strange Case of Private William Cathay," National Park Service.
27. "The Strange Case."
28. Spillers, "Interstices," 172.
29. Scott, "'The Harder They Fall' Review."
30. Scott, "'The Harder They Fall' Review."
31. Jeymes Samuel, dir., *The Harder They Fall*.
32. Spillers, "Interstices," 167.
33. Samuel, *The Harder They Fall*.
34. Amin, "We Are All Nonbinary," 114.
35. Spillers, "Mama's Baby, Papa's Maybe," 207, emphasis added.
36. Snorton, *Black on Both Sides*.
37. Samuel, *The Harder They Fall*.
38. Spillers, "'All the Things,'" 101, emphasis in the original.
39. Spillers, "'All the Things,'" 102.
40. Spillers, "'All the Things,'" 101.
41. Spillers, "*The Crisis of the Negro Intellectual*."
42. Spillers, "*The Crisis of the Negro Intellectual*," 81.
43. Spillers, "Interstices," 159, 173.

Works Cited

Amin, Kadji. "We Are All Nonbinary: A Brief History of Accidents." *Representations* 158 (2022): 106–19.

Baron, Dennis. "The Oldest Genderless Pronouns Are Lo and Zo, for French, and E, Es, Em, for English." *Web of Language*, July 16, 2020. https://blogs.illinois.edu/view/25/667453458.

———. "Thon Was Word of the Year in 1884." *Web of Language*, January 5, 2018. https://blogs.illinois.edu/view/25/597154.

Bird, Sarah. *A Daughter of a Daughter of a Queen: A Novel*. New York: St. Martin's Press, 2018.

Blanton, DeAnne. "Cathay Williams: Black Woman Soldier, 1866–1868." *Minerva: Quarterly Report of Women and the Military* 10, no. 3 (1992): 1–12. https://www.buffalosoldier.net/CathayWilliamsFemaleBuffaloSoldierWithDocuments.htm

"A Brief History of Singular 'They.'" *Oxford English Dictionary Blog*, September 4, 2018. https://public.oed.com/blog/a-brief-history-of-singular-they.

"Cathay Williams Story." *St. Louis Daily Times*, January 2, 1876.

Converse, C. C. "A New Pronoun." *The Critic and Good Literature*, August 2, 1884, 55.

"The Epicene Pronoun: The Word that Failed." *American Speech* 56, no. 2 (1981): 83–97.

Funk and Wagnalls New Standard Dictionary of the English Language, vol 4: Sabi to Z. s.v. "Thon." New York: Funk and Wagnalls, 1929.

Hammonds, Evelynn. "Black (W)holes and the Geometry of Black Female Sexuality." *differences: A Journal of Feminist Cultural Studies* 6, nos. 2–3 (1994): 127–45.

Hartman, Saidiya. "Seduction and the Ruses of Power." *Callaloo* 19, no. 2 (1996): 537–60.

"The History of 'Thon,' the Forgotten Gender-Neutral Pronoun." Merriam-Webster Dictionary, accessed May 27, 2020. https://www.merriam-webster.com/words-at-play/third-person-gender-neutral-pronoun-thon.

"How 'Harder They Fall' Was Rolling Along until Murphy's Law Went into Overdrive." *Los Angeles Times*, December 29, 2021. https://www.latimes.com/entertainment-arts/awards/story/2021-12-29/jeymes-samuel-writing-directing-harder-they-fall.

Keeling, Kara. "LOOKING FOR M—: Queer Temporality, Black Political Possibility, and Poetry from the Future." *GLQ* 15, no. 4 (2009): 565–82.

Moten, Fred. "Blackness and Nothingness." *South Atlantic Quarterly* 112, no. 4 (2013): 737–80.

Oliven, John F. *Sexual Hygiene and Pathology*. Philadelphia, PA: J. B. Lippincott, 1965.

Puar, Jasbir. *The Right to Maim: Debility, Capacity, Disability*. Durham, NC: Duke University Press, 2017.

Quidnunc. "Thon: That's the Forewho." *American Speech* 48, nos. 3-4 (1973): 300–302.

Samuel, Jeymes, director. *The Harder They Fall*. Netflix, 2021.

Scott, A. O. "'The Harder They Fall' Review: A New Look for the Old West." *New York Times*, November 3, 2021. https://www.nytimes.com/2021/11/03/movies/the-harder-they-fall-review.html.

Snorton, C. Riley. *Black on Both Sides: A Racial History of Trans Identity*. Minneapolis: University of Minnesota Press, 2017.

Spillers, Hortense J. "'All the Things You Could Be by Now, If Sigmund Freud's Wife Was Your Mother': Psychoanalysis and Race." *boundary2* 23, no. 2 (1996): 75–141.

———. *Black, White, and in Color: Essays on American Literature and Culture.* Chicago, IL: University of Chicago Press, 2003.

———. "*The Crisis of the Negro Intellectual*: A Post-Date." *boundary 2* 21, no. 3 (1994): 65–116.

"The Strange Case of Private William Cathay." National Park Service. January 20, 2023. https://www.nps.gov/foun/learn/historyculture/william-cathay.htm.

2 Oracular Fever Medicine
A Time Travel Oracle for Hortense Spillers

ALEXIS PAULINE GUMBS

The week before Embody and Catalyze, the symposium honoring Hortense Spillers's retirement from Vanderbilt University, I sat far north of Nashville in the temporary office of the Pembroke archive in a building on what used to be the women's quad at Brown University. Not yet transferred to their home in the Hay Library, the boxes of the Black Feminist Theory Collection sat on metal shelves I could mostly reach myself. There amid the treasures, including a picture of Gayl Jones's listening face on the inside cover of the copy of *Corregidora* she gave to Ann duCille, Christina Sharpe's alphabetized printouts of the essays she reads and teaches from (including several by Spillers), Spillers's signed copy of visual artist Lorraine O'Grady's book of photomontages and many more, I found artifacts I knew that the other participants in the symposium would want to know about.[1] I reference and contextualize six of those artifacts (or sets of artifacts) here to remind us of Spillers's interconnection with other writers, her foundational role in the field I/we found already blooming, and her intentional commitment to the work of writing, listening, asking, opening.

    I opened up the Embody and Catalyze symposium at Vanderbilt the night we arrived at the welcome reception in a grand atrium with a group activity.

First, I asked everyone to breathe with me.

What a gift that Hortense Spillers was there with us to breathe in this praise at the symposium delayed multiple times by COVID. What a gift that she is here to breathe in chorus with us in this essay collection now.

And then I asked for dedication. Of course, everyone's presence was dedicated to Hortense Spillers, but who were the other people, not in the room, who had brought us to Spillers?

I dedicated my participation to Maurice Wallace, my PhD advisor. Rev Docta Wallace who read my first messy PhD student writing about Spillers work during my first semester as a graduate student and had enough grace and patience to encourage me to continue. I might have dedicated my participation to Farah Griffin, who put the first work of Black feminist literary criticism I ever read in my hands (Mae Gwendolyn Henderson's "Speaking in Tongues" when I was an undergraduate), but blessedly Farah was at the symposium in person![2]

Everyone turned to their neighbor and shared their dedication, becoming for a moment one of the congregations Spillers theorized in her dissertation "Fabrics of History: Essays on the Black Sermon."[3]

Next, I asked people to think of an intention for our weekend together and to associate that intention with a number. I think E. Patrick Johnson shared first, knowing he would have to leave the symposium early. In response to each intention, I offered an artifact from Spillers's history drawn both from her own papers and the papers of the late Cheryl Wall at the Pembroke archive.

And so here we are again. Gathering ourselves, remembering ourselves, deciding what we want, admitting what we need. Here we are again. And are you breathing? Notice the pace, the quality, the depth of your next six breaths. And who is with you (but not in the room with you) as you read this essay? Who touched your life such that you would end up here between these particular pages in the world Spillers makes imaginable? And finally, what are you wondering? What is the unresolved breakthrough you are living through in this moment, in your life, in your relationships, in your career? Find a question and inquiry or a place of wonder in your own life to ground your curiosity in this moment. Did you find it? Don't keep reading if you didn't find it! I mean for you to find your way to these questions now. If you prefer not to do that right now, read someone else's essay and come back. I'll wait.

Beloved reader, maybe you are like me. Maybe you don't like anyone telling you what to do or how to read or where to start or where to go. And good for you. And good for us! Can you imagine if Hortense Spillers only read how other people wanted her to read? The possibility stills the blood. But if you want to try something, to accept my guidance temporarily, you can follow these instructions or adapt them to your needs. But remain as critical as you are. After all we are readers in the tradition of Hortense Spillers. Which means when we read how we read . . . nothing is inevitable. No one is safe.

Did you find your question? Now choose a whole number between 1 and 6. That's where we'll start. Turn to the artifact that corresponds to that number and think about what it offers to your breakthrough. Feel into where it meets you. Does it affirm you, challenge you, stretch your perspective? I'd love to know. Then read through the rest of the artifacts with the same curiosity or come back for them later. Tell me what you learn.

1. Some Features of a Style

In 1969 as a PhD student at Brandeis, Hortense Spillers wrote an essay for a course she took with the poet, literary critic and translator J. V. Cunningham called "Some Features of a Style."[4] Cunningham himself had a very distinctive style that some call "classicist" and some call "anti-modernist." He used epigrams to write about the potential wisdom in how we choose to relate to mundane situations. A personal favorite line of mine is "We live in the given," from the book length poem To what strangers? What welcome?[5]

In her essay, Spillers, two years away from writing her dissertation proposal, identifies two ways her own writing manifests stylistically. She lives in the contrast between what she calls, "exercises in academic disinterestedness" and "soul spilling." Not to make too much of a connection I have already made an entire book out of between the name Spillers and the verb "spill," but Spillers's word choice here offers an image of the writer choosing between containment or flow. In the essay,

Spillers brings the critical eye that she will later bring to the poems of Gwendolyn Brooks and Audre Lorde, the fiction of Alice Walker, Margaret Walker, Ralph Ellison, and others to her own writing, including papers for other classes, a part of a novel draft and one of her own poems.

It would be wise for those of us constituted by the critical work Spillers is best known for to remember that her criticism has always come out of practice. She is an author of Black fiction, poetry, and theory who analyzes those practices from within. Finally, Spillers admits her intentions as a writer: "To be truthful and not affected, to be exact and not approximate are goals I want to reach as a writer."

At the Embody and Catalyze opening reception I transmuted myself into one of the preachers Spillers writes about in her dissertation and asked the gathered beneficiaries of Spillers career of writing and teaching whether she had reached those goals. Did she do it? I shouted. Of course! everyone indicated in their loud or quiet way, displaying different relationships to the practice of call and response, or at least its appropriateness in the halls of Vanderbilt.

But as I continue to sit with these goals, I realize the better question, and the question that has animated my infinite returns to Spillers's writing is "how?" How does she reach the goals of being truthful and not affected, exact and not approximate? We find examples of her success in the specificity of her verbs, in the infusion of vernacular into her psychoanalytic lines of unravelling, the way that the energy of multitudes sings through each precise sentence thanks to the specificity of its reference, not just in citation but in tone, in vibration. Every word is a brick she can lay in sound, scrape into solid collaboration. How could we not study that? How could we not wonder?

This is a question I bring not only to my own writing (even my rewriting of the sentences just prior) but also to each moment. How to be truthful, and not affected, exact and not approximate? What area of your life is asking you that question now?

2. Voices within the Pale: Proposal for a PhD Dissertation

On August 6, 1971, Hortense Spillers submitted her proposal for what would become the PhD dissertation "Fabrics of History: Essays on the

Black Sermon."⁶ In proposal form, the title was "Voices within the Pale." Spillers draws a throughline from her essay "Some Features of a Style" to her dissertation when she explains her interpretation of the idea of "idiom." "Of the five definitions of idiom," she explains, "one comes closest to the meaning I'm pursuing: 'The style of expression characteristic to an individual.'" But this is not about the dissertation as a place for Spillers to work out her writing style or to celebrate the stylistic articulations of the individual black sermonizers who populate her archive of inquiry. Spillers illustrates the stakes by explaining how she would change the definition of idiom, "I would change individual to a people, then, the spirit of the word, bending it to account for those forces that give shape to the dreams and reaching of 30 million black people in the United States." Spillers's work on idiom is not only accountable to the 30 million black people in the US, but to the "dreams and reaching" of that 30 million. Therefore, the idiom must go beyond the descriptive into the somatic, the prophetic, the poetic.

"In that sense," Spillers clarifies, "idiom is not only a way of saying things or a set of linguistic functions or occurrences, but also a way of feeling what is expressed, a way of perceiving and imagining what is to be known."

And you? To whom are you accountable, whose dreams, whose reaching? And what modes of expression does that accountability require?

3. Gratitude

On June 29, 1978 before publishing her essay "Gwendolyn the Terrible: Propositions on Eleven Poems" in the feminist anthology *Shakespeare's Sisters*, Hortense Spillers wrote a letter of gratitude to her favorite poet, Gwendolyn Brooks. Among her gratitudes was this: "I have found in your poetic voice mental strategies that help me feel empowered as a woman and a black woman at a particular time in a homicidal culture."⁷ She also asked for permission to excerpt the poems she examined in her essay. But the letter was returned to sender. The original letter remains in the Spillers archive, along with a handwritten note from Gwendolyn Brooks herself once it was all worked out.

The note reads:

Dear Ms. Spillers,

I hope that by now Harper has given you your "go-ahead."
I was certainly impressed by your brilliant work.

               Sincerely,
               Gwen Brooks

What is more of an affirmation? The adjective "brilliant" or the shortened given name "Gwen"?

And from whom are you seeking permission? And what exact permission do you seek? Also, why?

4. Birthday Number 40!

On April 24, 1982, also referred to in Hortense Spiller's day planner as "Birthday: Number 40," Hortense Spillers spoke in the gymnasium of Barnard College in Harlem at the Scholar and Feminist IX conference.[8] Her talk would become one of her most influential essays, "Interstices: A Small Drama of Words." The essay opens with a poem by Audre Lorde, a poet who stood on that same stage a year and a half earlier and while sharing poems told the audience, gathered for a fundraiser for the Women's Experimental Theater, how "inordinately proud" she was of her own silvering hair.

Spillers opens her essay with Lorde's "Who Said it Was Simple?" one of the poet's clearest theorizations of intersectional oppression as it plays out within progressive movements. And who better to begin with than the great Black Lesbian Feminist Warrior Poet theorist of erotic power Audre Lorde, since, as Spillers notes early in the talk, when she mentioned to a friend that she would be speaking about "sexuality as discourse" the friend laughed and said "Is that what you talk about when you make love?" Spillers thought to herself "there probably is at least one book to be written on erotic exclamations" but she explained to her audience that "the meeting of terms is both my point and beside it."

I return often to this essay on intergenerationally passed on language to describe sexuality and the important "lexical gaps" Spillers gets into, but to be honest, when I found Spillers's diary note, her drafts of the essay, and the typescript she used for her talk at Barnard what I thought most about was myself, and what was passing down intergenerationally to me as I sat among the dust of that fortieth birthday talk, a month before my own fortieth birthday and with the biography I was writing on Audre Lorde always on my mind. And I remember that Audre Lorde once called herself a "high priestess of 40" because she believed so deeply in the reclamation of power that she experienced when she turned forty and fully came out as a lesbian and redirected the energy she had spent hiding and worrying and fighting herself into creating the world she wanted. And I remember that Spillers insisted that what was at stake in this "small drama of words" was actually a "global restoration and dispersal of power."

And I wonder what you need to remember, now.

5. Absolutely

On July 15, 1984 foundational Black feminist literary scholar and now recent ancestor Cheryl Wall sent a glowing peer review to Indiana University Press for Hortense Spillers and Marjorie Pryse's coedited volume *Conjuring: Black Women, Fiction and Literary Tradition*.[9] Although Wall indicated on her review form that she was comfortable with her name and her report being shared with the authors, when I shared the report with her during the Embody and Catalyze Symposium Hortense Spillers says she never knew who the peer reviewers were for *Conjuring*. Now Cheryl Wall's archival papers and Hortense Spillers's archival papers sit next to each other as part of the Pembroke Center's Black Feminist Archive at Brown University.

It is clear from Cheryl Wall's review that she believed *Conjuring* had a crucial role to play in the establishment of a robust field of literary studies with a focus on Black women. And her answers do not leave any room for uncertainty about the value of the text as a whole, even though she does have slight critiques of certain essays. She uses superlatives, and adjectives such as "essential, crucial, excellent, outstanding, landmark," to describe the work and underlines her conviction with phrases like "without question" and "assuredly."

Wall answers the first question "Is this manuscript a significant contribution to the field?" with one word (followed by a period.): Absolutely.

To the second question "Does this manuscript reflect competent scholarship?" she replies that even "the least successful of these essays is competent, the best are brilliant drawing on a broad spectrum of critical approaches ranging from folkloristics to post-structuralism. Without question the volume contains the best criticism of black women's fiction extant."

In regard to what competition the book might face, Wall assures: "*Conjuring* can hold its own in any competition."

About sales: "I believe this book will sell at above average rates."

And when given the opportunity to say more, she goes on at length with a short essay explaining that

> Conjuring will assuredly stimulate widespread discussion and debate. It will be an essential text for academics whose professional interests include black women's fiction, for students, for general readers and I believe for the contemporary writers whose work is discussed herein. The critical issues it raises will give all these readers much to conjure with. . . . In sum, CONJURING is a landmark in Afro-American and feminist criticism.

"Much to conjure with" indeed. My ellipses above elide paragraphs of Wall's response. And generations. It goes without saying that the careers of most of the people included in this volume and the people reading and using this oracle right now, myself included, would not exist without the roles Wall, Spillers, Pryse and other scholars, writers and activists played in creating the field. But I won't ever leave it unsaid. And what are you supporting? And where are you eliding?

6. This Intramural Project

Hortense Spillers and Toni Morrison often moved through the same spaces. At gathering after gathering they had tried to sit and talk. Spillers also sent her publications to Morrison. On July 1984 Toni Morrison sent a note to Spillers's office at Haverford from her house on the Hudson River. She was clear about the value of Spillers work. "I was very much engaged by it, which is a heartfelt compliment," Morrison explained, "because generally when I read most criticism of Black women's literature, it seems so thin. You are quite the thinker."[10] She follows it with a request to "Please keep in touch, so we can finish the conversations we always begin when we meet."

From 1985 to 1989 Toni Morrison called on our beloved thinker, her own longed-for conversation partner, to theorize Black film as part of the Birth of Black Cinema Project Morrison mounted as part of her tenure as the Alfred Schweitzer chair of the Humanities at SUNY Albany in partnership with the New York State Writers Institute and with support from the National Endowment for the Arts. Haile Gerima, Toni Cade Bambara, Clyde Taylor, and others gathered along with Morrison and Spillers in November 1988 to share their thoughts on the emergence of Black film. Much of the film under discussion was created by the participants in what Clyde Taylor called the "LA Rebellion," an intentional collaborative effort by Black film students at UCLA film school from the 1960s to the 1980s to activate film as a tool for Black liberation, intervention, and transformed consciousness, which included filmmakers such as Julie Dash, Halie Gerima, Zeinabu Irene Davis, and many more.

Spillers was interested in the work under discussion because of its Black priorities. Or as she said in a narrative she mailed to Morrison, she was interested in Black Cinema as an opportunity for Black communities to creatively address each other beyond the white gaze: "In 'forgetting' that somebody is watching you, you/we dare to look inward. As far as I can tell, this intramural project is not only long overdue, but it is the only interesting one in this period of artistic realism."[11]

The November 1988 symposium held the opportunity to turn toward each other as a high priority. Featuring an opening treatise on the master narrative in film by Clyde Taylor, Toni Cade Bambara in conversation with Haile Gerima about *Embers and Ashes*, James Snead in conversation with St. Claire Bourne about his film *In Motion: Amiri Baraka*, and Hortense Spillers in conversation with Spike Lee about *School Daze*, the symposium did not marginalize the Q&A period but rather gave as much time for audience discussion as they did to each featured speaker. For better and worse. Listening to the recording, available now online via University of Albany's archives, I sometimes study the sound of Morrison's irritated breathing during particularly familiar sexist questions.

When Spillers took the stage, after Morrison introduced her, before she offered her thoughts on Spike Lee's work and sat with him in public conversation, she said "I have many things to thank Toni Morrison for, one of which being my posture, my status, which is to say inviting me here to have this role in this conference *despite* my status." She soon clarified, "I describe myself as an imposter because I spend the best days of my life in a classroom teaching about prose narrative . . . this is also the first time I have shared the stage with the subject. Mr. Lee is here!" She also admits that she bought a VCR specifically to watch *School Daze* four times. Her observations about colorism and institutional hypocrisy and the differential framing of the love scenes between the two major couples in the film incorporate not only her own nuanced reading of the film, but also her readings of the audience's responses and her discussions of the film with students on multiple campuses.

There was a long pause between her words and Spike Lee's eventual response. The audience laughs at whatever Spike Lee's face is doing as he moves through the overwhelm of answering the layered questions of the greatest reader of our time.

And what is your face doing now?

Notes

The title of this essay comes from Hortense Spillers, "A Hateful Passion, a Lost Love: Three Women's Fiction," in *Black White and In Color: Essays on American Literature and Culture* (Chicago: University of Chicago Press, 2003), 112. Spillers uses the phrase "what oracular fever" to wonder about Morrison's Eva Peace and how she decides to burn her son to death.

1. *Corregidora*, Box 3, Folder 9, Ann duCille Papers, Pembroke Archives, Brown University; Christina Sharpe's essay printouts, Box 4, Folder 22, Christina Sharpe Papers, Pembroke Archives, Brown University; Lorraine O'Grady's photomontage book, Box 20, Folder 34, Hortense Spillers Papers, Pembroke Archives, Brown University. Hereafter, Spillers Papers.
2. Mae Gwendolyn Henderson, "Speaking in Tongues: Dialogics and Dialectics and The Black Woman Writer's Literary Tradition," in *Changing Our Own Words*, ed. Cheryl Wall (New Brunswick, NJ: Rutgers University Press, 1989).
3. Hortense Jeanette Spillers, "Fabrics of History: Essays on the Black Sermon" (PhD diss., Brandeis University, 1974).
4. "Some Features of a Style," Box 3, Folder 9, Spillers Papers.
5. J. V. Cunningham, *To What Strangers, What Welcome: A Sequence of Short Poems* (Denver, CO: Alan Swallow, 1964).
6. Dissertation proposal, Box 3, Folder 17, Spillers Papers.
7. Letter to Gwendolyn Brooks, Box 10, Folder 2, Spillers Papers.

8. Spillers 1982 Calendar, April 24, Box 1, Folder 9, Spillers Papers.
9. Review of *Conjuring*, Box 26, Folder 15, Cheryl Wall Papers, Pembroke Archive, Brown University.
10. Note from Toni Morrison, Box 10, Folder 3, Spillers Papers.
11. Letter to Morrison, Box 10, Folder 3, Spillers Papers.

3 The Fineness of a Sentence, or, Hortense Spillers's Theoretical Acuity

KEVIN QUASHIE

Hortense Spillers theorizes at the level of the sentence, not just in regard to the particular fineness of what—how—she writes but especially in the way that the sentence becomes, for her, an apparatus for thought: the capacity and demands of the sentence, as a form and an enactment, inspires how Spillers thinks about blackness; animates how Spillers understands the object of black study (as a historical enterprise and also as a practice of the human); organizes her understanding of the limits and potency of black literary criticism.

The sentence is Spillers's unit for thinking about thinking and, as such, it confirms that hers is a practice of black formalism.

Formalism might seem like an unusual, even compromised, framework for appreciating Spillers's intellection. For one, literary traditions like New Criticism enact formalism in ways that make it seem foreign to or antagonistic with black creative praxis. Moreover, in the wake of a burning, raging world, a turn to formalism potentially ignores or obscures critical attention to the afterlife of transatlantic slavery, settler colonialism, late capitalism. As such, formalism might be too naïve for the urgency and insurgency of black art imaginaries.[1]

Formalist thinking surely has its limits. And still, Spillers's affinity with formalism is undeniable, a commitment notable in essay titles like

"Formalism Comes to Harlem," "Interstices: A Small Drama of Words," "Changing the Letter: The Yokes, the Jokes of Discourse, or, Mrs. Stowe, Mr. Reed." To my mind, Spillers resides as kin of a vanguard tradition of black feminist criticism informed by close reading and aesthetic discernment—or formalism by another name. These scholars include Barbara Christian, Toni Morrison, Deborah McDowell, Cheryl Wall, Joyce Ann Joyce, Trudier Harris, Claudia Tate, Nellie McKay, Ann duCille, Hazel Carby, Mae Henderson, Madhu Dubey—others too. In a different and richer light, we might appreciate these scholars as practitioners of deconstructionism alongside Barbara Johnson, Jacques Derrida, and Roland Barthes, since they all revel and grapple with textual pleasures and the differential significations of words.[2]

I want to consider, then, Spillers's word-work, to explore the materiality of and urgency in tarrying with sentences.[3] In her doing, the sentence becomes an aesthetic unit both for conceptualizing the activity of black reading and thinking, and for clarifying the ethical habitus of literary studies. I want to engage Spillers toward enunciating a black tradition of critical formalism that calls us back to the fine small doings of the word.

By emphasizing Spillers's formalist proclivities, I am expanding our tendency to privilege her iconic essay on the scene of subjection, "Mama's Baby, Papa's Maybe: An American Grammar Book," the way that this formidable theorization of gender's material and idiomatic violences constitutes the predominating terms on which we appreciate Spillers's contributions. And though "Mama's Baby" is singularly a study of subjection's calculus, it also signals Spillers's investments in aesthetics and the rhetorical: For one, its first half title—"mama's baby, papa's maybe"—turns on a vernacular wordplay, a bluesy signifying rhyme that enunciates the kinlessness made by enslavement. Right there, in the chiasmic juxtaposition of the black mother's traceable relation to the child—a relation that holds no legal claim—next to the father's wily feasibility, Spillers ideates a linguistic deformation of Western patriarchal lineage. Relatedly, the second half title declares slavery's constitutive gender terror as a "grammar book," securing the intersection between rhetoric (law), pedagogy and epistemology, and materiality (embodiment). Or, words and flesh, flesh and words.

Indeed, even finer than the titular poetics is Spillers's use of an ambivalently active verb to declare the condition of black female unspeakability and to confound the very idea of what speaking is; early on, Spillers writes: "I *describe* a locus of confounded identities, a meeting ground of investments and privations in the national treasury of *rhetorical* wealth. My country needs me, and if I were not here, I would have to be invented."[4] "Describe" here becomes an action of objectification—the one who inhabits this capacity to describe is not really the agent of the description as much as she is its object, the figure deployed to express/delineate rather than the one expressing/delineating. One might recall that this reluctant—ambivalent—expressiveness is preceded by two moments that idiomize language and performativity, first the essay's dramatic opening imperative, "Let's face it," which is followed by an admission of misnaming and a catalog of epithets, scared with quotation marks (as in, "'Peaches' and 'Brown Sugar,' 'Sapphire' . . . 'Aunty'"). Which means that the essay commences its theorizing with three syntactical flourishes that establish a drama of words, articulated clearly in an oft-cited sentence about the sentence:

> In order for me to speak a truer word concerning myself, I must strip down through layers of attenuated meanings, made an excess in time; over time, assigned by a particular historical order, and there await whatever marvels of my own inventiveness.[5]

Together, these four moments constitute the syntactical acuity of theory—the preciseness of the word and of word-work in the essay's thinking to come.[6]

Spillers's sentences are always fine, always astute and trembling with the impossible yearning totality of an idea. The sentences are poetic but they are also poiesis, in the way that they make and unmake the idea and the speaker, propelling along something astonishing and vital and new—again, word and work, word as work.

First, to the matter of Spillers's sentence-work as an avenue into thinking about study: In "Peter's Pans: Eating in the Diaspora," the introduction to her collection *Black, White, and in Color*, Spillers considers the formative capacity and limits of black studies. Early in that essay, she diagnoses the theorization of blackness as a conundrum:

> the puzzle remains how an oxymoron, with an actual and material dimension, is to be expressed, when it lays hold of a cultural semantics rather than a *locality of sentences*. Even if we grasp a general economy of practices all at once, it can still only be "said" *bit by bit* and *part by part*.[7]

This insight advocates the sentence as a possibility for black studying because of its localized intensity, its accretion of knowing that refuses the totalizing move. Spillers turns to language-thinking to caution against the danger of language-thinking, especially as this danger resides in the urgency of black studies as a field motivated by enunciating the conditions of black life and rectifying the ideologies that misname black being. At such an intersection, Spillers emphasizes the partial and approximative qualities of writing that bypass the assumptions of "a general economy" in favor of an intelligence materialized "bit by bit," "part by part."[8]

Spillers embraces the perplexing granular affair of the rhetorical, adopting its terms—"meditation/meditation," "translation"—to enunciate what black critical practice might be.[9] She proposes that

> black writers . . . must retool the language(s) that they inherit. The work of logological refashioning not only involves the dissipation of the poisons of cliché and its uncritical modalities but it also takes a stab at the pulsating infestations that course through the grammars of "race," on "blackness" in particular.[10]

In this moment, Spillers is appraising Ralph Ellison's *Invisible Man*, and she leans into its conjugation of narrative and subjectivity to assert that blackness is a "<u>critical</u> posture"—that blackness invites and invokes criticality through rhetoricity.[11]

The sentence, for Spillers, is a locality of the struggle with the (im)precise force of the word, a locality for sustaining the distinction between blackness as it is lived in the human who is black, and blackness that becomes an occasion for thought. She wants to refuse a simplistic collation of black identity and black study, announced in this crisp claim:

> Even though it seemed that there was only slight difference between the subject(s) of "activism" and the subject(s) of meditation/mediation, there actually yawned enough of a spatio-temporal *beance* or break between one and another to give birth to anxieties of displacement and misorientation simultaneously emergent with the event itself.[12]

That is, Spillers disaggregates black subjects—as historical actors—from blackness as subject or figure for thought/study. This difference animates her exploration of critical practice as an upheaval inaugurated by words:

> At the suggestion of one of my most formidable teachers, J. V. Cunningham, I was trying to learn to write "idiomatically," according to what he had called the "abiding centrality of the word," and to my mind, that meant the creation of sentences that could *not* be anticipated, that violated the rules within the sights of grammar. What, for me, would a sentence sound and "feel" like that was not *oratorical*? For one who had grown up listening to the rich rhetorical babble of southern black Baptist preaching and still admire it, Cunningham's idea was a most peculiar one to me both in the ear and off the tongue. The stylistic elements of the idiomatic were (and remain) for me a *political* choice, inasmuch as I have wanted, as a critico-theoretical practitioner, to *surprise* the most blatant of the racist presumptions that invade every field of discourse.[13]

Across Spillers's recollections, writing arrives as an apparatus for theorizing blackness as the discursive made material and the material made discursive.[14]

Spillers's arguments about black intellectual production are realized fully in "*The Crisis of the Negro Intellectual*: A Post-Date," particularly in her astuteness about community as a dilemma for black studies. Crucially, she acknowledges community as idealization that—especially in the latter quarter of the twentieth century—fractures under the weight of the grim realities of black life, realities that produce and reinforce a dissonance between the scholar who theorizes community and the collective that represents such theorizations. In this regard, "community" becomes the spectral object of black study, even the spectral object of the object-of-black-study as the intellectual's work is haunted by justifying her isolation from this fictive community:

> Perhaps the "purest" object that the black creative intellectual always imagines as the unmediated "thereness" is situated in his/her concept of natal community. But, in my view, the time has come for us to rethink community, if we dare, precisely as an "object of knowledge," beginning with our false relations to it as an "unchanging same."[15]

Spillers announces the intramural as a troubling vector of black study as she takes stock of a discursive seamlessness that falsely authorizes black intellectual productivity—that we have blackness in common as our mark of degeneration across time and space. It is not that Spillers doubts the fact of degeneration but more that she wants to nuance how we understand that fact as an agent of intellection, especially twenty-five years after Harold Cruse's book. (*Crisis* was published in 1967, Spillers's reassessment in 1994.) At least two nuances are at work here: one is Spillers's refusal of the complacency that flattens the differences between black people; the other is her interest in the question of the creative intellectual's object. To that end, early on, Spillers tracks—and contextualizes—the relative material success of a subset of black folks:

> Although African American intellectuals as a class have gained greater access to organs of public opinion and dissemination, although its critical enterprise has opened communication onto a repertoire of stresses that traverse the newly organized humanistic field, and although we can boast today a considerably larger black middle class and upper-middle class, with its avenues into the professions, including elective office, some corporate affiliation, virtually *all* of the NBA, and the NFL, and a fast break into the nation's multimillion dollar "image" industries, the news concerning the African American life-world generally is quite grim.[16]

That passage closes with a declaration of grimness that helps Spillers to differentiate experience across class, as if to pronounce the small size of this resourced demographic. And in that differentiation, Spillers is trying to expose the impact that grimness has on conceptualizing black intellectualism. Admittedly, the clarity here turns on a complicated, almost contradictory, appreciation of grimness as both materially specific and ideologically capacious, as an abiding textuality that inflects the intellectual's struggle with her situatedness. Across two passages, Spillers writes the following:

> The decline of the American market ... has joined forces with late-capital schemes of global reorganization in a dizzying velocity of change that has shifted the very imaginary object on which the black creative intellectual had worked at one time—a stake in the soil, actually bound by coordinates on the map of the inner city, the old "community" is neither *what* nor *where* it used to be; the tax base could not but have followed the wealth—both in and of itself and of labor's potentials—to the city's rim and well beyond.
>
> ... From my point of view, this marks the ace development that today's black creative intellectual neither grasps in its awful sufficiency nor wants to bear up under since she is implicated in its stark ramifications. (We instead chase after fantastic notions, quite an easier pastime than looking at what has happened to community.)[17]

These might seem like indictments of the intellectual who is severed from the community about which she writes, but I understand Spillers to be exploring the discursive operations of black intellectualism, as if to query *what motivates the work, what is the object of the work*. I read Spillers as trying to theorize the positionality of a black thinker thinking through blackness in ways that don't conflate the thinker (or the thinker's black body) with her subject matter, in ways that appreciate thinking as work that is related to but distinct from the inhabitance of racialized being. I read Spillers as offering a calculus of critical practice, one that sustains the fact that in the world of black thought, "The personal pronouns are offered in the service of a collective function."[18]

Across the essay, Spillers calls into question the blackness of black study, the blackness that seemingly authorizes black study.[19]

To that end, she gently offers the following—*gently*, I say, especially in keeping with the tender mood of subjunctivity:

> Might we suggest that *before* the black creative intellectual can "heal" her people, she must consider to what extent she must "heal" herself, and that *before* the intellectual can offer a salvific program against crack and crack-up, she is called upon to consider what immediate conversion she must herself undergo? And is it too much to imagine that what is wrong with "the community" is wrong with oneself? And furthermore, could we say that the black creative intellectual, like the black musician whom she so admires, has an object in fact, but that she is not always interested in what it is?[20]

This diagnosis, as a series of questions, dramatizes the figure of the intellectual—not what the intellectual produces, not the arguments she makes, but how it is her thinking works.

Spillers wants to disentangle the black thinker from easy iterations of intellectualism, an inclination that provokes a sustained analogy between the musician and the intellectual:

> [For the musician] though ego-consciousness is necessary, it is the *performance* that counts here, apparently, as we know black musicians and remember them by the instruments of their performance.... In other words, music in black culture achieved its superior degree of development, in part, because its ancestral forces were *occasioned, allowed*. The culture's relationship to language is the radically different story too familiar to repeat.[21]

In this instance, Spillers surmises that the musician's fluency and praxis are animated by the historical forces of slavery's injunctions but also, importantly, by the refinement of ego-consciousness necessitated in the relation between artist and object (instrument). Her idealized musician develops a relationship to their instrument, a relationship that surpasses the language of control and that constitutes their creative habitat, a dynamic I might summarize via chiasmus: a fluency of praxis, a praxis of fluency. Spillers's gambit, then, is to wonder if this mode can be a model for the creative intellectual: "the black creative intellectual does not make music, as it were, and should not try, but he *can* 'play.'

What, then, is his 'instrument'?"[22] How can the processual dimensions of the musician working to make music resonate with the creative intellectual's making? What is the instrument and what is the orientation to that instrument? The analogy might not be entirely analogous given music's provenance as a black enactment; and still, Spillers presses us to adopt (and adapt) the idiomatic musician's ego-work as an amplitude for contemplating subjectivity's function in the persona of the black intellectual.[23]

In Spillers's formulation, the creative intellectual must persist to decipher knowledge as an object of study, must bear asking *what kind of work is black knowledge making?* I say *bear* because Spillers is sensitive to the ways that the ideals of intramurality can interfere with encountering the utility/futility of intellectual labor:

> The black creative intellectual, then, is rarely afforded *the occasion of the moment* clean; either he will remind himself, or someone else will, of the "big picture," let's say, of the material scene through which he is moving. The very ability to *differentiate* oneself as an *intellectual worker* under the historicizing conditions of African-American culture, long constituted in and by dominance as a mute *facticity* and *tactility*, has barely been achieved by African-Americans across the life-world.[24]

In "*Crisis*," Spillers theorizes the matter of black intellectual creative agency—she theorizes the impediments to the freedom to think, including the willingness to deliberate the manner and process and discourse of (one's) thinking. Spillers is in pursuit of the fineness—the constitutive magnetic components—of black thinking and, to that end, she heightens the distinction between the ideation of self, the ideation of doing, and the apprehension of the prerogatives of blackness. Hers is a mighty attempt "to reconfigure the relation between a knowing subject and how he arrives at knowing—in other words, the latter is neither given in the thing itself, nor is it the transparent transcendent."[25] I borrow this formulation from Spillers's explication of Louis Althusser's critique of Karl Marx because it amplifies the earlier question about the intellectual's instrument. Indeed, Spillers clarifies the query and offers an answer:

> What is the work of the black creative intellectual, *for all we know now*?
>
> The short answer is that the black creative intellectual must get busy *where he is*. There *is* no other work.[26]

The resignation and definitiveness here might reflect how intractable this terrain is—intractable, since the "doing" is thinking which is hard to make legible, hard to make viable in the discursive context of neoliberalism as well as in regard to black ideations of meaningful work; since the "instrument" might be words and sentences which are both the materialities with which one works and the materialities that are one's trouble (the trouble to make words say, the trouble words make in enunciating black subjection). And still, if the black creative intellectual has to "get busy where he is," then that <u>where</u> might be in the praxis made by the page of ideas, in the word-work of the sentence. Or, as Spillers writes in a later essay: "In order to say the 'not-sayable,' I must say—must enter the chain of significant differences inscribed by the sentence."[27] For Spillers, the sentence is the scene—the locality—of black study's criticality.[28] Which means that the sentence is a site of black specificity, black tautness, black proximity, black enactment and creativity, black vitality, black intramurality, black work, black deciphering and delineating, black art. The sentence is an instance and praxis of black aesthetic inhabitance manifested via the rhetorical instability of words and signs, a compass toward an evanescence of black thinking.

Spillers's ideations of the sentence conspire with her iteration of the sermon as a technology of black empowerment—the sermon as an instrument of the rhetorical. In "Moving On Down the Line: Variations on the African American Sermon," Spillers once again explores community as a potential shaped by language-work. Her argument begins with a conclusion about the black churches in the American south via comparison with the great churches of Europe:

> what the feast of the gaze is to the great churches of Europe, . . . the feast of hearing is to the church of the insurgent and dispossessed. . . . In the

church of the prince, ecclesiastical architecture accomplishes the project of awe through the play of light, the immediated spaces along the line of horizontal vision, the sweep, the curve of the soaring angle. The *eye* initiates a vault, a leap of faith. In the church of the insurgent, the hierarchy of the ecclesia, of the political body, is razed, as nuance is stripped down to its bare, necessary minimum. In this church of democratic forms, attested to by far humbler architectural display, the listening *ear* becomes the privileged sensual organ, as the sermon attempts to embody the Word. Between eye and ear, there is not much to choose regarding human status in the places of the Holy. We are small there. But through the Protestant sermon's rhetoric of admonition, through the African-American's sermon of exhortation, "I" improve; "I" "hear"/"have" the Word, at last, in a gesture of intervention that the physical and psychic violence of the North American slave trade neither anticipated, nor could ward off. The African-American church, therefore, sustains a special relationship of *attentiveness* to the literal Word that liberates.[29]

Spillers does remarkable things in this passage, including dislodging the praxis of the black church from the singular clutches of Christianity. More importantly, she conceptualizes the small insurgent church as a structure that operates on the force of the aural, where the siege of engagedness travels through the altitude and amplitude of the word. For her, this black church assembly materializes in the ecology of the word as a force in relation to the body who is attending to the word— not the visual spectacle of majestic architecture, but the potency of the body sutured to the word. In the essay's opening move, Spillers underscores black culture's "special relationship of *attentiveness* to the literal Word that liberates," sermonic work as a praxis of human insurgency.[30] It is in this regard she can hypothesize that the "preacher and the sermon [are] the first-run event of an African *critical* subject-position" in a New World context.[31]

The sermon stands as the occasion of black critical work, the intellectual embodied labor of being with the word, the call to criticality akin to Baby Suggs's invocation to the congregants gathered in the Clearing: "Here ... in this here place, we flesh." That moment from Toni Morrison's *Beloved* is an iconic scene of activation, Baby Suggs inviting or enunciating or demanding that the gathered ones be with the word, that they decipher its sermonic force. Indeed, Baby Suggs's incitement narrativizes the intramural potentiality Spillers theorizes in "Moving," as each congregant is engaged in an experience of wrestling with the word as well as wrestling with the shared communion of being with others in this wrestling. This distillation of collectivity sustains Spillers's earlier unease about tendency to flatten the differences in community, since the experience of being with the word is inhabited in each one and across the many ones. What else is crucial here—and it echoes the dimensions of Baby Suggs's sermon too—is Spillers's insistence that the congregants are "readers" even as they are "hearing" the sermon. In this sly small move, Spillers expands the epistemology of literacy, refusing the normative designation of reading, animating sermon-attending as an intelligence of deciphering and discerning. "We address here the requirements of literacy as the ear takes on the functions of 'reading,'" she announces, which dramatizes the critical practice at stake in the church's insurgent word.[32] In Spillers's logic, the congregants are readers of the word which means that they are engaged in word-work: they are practitioners of deconstructionist deliberating and reordering signs and signifiers. These congregants are intellectual workers and Spillers revives for us the dynamism of their attentiveness, their thinking, their critical labor.[33]

In conceptualizing the sermon's intellectual criticality, Spillers exploits its underacknowledged paradox:

> An aspect of the sermon's miracle is that its audience already knows that there are no suspended or ironic conclusions to the tales that sermons project. In fact, there is only *one* sermonic conclusion, and that is the ultimate triumph over defeat and death that the Resurrection promises. In this case, the processes of hearing/reading lose their character of uncertainty in the Single Surprise that matters. I would go so far as to say that this rewarded anticipation of an outcome is the most prominent feature of temperament in a reading/auditory variable that distinguishes an African-American readership from other constituent reading communities trained in and on the economies of irony.... The sermon itself has formal success only to the extent that the preacher knows that his or her "readers"

choose to agree with the sermon "contract"—to obey the rules of listenership that obtain in the situation.[34]

Again, Spillers emphasizes the *work* that a reader has to do to engage—encounter—the sermon, this critical pursuance that includes surrendering to the lure of the object of study.[35] There is no other miracle to the sermon than this, this call to work, and Spillers's formulation of sermon-reading rightly orients us to the reader (congregant) rather than to the preacher, to the condition of audition that Maurice Wallace describes as a black cultural co-production that merges body, voice, language. I am compelled, further, that Spillersian reading dares to conceptualize understanding and knowing and thinking beyond an encounter with the written word, but also beyond the specific sensibility of orality; this reading is about hearing's contemplative wonder.[36]

The "sermon's miracle," which is the miracle of critical praxis, is not complicated: the miracle arrives in coming to know through the rigor and intensity and surprise and intimacy of reading closely.

Near the end of "Moving," after studying through the sermons of John Wesley Edward Bowen, a Methodist clergyman and nineteenth century black intellectual, Spillers secures the case for the sermon as a technology of black empowerment:

> At this place of fracture, we listen attentively for the moving line that is made articulate to living. In this case, the sermonic word does not soar; it does not leap, it never leaves the ground. It *scatters* instead through the cultural situation and, like the force of gravity, hold us fast to the mortal means. Bound to this earth by the historical particularity of the body's wounding, the community comes face to face with the very limit of identity—the indomitable, irremediable otherness of death, metaphorized, in this instance, by the institution of slavery. But this apparent fatality, in binding speakers and hearers/readers to the material situation, quickens us all the more to the radicalizing move. It seems to me that it is the role of the sermon to replay not only *this* narrative, but its *outcome* on the other side of disaster, as Bowen's "good time coming" would have us believe.[37]

Most stunning is this idiomization of *the moving line*, which I understand as an aphorism for the sentence and its force of impact, the materialization of being in collectivity, an episteme for a reader's reading. In explicating this episteme, Spillers declines from valorizing (spiritual) transcendence and instead describes the "sermonic word" as something immanent, embodied, enfleshed: it is of and on the ground, sutured to the body and its mortality, animating through the body's labor to behold the word—as in, "Here, we flesh." The radicality, then, of black encounter with enduring fatality exists in this conceptualization of reader reading and thinking and living through the sentence. This specificity lives in the particularity of the words "fracture" and "scatter" in the passage above, these inflections of breaking and dispersal that signify both the New World subjection of blackness and the disruption that is any act of reading. One is moved by the transgression that is the sermon's moving line. And in emphasizing hearing as critical discernment, Spillers recites sermon's intramural dimension—hearing, which radiates through the one and through the plural; hearing, which is multisensory (it is reading, deciphering, embodied varyingly).[38]

"Word work is sublime . . . because it is generative," Morrison proffers, and Spillers reminds us that this sublime generativity could be—is—of black intellection, a moving line that collates word and body and transgression, a reading that is being with the moving line.[39]

In conceptualizing word-work as black-work, Spillers is in company with Toni Morrison, especially how Morrison theorizes the reader as a writer and therefore constitutes reading as activity of profound responsibility.[40] Significantly, Morrison's theorization of the reader aims to undermine the two-part "semantic crisis" that generates from American racial logics: first, the dissonance between blackness objectified in the black text juxtaposed against the black human who is never idealized as that text's reader; second, the white reader who, idealized as the audience, is licensed to experience—passively—the text's spectacle of black life. Morrison's theorizing yearns for something other than this intersecting lethargy, for a "new [American] reader" capable of bearing the responsibility of reading.[41] This determination is announced in the preface of *Playing in the Dark*, where Morrison sutures together writing and reading:

> Writing and reading are not all that distinct for a writer. Both exercises require being alert and ready for unaccountable beauty, for the intricateness

or simple elegance of the writer's imagination, for the world that imagination evokes. Both require being mindful of the places where imagination sabotages itself, locks its own gates, pollutes its vision. Writing and reading mean being aware of the writer's notions of risk and safety, the serene achievement of, or sweaty fight for, meaning and response-ability.[42]

Here, Morrison advocates for reading as a critical enactment akin to writing, a commitment she articulates via the metaphor "invisible ink" as that which "lies under, between, outside the lines, hidden until the right reader discovers it."[43] For Morrison, this is reading as an art rather than merely reading as a skill, by which she means discernment with the text and its disturbances: "I want my fiction to urge the reader into active participation in the nonnarrative, nonliterary experience of the text, which makes it difficult for the reader to confine himself to a cool and distant acceptance of data."[44] Across her oeuvre, Morrison emphasizes reading as an apparatus for thinking about thinking—for thinking about the thinking that happens in writing—as well as an aesthetic frame for thinking about critical practice, even critical inhabitance.[45]

Reading and writing, yoked in chiasmus, constellate as terms of "meaning-invention," which is how Patricia J. Williams terms it in a passage from *The Alchemy of Race and Rights* that harmonizes with Morrison and Spillers:

> I am trying to create a genre of legal writing to fill the gaps of traditional legal scholarship. I would like to write in a way that reveals the intersubjectivity of legal constructions, that forces the reader both to participate in the construction of meaning and to be conscious of that process. Thus, in attempting to fill the gaps in the discourse of commercial exchange, I hope that the gaps in my own writing will be self-consciously filled by the reader, as an act of forced mirroring of meaning-invention. To this end, I exploit all sorts of literary devices, including parody, parable, and poetry.[46]

In trying to describe method, Williams settles on the force of the sentence, its line as a locus of deliberation and surprise and wonder—the invitation of sentence work as the poiesis of invention. Or reading.

At the heart of considering Spillers's investment in the sentence is the fact that thinking is hard to represent materially and therefore hard to value, black thinking even more so. Indeed, we are inundated with ideations of black performance where the black body is emblematic of doing and working, but the ideation of black thought, visually or otherwise, is hard to sustain.[47]

Thinking is hard to materialize—that is one dimension animating Spillers's formalism; another is the role that writing has played in the conceptualization of blackness, especially writing as an agent in black theorizing the matter of being. Remember that Spillers frames blackness as a problem for thought by proclaiming that "the puzzle remains how an oxymoron, with an actual and material dimension, is to be expressed," a framing that signifies on the long intersection between black being and black writing.[48] In Spillers's intelligence, thinking, as an apparatus of reading-writing, scales the matter of being to the always-failing preciseness—the ambition for preciseness—of the sentence, "a locality" that is realized "bit by bit and part by part."[49]

Spillers locates her theorizing in aesthetics and formalism, in the intensity and architecture and inventiveness made by encountering words and their approximative capacities. Hers is a black sentence-work, an intellectual labor made material.

How big the world a sentence can make, how big the burden and the sweep, how precise, how small, how right there in one's hand or on one's tongue or in one's reading imaginary, how right there—right here—and demanding and embracing is sentence work.

In the world of reading and thinking that Spillers authors, criticism is an ordinary common act: it is what every reader does, like those congregants of the sermon, surrendering to the lure of words and sinking down into the praxis of discernment. Ordinary, in the way that Morrison conceptualizes the reader as a writer, ordinary and necessary and conditioned by the surprise, wonder, unsettledness—the estrangement—that aesthetics makes.[50]

In Spillers's imagination, the sermon operates as a form of criticality; the sermonic call to reading, that fracturing and scattering, imagines the reader as one who is thralling in and with the text. The preacher might say "sing your song in this foreign land" but it is the sermon's reader, the one hearing and thinking and sussing the words in the company of the church—it is the sermon's reader who is doing the finding.[51] It is a deconstructionist practice.

"A writer," Roland Barthes claims, "is not someone who expresses his thoughts, his passion, or his imagination in sentences but *someone who thinks sentences*: A Sentence-Thinker (i.e., not altogether a thinker and not altogether a sentence-parser)."[52] Which is to say that a writer thinks in and through sentences, that sentence-making cannot be separated from thinking and vice-versa. Again, someone who thinks sentences: that is Spillers.[53]

Reading and thinking, aesthetics and formalism, the intramuralities of black study, the vitality of the sentence, the idiomatic "moving line": these are constitutive elements of Spillers's deconstructionism, her theoretical engagement with the terrible possibilities in language. It is poiesis as R. A. Judy delineates in *Sentient Flesh*:

> Precisely because poiēsis formally exhibits what it exposits, change in action in a duration of time, we can understand it to connote human creating in semiosis, in saying possibility. . . . The relationship between language, perception, and imagination as a technology of life, which is where the poetic and sociality meet.[54]

Spillers's poiesis is intellect in action, thinking in action—even "thinking-in-disorder," where thinking is not in contradistinction to the body but instead is a condition of embodiment.[55]

In this way, Spillers enacts an idea of critical practice—of criticism—that extends beyond its specialized name in the humanities; criticism, here, is the instance of any reader encountering the word—or the world—and willing themselves to behold what they are encountering. Ordinary criticism: maybe every reader is a critic; in sermonic practice, maybe every reader is a critic.[56]

Such is Spillers's formalism, a fineness of thinking and of thinking-in-action that ordinates through specificity, detail, and intensity—the attentiveness and surprise and surrender of reading, this fineness that constitutes a beautiful urgent black aesthetic labor.

Notes

Thank you to Fabrizio Ciccone, Margo Crawford, C. Riley Snorton, and Gianna Mosser for their engagements of this essay; thank you to Hortense J. Spillers for invitation upon invitation to think.

1. Across the twentieth and twenty-first centuries, there have been various arguments in black literary studies for, against, and about form and formalism; often these arguments are framed by politics as such is positioned vis-à-vis form(al- ism). In regard to the Harlem Renaissance, for example, one sees these arguments navigated in David Levering Lewis's historical study *When Harlem Was in Vogue* or in Houston Baker's *Modernism and the Harlem Renaissance*; writers like Ralph Ellison (see *Shadow and Act*) and James Baldwin (see, as one example, *Notes on a Native Son*) engage these debates across the middle part of the last century; and the matter of form—of a black rather than a universal form— is nearly the genesis of the Black Arts / Aesthetic Movement as Evie Shockley (*Renegade Poetics*) and Margo Crawford (*Black Post Blackness*) showcase. In the 1980s, Baker and Henry Louis Gates Jr. (in *The Signifying Monkey* and as editor of *Black Literature and Literary Theory*) emerge as two prominent theorists of formalism, but they are not alone, as the next note will emphasize. Some of the debate about formalism is summarized in Norman Harris's essay "'Who's Zoomin' Who': The New Black Formalism."

    The conversation about formalism often is amplified as a discourse about aesthetics and about criticism; in the contemporary landscape of black literary/ cultural theory—or even black studies more broadly—the matter of formalism overlaps with considerations of the enduring intertwined violences of racial slavery, settler colonialism, and capitalism. One could even make the case that afropessimism, as a broad school of thought, enunciates a formalism and an aesthetic sensibility as much as it disavows the value of formalist/aesthetic- thinking in the midst of such horrors. In making this latter claim, I am thinking of the critical particularities in Frank B. Wilderson's *Red, White & Black* or Saidiya Hartman's keen method work in *Wayward Lives* (or the case of critical fabulation advanced in "Venus in Two Acts"). It has to be noted that Hartman doesn't necessarily declare herself as an afropessimist, even as her work is often cited as informative of that school; in that context, someone like Fred Moten, especially his thinking from *In the Break*, is certainly engaging aesthetics, formalism, and black criticality. Some work relevant to this breadth includes Paul Taylor's *Black Is Beautiful*, Stephen Best's *None Like Us*, Daphne Lamothe's *Black Time and the Aesthetic Possibility of Objects*, Rizvana Bradley's *Anteaesthetics*, Phillip Brian Harper's *Abstractionist Aesthetics*, Fumi Okiji's *Jazz as Critique*, David Lloyd's *Under Representation*, Kandice Chuh's *The Difference Aesthetics Makes*, Caroline Levine's *Forms*, Anna Kornbluh's *The Order of Forms*, and Michael Kelly and Monique Roelofs's edited *Black Art and Aesthetics*. Implicit and explicit across literary assessments of formalism is the specter of New Criticism; see

Andy Hines's *Outside Literary Studies*, Fredric V. Bogel's *New Formalist Criticism*, Miranda B. Hickman and John D. McIntyre's *Rereading the New Criticism*, Verena Theile and Linda Tredennick's *New Formalism and Literary Theory*, W. J. T. Mitchell's "The Commitment to Form; Or, Still Crazy after All These Years," Joseph North's *Literary Criticism: A Concise Political History*, and Lindon Barrett's *Blackness and Value* (especially chapter four). Finally, I want to mention Sylvia Wynter's critique of and caution toward aesthetics and formalism in "Rethinking 'Aesthetics': Notes toward a Deciphering Practice," which cautions about the ways that criticism aesthetics (which Wynter means largely as a discourse of valuation) reiterate the figure of man/Man as the order of things. Wynter offers deciphering as an alternative: "Rather than seeking to 'rhetorically demystify' . . . a deciphering turn seeks to decipher *what* the process of rhetorical mystification *does*. It seeks to identify not what texts and their signifying practices can be interpreted to mean but what they can be deciphered to *do*" (266–67). In some ways, this claim about deciphering will resonate with the case I make for Spillers and sermonic reading in the pages to come. In regard to thinking further about Wynter, aesthetics, and black studies, see Zakiyyah I. Jackson's "Against Criticism" and Katherine McKittrick's *Dear Science* and especially "Dear April: The Aesthetics of Black Miscellanea." And even in its breadth, this note excludes many other citations that have been formative to my thinking about the matter of aesthetics.

2. Part of the claim here is to acknowledge the contributions that black feminist scholars made to what we might understand as deconstructionism. That is, Houston Baker and Henry Louis Gates Jr. are regularly recognized as vanguard figures in black literary theory and even specifically as contributors to deconstructionist thinking, but this is less the case with the cohort of writers named here. In brief, in citing these writers, I am thinking of Barbara Christian's *Black Women Novelists*, *Black Feminist Criticism*, and the iconic "The Race for Theory"; Toni Morrison's close reading of her work in "Unspeakable Things Unspoken" and the argument about reading and writing in *Playing in the Dark*; Deborah McDowell's *"The Changing Same"*; Cheryl Wall's edited collection *Changing Our Own Words*; Joyce Ann Joyce's "'Who the Cap Fit'" and *Warriors, Conjurers and Priests*; Trudier Harris's *From Mammies to Militants*; Claudia Tate's *Domestic Allegories of Political Desire*; Nellie Y. McKay's *Critical Essays on Toni Morrison*; Ann duCille's *Skin Trade* and "Phallus(ies) of Interpretation: Toward Engendering the Black Critical 'I'"; Hazel Carby's *Reconstructing Womanhood*, Mae G. Henderson's "Speaking in Tongues," Madhu Dubey's *Black Women Novelists and the Nationalist Aesthetic* as well as *Signs and Cities*. I could add Susan Willis's *Specifying*, Michael Awkward's *Inspiriting Influences* and *Negotiating Difference*, and Marjorie Pryse and Spillers's edited collection *Conjuring* as part of a canon of black feminist scholars for whom the deconstructionist practice of critical reading was central. It is worth noting, also, that Barbara Johnson, in *The*

Critical Difference and especially *A World of Difference*, bridges the gap between black (women's) literary studies and institutional deconstructionism (that is, the Yale cohort as Marc C. Redfield explicates in *Theory at Yale*).

3. Though the phrase might be common, my use of "word-work" borrows from Toni Morrison who proclaims "word work is sublime . . . because it is generative." Morrison, "The Nobel Lecture," 106.
4. Spillers, "Mama's Baby, Papa's Maybe," 203. Emphasis added.
5. Spillers, "Mama's Baby, Papa's Maybe," 203.
6. As I. Augustus Durham does, one might notice the echo of Ralph Ellison's "The Little Man at Chehaw Station" here, with Ellison, in 1978, writing "But out of a stubborn individualism born of his democratic origins, he insists upon the cultural necessity of his role, and argues that if he didn't exist he would have to be invented. If he were not already manifest in the flesh, he would still exist and function as an idea and ideal because—like such character traits as individualism, restlessness, self-reliance, love of the new, and so on—he is a linguistic product of the American scene and language, and a manifestation of the idealistic action of the American Word as it goads its users toward a perfection of our revolutionary ideals." *Going to the Territory*, 7–8. Spillers, of course, is deeply engaged with Ellison—including in "Peter's Pans" and in "Ellison's Usable Past"—so much so that Durham, in *Stay Black and Die*, claims Ellison as Spillers's "otherfather" (100). More than this, Spillers takes up the enduring significance of Ellison's essay in her 2003 piece, "'The Little Man at Chehaw Station' Today." I am also grateful to Victoria Davidjohn for extended meditations on Spillers's use of "I describe" in "Mama's Baby."
7. Spillers, "Peter's Pans," 3. Emphasis added.
8. Across this essay and in some current work, I am engaging Spillers's language-thinking in conjunction with Toni Morrison's. As such, I want to note resonances between the former's claim about sentences and (black) totality, and the latter's declaration in the Nobel lecture: "language can never live up to life once and for all. Nor should it. Language can never 'pin down' slavery, genocide, war. Nor should it yearn for the arrogance to be able to do so. Its force, its felicity is in its reach toward the ineffable." Morrison, "The Nobel Lecture," 106.
9. Spillers, "Peter's Pans," 4.
10. Spillers, "Peter's Pans," 4.
11. Spillers, "Peter's Pans," 5.
12. Spillers, "Peter's Pans," 4. Emphasis in original.
13. Spillers, "Peter's Pans," 7. Emphasis in original.
14. Though I am not engaging the full arc of Spillers's essay, it is important to acknowledge that she uses the introduction as an occasion both to think again with her published work and also to conceptualize the praxis of thinking materialized in/across that work. This enactment reinforces my appreciation of

Spillers's suturing of writing and thinking. I want to note, also, that Spillers's use of "surprise" (as in "to surprise the most blatant of the racist presumptions") echoes Barbara Johnson's ideation of surprise as a deconstructionist principle; see "the surprise of otherness" as she articulates it in *A World of Difference*, a phrase which becomes the subtitle of *The Barbara Johnson Reader*. Relatedly, the notion of the unexpected semantic emergence is central to Barthes's thinking in *The Pleasure of the Text*. Finally, my occasional use of the phrase "critical practice" is a nod to Catherine Belsey's book of the same name.

15. Spillers, *"Crisis of the Negro Intellectual,"* 458.
16. Spillers, *"Crisis of the Negro Intellectual,"* 430. Emphasis in original.
17. Spillers, *"Crisis of the Negro Intellectual,"* 432–33. Emphasis in original.
18. Spillers, "Mama's Baby, Papa's Maybe," 203.
19. In using the phrase "the blackness of black study" I am signifying on Spillers's affinity for Ellison's *Invisible Man* and its meditation on "the blackness of blackness."
20. Spillers, *"Crisis of the Negro Intellectual,"* 434. Emphasis in original.
21. Spillers, *"Crisis of the Negro Intellectual,"* 451. Emphasis in original.
22. Spillers, *"Crisis of the Negro Intellectual,"* 444–45. Emphasis in original.
23. Elsewhere in the essay, Spillers notes that "The black creative intellectual, from Ralph Ellison, in *Invisible Man*, to Imamu Baraka, in *Home*, to Toni Morrison, in interview, to name some of the most eminent cultural figures, embraces the black musician and his music as the most desirable model/object." Spillers, *"Crisis of the Negro Intellectual,"* 450.
24. Spillers, *"Crisis of the Negro Intellectual,"* 444–45. Emphasis in original.
25. Spillers, *"Crisis of the Negro Intellectual,"* 453.
26. Spillers, *"Crisis of the Negro Intellectual,"* 450. Emphasis in original.
27. Spillers, "Black, White and in Color, or Learning How to Paint," 288.
28. In "The Idea of Black Culture," Spillers extends her engagement with the discourse of black study, nuancing the astuteness that blackness as an identity is not simplistically coequivalent with black culture as either product or a "method." We could collate Spillers's exploration of object with work by Alexander Weheliye (*Habeas Viscus*), Robyn Wiegman (*Object Lessons*), Ann duCille ("The Occult of True Black Womanhood"), Robert Reid-Pharr ("Cosmopolitan Afrocentric Mulatto Intellectual"), Jennifer Nash (on possessiveness in *Black Feminism Reimagined*), and Fred Moten ("The Case of Blackness").
29. Spillers, "Moving On Down the Line: Variations on the African American Sermon," 251–52. Emphases in original.
30. Spillers, "Moving On Down the Line," 252.
31. Spillers, "Moving On Down the Line," 263. Emphasis in original.
32. Spillers, "Moving On Down the Line," 252.
33. Spillers's engagement of these two idioms—community and the aural—extends across pages 252–59. For further critical considerations of oral, aural, and writing,

see Alexander Weheliye's *Phonographies*, Maurice Wallace's *King's Vibrato*, Emily Lordi's *Black Resonance*, and Peter Szendy's *Listen*.
34. Spillers, "Moving On Down the Line," 263. Emphasis in original.
35. This irony, Spillers argues, is "the revelation of an already anticipated subject and outcome" that Roland Barthes calls the "hermeneutic narrative." "Moving On Down the Line," 264. I am using the word *lure* as a specific term of aesthetics, à la Steven Shaviro in *Without Criteria*.
36. See Wallace's *King's Vibrato*, especially pages 1–9. Notable, too, is the way that Spillers's aurality situates us away from the culturally masculine imperative of orality and also resolves the Derridean speech-writing fracture. In making this brief note, I am thinking in conjunction with the citations in note 10 as well as the arguments about the discursive privileging of black orality; see Harryette Mullen's "African Signs and Spirit Writing"; Madhu Dubey's *Signs* (especially chapter 1); and Lordi's *Black Resonance* (especially pages 18–19).
37. Spillers, "Moving On Down the Line," 276. Emphasis in original.
38. Thanks to Fred Moten whose questions, in a May 2023 conversation at the University of Pittsburgh, pressed me to attend more particularly to "fracture" and "scatter."
39. Morrison, "The Nobel Lecture in Literature," 106. Here, I am also thinking with Mae G. Henderson's engagement of Mikhail Bakhtin in "Speaking in Tongues."
40. In the opening of her Nobel lecture, Morrison characterizes the old woman—a figure whose thinking is voiced largely through Morrison's speculation—thusly: "Being a writer she thinks of language partly as a system, partly as a living thing over which one has control, but mostly as agency—as an act with consequences. So the question the children put to her: 'Is it living or dead?' is not unreal because she thinks of language as susceptible to death, erasure; certainly imperiled and salvageable only by an effort of the will. She believes that if the bird in the hands of her visitors is dead the custodians are responsible for the corpse" (103).
41. The phrase "semantic crisis" and the idea of a new American reader come from Michael Nowlin's "Toni Morrison's *Jazz* and the Racial Dreams of the American Writer"; see 157–60. For a further explication of the matter of audience and the imagined/idealized black reader, see Kevin Quashie's *Black Aliveness*, especially pages 1–14.
42. Morrison, *Playing in the Dark*, xi.
43. Morrison, "Invisible Ink," 348.
44. Morrison, "Memory, Creation, and Fiction," 328
45. I am thinking especially of *Playing in the Dark* and the essays "Rememory," "The Nobel Lecture," "Invisible Ink," "Race Matters," and "Memory, Creation, and Fiction," all collected in *The Source of Self-Regard*, as well as "Strangers" published in the *New Yorker*. Morrison regularly tells us that reading-writing is the formative idiom of her intellection; indeed, Morrison's understanding

of writing as creatively intransitive (that is, it is not writing with a direct purpose/argument, but writing as a process of intellection that generates its own force and momentum) resembles some tenets of deconstructionism. And still, Morrison also critiques the (deconstructionist) demotion of the author/writer as reaction to the rise of black/diasporic women's writing (see "Unspeakable Things"). In addition to the essays noted above, see Morrison's interview with Mavis Nicholson for the show *Mavis on Four*.

46. Williams, *The Alchemy of Race and Rights*, 7–8.
47. In thinking about the work and legibility of thinking, see Lordi's arguments in *Black Resonance* about the labor and craft and intelligence of music-making. Lordi continues these investments about craft and labor in *The Meaning of Soul*. (Thanks to Lloyd Pratt for the helpful question that reminded me of Lordi's work.) For other explications of the problem of black thinking, see RA Judy's introduction to *Sentient Flesh* and Nahum Chandler's *X: The Problem of the Negro as a Problem for Thought*; also useful are the explorations of thinking, affect, and language in Mel Y. Chen's *Animacies* and Sianne Ngai's *Ugly Feelings* and Hannah Arendt's general explication of thinking in *The Life of the Mind* and *The Human Condition*.
48. Spillers, "Peter's Pans," 3.
49. Spillers, "Peter's Pans," 3.
50. Across this essay, in thinking about reading, I am leaning on work by Louise Rosenblatt (*The Reader, the Text, the Poem*), Naomi Schor (*Reading in Detail*), Roland Barthes (the emphasis on rereading in *S/Z*), Alberto Manguel's *A History of Reading* (especially the idea that reading is intransitive, which Manguel comes to via Barthes's *ecriture*; see page 184), in addition to works cited in the first note about formalisms. Here, as throughout, I am engaged with the enthusiasm for reading and word in Derridean deconstructionism, though I am interested also in the phenomenology of reading in a way that runs against Derrida's critique of phenomenology (in *Speech and Phenomena*; see David B. Allison's "Derrida's Critique of Husserl and the Philosophy of Presence"). And it is deconstruction that helps me to advocate for reading, words, and text without deploying the political naivete of New Criticism. Finally, I am indebted to Zadie Smith's writing about reading as an aesthetic practice; see especially *Changing My Mind*.
51. The quoted line is a borrowing from Psalms 137, verse 4.
52. Barthes, *The Pleasure of the Text*, 51. Emphasis in original.
53. For more on sentence thinking, see Renee Gladman's work, including *Plans for Sentences*, *Prose Architectures* (where, in the afterword Fred Moten asks "Is there a refuge in the sentence? Is there an underground railroad in the sentence?" [112]), and "The Sentence as a Space for Living: Prose Architecture"—as well as Evie Shockley's thinking about reading—vis-à-vis Gladman—in "On Seeing and Reading the 'Nothing': Poetry and Blackness Visualized." And because they

have been useful to my work overall, I want to cite William Gass's *The World within the Word*, especially "The Ontology of the Sentence" and Jan Mieszkowski's *Crises of the Sentence*, with gratitude to Margo Crawford, Lawrence Stanley and Zach Sng for engagements herein.

54. Judy, *Sentient Flesh*, 13
55. Judy, *Sentient Flesh*, 19
56. My turn to engaging criticism reflects the fact that the name "critic" can be given to people working in different contexts; see Adam Gordon's *Prophets, Publicists, and Parasites* and Evan Kindley's "Criticism's Context." But I am also interested in the disciplinary conversations about criticism across a number of forums, including Los Angeles Review of Books's "No Crisis" on the state of criticism (2015), *American Literary History*'s The Function of American Literary Criticism at the Present Time (2022), Nicholas Gaskill and Kate Stanley's *PMLA* Theories and Methodologies forum "Aesthetic Education without Guarantees" (2023)—as well as books like John Guillory's *Professing Criticism*, Paul A. Bové's *Love's Shadow*, and Hines's *Outside Literary Studies*. And, of course, I am thinking about some black writers—Morrison, Ralph Ellison, James Baldwin, June Jordan, Zadie Smith—whose writing about the function of the black writer/artist engages the conversation about criticism.

Works Cited

Allison, David B. "Derrida's Critique of Husserl and the Philosophy of Presence." *Veritas* 50, no. 1, (2005): 89–99.

Arendt, Hannah. *The Human Condition*. Chicago: University of Chicago Press, 2018.

———. *The Life of the Mind*. New York: Mariner, 1981.

Awkward, Michael. *Inspiriting Influences: Tradition, Revision, and Afro-American Women's Novels*. New York: Columbia University Press, 1989.

———. *Negotiating Difference: Race, Gender, and the Politics of Positionality*. Chicago: University of Chicago Press, 1995.

Baker, Houston. *Modernism and the Harlem Renaissance*. Chicago: University of Chicago Press, 1987.

Baldwin, James. *Notes on a Native Son*. Boston: Beacon Press, 2012.

Barrett, Lindon. *Blackness and Value: Seeing Double*. Cambridge: Cambridge University Press, 2009.

Barthes, Roland. "The Death of the Author." In *Image-Music-Text*, translated by Stephen Heath, 142–48. New York: Hill and Wang, 1977.

———. *The Pleasure of the Text*. Translated by Richard Miller, Hill and Wang, 1975.

———. *S/Z*. Translated by Richard Howard, Hill and Wang, 1975.

Belsey, Catherine. *Critical Practice*. London: Methuen, 1980.

Best, Stephen. *None Like Us: Blackness, Belonging, Aesthetic Life*. Durham, NC: Duke University Press, 2018.
Bogel, Fredric V. *New Formalist Criticism: Theory and Practice*. New York: Palgrave Macmillan, 2013.
Bové, Paul A. *Love's Shadow*. Cambridge, MA: Harvard University Press, 2021.
Bradley, Rizvana. *Anteaesthetics: Black Aesthesis and the Critique of Form*. Palo Alto, CA: Stanford University Press, 2023.
Carby, Hazel. *Reconstructing Womanhood: The Emergence of the Afro-American Woman Novelist*. Oxford: Oxford University Press, 1989.
Castronovo, Russ and Gordon Hunter, eds. "The Function of American Literary Criticism at the Present Time." Special issue, *American Literary History* 34, no. 1 (spring 2022).
Chandler, Nahum. *X: The Problem of the Negro as a Problem for Thought*. New York: Fordham University Press, 2013.
Chen, Mel Y. *Animacies: Biopolitics, Racial Mattering, and Queer Affect*. Durham, NC: Duke University Press, 2012.
Christian, Barbara. "The Race for Theory." *Cultural Critique*, no. 6 (spring 1987): 51–63.
Chuh, Kandice. *The Difference Aesthetics Makes: On the Humanities "After Man."* Durham, NC: Duke University Press, 2019.
Crawford, Margo. *Black Post Blackness: The Black Arts Movement and Twenty-First-Century Aesthetics*. Urbana: University of Illinois Press, 2017.
Derrida, Jacques. *Speech and Phenomena And Other Essays on Husserl's Theory of Signs*. Translated by David B. Allison. Evanston, IL: Northwestern University Press, 1973.
Dubey, Madhu. *Signs and Cities: Black Literary Postmodernism*. Chicago: University of Chicago Press, 2003.
duCille, Ann. "The Occult of True Black Womanhood." *Signs: Journal of Women in Culture and Society* 19, no. 3 (1994): 591–629.
———. "Phallus(ies) of Interpretation: Toward Engendering the Black Critical 'I.'" *Callaloo* 16, no. 3 (1993): 559–73.
———. *Skin Trade*. Cambridge, MA: Harvard University Press, 1996.
Durham, I. Augustus. *Stay Black and Die: On Melancholy and Genius*. Durham, NC: Duke University Press, 2023.
Ellison, Ralph. "The Little Man at Chehaw Station: The American Artist and His Audience." In *Going to the Territory*, 3–38. New York: Vintage, 1987.
———. *Shadow and Act*. New York: Vintage, 1995.
Feuerstein, Melissa, Bill Johnson González, Lili Porten, and Keja L. Valens, eds. *The Barbara Johnson Reader: The Surprise of Otherness*. Durham, NC: Duke University Press, 2014.
Foucault, Michel. "What Is an Author?" Translated by J. V. Harari. In *The Foucault Reader*, edited Paul Rabinow, 101–20. New York: Pantheon Books, 1984.

Gaskill, Nicholas, and Kate Stanley. "Aesthetic Education without Guarantees: An Introduction." *PMLA* 138, no. 1 (2023): 127–36.

Gass, William H. *The World within the Word*. New York: Knopf, 1978.

Gates Jr., Henry Louis, editor. *Black Literature and Literary Theory*. London: Methuen, 1984.

———. *The Signifying Monkey: A Theory of African-American Literary Criticism*. Oxford: Oxford University Press, 1988.

Gladman, Renee. *Plans for Sentences*. Seattle: Wave Books, 2022.

———. *Prose Architectures*. Seattle: Wave Books, 2017.

———. "The Sentence as a Space for Living: Prose Architecture." *Tripwire* 15 (2019): 91–109.

Gordon, Adam. *Prophets, Publicists, and Parasites: Antebellum Print Culture and the Rise of the Critic*. Boston: University of Massachusetts Press, 2020.

Guillory, John. *Professing Criticism: Essays on the Organization of Literary Study*. Chicago: University of Chicago Press, 2022.

Harper, Phillip Brian. *Abstractionist Aesthetics: Artistic Form and Social Critique in African American Culture*. New York: NYU Press, 2015.

Harris, Norman. "'Who's Zoomin' Who': The New Black Formalism." *Journal of the Midwest Modern Language Association* 20, no. 1 (1987), 37–45.

Harris, Trudier. *From Mammies to Militants: Domestics in Black American Literature from Charles Chesnutt to Toni Morrison*. Philadelphia: Temple University Press, 1982.

Hartman, Saidiya. "Venus in Two Acts." *Small Axe* 12, no. 2 (June 2008): 1–14.

———. *Wayward Lives, Beautiful Experiments: Intimate Histories of Riotous Black Girls, Troublesome Women, and Queer Radicals*. New York: Columbia University, 2019.

Henderson, Mae. "Speaking in Tongues: Dialogics, Dialectics, and the Black Woman Writer's Literary Tradition." In *Changing Our Own Words*, edited by Cheryl Wall. New Brunswick, NJ: Rutgers University Press, 1989.

Hickman, Miranda B,. and John D. McIntyre, eds. *Rereading the New Criticism*. Columbus: Ohio State University Press, 2012.

Hines, Andy. *Outside Literary Studies: Black Criticism and the University*. Chicago: University of Chicago Press, 2022.

Howard, Richard. "A Note on the Text." In *The Pleasure of the Text*, v–viii. New York: Hill and Wang, 1975.

Jackson, Zakiyyah I. "Against Criticism: Notes on Decipherment and the Force of Things." *No Humans Involved* (exhibition catalogue), Hammer Museum, 2021, 70–81.

Johnson, Barbara. *The Critical Difference: Essays in the Contemporary Rhetoric of Reading*. Baltimore, MD: Johns Hopkins University Press, 1985.

———. *A World of Difference*. Baltimore, MD: Johns Hopkins University Press, 1989.

Joyce, Joyce A. *Warriors, Conjurers and Priests: Defining African-Centered Literary Criticism.* Chicago: Third World Press, 1994.

———. "'Who the Cap Fit': Unconsciousness and Unconscionableness in the Criticism of Houston A. Baker, Jr. and Henry Louis Gates, Jr." *New Literary History* 18, no. 2 (winter 1987): 371–84.

Judy, R. A. *Sentient Flesh: Thinking in Disorder, Poiēsis in Black.* Durham, NC: Duke University Press, 2020.

Kelly, Michael and Monique Roelofs, eds. *Black Art and Aesthetics: Relationalities, Interiorities, Reckonings.* London: Bloomsbury, 2023.

Kindley, Evan. "Criticism's Context." *American Literary History* 34, no. 2: 635–43.

Kornbluh, Anna. *The Order of Forms: Realism, Formalism, and Social Space.* Chicago: University of Chicago Press, 2019.

Lamothe, Daphne. *Black Time and the Aesthetic Possibility of the Object.* Chapel Hill: University of North Carolina Press, 2024.

Levine, Caroline. *Forms: Whole, Rhythm, Hierarchy, Network.* Princeton, NJ: Princeton University Press, 2015.

Lewis, David Levering. *When Harlem Was in Vogue.* New York: Penguin, 1997.

Lloyd, David. *Under Representation: The Racial Regime of Aesthetics.* New York: Fordham University Press, 2019.

Lordi, Emily. *Black Resonance: Iconic Women Singers and African American Literature.* New Brunswick, NJ: Rutgers University Press, 2013.

———. *The Meaning of Soul: Black Music and Resilience since the 1960s.* Durham, NC: Duke University Press, 2020.

Manguel, Alberto. *A History of Reading.* New York: Penguin, 1997.

McDowell, Deborah. *"The Changing Same": Black Women's Literature, Criticism, and Theory.* Bloomington: Indiana University Press, 1995.

McKay, Nellie Y. *Critical Essays on Toni Morrison.* Boston: G. K. Hall, 1988.

McKittrick, Katherine. "Dear April: The Aesthetics of Black Miscellanea." *Antipode* 54, no. 1 (September 2021): 3–18.

———. *Dear Science and Other Stories.* Durham, NC: Duke University Press, 2021.

Mieszkowski, Jan. *Crises of the Sentence.* Chicago: University of Chicago Press, 2019.

Mitchell, W. J. T. "The Commitment to Form; Or, Still Crazy after All These Years." *PMLA* 118, no. 2 (2003): 321–25.

Moten, Fred. "The Case of Blackness." *Criticism* 50, no. 2 (spring 2008): 177–218.

———. *In the Break: The Aesthetics of the Black Radical Tradition.* Minneapolis: University of Minnesota Press, 2003.

Morrison, Toni. "Interview: Mavis on Four." Youtube, uploaded by Thames TV, Aug 6, 2019, https://www.youtube.com/watch?v=UAqB1SgVaC4

———. "Invisible Ink: Reading the Writing and Writing the Reading." In *The Source of Self-Regard*, 346–52. New York: Vintage, 2019.

———. "Memory, Creation, and Fiction." In *The Source of Self-Regard*, 326–33. New York: Vintage, 2019.
———. "The Nobel Lecture in Literature." In *The Source of Self-Regard*, 102–9. New York: Vintage, 2019.
———. *Playing in the Dark: Whiteness and the Literary Imagination*. New York: Vintage, 1993.
———. "Rememory." In *The Source of Self-Regard*, 322–25. New York: Vintage, 2019.
———. "Strangers." *New Yorker*, October 12, 1998.
———. "Unspeakable Things Unspoken: The Afro-American Presence in American Literature." In *The Source of Self-Regard*, 161–97. Vintage, 2019.
Mullen, Harryette. "African Signs and Spirit Writing." *Callaloo* 19, no. 3 (summer 1996): 670–89.
Nash, Jennifer. *Black Feminism Reimagined: After Intersectionality*. Durham, NC: Duke University Press, 2019.
Ngai, Sianne. *Ugly Feelings*. Cambridge, MA: Harvard University Press, 2007.
North, Joseph. *Literary Criticism: A Concise Political History*. Cambridge, MA: Harvard University Press, 2017.
Nowlin, Michael. "Toni Morrison's *Jazz* and the Racial Dreams of the American Writer." *American Literature* 71, no. 1 (March 1999): 151–74.
Okiji, Fumi. *Jazz As Critique: Adorno and Black Expression Revisited*. Palo Alto, CA: Stanford University Press, 2018.
Pyrse, Marjorie, and Hortense Spillers, eds. *Conjuring: Black Women, Fiction, and Literary Tradition*. Bloomington: University of Indiana Press, 1985.
Quashie, Kevin. *Black Aliveness, or A Poetics of Being*. Durham, NC: Duke University Press, 2021.
Redfield, Marc C. *Theory at Yale: The Strange Case of Deconstruction in America*. New York: Fordham University Press, 2015.
Reid-Pharr, Robert. "Cosmopolitan Afrocentric Mulatto Intellectual." *American Literary History* 13, no. 1 (spring 2001):169–79.
Rosenblatt, Louise. *The Reader, the Text, the Poem: The Transactional Theory of the Literary Work*. Carbondale: Southern Illinois University Press, 1994.
Schor, Naomi. *Reading in Detail: Aesthetics and the Feminine*. London: Methuen, 1987.
Shaviro, Steven. *Without Criteria: Kant, Whitehead, Deleuze, and Aesthetics*. Boston: MIT Press, 2012.
Shockley, Evie. "On Seeing and Reading the 'Nothing': Poetry and Blackness Visualized." *New Literary History* 50, no. 4 (2019): 499–528.
———. *Renegade Poetics: Black Aesthetics and Formal Innovation in African American Poetry*. Iowa City: University of Iowa Press, 2011.
Smith, Caleb, Sarah Mesle, and Merve Emre, eds. "No Crisis." Special series of *Los Angeles Review of Books*, 2015.
Smith, Zadie. *Changing My Mind: Occasional Essays*. New York: Penguin, 2009.

Spillers, Hortense. "Black, White, and in Color, or Learning How to Paint: Toward an Intramural protocol of Reading." In *Black, White, and In Color: Essays on American Literature and Culture*, 277–300. Chicago: University of Chicago Press, 2003.

———. "Changing the Letter: The Yokes, the Jokes of Discourse, or, Mrs. Stowe, Mr. Reed." In *Black, White, and In Color: Essays on American Literature and Culture*, 176–202. Chicago: University of Chicago Press, 2003.

———. "*The Crisis of the Negro Intellectual*: A Post-Date." In *Black, White, and In Color: Essays on American Literature and Culture*, 428–70. Chicago: University of Chicago Press, 2003.

———. "Ellison's Usable Past: Toward a Theory of Myth." In *Black, White, and In Color: Essays on American Literature and Culture*, 65–80. Chicago: University of Chicago Press, 2003.

———. "Formalism Comes to Harlem." In *Black, White, and In Color: Essays on American Literature and Culture*, 81–92. Chicago: University of Chicago Press, 2003.

———. "The Idea of Black Culture." *New Centennial Review* 6, no. 3 (winter 2006): 7–28.

———. "Interstices: A Small Drama of Words." In *Black, White, and In Color: Essays on American Literature and Culture*, 152–75. Chicago: University of Chicago Press, 2003.

———. "'The Little Man at Chehaw Station' Today." *boundary 2* 30, no. 2 (2003): 5–19.

———. "Mama's Baby, Papa's Maybe: An American Grammar Book." In *Black, White, and In Color: Essays on American Literature and Culture*, 203–29. Chicago: University of Chicago Press, 2003.

———. "Moving on Down the Line: Variations on the African-American Sermon." In *Black, White, and in Color: Essays on American Literature and Culture*, 251–76. Chicago: University of Chicago Press, 2003.

———. "Peter's Pans: Eating in the Diaspora." In *Black, White, and In Color: Essays on American Literature and Culture*, 1–64. Chicago: University of Chicago Press, 2003.

Szendy, Peter. *Listen: A History of Our Ears*. Translated by Charlotte Mandell. New York: Fordham University Press, 2008.

Tate, Claudia. *Domestic Allegories of Political Desire: The Black Heroine's Texts at the Turn of the Century*. Oxford: Oxford University Press, 1992.

Taylor, Paul C. *Black Is Beautiful: A Philosophy of Black Aesthetics*. New York: Wiley, 2016.

Theile, Verena, and Linda Tredennick, eds. *New Formalism and Literary Theory*. New York: Palgrave Macmillan, 2013.

Wall, Cheryl, ed. *Changing Our Own Words*. New Brunswick, NJ: Rutgers University Press, 1989.

Wallace, Maurice O. *King's Vibrato: Modernism, Blackness, and the Sonic Life of Martin Luther King Jr.* Durham, NC: Duke University Press, 2022.

Weheliye, Alexander. *Habeas Viscus: Racializing Assemblages, Biopolitics, and Black Feminist Theories of the Human.* Durham, NC: Duke University Press, 2014.

———. *Phonographies: Grooves in Sonic Afro-Modernity.* Durham, NC: Duke University Press, 2005.

Wiegman, Robyn. *Object Lessons.* Durham, NC: Duke University Press, 2012.

Wilderson III, Frank B. *Red, White & Black: Cinema and the Structure of US Antagonisms.* Durham, NC: Duke University Press, 2010.

Williams, Patricia. *The Alchemy of Race and Rights: Diary of a Law Professor.* Cambridge, MA: Harvard University Press, 1992.

Willis, Susan. *Specifying: Black Women Writing the American Experience.* Madison: University of Wisconsin Press, 1987.

Wynter, Sylvia. "Rethinking 'Aesthetics': Notes toward a Deciphering Practice." *Ex-Iles: Essays on Caribbean Cinema*, edited by Mbye Cham, 237–79. Trenton, NJ: Africa World Press, 1992.

```
224 River Road
Grand View-on-Hudson, NY  10960

9 July 1984


Hortense J. Spillers
5 College Circle
Haverford, PA  19041


Dear Hortense,

I suppose you're in Italy now, but I wanted to thank you for sending
me your article.  I was very much engaged by it, which is a heart-
felt compliment, because generally when I read most criticism
of Black women's literature, it seems so thin.  You are quite a
thinker.

Please keep in touch, so we can finish the conversations we
always begin when we meet.


Regards,

Toni Morrison


TM/jp
```

ARCHIVAL FRAGMENT 2: A letter from Toni Morrison to Hortense Spillers, 1984

4 When Hortense Spillers and Toni Morrison Meet in the Clearing

The Hieroglyphics of Marking and Unmarking

MARGO NATALIE CRAWFORD

> I am a marked woman. . . . I describe a locus of confounded identities.
>
> —Hortense Spillers, "Mama's Baby, Papa's Maybe"

> "Mark me, too, I said. 'Mark the mark on me too.'" Sethe chuckled.
> "Did she?," asked Denver.
> "She slapped my face."
>
> —Toni Morrison, *Beloved*

When we revisit these resonant words in Hortense Spillers's "Mama's Baby, Papa's Maybe" and Toni Morrison's *Beloved*, we need to appreciate what is in the margins of a draft of "Mama's Baby, Papa's Maybe" in the Hortense Spillers archive at Brown University. In a typed manuscript page, after the list of names that "mark" black women ("Peaches," "Brown Sugar," "Sapphire," "Earth Mother," "Aunty," etc.), there is a handwritten sentence in an early work-in-progress version of "Mama's Baby, Papa's Maybe." Spillers writes, "I know no living woman, for example, who gauges herself by [unreadable words] them."[1] Underneath the crossing out of other words, this partially unreadable sentence floats mysteriously. The trace of the unreadable looks like it could be "thinking about." The full sentence could be: "I know no living woman, for example, who gauges herself by thinking about them." I am struck by the fact that Spillers initially wanted to include this focus on the fact that "living" black women do not gauge themselves through the categories Spillers includes as examples of the "marked woman" ("Brown Sugar," "Aunty," etc.) The removal of this sentence does not erase this confession from the essay. Throughout "Mama's Baby, Papa's Maybe" and throughout Spillers's larger body of work, we feel the presence of the absence of the need to resolve complicating factors as Spillers stays in the brilliance and vulnerability of what she has described as "sustained doubt."[2]

Spillers moves from the marking ("I am a marked woman") to what is an unmarking ("I describe a locus of confounded identities"). This move from the marked to the almost unmarked helps us understand why Spillers's words at the end of "Mama's Baby, Papa's Maybe" keep resonating—that call to "gain the *insurgent* ground."[3] The unsettled tilt of black feminist insurgent ground refuses the idea of the always already marked. The attention in Spillers's work to both the legible, familiar, recognizable marking of black bodies and the "confounding" of the marking creates room for a rethinking of Frantz Fanon's theory of epidermalization—"the slow composition of my *self* as a body in the middle of a spatial and temporal world."[4] Spillers reshapes Fanon's epidermalization into the slow rediscovery of my *self* as flesh in the middle of a steady attempt to mark the space and time of the black body. Spillers conveys the idea of marking and unmarking in the words "the hieroglyphics of the flesh." Hieroglyphics may be Spillers's image of marks so convoluted they convey a sense of the undoing of the signifying power of marks. When Zora Neale Hurston, in "Characteristics of Negro Expression," claimed the "Negro" "thinks in hieroglyphics," she was anticipating Spillers's move to hieroglyphics of the flesh as a way of thinking about the limits of the idea of the "marked" black subject.[5] Spillers, on the lower frequencies, in "Mama's Baby, Papa's Maybe," reshapes the opening words "Let's face it. I am a marked woman" into "Let's face it: I am hieroglyphics of the flesh."

The practice of unmarking gains shape in Spillers's practice of saying the unsayable. In "Black, White, and in Color, or Learning How to Paint: Toward an Intramural Protocol of Reading," Spillers writes, "In order to say the 'not-sayable,' I must say."[6] These words allow us to hear her commitment to simultaneously facing a discourse of the marked ("I am a marked woman") and the limits of the idea of always already marked black people. The simultaneity of the lived markedness and unmarkedness is the unsayable. When Toni Morrison, in *Beloved*, imagines the scene of refusing the continued marking, we feel Spillers's marked woman refusing to take part in the passing on of the mark. Here is the crucial scene of the refusal of the passing on of the "mark" in *Beloved*.

> She picked me up and carried me behind the smokehouse. Back there she opened up her dress front and lifted her breast and pointed under it. Right on her rib was a circle and a cross burnt right in the skin. She said, "This is your ma'am. This," and she pointed. "I am the only one got this mark now. The rest dead. If something happens to me and you can't tell me by my face, you can know me by this mark."
> Scared me so. All I could think of was how important this was and how I needed to have something important to say back, but I couldn't think of anything so I just said what I thought. "Yes, Ma'am," I said. "But how will you know me? How will you know me? Mark me, too," I said. "Mark the mark on me too." Sethe chuckled.
> "Did she?," asked Denver.
> "She slapped my face."[7]

Sethe's mother cannot bear the thought that her daughter would ask to be marked (and would ask her mother to be the person who marks her). The mother's reaction to the words "mark the mark on me too" must stem from the fact that the mark is a wound. She cannot understand how her daughter could want to be wounded in the same way that she, her mother, has been wounded. When she slaps Sethe, she is violently refusing the passing on of the violence of the mark-making. If this mark on her mother is a branding of the skin, created so that a slave master can mark his property, the power of this scene is the mother's refusal to accept the idea that her daughter will be marked as a slave and that their shared marking (as a slave) will be the only way that they will recognize each other. The slap signals that, for Sethe's mother, the words "mark me too" are painful to hear. The words remind her that her young daughter does not understand that the mark was never a choice and that she would never choose to hurt her daughter in the manner that she has been hurt.

When Spillers imagines "hieroglyphics of the flesh" as "undecipherable markings on the captive body," she gives us a way of understanding why Sethe's mother slaps her daughter and why Sethe asks her mother to "mark the mark on me too." Sethe's mother points to the mark (the "circle and a cross burnt right in the skin"), but the pointing cannot be contained. She is asking her daughter to see the "undecipherable." Sethe, as a child, is trying to understand the "undecipherable" when she asks to be marked. Sethe has inherited the hieroglyphics of the flesh. Spillers, in "Mama's Baby, Papa's Maybe," poses the core question about the generational "transfer" of "marking and branding." She writes, "We might well ask if this phenomenon of marking and branding 'transfers' from one generation to another, finding its various symbolic substitutions in an efficacy of meanings that repeat the initiating moments? . . . This body whose flesh carries the female and the male to the frontiers of survival bears in person the marks of a cultural text whose inside has been turned outside." When Sethe, as a child, asks her mother to "mark the mark on me too," Morrison dramatizes her mother's pain upon hearing her child expect the direct transfer of the "marking and branding." Spillers wonders about the "symbolic substitutions" that might create less legible transfers of this marking and branding. Spillers's turn to the transfer of the substitution marks is a profound opening of space for an afterlife of slavery discourse that traces the complexity of the repetition of the "initiating" brands.

The complexity of the new marks, the substitute marks, does not make it harder to identify slavery and its afterlife as the reason for the marks. Morrison and Spillers meet in the space where the complexity of the new marks, the substitute marks, deepens our understanding of the complexity of Black life after slavery. I grew up hearing that we were never meant to survive. Blackened subjects have been hailed as impossible survivors. When Spillers, in Arthur Jafa's 2014 film *Dreams*

Are Colder than Death, makes her words "We were available" sound like the very words hurt her vocal cords, we hear those who have been hailed as impossible survivors. The focus on "being available" emerges in this film and in her 2018 public lecture "To The Bone: Some Speculations on the Problem of Touch."[8] Just as Morrison at the end of *A Mercy* emphasizes that "there is no protection," Spillers with "availability" emphasizes that enslaved Africans could not protect their own bodies. Spillers uses "we" in a most crucial manner ("We were available"). The generational transfer of being dispossessed from your own body is what Spillers aims to uncover when she theorizes the "hieroglyphics of the flesh."[9]

Fred Moten powerfully imagines being possessed by dispossession. Dispossession, for Moten, is the escape from the logic of possession tied to consenting to be a single being. Moten calls for "acknowledging what it is to own dispossession, which cannot be owned but by which one can be possessed."[10] Spillers's way of saying "we were available" articulates deep pain, but Spillers's voice when she delivers these words in *Dreams Are Colder than Death* also makes us hear a plea for us (blackened subjects) to remain available to being possessed by dispossession. When Spillers, in this same film, says, "Another word for this is empathy," we enter what Morrison, in the novel *Paradise*, describes as the "endless work" to be done "down here in Paradise."[11] The endless work of empathy emerges when one is living the hieroglyphics of flesh and feeling like what Morrison describes, in *Paradise*, as an "open body."[12]

Spillers and Morrison meet, on the lowest frequencies, when they both begin to theorize about the "open body." For Morrison, the practice of the open body appears when the character Consolata teaches the other Covent women how to imagine a type of art therapy that is a re-marking of an open outline of their marked bodies. Morrison uses the word "open body" as she imagines outlines of bodies being drawn on a floor and then being painted and marked as the women try to release the trauma they have been carrying. For Spillers, the idea of the open body appears when she, in "A Hateful Passion, A Lost Love: Three Women's Fiction," thinks about Morrison's character Sula as a "potential being."[13] This idea of a potential being shows how Spillers reaches for a grammar that will make blackness feel less always already marked. When Sula thinks, "Wait'll I tell Nel," she is dying and realizing that death is not the end of the world.¹⁴ Sula is, at this point in the novel, ready to "tell" but she must wait because she is *passing*. Sula embodies the power of potentiality (the power of being a character who always remains an identity in formation). The slide of a process of formation in the often-cited words in *Sula* ("We was girls together ... girl, girl, girlgirlgirl") deliver the sound of potential being as the only type of being that matters in an antiblack world of the always already marked. As Morrison expresses this layering of "girl," we feel Spillers's notion that Sula, on the deepest registers, represents a "potential being."¹⁵

In *Beloved*, Morrison makes Baby Suggs's sermon in the Clearing a meditation on the potential being of black flesh. This iconic sermon begs to be re-read through Spillers's study of the black sermonic tradition. When we allow Morrison and Spillers to talk to each other in the clearing created by the meeting of black feminist theory and black women's literature, Spillers's focus on the black sermonic tradition of the "gaze of the ear" (as opposed to the violence of the "feast of the gaze") gains new dimensions.¹⁶ Baby Suggs's sermon in the Clearing signals the power of a black collective, outdoor love and reclamation of blackened flesh. When we re-read this scene through the lens of Spillers's study of the black sermonic tradition, Morrison's turn to the sonic (what Spillers calls the "gaze of the ears") matters. Morrison writes, "Saying no more, she stood up then and danced with her twisted hip the rest of what her heart had to say while the others opened their mouths and gave her the music. Long notes held until the four-part harmony was perfect enough for their deeply loved flesh."¹⁷ When Spillers's theory of the black sermon meets Morrison's imaging of Baby Suggs's sermon, we *hear* the "long notes held" of this flesh we might call a body. It matters that the publication of Spillers's theory of flesh, in "Mama's Baby, Papa's Maybe" happens at the same time as Morrison gives us Baby Suggs's sermon on flesh. Spillers, in "Moving on Down the Line: Variations on the African-American Sermon," thinks about the black sermonic word that "never leaves the ground" even as it "scatters."¹⁸ The idea of a nontranscendent transcendence emerges in this essay. If we do not let the "long notes held" (in Baby Suggs's sermon) matter as much as Suggs's call for a "holding" of the neck ("So love your neck, put a hand on it, grace it, stroke it and hold it up"), we miss Morrison's and

Spillers's work of simultaneously marking and unmarking black pain. Baby Suggs's opening words "we flesh," in her sermon, echo in Hortense Spillers's performance in the film *Dreams Are Colder than Death*. At a charged moment of pause in this film, Spillers simply says, "that's flesh" and the film then has the mood of "long notes held." Spillers captures the embodiment of this blackness—"that's flesh"—and then she lets that "captive body" go. She, like Baby Suggs, needs the "long notes held" to loosen the hold that would make the hold on the neck become a holding "down" and not the love that can "hold it up."

Spillers describes the black flesh of "long notes held" as "iconic folds" and a "grid of associations."[19] When Baby Suggs asks her outdoor congregation to touch their flesh and hold it, she calls for a holding of Spillers's "potential being," a holding of "iconic folds." When Spillers imagines black flesh as "iconic folds," she adds new dimensions to her practice of creating a discourse that marks and unmarks the impact of antiblackness on the formation of black being. "Iconic folds" signal marked surface and the multiplication and fracturing of marked surface. "Iconic folds" signal a hidden area created by the process of marking and remarking but not legible in the "feast of the gaze."[20] Spillers proposes, in "Moving on Down the Line: Variations on the African-American Sermon," that the black sermonic tradition has found refuge away from an external gaze through a shared black space of inwardness. We need more focus on the relation between Spillers's theory of oneness and this black shared inwardness. For Spillers, the question is not do we choose the one or the mass, but rather how to find the new grammar that allows us to feel the one-in-the-mass. Spillers recognizes the need, in black study and black life, for a "concept of the one" that does not become an individualism set apart from the black masses. Spillers, in "'All the Things You Could Be by Now, If Sigmund Freud's Wife Was Your Mother': Psychoanalysis and Race," reminds us that the discourse of slavery is always liable to reproduce the cancelling out of "the one" that the Middle Passage created. In "'All the Things You Could Be by Now,'" Spillers argues that "before the 'individual,' properly speaking, with its overtones of property ownership and access, more or less complete, stands the 'one.'" If the idea of the *one* takes us out of the individual/collective binary, oneness is shared interiority (a black public interiority).

In "Who Cuts the Border? Some Readings on America," Spillers evokes the lucid notion of the "commotions" created when one feels that one's interiority is being marked. As she analyzes the often-cited Black butler scene (with the young Sutpen) in *Absalom, Absalom!*, she arrives at the idea of the "commotions stirred up on the interior" and the "markings of . . . an interior space."[21] When these words are felt alongside "Let's face it. I am a marked woman," the marking is so much more than all of the names listed—"Peaches and Brown Sugar," "Sapphire" and "Earth Mother," "Aunty," "Granny," God's "Holy Fool," a "Miss Ebony First," or "Black Woman at the Podium." The opening words—"I am a marked woman, but not everybody knows my name"—when read alongside "Who Cuts the Border? Some Readings on America" begin to sound like a twist of what Spillers says about young Sutpen's discovery of his class (and race) position—"he is not who he thought he was."[22] Re-reading this opening line of "Mama's Baby, Papa's Maybe" as what Fred Moten calls "cut interpellation," or "incomplete christening," allows us to remember Eagleton's sense that there are many ways of responding to the hailing.[23] Eagleton writes, "What if we fail to recognize and respond to the call of the Subject? What if we return the reply: 'Sorry, you've got the wrong person'? . . . There are, after all, many different ways in which we can be 'hailed,' and some cheery cries, whoops, and whistles may strike us as more appealing than some others."[24] Spillers keeps teaching us how to not turn when we feel that "hey you" hailing us.

Black flesh in motion is a marked body that feels marked and unmarked. The most compelling aspect of Spillers's theory of flesh may be the idea that we need to find language that begins to capture what it means to "negotiate between the tenses" of "Let's face it. I am a marked woman" and the speculative wonder of the proposition of the "hieroglyphics of the flesh."[25] The *speculative* tense of a hieroglyphics that has not yet become a recognizable language is embedded in Spillers's turn to the opacity of the hieroglyphic after beginning "Mama's Baby, Papa's Maybe" with the declaration "Let's face it. I am a marked woman." Spillers writes, "In that sense, before the 'body' there is the 'flesh,' that zero degree of social conceptualization that does not escape concealment under the brush of discourse or the reflexes of iconography."[26] "Flesh," for Spillers, is not a way of strategically essentializing blackness. It is a form of strategic abstraction, a way that she finds a new grammar to move away from the idea of a legibly gendered black body and the idea of an intact body tied to an intact sense of self. When she adds the word "hieroglyphics" to "flesh" ("hieroglyphics of the flesh"), she makes us feel this notion of flesh as not "writing *on* the body" but a marking that disrupts the binary of surface and depth, a marking that makes the word "body" seem too concrete.

The flesh work of unmarking is the practice of refusing to lapse into narratives of the *black body* that cancel out the *hieroglyphics of the flesh*. R. A. Judy, as he engages Spillers, in *Sentient Flesh*, describes the simultaneity of being outside and inside the enclosures that make black subjects become the "enslaved captive body."[27] Judy rethinks Spillers's hieroglyphics of flesh as Spillers moves from the architecture of the vestibule to the abstraction of "vestibularity." For Judy, this vestibularity is the "disciplining action of culture on the flesh."[28] When Judy thinks about the vestibule as the space where the "traces of being outside, such as shoes and outerwear, are left," the vestibularity of flesh becomes the in-between space when and where one is becoming the "enslaved captive body" even as the traces of being outside of that pure and total captivity remain.[29] The traces of being outside of the epidermalization of blackness are felt by blackened subjects in ways that are still opaque and illegible (in ways that are too opaque and illegible to continue to be visualized as double consciousness).

Spillers's practice of annotation (her marginal marks on the pages in her archive at Brown University) reveals her steady unmarking of the impulse to mark and re-mark the black body. Her *marks* in the margins of the draft of Toni Morrison's play *Dreaming Emmett* offer a new way of understanding how her early work relates to her recent work, in her "Afropessimism and Its Others" lectures, on unmarking Afropessimism's naturalizing of the idea that the ontology of the black subject equals the ontology of the slave. In 1985, Spillers was invited to deliver a lecture (at Capital Repertory Theatre in Albany, NY) on a draft of Toni Morrison's *Dreaming Emmett*. Just as Spillers and Morrison converged, in 1987, when they both set "flesh" in motion (when Baby Suggs's sermon meets Spillers in the clearing), Spillers and Morrison meet on the page when we read the annotated pages of the Morrison script in the Spillers archive. Spillers marks a key part of the play when Emmett asserts:

> What do they know? They killed me and they don't know who I am. You weren't even alive then, and you act like you know me better than my mother. Fourteen? Black? Male? Chicago? White Woman? Photograph? What does that mean? That doesn't equal me. That's not who I am. You can't breathe, you say, because of a newspaper headline.[30]

In the margins, Spillers notes, "a summation of selective identities doesn't equal the person." Early style Spillers was predicting the afropessimist tendency to suggest that the structural must be ontological.

At the end of *Dreaming Emmett*, the character Tamara asks Emmett, "Will you keep on—dreaming Emmett? Do you have to?" Emmett replies, "Not if you do. If you remember, if anybody does. I won't have to. I can get *on*!" Spillers writes in the margins, "episodes of the historic." When I read the end of Morrison's play with Spiller's marginal notes, I had to return to Spillers's essay "Who Cuts the Border? Some Readings on America" and find that key moment when she refers to "locating a site for new, or over-inscriptions."[31] Morrison and Spillers meet at the end of this play "Dreaming Emmett" when Emmett's final monologue becomes an echo of Spillers's words—"locating a site for new, or over-inscriptions." In the final movement of the play, Tamara asks, "On?" and Emmett muses:

> Yeah. On. Do you know that the grass in the sea is always green and moving? And there's dark velvet alleys in between snow caps? You can look at the sun as an equal and then you feel sorry for it because it only has one world. Just one! Tomatoes scream when you cut them and there never was a beginning. There never was a nothing. And there never will be a nothing. It's not empty. It's not. It's, it's—loaded! *You* dream it! I have to get out of here. I have to go! [He disappears. The kite rises and gleams.]

Morrison is not abstracting Emmett Till's murder. She is doing what Spillers describes as "locating a site for new, or over-inscriptions."[32]

Reading these last words written by Morrison, I then returned to Spillers's annotations at the beginning of the script, in the margin of the lines in which Morrison describes the play's approach to the dreamscape. Spillers writes, "To seek to provide systematic distortions and displacement as in dreaming ... no intermission, but blackouts ... a scene of violence abandoned."[33] The non-dreamy dreamscape of *violence abandoned* is Spillers's and Morrison's attempt to denaturalize the marked. Morrison paused her writing of *Beloved* to write this play. Baby Suggs' sermon on flesh was emerging, just as Spillers's theory of flesh was in process of emerging, when she received Morrison's draft *Dreaming Emmett*. Morrison and Spillers meet in a "clearing" that is the space of Baby Suggs' outdoor sermon and the space of unapologetically black critical theory--a space that Spillers refers to, in "Peter's Pans: Eating in the Diaspora," as "talk[ing] *that* talk in *that* place."[34]

Clamoring for a Join: When Spillers and Morrison "Talk that Talk"

Spillers muses, "But what did it mean to talk *that* talk in *that* place?"[35] The talk that Spillers is talking about is described, earlier in this essay, as the "street talk" and the church podium talk. As Spillers thinks about the movement of black critical thought from the street, the church, and black everyday life to the ivory tower of the academy, she recalls a sense of wonder at the suddenness of the circulation of black talk from the space of the black streets to the space of academic institutions. She writes, "Suddenly a curricular object, 'Black Studies' was the name in the morning of a set of impulses that had been called the 'movement' only the night before."[36] The texture of Spillers's theoretical style stays this sense of wonder about the tension, in black critical theory, between the movement and the institutionalizing of ideas and impulses.

The deepest dimension of the clearing of black critical theory where Spillers and Morrison meet is the sense of ideas that are struggling in a discourse that is not yet here. For Morrison, that clearing of space for *talking that black critical talk* in her novels can be seen when she explains why she regrets not keeping the words "clamor for a join" (as opposed to "Certainly no clamor for a kiss") in the penultimate sentence in

Beloved.³⁷ Morrison's editor felt "clamor for a join" was "too dramatic, too theatrical."³⁸ As Morrison laments not keeping the original version, she explains, "The trouble it takes to find just one word and know that it is that note and no other that would do is an extraordinary battle. To have found it and lost it is in retrospect infuriating."³⁹ Just as Morrison thinks about clamoring for "a join" as being remarkably different from clamoring for "a kiss," Spillers's decision to remove the words "I know no living woman, for example, who gauges herself by [unreadable words] them" (from the final version of "Mama's Baby, Papa's Maybe") signals that the emphasis on the marked woman obscures the harder to grasp marks of ungendered black womanhood that are not standard, institutionalized grammar in Black Studies. Spillers begins to *talk that real talk* in this sentence in the earlier draft. She winks to the readers who might also be blackened, ungendered women who "know no living woman . . . who gauges herself by . . ." When Morrison imagines Baby Suggs hailing, in the Clearing, a new subject position called "flesh," she is also talking that talk that is not standard, institutionalized grammar. When Baby Suggs proclaims, "we flesh," we can hear what Morrison feels about the word "join" in the original ending of the novel—"it is that note and no other that would do."⁴⁰ The words "we flesh" are a "clamor for a join," a yearning for a black talk about blackness that decenters any desire to continue clamoring to kiss the dominant institutional forces that need blackness to be marked and easy to read.

Spillers and Morrison call for a joining of the work with abstractions that often create the difficulty of critical theory and the resonance of Black American everyday discourse. Their shared clamoring for a join of a black opacity and black lucidity creates the deepest meaning of Spillers's idea of "talk[ing] that *talk* in *that* place." When Spillers, in "Mama's Baby, Papa's Maybe," writes, "If I were not here, I would have to be invented," the profundity of everyday talk slides, with ease, into an example of a poetic line that could almost make it into a spoken word slam performance poem.⁴¹ This line is a little too opaque to resonate (with immediate, *nod your head* clarity from a slam poetry audience). The listeners might be ready to clap and then hold the applause, waiting for the full explanation. The Spillersian sentences *talk that talk in that place* where black listeners are waiting for a discourse that invents them.

Morrison is wonderfully confused about what kind of *talk* might invent black readership when she, in 1975, insists that she is writing:

> For all those people in the book who don't even pick up the book . . . all those non-readers, all those people in *Sula* who (a) don't exist and (b) if they did wouldn't buy it anyway. But they are the ones to whom one speaks. Not to the New York Times; not to the editors; not to any distant media; not to anything. It is very private thing. They are the ones who say, "Yeah, uh huh, that's right."[42]

This peculiar, puzzling sense of writing to an ideal reader *who does not exist* shows, that like the inclusion of the "uh huh," Morrison is searching for words that begin to explain what it feels like to practice the Spillers notion of "talk[ing] *that* talk in *that* place" where the ideal black readers do not yet exist.[43]

Spillers and Morrison have created space where the "Yeah, uh huh, that's right" reader response can come at the unexpected moments when their words spiral the most and become most hieroglyphic. In "Interstices: A Small Drama of Words," Spillers explains that "first-order" words "seem to come off the human tongue and need not be referred back to a dictionary in order to be understood."[44] Her clamoring for the join of first-order language and what she calls "words that talk about other words" shapes how she insists on both the connection *and* the difference between structures of power and the lived experience of actual Black people.[45] Spillers ends one of her "Afropessimism and Its Others" lectures, in 2021, with Kevin Quashie's turn to "black aliveness" after she troubles the afropessimist inability to separate "positions in discourse" from "real people."[46] In this lecture, Spillers insists that "there is a Black world." In "Interstices," she analyzes the "culture of feeling" that emerges in *Drylongso: A Self-Portrait of Black America* (1980) as African American anthropologist, John Gwaltney, tries to make his 1970s recordings of what he calls "core black culture" be heard, on the page, with as little mediation and translation as possible.[47] The speakers recorded in *Drylongso* discuss race, gender, sexuality, and survival. In the introduction to *Drylongso*, Gwaltney writes, "It is evident that black people are building theory on every conceivable level."[48] Spillers, in "Interstices," focuses on the recording and translation of the "first-order language" in *Drylongso* and reveals her deep interest in a type of black critical theory that can attend to the complex relationship between what she refers to as "positions in discourse" and "real people."[49] As Spillers analyzes (in "Interstices") the words of the black women speakers in *Drylongso*, her own theory (her own "words that talk about other words") creates a bridge between the study of "positions in discourse" and the practice of trying to listen to black working-class women who use their own words to talk about their lives and are not intending to shape this talk into any form of study for an external gaze. Her analysis of the recorded speakers in *Drylongso* has subtle moments when her focus on *talking that talk in that place* (of the academy) shifts into talking that talk with a black working-class "culture of feeling."[50]

Here is the crucial passage, in "Interstices," when Spillers carefully "clamors for the join" of black "cultural feeling" and the study of "positions in discourse." As Spillers analyzes the "first-order" words of Nancy White (fictional name used by Gwaltney), she writes:

> The leisure that Mrs. White does not perceive that she has had to contemplate her sexuality as an isolated ontological detail marks a classically schismatic feature between African-American and Anglo-American historical passage. I observe a tendency, if not a law. A mediation in this case between a first-order expression of sexual practice and the discourse of sexuality would try to elicit the hierarchies of value that the respective terms stand for. "Body," for example, is not a polyvalent or ambiguous referent for a Mrs. White. At the level of analysis and experience, we witness no arbitrary bonding between a signifier and a signified so that for Mrs. White the word, the gesture that fulfills it, and the actual consequences of both converge on a literal moment of time.[51]

Spillers creates the space where the "analysis and experience" can be the same level. Critical discourse makes the constantly used words "the black body" sound like a theoretical matter separated from the people who live within that body. Spillers shows that this working-class black woman critical thinker, Nancy White, does not speak the language that scholars writing about working-class black women speak, but talks about her body (in relation to race, gender, class, and sexuality) in a manner that makes her very use of the word "body" sound like her full inhabitation of what she is "gestur[ing]" to. Gwaltney records Nancy White saying, "When you lose control of your body, you have just about lost all you have in this world!"[52]

Spillers teaches us how to see the "convergence" of Nancy White's telling and showing (her use of the word "body" and her refusal to make her talk about her own body become any type of distance from her own body). When Spillers writes, "and the actual consequence of both [using words and being the non-arbitrary signified of the signifiers] converge on a literal moment of time," she enables us to feel Nancy White's words as such a powerful point of convergence of experience and analysis (in this case, "sexual practice" and the "discourse of sexuality").

When Spillers creates this room, in "Interstices," for a black feminist convergence of experience and analysis, she is doing much more intellectual and political work than the longstanding [white] feminist discourse of writing from the body. Spillers gestures to the idea of a black feminist critical thought that is a practice of thinking in the flesh (in a zone of shared embodied disembodiment where one cannot *talk that talk* of inseparable analysis and experience, if one is not in the Clearing that is the space of black freedom movement). Toni Morrison and Spillers stay stuck in the Clearing when we recognize that Baby Suggs's words "We flesh" are also what Spillers describes as the "literal moment" when "at the level of analysis and experience, we witness no arbitrary bonding between a signifier and a signified."[53] Morrison imagines Baby Suggs' words "we flesh" leading to Suggs asking the congregants in her outdoors church to take "hold" of their flesh.[54] This moment in this iconic literary scene of black liberation theology is a tremendous display of the nonarbitrary bonding of the word "flesh" and the people who share that flesh. When Morrison and Spillers meet in the clearing their writing creates, we feel more space for what Spillers refers to as the "mediation" needed between first-order expressions of black lived experience and the discourse that is not as easy to "pass on." "This is not a story to pass on" (at the end of *Beloved*) can be read as Morrison's refusal to simplify analysis even as she foregrounds first-order language of experience.[55] In *Jazz*, there is a prayerful, Baby Suggs-like, sermonic passage when Morrison's voice as a theorist sounds like Spillers's enchantment, in "Interstices," with a practice of *talking that talk* that makes words inseparable from the "gesture that fulfills" what the words are trying to produce (trying to do). As Morrison's narrator contemplates Golden Grey's amputated existence, the text reads: "I will locate it so that the severed part can remember the snatch, the slice of its disfigurement. Perhaps then the arm will no longer be a phantom, but will take its own shape, grow its own muscle and bone, and its blood will pump the loud singing that has found the purpose of its serenade. Amen."[56] Imagine Baby Suggs' sermon in the Clearing including a call for the "severed part" to "remember the snatch." If we cannot imagine these seemingly more abstract words in the same sermon with the words "We flesh," we fail to believe Spillers's insight that there are "gestures that fulfill" words (that as Baby Suggs says the words "remember the snatch," her outdoor congregants would touch their bodies, as Suggs' sermon counsels, and feel what Spillers describes as the "undecipherable markings on the captive body."[57]

As Morrison and Spillers clamor for the join of flesh experience and flesh analysis, their black feminist work of marking and unmarking complicates any simple reading of the opening words in "Mama's Baby, Papa's Maybe"—"Let's face it. I am a marked woman." Spillers and Morrison teach us: Let's face it. We need theory that can conceive of marked Black women whose experience in this flesh we might call a body complicates the binary of marked and unmarked. When Spillers and Morrison meet in the Clearing of their meditations on *flesh*, on the margins of *Dreaming Emmett*, and in the interstices of *Sula* and *Jazz*, they gesture to a new grammar that makes the idea of marked blackness matter most as a way of understanding what Spillers names "potential being."[58] What Spillers says about Morrison's character Sula and potential being is also a meta-view of what is at stake in the type of Black Study practiced by these two visionary writers: "no longer bound by a rigid pattern of predictions, predilections, and anticipations . . . the will toward rebellion itself *is* the stunning idea."[59] Spillers is one of the space-clearing theorists Morrison thanks in "Race Matters" when she writes:

I applaud and am indebted to scholars here and elsewhere who are *clearing* (theoretical) space where racial constructs are being forced to reveal their struts and bolts; their technology and their carapace, so that political action, intellectual thought, and cultural production can be generated.[60]

Notes

1. Box 15, Folder 15, Hortense J. Spillers Papers, Ms.2019.013, Pembroke Center Archives, John Hay Library, Brown University. Hereafter Spillers Papers.
2. During the 2022 "The Nicknames of Distortion: A Hortense Spillers Symposium," at Brown University, Spillers explained that she now views her investment in the essay form (as opposed to book-length analyses) as her interest in "sustained doubt."
3. Spillers, "Mama's Baby, Papa's Maybe," 229.
4. Fanon, *Black Skin, White Masks*, 111.
5. Hurston, "Characteristics of Negro Expression," 80.
6. Spillers, "Black, White, and in Color," 288.
7. Morrison, *Beloved*, 61.
8. Spillers describes this study of touch in the following manner: "The question of touch, to be at hand without mediation or interference, might be considered the fundamental element of the absence of self-ownership. It defines at once the most terrifying personal and ontological feature of slavery's regimes across the long ages; yet touch, for twentieth-century critics, notably poet Audre Lorde, reverts to the realm of the erotic. 'To the Bone' attempts an entry into this paradox as an exploration of a troubled legacy." Hortense J. Spillers, "To the Bone: Some Speculations on Touch," YouTube, posted by Studium Generale Rietveld Academie, June 27, 2018, https://www.youtube.com/watch?v=AvL4wUKIfpo.
9. Spillers, "Mama's Baby, Papa's Maybe," 85.
10. Moten, *Black and Blur*, 85.
11. Morrison, *Paradise*, 318.
12. Morrison, *Paradise*, 265.
13. Spillers, "A Hateful Passion," 118.
14. Morrison, *Sula*, 149.
15. Spillers, "A Hateful Passion," 118.
16. Spillers, *Black, White, and in Color*, 26.
17. Morrison, *Beloved*, 104.
18. Spillers, "Moving on Down the Line," 276.
19. Spillers, "Mama's Baby, Papa's Maybe," 210.
20. Spillers, *Black, White, and in Color*, 26.
21. Spillers, "Who Cuts the Border?," 334.
22. Spillers, "Who Cuts the Border?," 334.
23. Moten, *In the Break*, 69.

24. Eagleton, "Ideology and its Vicissitudes," 217.
25. McDowell, "Negotiating between Tenses," 144.
26. Spillers, "Mama's Baby, Papa's Maybe," 206.
27. Judy, *Sentient Flesh*, 184.
28. Judy, *Sentient Flesh*, 184–85.
29. Judy, *Sentient Flesh*, 184.
30. Box 13, Folder 50, Spillers papers.
31. Spillers, "Who Cuts the Border?," 333.
32. Spillers, "Who Cuts the Border?," 333.
33. Box 13, Folder 50, Spillers papers.
34. Spillers, "Peter's Pans," 3.
35. Spillers, "Peter's Pans," 3.
36. Spillers, "Peter's Pans," 3.
37. Morrison, *Beloved*, 134.
38. Morrison, *Beloved*, 134.
39. Morrison, *Beloved*, 134.
40. Morrison, *Beloved*, 134.
41. Spillers, "Mama's Baby, Papa's Maybe," 203.
42. Lecture at Portland State University in May 1975.
43. Spillers, "Mama's Baby, Papa's Maybe," 3.
44. Spillers, "Interstices," 169.
45. Spillers, "Interstices," 169.
46. Spillers, "Afropessimism and Its Others."
47. Spillers, "Interstices," 171; Gwaltney, *Drylongso*, xxii.
48. Gwaltney, *Drylongso*, xxvi.
49. Spillers, "Afropessimism and Its Others."
50. Spillers, "Interstices," 171.
51. Spillers, "Interstices," 172.
52. Gwaltney, *Drylongso*, 147.
53. Spillers, "Interstices," 172.
54. Morrison, *Beloved*, 88.
55. Morrison, *Beloved*, 275.
56. Morrison, *Jazz*, 159.
57. Morrison, *Beloved*, 187.
58. Spillers, "A Hateful Passion," 118
59. Spillers, "A Hateful Passion," 118
60. Morrison, "Race Matters," 138. Italics mine.

References

Eagleton, Terry. "Ideology and its Vicissitudes in Western Marxism." In *Mapping Ideology*, edited by Slavoj Žižek. London: Verso, 1994.

Fanon, Frantz. *Black Skin, White Masks*. Translated by Charles Markmann. New York: Grove Press, 1967.

Gwaltney, John. *Drylongso: A Self-Portrait of Black America*. New York: The New Press, 1993.

Hurston, Zora Neale. "Characteristics of Negro Expression." In *Within the Circle: An Anthology of African American Literary Criticism from the Harlem Renaissance to the Present*, edited by Angelyn Mitchell. Durham, NC: Duke University Press, 1994.

Judy, R. A. *Sentient Flesh: Thinking in Disorder, Poiesis in Black*. Durham, NC: Duke University Press, 2020.

McDowell, Deborah E. "Negotiating between Tenses: Witnessing Slavery After Freedom—*Dessa Rose*." In *Slavery and the Literary Imagination*, edited by Deborah E. McDowell and Arnold Rampersad. Baltimore: Johns Hopkins University Press, 1989.

Morrison, Toni. *Sula*. New York: Vintage, 1973.

———. *Beloved*. New York: Vintage, 1987.

———. *Jazz*. New York: Plume, 1992.

———. "Race Matters." In *The Source of Self-Regard: Selected Essays, Speeches, and Meditations*. New York: Knopf, 2019.

———. *Paradise*. New York: Knopf, 1997.

———. *A Mercy*. New York: Vintage Books, 2008.

Moten, Fred. 2003. *In the Break: The Aesthetics of the Black Radical Tradition*. Minneapolis: University of Minnesota Press, 2003.

———. *Black and Blur (Consent Not to Be a Single Being)*. Durham, NC: Duke University Press, 2017.

Spillers, Hortense. "Afropessimism and Its Others: A Discussion between Hortense J. Spillers and Lewis R. Gordon." YouTube, posted by Soka University of America, May 24, 2021. https://youtu.be/Z-s-Ltuo6NI.

———. *Black, White, and in Color: Essays on American Literature and Culture*. Chicago: University of Chicago Press, 2003.

———. "A Hateful Passion, A Lost Love: Three Women's Fiction." In *Black, White, and in Color*, 93–118. Chicago: University of Chicago Press, 2003.

———. "Interstices: A Small Drama of Words." In *Black, White, and in Color*, 152–75. Chicago: University of Chicago Press, 2003.

———. "Mama's Baby, Papa's Maybe: An American Grammar Book." In *Black, White, and in Color*, 203–229. Chicago: University of Chicago Press, 2003.

———. "Peter's Pans: Eating in the Diaspora." In *Black, White, and in Color*, 1–64. Chicago: University of Chicago Press, 2003.

———. "To the Bone: Some Speculations on Touch." YouTube, posted by Studium Generale Rietveld Academie, June 27, 2018. https://www.youtube.com/watch?v=AvL4wUKIfpo.

5 Performance and Preformance

FRED MOTEN

> ... what classical political economy does not see, is not what it does not see, it is *what it sees*; it is not what it lacks, on the contrary, it is *what it does not lack*; it is not what it misses, on the contrary, it is *what it does not miss*. The oversight, then, it is not to see what one sees, the oversight no longer concerns the object, but *the sight* itself. The oversight is an oversight that concerns *vision*: non-vision is therefore inside vision, it is a form of vision and hence has a necessary relationship with vision.
>
> —Louis Althusser et al., *Reading Capital*

> The "real-concrete" question, then, that is posed to black creative intellectuals—What will you do to save your people?—and its thousand and one knee-jerk variations, is therefore misplaced. It seems to me that the *only* question that the intellectual can actually *use* is: To what extent do the "conditions of theoretical practice" pass through him or her, as the *living site of a significant intervention*? In other words, as it passes through "I," what alterations of its properties does the "I/eye" perform? Quite obviously I mean to say that the shifter in the formulation need not refer, *at all times*, to an autobiographical itinerary but might inscribe an *ensemble* of efforts ... defined along particular lines of stress.
>
> —Hortense Spillers, "The Crisis of the Negro Intellectual: A Post-Date"

Spillers's Fall

Hortense Spillers's 1994 essay "*The Crisis of the Negro Intellectual*: A Post-Date" is a typically rich and complex apparatus of opening, a characteristically Spillersian hinge, and hall and haul and call and caul, and fall; veiled, vexed, "vestibular" cause and gone. Her reconsideration of Cruse's classic text sounds a problematic of music, of performance, of multigraphic shift, in its veered interrogation of black intellectuality's relation to its aim(s). And insofar as it moves in varied address of Althusser's question concerning the nature and fate of reading, Spillers asks black creative intellectuals to re-assess their relation to their favored objects in a new elaboration of "the concept of the object." Her essay is a second-sighted site of concern with sight, oversight, and reading at sight, theorizing and enacting a retroprojective literacy of displacement that will have been both before and after reason's vaunted foresight whose generally consensual irruption accesses and exceeds African-American music as a "form of cultural production that the life-world can 'read' through thick and thin" in the name of a performative ethics for which musicking is neither object, nor example, but a deviant way to deviant theoretical practice. In working something like Althusser's "*ever-already* complex raw material, a structure of 'intuition' or 'representation' which combines together in a particular '*Verbindung*' sensuous, technical and ideological elements," Spillers seems to recall, through music, and re-imagine for contemporary scholarship an approach whose critical sensitivities bend reconstruction of the concept of the object toward concept's and object's disappearance. This capacity to see (through) what is seen, through whatever one it is that some one or other sees in mutual (de)constitution and (mis)recognition, which is a mode of reading Althusser may desire without ever quite achieving, is the improvisatory track Spillers is on and extends. Her tensile, supple, angelically critical reading looks backward not so much at but with and in disaster and its exhaust, blown forward in and into retrospection as close topographical attitude given in touch-sensitive engagement as if the tightest kitchen curls were set to till the ground and sea they brush in common wind. To see is to dig, and to caress, in this regard of the zero degree. And Spillers is hip to how music's aural aroma, its auricular flavor, helps us get to(, at, with, beyond, and beside the point where we are beside ourselves) what single(-minded) seeing blindly thinks it has. Again, she not only illuminates Allthusser's understanding of Marx's disruption of "reading at sight," she has tapped into and amps up black intellectuality's anticipation of that disruption, occurring precisely at the intersection of music and writing, precisely at the troubled, troubling occasion wherein the music's ancestral forces are allowed, as it were, *by force*, to carry out the cut operations of its opening foreclosures, against the threat of being derailed by a desire for inaugural purity that demands disavowal of those forces, a desire that attunement to errant, deviant, criminal, *hard* beauty requires that we disavow. This is not just about sound's disruptive augmentation of sight; it is about the way that certain ante-intellectual infatuations with the "real objects" that are given at first sight are broken in (Lindon Barrett's) double vision, a blurred clarity that will have come, as it were, before its simple precedent and which opens us to a discourse of palpable and "culpable" depth that Althusser associates with the Freudian discovery of the unconscious and which we might associate, by way of Spillers, with the discovery of the (under)ground, the fugitive site of blackness *as* black intellectuality, blackness as a concern with and an enactment of soul or, more precisely, the aerate surfaces and surfacings of animate flesh.

Are the black creative intellectual's "object" and the composite lost love object (what she calls our endangered "natal population" [or, elsewhere, that "natal community" which one can now no longer, but which one perhaps never could "swear one knows"] and the customary discourses that operate in a relation to that loss that is, itself, yet to have been fully determined) the same? Or is the (perhaps necessarily) lost object "the apparent homogeneity of the mass, which black life offered to the imagination in the late sixties" and which has been "more or less revealed now as the necessary fiction that has come unraveled at the seams"?[1] At stake here is the ongoing development, or the ongoing flight, of the concept of the object. At the same time, however, as we move critically within the distinction between the real object and the concept of the object, at the same time as we open ourselves up to the liberatory force of such abstraction, we must also investigate the distinction between the object—ennobled by representation even at the level of its "reality"—and the thing. This is in the interest of a certain re-materialization of the abstract. In other words, after one's critical capacities are initialized and honed—precisely in their relation to black social life in what might be called its actuality—by something like an ontological distinction between blackness and black people or the black community, one then requires some understanding of blackness in its materiality—precisely in its relation to black social life in what might be called its possibility. This might all be related to another question, the one concerning the relation between black intellectuality (where the question of its object is bound to the question of its status *as* object) and what Antonio Negri—moving in the usually unacknowledged wake of C. L. R. James—calls "mass intellectuality," a question re-opened now precisely at the moment when the strident dismissal of the mass's apparent homogeneity seems all too prone to an immediate slide into the dismissal of the very idea of the (black) mass itself as well as the black intellectual's critical relation to / improvisational embodiment of it. (To paraphrase Amiri Baraka—in full acknowledgment of the long, differential grain of his thoughtful celebration of the black mass—this matter concerns class struggle in black studies, a problematic whose deep surface we have only begun to scratch.)

What prompts that slide? Is it what Spillers calls "the *theatricalization* of culture analysis and the object of knowledge ... impoverished public discourse" or is there, in fact, an impoverished notion of theatricality, an undeveloped notion of the object (of knowledge) that will have structured a given public discourse precisely in and as a given poverty?[2] This is a Zora Neale Hurston question given by way of a certain preformative amplification of the performative that Spillers deploys to place some stress on—to distress or stress out—Althusser. In other words, Spillers enacts and inhabits a crucial distinction between performance (as mere elaboration of a repertoire of gestures and utterances, an ego-driven going through the motions) and preformance (as the improvisatory enactment of theoretical practice *by the putative object* of theoretical practice given in no-thingly, new-thingly resistance to already given protocols). We would do well to linger in that distinction for a long, perhaps interminable, moment. This is one way to think the "hiatus" of which she speaks late in the essay: "the break from dailiness, the distancing time" that signals the necessary reflection of the object on and in its field, a certain irruption of a "question for theory" that asks "what contribution the thought-object can make to exposing and illuminating it."³ The hiatus is a stage, a break, a preformative occasion, the ordinary irruption of the extraordinary in the ordinary: *blackness*—the black mass in all the richness and diversity of its becoming-object, its interior interobjectivity—*thinking* in the wrought social informality of imagining black things.

What's at stake is something Spillers refers to as a refusal to *"perform personality* rather than using the latter to execute the former"; something on the order of a refusal of the *commercialization* of black studies. That refusal is all bound up with a concern for quality over marketable quantity. In the meantime, the refusal both Spillers and Cruse exemplify is no easy feat, especially when the academy has now become so much more than ever the unhappy and unwelcoming home of intellectual work; especially when the academy remains the site of a mundane refusal of black intellectual existence that redoubles its duplicitous and exclusionary incorporation of the life of the mind. How can we refuse what is continually refused us? Perhaps by recalling that our ongoing flight is a history of such refusal while considering that if writing does follow from (inhabitation's ordinary, ambulatory, all but bass-ic) exodus, as Spillers intimates by way of Michel de Certeau, then none ought to know more about trying to figure out how to know more about such a "thematics of flight" in its subtle difference from and relation to diaspora, than the creative black intellectual. When reading Cruse by way of Spillers, and when one therefore takes the opportunity to read Spillers in the light of Cruse, one realizes that the sense of the endangerment of the natal population, and the unknowability of a natal community defined by a fantasy of homogeneity, had already, insistently, marked Cruse's magisterial work, as its very condition of possibility. When Spillers reads and invokes Cruse she does so as a traveler along tracks that he laid down. Certain unnecessarily disrespectful critiques of the discourse of crisis, whose inability to understand the irreducible relation between crisis and critique is manifest as the servile willingness to step to and fetch any old knock-off version of the profession's fetish for anti-essentialism, won't go there and probably won't go anywhere other than where wherever one goes to exercise the paralytic right to personality. The question before us, if we choose to follow in Spillers's tracks, concerns our destination and direction, our object and our aim, at a moment when the most visible signs of our success, as well as the most undeniable symbols of our failure, are inextricably bound to a sense of loss. We'll have to remember that this particular state of affairs only seems new. Certainly, black intellectuality has always been particularly attuned to the strange interplay of mourning and celebration. All we can do is think about that. All I do is think about you. I love you. You were always gone. Let's stay together. Come on, let's go. Perhaps, if we take up that attunement again, not only as method but also in the way that it manifests both a properly improper stance toward our critical object (that which is called "Western Civilization") and an inappropriably appropriate reaching for our imaginative aim (blackness as an alternative, common, non-exclusionary form of life), then we can also claim the honor of moving (with) Cruse down tracks that Spillers now lays down. Let's see what that looks like. Let's see who looks like that. Let's see if we can look like that with them.

stewart's feast

> And then I would do a painting and it would take a couple of days to find out that it's a disaster. But with photography, I had 36 images to find out that they were all disasters, quickly.
>
> Something I'm curious about is how reality changes through the medium.... Well, you know, the thing that's happening through the medium is your capturing light on surface, right? . . . That's part of the intelligence of the medium. It's that this is the best tool to capture light on surface. I mean that's what it's all about for me.
>
> I'm working not only with the subject matter, but I'm working with the medium and trying to stretch the medium out. I'm using a flash like a brush. The light of a flash like a brush and I am bouncing it off the floor, so you get a different perspective of where the light comes from. There's motion and I am stopping the motion with the light. And she fits into that space. She's bending over backwards and she's filling up that space.

> At this point I'm experimenting with the medium anyway. I don't know what's going to happen. You don't know how it's going to change through the medium. This is negative black and white. It's not digital, so you can't see it right away. I don't know what I'm going to get until I get into the dark room. That's a whole other gestation there.[4]
>
> Frank Stewart

Nexus and journey go together because they don't. Focus, center, crossroads, hub, a bunch of ways gone through, a pointless point of collection and release, gathering and dispersal, both beginning and end and neither, where one and one make three and none in constant proof of one stillborn in motion, of one and one's impossible afterlife in solid air. The natal occasion is tragicomically avoided one mo'gin in the bad, expectant faith we keep with fate and time. Meanwhile, Frank Stewart regularly celebrates a feast of the senses, that's the day constantly before the day that Christ's body went into Heaven, when all is in the wake and on the edge. Stewart is interested in the intraplay of the material and the immaterial in their differential inseparability, not just when sensual experience becomes nonsensual and meaning is made (to go off), but also when a certain madness of brushed light and bent or tangled form pervades the image and evades the imaged, and when sensual experiences move over or across the boundaries that are supposed to separate sensual registers. In these ways, index turns on itself as meaning unravels, while content and form collude in brokenness. This is to say that surface is broken open, and seeing feels like breathing. The image and the imaged are affected, vulnerable. They are foregiven in and as the next disaster, where Stewart makes findings in the art of loss. What's sacramental in Stewart's work is that it makes conditions in which the viewer can all but walk or rise or, deeper, fall into the photographic space. We are required and allowed to be made aware of having joined him in grave somersault and low-ride tumble. What light we are, or have, is transferred, too, and shared, in barely airborne surfacing. This pandimensionality is as miraculously close as heathens get to divine experience, but it is, as when Jesus rises, an experience of the flesh and of the senses. Not resurrection so much as an insurrection, this feast is given also, and all but primarily, as aroma. Now, how does somebody who's not trying to make a picture of scent, make such great pictures of what it is to have been sent by scent, and to it? There's some kind of alchemical and pansensual sorcery going on. It's a matter of spirit and Stewart preaches the gospel of barbecue, using a flash like a brush to share light from one surface to another. And light is the surface in question, and the implement that turns surface into instrument. *All this arranging and deepening where surface, medium, and instrument are inseparable is surfacing.* The interplay of foreground and background is not the point. What matters is the pointlessness, the intra-active nonlocality, which is given when the very idea of foreground and background are no longer backdrop and foregone conclusion. We're not lost in the photograph but we find that we can't quite be found. For the moment, in the moment, we see no looking at, just looking with. Moreover, there's gone, too, and so is here. Even now is given over to presencing, where reality changes and emplotment fails. Having been taken by the club by in a chain of Phineas Newborn, and on the road with Ahmad Jamal, Stewart has long been engaged in mobile, anthemic, anathematic, ana-mathematical monasticism. Jazz pianists' extended tilling of the trio field, in the ancient neoplasticism of the Plantation Inn's or Small's or Lola's or some other cup of trembling, where one and three are subject to under-trinitarian confusion, forms a school for surfacing, where number gives way to recess and felt curve. It's like when somebody singing a song about a creek to the creek that accompanies her becomes the sound shining in a photograph of light applied to light with light in shade. In and through Frank Stewart's immersed, immersive, echomusecological photography, we see the glorious rise and even more glorious fall of the black creative intellectual.[5]

This essay is just some questions laid out on top of one another, augmenting and obscuring one another, addi(c)tive and redactive and diffractive in all this compulsive pointing, and invasive seeing, and violent, loving regard. Maybe this essay *are* some questions. There might be no (such thing as an) essay, at all, all this incompleteness all for naught in constant seeking. Questions laid out, not posed. This layering gets deep when matter and medium lay down with one another and get

FIGURE 5.1. Frank Stewart (b. 1949), *Smoke and the Lovers, Memphis (or Smoke and the Lovers, Hawkins Grill)*, 1992 (printed 2009), gelatin silver print, 12⅜ × 18½ in., The Museum of Modern Art, New York, David H. McAlpin Fund. © Frank Stewart, used with permission

(us) involved. It's like what happens when you close this book and the compact of surfacing goes mad, light on light in light all heavy with and through one another. Light, which is said to reveal, covers over some other layer of itself, as if in recovery of certain shades of the blues and the abstract truth, wherein a mystery is shown but not divulged. After hours, there's no telling what goes on in a book like this. And after unfolding, when the light goes on, stillness can't quite hide the sound of rearrangement, shit getting itself correct in secret resistance to every point of view; mantic, Pan-African approach divining all the way to China. The rub is this rubbing of the photographs and the various flavor it induces. Smoke, as in *Smoke and the Lovers*, reveals some drawn out sharing of attention. Light turns the surface, seasons it, lightning lightening the heavy paper; but the paper, the surface, having been held in light's (ab)solution, its foregiveness, is not to be seen beneath the appearances that tell of it and tell on it, thereby disclosing its inexistence like an aura, all but aural, in études of elemental fade.[6] Isn't that how overtone bears fundament out into nothingness? Out into was it ever there? Out into was there ever any surface underneath this practicing of surfacing that light takes up in and with and through its medium?

Out into "I'm curious about how reality changes through the medium"? Light's medium is photography. Photography's medium is Frank Stewart. Frank Stewart's medium is the open secret.

Surfacing is the diffusion, dispersion, disruption, and deepening of surface. In the digitalization of photography, what is the fate and practice of surfacing's ongoing intensification of the refusal, in rehearsal, of surface? Can brushing light survive cybernetics' arrest of development? A certain motion of light in water, or movement of light through fluid, seems necessary.[7] More questions concerning the alignment visage and portraiture emerge with others concerning the entanglement of medium and pigment. These are questions Glenn Ligon has asked of and by way of Chris Ofili and David Hammons.[8] These are Sam Gilliam's questions for drapery, and Jack Whitten's questions of fabric(ation). These are questions for laundresses and seamstresses and quilters and schoolteachers, questions Stewart asks, in light, of Alma Thomas. These are kitchen table questions for cooks and collagists and painters and photographers. These are tense questions. These are Spillers questions. Such questions of wave and vapor are concerned not only the specific problem of the

FIGURE 5.2. Frank Stewart (b. 1949), *Alma W. Thomas (or Alma Thomas, Painter)*, 1976 (printed 2019), gelatin silver print, 7 × 10 in. (image), Bowdoin College Museum of Art, Brunswick, Maine, Museum purchase, Gridley W. Tarbell Fund. © Frank Stewart, used with permission

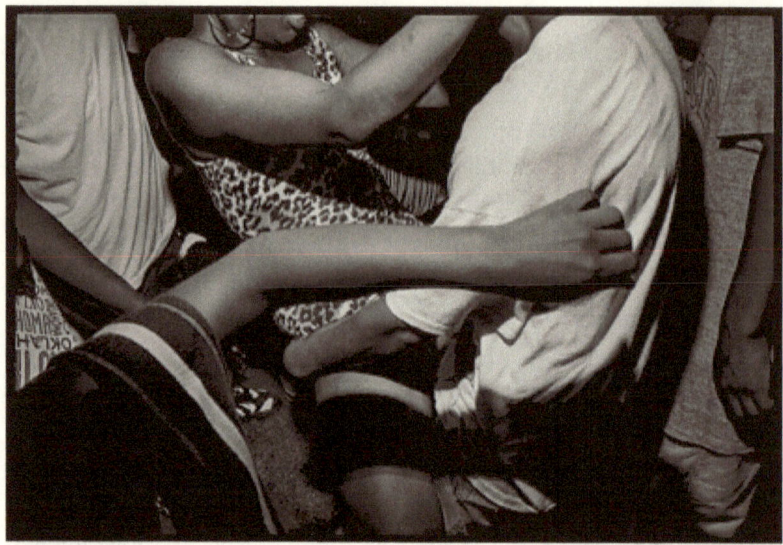

FIGURE 5.3. Frank Stewart (b. 1949), *Juneteenth '93*, 19th of June Celebration, Mexia, Texas, 1993, gelatin silver print, 7¾ × 11½ in., collection of the artist. © Frank Stewart, used with permission

non-particular but the general problem of the pre-particulate, where the convergence of light, pigment, instrument, medium and surface is fabulous and fabulant. When Stewart's description of his practice as brushing light with light is endowed with absolute clarity, then the very nature of reality, and not just its representation or reproduction, comes into the play of changes. Who gets to these questions? Who has to ask these questions? Because they are unsettling it should come as no surprise that the unsettled ask them best and with the most terrible precision. These questions of framing are sacraments of the enframed. Abstract truth is blue's (people's) special concern. It is played out in black (and white). There, it's read, and understood, by students of the frame. They abstract persons from the frame, suspending personality in the frame in favor of shook arms and moved forms. They know what it means that, for the sake of movement, motion is stopped with light. They stay on the scene, they stay with the seen, where there's some work going on, people working shit out, working their way out of something.

It looks like the unowned, the un-self-possessed, are working their way out of work, and of the work, and we're all up in there with them, and Stewart's all up in there, too. Light's been rubbed around up in there—you can taste it. They're studying, but they ain't studying you, or any human calculation. The passionate attachment of the people is impersonal. If you want to know what disaster, here it is. There is no concept of the human that will have been able to withstand the distinction between the owned, ownable, but incapable of owning and the owner. And it's in this regard, by way of this distinction, that the human fully comes into his own, as enacted self-possession, to which he submits in and as the image, the picture, *das Bildung im Gestell*. This, in its turn, both requires and allows us to consider the relation between the owned, ownable, but incapable of owning and those who improve and are improved, and who conceive and are conceived. The problem is given already in the concept, and in conceptualization, and in their relation to the interplay of separation and grasp by which self-picturing and self-regard are held. And the problem this problem bears and hides is a wound at the heart of the human insofar as all ownership begins with the separative self-possession of the one who owns. The extent to which the owner must be self-owned is the extent to which the owner is always already revealed as incapable of owning. His picture of himself is incomplete, though the frame is absolute for him and absolutely brutal for those he sees as owned and owns. For the one who will have owned all this is, as it were, inconceivable. Self-consciousness looks outward for itself. You can't look out for yourself like that. You can't understand yourself that way. It is the inconceivable, generalized as a generative non-conceptuality, that we share, in/as practice.[9] But you can't stand where we ground together. Man, we be grounding without ground. I wish this essay were a brush, or a sheaf of sheaves of light, on photography as a kind of grounding, a kind of surfacing. I wish it could reveal and then abjure the relays between institution and personality, taking and having.

The question concerning the taking of the photograph is one of attitude. Consider by way of the undergeometrical in Spillers, who refuses the norms of verticality in and as grounding rather than in and as the having, which is to say the standing, of ground or the occupation of a point of view. The point of flew, or flown, in grounding, in touching in approaching, is that the medium is intimate. Spillers and Stewart are homelessly homegrown confidants of the zero-degree of social (non) cenceptualization.[10] He whispers, look where this light is coming from and her reply is, "the empathic luminosity we share." But here's a paradox: the way to get (the) people out of being-framed is to get down in it and irrupt. It is to prefer the horizon(t)al in approaching, surfacing, in relation to a sociological hesitation, a solicitation, a rhythm-n-ing that is before the concept, as its depth charge. At the same time, there's a de-objectification of the real that's intimated in the thought that it must change, that it's already otherwise, and that this is what photography reveals. If the concept of the object is a remedy for the simplifications and ossifications of the real object it is not, finally a de-objectification but is, rather, a re-objectification whose power of abstraction and extraction is too awesome. This is why the re-materialization of work is crucial, why Spillers reads the way Althusser reads Marx so closely and tells them all about themselves. She's working with the people who be working something out. Stewart all but puts it this way: "At this point [we're] experimenting with the medium anyway. [We] don't know what's going to happen. You don't know how it's going to change through the medium. This is negative black and white. It's not digital, so you can't see it right away. [We] don't know what [we're] going to get until [we] get into the dark room. That's a whole other gestation there." They're experimenting in the dark room, in the basement at the house party on Juneteenth, in the corner booth by the juke box at Hawkins Grill. That abstraction and extraction from the bodies of the workers, which is crucial to the operation and the critique of capital, demands another intellectual and affective (dis)comportment that bears sufficient attunement to the terrible utility of the concept is a matter of concern for photography. A re-materialization, a surrealization of work, in the flesh, in and as our monstrous claim upon the monstrous, which is manifest as sharing, in open and empathic handing, is at hand in Stewart. The echology is maternal. The passage is eternal. The middle lasts forever. The medium is massage. Spillers and Stewart share expectation in Memphis, which opens on the delta, where things change. They see with what they see, not so much catching people in the act but rather studying with them their releasement, their preformative practice, before the act, and their critical practice in the aftermath of what never, finally, passes for the act. There's a culinary and intoxicant sociality in flavor's

FIGURE 5.4. Frank Stewart (b. 1949), *Self-portrait*, Dominican Republic, 1986, gelatin silver print, 16 × 20 in., collection of the artist. © Frank Stewart, used with permission

entire sensual range. This is all essence, but it's estuarial, too, something flown and flowing through, where the idea of the natal community is all but always already dispersive, a cosmopolitan slide, some kind of phono-photographic gliss that animates (the) work. Call it unrest, or restlessness, or nervous muscularity; something ante-kinetic; some new, and off, an ante-genetic rebirth of the newly neverborn.

soul's feel

Scene set, sound seen, light table overturned. Turn, is that the set you see? Descend. Let's try approaching surfacing again. Is photography contingent on its printing? Is photography the print, the thing in hand? Now, after the digital, where is photography? When does it happen? Does the photograph give photography or is the photograph what photography withholds? Or, what if the thing photographed, as if it were some idea of the thing itself, is what photography withdraws? It seems that the essence, or maybe the condition, or maybe the instance of the photograph is never there before us. What you hold in your hands, or what you behold on the wall, is not quite there. What if the central fact of the photograph is not that it captures but, rather, that it withholds? When it seems like it's all right there in front of us, showing or representing itself or its making or its maker, it's hiding, sliding, moving on in plain sight as if it were plainsong.

Photography removes in drawing with and drawing on. Photography is given in the withdrawal of and in the photograph; not only of what's photographed, but also of the photograph's own wane, when it loses all it has, or all that has been taken. With the chemistry of the polaroid, which emerges before our eyes and fades in our hands, a scene is set, and seen, and then recedes, in a kind of fluidity, as when a river shines and sways. This recess and recession, this double session of retreat, words written out in chalk and palimpsestically, in and as the residue of all that has been written, of all the anerasive noise through which the figure, or the shape, or the form, or the word emerges, and back into which it falls or lays, is photography. Is drawing also always the withdrawn? Such intraplay of abandon and accompaniment is given again and again in folded service (I mean surface).

To describe rather than depict, rather than explain; to view with rather than provide a theoretical overview; to see with the seen when they are seeing: all these are to do much more than merely see them. Moreover, such withness is so much more than witnessing. Photophenomenological description shares experience for whom no person, and never the merely personal, comes first. There's no question of or questing for personality. At stake, instead, is something of preformance. Is the *per* in person(ality) the same as the *per* in perform(ance)? There's something of completeness, of finishing, of being-through that demands and justifies refusal. What would it mean to pass, or go past, through? What is it to sound this passing through, never getting through it, or over it, never being-through with it? This sojourn on the road, this big road blues, this constant delta, is the holding and releasement of intelligence. It's the simultaneous sharing and keeping of a secret, where the sharing of the secret keeps it safe. There's something withdrawn in the telling, this doubleness of holding out, this cutting seriality of perseverance, dis continuity, dis place/meant. Perhaps in some continual withdrawal of telling, even of the telling of a story, something is said. What's the difference between the saying, or the sharing, and the telling of a secret? Is there an opening of the secret into which the secret withdraws? We go there with it, into that sousveilant recess to find that the rendezvous of victory is involvement. This is a C. L. R. James / Aimé Cesaire / Martin Carter imperative, a Pancaribbean affordance when Memphis is aberrantly seen as sea's upper partial.[11] T/here, in study, the figure of the intellectual gets up to get down.

So it is that the "homegrown" intellectual is addressing her hermeneutic demand not only to the cultural dominant but to her natal community as well. Furthermore, it is by sectors of both that she is, in effect, interpellated, or summoned, as a responsible subject and subjectivity. And how could it be otherwise? How could it not be double trouble that her very vocation is itself a space not yet entirely cleared out, as it were, by a culture that maintains no obligation at all to believe her, especially; to treat her, to imagine her, as a credible discursive subject, working on an intellectually identifiable object, at the same time that she encounters it as contradictory, if not adversarial, that she moves on in a "negative capability"? The other tale, then, that the black creative intellectual confronts marks the weave of contradiction as a fruitful one, but only if . . . It is, perhaps, too soon here to speak of bravery, but I suspect that that must be our destination through the reversals of assumption that now make it difficult, if not impossible, to (1) reconstitute a "talented tenth," which is itself the culminative position of the myth of representation (as both Du Bois and Cruse embraced it from their common historic past); (2) sustain the idea of the intellectual as a leading and heroic personality rather than a local point of oscillation among contending conceptual claims; and (3) continue to pursue a theory and practice of intellectual or cultural work that is performative rather than, for lack of a better word, unfortunately, "scientific," or responsible to a "cognitive apparatus," or a "thought-idea."[12]

What if the primary way to sustain the idea of "the intellectual as . . . a local point of oscillation" is photography? What if photography is such oscillation's field, its radical nonlocality? The leading and heroic personality of the black intellectual fades in the impersonality of working through the work. If personhood persists in performance rather than posture, then *preformance* is dis place/meant of the person.

Furthermore, if Steiner and Foucault were right, man is not only no longer the linchpin of historical movement but history itself demonstrates a minimal resiliency of meaning as a self-reflective tool in the current inventory of media-inspired, constructed punctualities. Certain idols of narrative have lost their explanatory power for American culture in general and for African American culture, in particular, if its contemporary music tells us anything, so that the key question for the black creative intellectual now is: How does one grasp her membership in, or relatedness to, a culture that defines itself by the very logics of the historical? Or, as I queried earlier, What is the work of the black creative intellectual, *for all we know now*?

The short answer is that the black creative intellectual must get busy *where he/she is*.[13]

Get busy. Get down. Fall through. Where s/he is all up in there; and man, above, is mere "media-inspired, constructed punctuality." That's all. The human will have been the generalization of that point, that particle, but still. No way that where we are is here, says Nathaniel Mackey; like he was really nowhere, says Amiri Baraka.[14] And Stewart shows dis place/meant, here and now, is nowhere in presencing, which is approaching, surfacing. If the contemporary is generally understood as now/here, this spatio-temporal coordination, this posture, this emplotment, which will have then been placed on the move, in history, the timeline spread brutally out in smooth-curved plane all over the globe, then Afro-dis place/meant's work, its spirit-physics, its crowds of commonanima, bespeak the strange anacontemporaneity of no/where, its anarhythmia.[15] What if the incessant photography of black artists, in the recesses of black social life, in the wake and on the edge of catastrophe, asks us to ask again? What if play, in/as dis place/meant, is the condition in which "the black creative intellectual" becomes instrument or God's trombone? If, as Spillers says, ". . . the intellectual has imagined flight only in its negative instance as a supposed rejection, when his very status, or standing, *as an intellectual requires* that he take on a language and disposition that are 'foreign,'"[16] then photography, for Stewart, is where a preference for fallenness is exercised. To see with him as he sees with them is soul, as feeling depth, Aretha breathes, as again, Spillers lays it out and lays it down in Memphis blue. If,

FIGURE 5.5. Frank Stewart (b. 1949), *God's Trombones*, Harlem, New York, 2009 (printed 2022), inkjet print on aluminum, 48 × 60 in., collection of Marquise Stillwell. © Frank Stewart, used with permission

in other words, the work of the academy [or of the museum, or of the gallery], or more specifically, the "cognitive apparatus," is defined, symbolically speaking, as "not-mother," a "not-my own" ... [then] I am referring less to the maternal and paternal objects here as gendered actants of precisely defined sexual role than the *ground of intimacy* that the subject assumes: the more or less harmonious ensemble of impressions that bound me not only to my body, but my body as it is reflected back to me in the eyes of others that I recognize *as like myself*.[17]

then the *grounding of intimacy*, as reflection fades in our black share, all over the world till earth is seen before world's end, is photography, which is surfacing, which is the medium of its media, Frank Stewart and Hortense Spillers, the black creative intellectuals to end them all.

Notes

This essay is a revised and expanded version of an essay by Fred Moten, "Feast for the Senses," that appeared in the publication Frank Stewart's *Nexus: An American Photographer's Journey 1960s to the Present*, published by Rizzoli Electa in 2023. Copyright © The Telfair Museums.

1. Spillers, *"The Crisis of the Negro Intellectual*: A Post-Date," in *Black, White, and In Color: Essays on American Literature and Culture*, 428–70 (Chicago: University of Chicago Press, 2003), 435.
2. Spillers, *"The Crisis of the Negro Intellectual,"* 460.
3. Spillers, *"The Crisis of the Negro Intellectual,"* 462.
4. Victoria L. Valentine, "Culture Talk: Frank Stewart on his Jazz Photographs, Approach to Image Making, and Forthcoming Museum Retrospective," *Culture Type*, June 18, 2020, https://www.culturetype.com/2020/06/18/culture-talk-frank-stewart-on-his-jazz-photographs-approach-to-image-making-and-forthcoming-museum-retrospective.
5. Steven Feld, "From Ethnomusicology to Echo-Muse-Ecology: Reading R. Murray Schafer in the Papua New Guinea Rainforest," *Soundscape Newsletter*, no. 08, June 1994; posted to Squarespace, March 2, 2007, https://static1.squarespace.com/static/545aad98e4b0f1f9150ad5c3/t/5465b2bee4b0c4e0caea1605/1415951038575/1993+From+Ethnomusicology+to.pdf.
6. Wallace Stevens, "The River of Rivers in Connecticut," in *The Collected Poems of Wallace Stevens: The Corrected Edition* (New York: Vintage, 2015), 564.
7. Samuel R. Delany, *The Motion of Light in Water: Sex and Science Fiction Writing in the East Village* (Minneapolis: University of Minnesota Press, 2004).
8. Glenn Ligon, "Blue Black," in *Chris Ofili: Night and Day*, ed. Massimiliano Gioni (New York: Rizzoli, 2014); and Glenn Ligon, *Blue Black* (St. Louis: Pulitzer Arts Foundation, 2017).
9. See Hans Blumenberg, *Begriffe in Geschichte* (Frankfurt am Main: Bibliotheke Suhrkamp, 2016); and Hans Blumenberg, *Theorie der Unbegrifflichkeit* (Frankfurt am Main: Bibliotheke Suhrkamp, 2019).
10. See Hortense Spillers, "Mama's Baby, Papa's Maybe: An American Grammar Book," in *Black and White and In Color: Essays on American Literature and Culture*, 203–29 (Chicago: University of Chicago Press, 2003).
11. Martin Carter, *Selected Poems/Poesías Escogidas*, trans. Salvador Ortiz-Carboneres, (Leeds: Peepal Tree Press, 1999); Aimé Césaire, *The Collected Poetry*, trans. Clayton Eshelman and Annette Smith. (Berkeley: University of California Press, 1983); and C. L. R. James, *At the Rendezvous of Victory: Selected Writings* (London: Allison and Busby, 1984).
12. Spillers, *"The Crisis of the Negro Intellectual,"* 445.
13. Spillers, *"The Crisis of the Negro Intellectual,"* 450.

14. See Amiri Baraka, *S O S: Poems, 1961–2013* (New York: Grove Press, 2016); Nathaniel Mackey, *Splay Anthem* (New York: New Directions, 2006); and M. NourbeSe Philip, *A Genealogy of Resistance and Other Essays* (Toronto: Mercury Press, 1997).
15. Julius S. Scott, *The Common Wind: Afro-American Currents in the Age of the Haitian Revolution* (London: Verso, 2020).
16. Spillers, *"The Crisis of the Negro Intellectual,"* 460.
17. Spillers, *"The Crisis of the Negro Intellectual,"* 460.

Sunday, March 4, 1973
10:30 p.m.

I met Gwen Brooks tonight. She is a person of great humility — no pretenses or sham polish. Though the Wellesley setting was hospitable enough, it would have been good, too, to have talked to her in a more informal atmosphere; everybody was so much on his P's & Q's tonite that a good deal of the talk was "cocktail" repartee. I would like for her to read one of my stories.

I talked to Gwen Brooks about her interpretation of her poem, "Mother" (the act of abortion and a woman's reflections concerning it), as she read the poem, there was nothing particularly striking or earth-shaking about the event. Her reading seemed, to me, very light, almost whimsical. I asked her if she felt that way, and she said no — that the poem was very serious. I thought so too. At the times when I've read the poem in various classes, I've given it a very solemn, really sorrowful emphasis. Her own reading was an articulate one, but a very different register prevails of. She is a very gentle person — not at all worried about anything apparently.

She said that it didn't matter at what age a person starts writing. That's good! I told her about

ARCHIVAL FRAGMENT 3: Journal Entry on Gwendolyn Brooks

my ten year "old" novel — — the one I launched ten years ago. I still have the carcass lying about. It's funny, but it's there for the record. I asked her where she thought black people were going, she

laughed. Well, she said she'd like to think that we're steadily moving toward some dynamic liberation, but that we're not moving steadily — rather limpingly, faltering. A few backward steps now & again. Then in her own quiet way, she asked: "Are you worried?" I assured her that I was and wanted to go on about how worried, but she had to autograph some more anthologies and say "goodbyes" etc, to some people, once we were all getting ready to leave them. I'm glad I know her.

Gentle Lady — — Large-eyed and strong. Very quick, sudden, with her sudden questions. —

Who's afraid of Gwen Brooks? I am!

6 Black Reconstruction, or, Names for Love

Hortense Spillers as Reader

ANTHONY REED

This essay aspires to an account of Hortense Spillers as *reader*, an aspect of her work that reveals itself both in the texts she finds and examines, and the ways she examines them. More modestly, this essay will trace the protocols and "dispositions of reading" that animate her intellectual project between Feminist Studies (defined institutionally by the protocols and norms of mostly middle-class white women) and Black Studies (defined institutionally by the protocols and norms of mostly middle-class African American men). I put her reading practice in conversation with debates on the reparative that emerge from queer theory in order to draw out what I describe as the work of Black Reconstruction in her work. (Though the phrase echoes Du Bois, I am not otherwise claiming a link between their projects.) Even if it is justified, invoking queer theory, to which Spillers makes very occasional reference, is not without risk. My gambit is that reading is flexible enough a category in her work to allow me to comment on Spillers's tremendous innovations in *method*, which do not always surface when her work is read for the *content* of her arguments. A short essay can only begin to take up such a large question, so I will limit my consideration of reading primarily to her early essays, drawing out the ways she engages psychoanalytic and adjacent theory in pursuit of more accurate naming of Black positionality within the field of culture. I hope in this essay to make some preliminary observations about Spillers's way of posing and interrogating questions with precision and clarity, her way of positing *grounds*—"some basic point[s] of structure that would grant the free flow of movement among various appointments"—with reading being one essential component of her project.[1]

Reading, at once process, concept, and metaphor, links these two through a more prominent notion of text, irreducible to print. Text makes a politics of (diasporic) reading appear as something other than a position within ongoing professional debates about reading's status. Spillers asks, "If psychoanalytic theory offers the analysand a narrative, a text in the 'place' of a dropped-out content, or a content that was never there, then what is the relationship between a fictional text and the historical, or the community in history, both *inventing* and *invented* by its texts?"[2] Reading, active decoding in order to rearrange one's living in an object world, becomes a key point of entry into the "larger sociality that shapes our becoming."[3] Reading encourages recommitment to acts of collective care and concern that, however tentatively, short-circuit the impersonal structures, myths, and legends that, borrowing a phrase from Lauren Berlant that rhymes with Spillers's account of race and psychoanalysis, "conventionalize desire, intimacy, and even one's own personhood."[4] Doing so is not a fictional encounter with things as they really are in a positivist sense, denuded of all self-delusion and unburdened from fantasy or attachment, but instead a reawakening to the contingency of the world as it is and a disenchantment with our frames of knowing and speaking through which we might loosen the *self*, bound as it is to particular histories and matrices of desire, to make room for new desires and attachments that in the absence of a less contentious term I will call love.

Though queerness, like gender in Spillers's work, may not be chiefly organized around sexual difference—may, indeed, be shadowed by ungendering and the denial of object *choice* central to liberal love-is-love framing in the US—in the history of the African diaspora, I want to be cautious about the ways I'm staging a conversation with queer reading and Spillers's Black feminist reading.[5] As early as her groundbreaking "Interstices: A Small Drama of Words," Spillers has insisted that because of the ways slave societies made Blackness a figure of "what a human being was *not*," "black is vestibular to culture" and, moreover, "the prerogatives of sexuality are refused her [the Black woman] because the concept of sexuality originates in, stays with, the dominative mode of culture and its elaborate strategies of thought and expression."[6] Revisiting that essay, she writes, "the black life-world figures into the sexual universe at different velocities, even ferocities, I think we could say, but those mythemes that I am identifying are not empowered to register either nuance over time (synchrony), or intricate pulse in time (diachrony). And that absence of variation gauges precisely what I mean by the 'interstitial'—those punctualities (in a linked sequence of events) that go unmarked so that the mythic view remains undisturbed."[7] As a way of marking an unmarked fulness (heterosexual, able-bodied, white patriarchal masculinity), Blackness is a coordination of tropes and grammars that allows human worlds to appear natural. "Blackness," as a category of critical interpretation or explanation, is at once central to the development of conceptual matrices such as the sexual universe and must be repressed (except as deviance) to uphold the "mythic view." To function, the "mythic view" requires the displacement of African personality in order to cover the broader social articulation of sexual desire, kinship, power, and property—constitutive of the imperialist hetero-patriarchal capitalist social order—that was not, and could not be, limited to people thenceforth known as Black.

Black sexuality can neither be reduced to "a neutral reference to a set of practices that would circumscribe all the discriminations of gendered forms" or "a class-bound narrative firmly situated in the mythemes of the 'nuclear family'" because those categories already require "an elaboration and complication of competing, overlapping, and complementary discourses," or reading, to resist the seductions of the universal that, here, would be a misreading of the historical text.[8] As Spillers argues, "Whether we are talking about sexuality, or some other theme, we would identify this process of categorical aligning with prior *acts of the text* as the subtle component of power that bars black women, indeed, women of color, as a proper subject of inquiry from the various topics of contemporary feminist discourse."[9] Yet, in distorted forms, Black women do have a way of showing up, which requires ways of reading that undermine the forms and phases of "symbolic *value* that conform precisely to equations of political power."[10]

In passages like these, for which reading is always at least a shadow referent, it is clear that reading, like naming, is never neutral or innocent, but always engaged and guilty; not passive but dynamic, not a display of mastery but open-ended; historically contingent and *motivated*. To read truly requires engaging what she calls the "socionom" or, invoking Barbara Herrnstein Smith, "The ground for locating competing interpretive interests . . . for placing them in relation to one another" in accord with "one's leanings and inclinations toward one system, or logics of representation, and not another."[11] Students of her work will have noted that her analyses of culture always emerge from situated readings of texts: sermons, Harold Cruse's *The Crisis of the Negro Intellectual*, Paule Marshall's *Chosen Place, Timeless People*, Calvin Hernton's *Sex and Racism in America*, Daniel Patrick Moynihan's *Report on the Negro Family*, Gwendolyn Brooks's *Maud Martha*, and so many others, contexts that scholars who go to Spillers work seeking theory—portable frames and concepts—tend to lose sight of. Part of what I want to indicate via these genres and proper names is that to fully grapple with the contours of Spillers's thought requires acknowledgment that *what* she thought is not easily extricable from *how* or *with whom* she engaged in writing. This is not just a scholastic exercise but a matter of tracking the work of pleasure in the scene of Black study through which genuinely alternative ways of thinking, of valuing the known but not thought *in these terms*, might emerge. Referring to a book that "makes us comfortable, gives us feelings of coziness and charm," Spillers argues that writing makes intramural conversations "a naming," which give them "significance or record beyond the transitory business of our daily lives."[12] Reading reactivates that significance, drawing attention to a "historical basis [that] is not totally exhausted by 'race,' 'class,' 'gender,' 'previous state of servitude,' 'sexual preference,' 'last name,' 'region of birth,' 'religious faith,' etc."[13] "These elements of social modality," she continues, "come to bear on the historical situation [which she glosses as *enunciative conditions*] of the text, the writer, and various constituent reader-groups that 'choose' the text."[14]

Understanding reading to be active—a range of activities that coordinate attention and care to the text before us, the "enunciative conditions" of its emergence and other facts of its historical situation without fully effacing one's own attachments to and desires for the world. In other words, reading is a way of loving as much as it's a way of living. It is a way of being in the world, bringing the world in, inhabiting and making space in the world, rethinking the world so there is room to breathe. Invoking Ralph Ellison, reading offers one way of "seeing around corners" and beyond the suffocating contours of what one derives from those analyses of Blackness whose austere and seductive accounting of slavery make slavery present in daily life without saving room for the personality of the enslaved, the daily character of living and loving.[15]

Although theory persists as a prestige category, however evasive its meanings are, literary *methods* give "us a clue to the text of our own experience."[16] "Criticism" and "theory," Spillers has recently argued, "are not only mutually supportive, but *interpenetrative* in the relay of emphasis and competence that they evoke at varying moments of reading and analysis."[17] "Reading" and (textual) "analysis," however, are not primarily about narrowly conceived literature or writing but the signs and symbols by which make their work intelligible and shareable. Two important interlocutors for this more expansive interpretation of reading are Julia Kristeva and Roland Barthes. Spillers is one of Julia Kristeva's most astute readers. For the latter's account, inflected by psychoanalysis and semiotics, text *produces* the subject rather than simply being produced by her. Text gathers non-referential systems (like grammars) and figural systems (i.e., sign systems). The interaction of these two systems, invoking Roland Barthes, situates text "at the limits of the rules of the speech-act (*énunciation*)."[18] Reading discloses the mechanisms of power in meaning-making,

But that's not all reading (or criticism) does. To reiterate an earlier claim, the present essay about reading is also about love. Not the love balanced on the scales of the economism around which the "calculus of motives that we call 'modernity'" has fashioned itself, which is no love at all.[19] Rather, as an "abeyance of closure," that space held open, the intramural becomes tactile, legible as texture and text.[20] Spillers does not, as I read her work, produce "strong theory" in Eve Kosofsky Sedgwick's sense—a totalizing paranoiac theory that gathers and organizes disparate features of the world into its textual production of Truth. Coded into the terms of the text I've started to outline, a strong theory requires a transcendental signified that arrests the play of grammar and reference by subverting the grammatical code itself to produce meaning. Paranoia, its faith placed in exposure of what is harmful or threatening, reproduces versions of itself by downplaying or minimizing the richness, complexity, and irresolute nature of the objects it studies, reducing them in scale so that they no longer pose a threat to the investigator's ego. Paranoia bolsters that ego by granting the investigator the status of the undeceived, the one who possesses knowledge that will, somehow, lead to greater freedom.

Spillers's salutary distinction between analyses of Blackness ("modern Western racialized perceptions of reality"), which seem to commit the critic to a paranoid position, and Africanity, which refuses a distinction between Africa and the West, inclines toward the reparative.[21] Or perhaps simply the dialectical. At an earlier moment, Spillers argued that "So much of the work of domination appears to be aided by an erstwhile 'outside,' reproduced within the very precincts of the dominated, that a rigid demarcation of the social order into cultural dominant, and dominated, positions seems ever more inadequate."[22] What fantasies and unspoken desires subtend the predication of the world itself as antiblack, understanding as I do that "world" in those accounts attempt to name a particular textualization (or, more polemically, a reification) of the human ecosystem as natural or neutral? The mechanism by which one "sees around" such a formation, I have been arguing, is reading, but it is a reading that requires surrendering commitment and perverse attachment to those scenes of disappointment whose austere refusal of consolation and air of self-denial grants the critic an aura of truth. One familiar solution is emotional distance, which Spillers glosses as "ambivalence"—that abeyance of closure, or *break* in the passage of syntagmatic movement from one more or less stable property to another, as in the radical disjuncture between "African" and "American."

But recourse to critical *distance*, whose original description of relative space becomes more urgent in light of the radical disjuncture Spillers names, raises a question that perhaps once seemed settled: From what position does one perform that analysis and, as Spillers asks, "would a radical shift of *consciousness* adequately effect the kind of root change" those analyses intend?[23]

Fred Moten, whose work one can read as in constant dialogue with Spillers's (among others), wonders "what is it, to think from no standpoint; to think outside the desire for a standpoint? What emerges in the desire that constitutes a certain proximity to that thought is not (just) that blackness is ontologically prior to the logistic and regulative power that is supposed to have brought it into existence but that blackness is prior to ontology."[24] Blackness, he continues, "is ontology's anti- and ante-foundation, ontology's underground, the irreparable disturbance of ontology's time and space." Yet at that remove it's hard to know how to think the "community of texts and propositions" so central to Spillers's investments in reading or the intramural. Where Moten indexes his thinking without standpoint to the slaveship's hold, Spillers argues that "no single aspect/event of the socionom (the web of identity) can be perfectly isolated, nor can it occupy, from its local and particular site, the sovereign position."[25] She continues: "This ground for locating competing interpretive interests—Barbara Herrnstein Smith calls them 'communities'—for placing them in relation to one another is made up of one's leanings and inclinations toward one system, or logics of representation, and not another." One might say it depends on one's *position*.

Here I think it would be helpful to talk about Spillers's protocols of reading as communal, and a brief comparison with Eve Sedgwick's account of paranoid versus reparative reading will help. Within the psychoanalytic tradition developed by Melanie Klein, the position takes the place of progressive stages, personality types or structures to refer to the ego's characteristic ways of relating to its objects. This is to say the ego never appears in isolation, but always in relation to other objects. The paranoid position—"a position of terrible alertness to the dangers posed by the hateful and envious part-objects that one defensively projects into, carves out of, and ingests from the world around one"—is the tendency that, for Sedgwick, accounts for a certain style of producing theory as a way of relating to the world. As alternative to the paranoid position, Sedgwick describes the depressive position as "the position from which it is possible in turn to use one's own resources to assemble or 'repair' the murderous part-objects into something like a whole—though, I would emphasize, *not necessarily like any preexisting whole*. Once assembled to one's own specification, the more satisfying object is available both to be identified with and to offer one nourishment and comfort in turn. Among Klein's names for the reparative process is love."[26]

It's not a reading of Klein (or Sedgwick), much less a critique, to observe that the term "repair" in her metaphor usually refers to mending, to making whole something that has been broken, to patching something up that's not functioning so that it can work again. The relationship Black Studies, as Spillers develops it, has to the object world—and to its objects of knowledge—is less one of repair than of reconstruction. Echoing Du Bois, but meaning something different by the phrase, this is a project of Black Reconstruction—making something new out of what has failed or caused harm. One of the animating conditions of Spillers's work is the unrequited, even misplaced optimism some Afro-descendant people have for the world, surely a one-sided attachment tinted by dread. But this is countervailed by what she calls an "interior intersubjectivity." That analysis starts from the observation that "So much of the work of domination appears to be aided by an erstwhile 'outside,' reproduced within the very precincts of the dominated, that a rigid demarcation of the social order into cultural dominant, and dominated, positions seems ever more inadequate."[27] The separation of Black practices from oppressive regimes is, in other words, often self-delusion. "A psychoanalytic culture criticism would not only attempt to name such contradictions but would establish the name of inquiry itself as the goal of an *interior intersubjectivity*."[28] This strategy of reading and analysis requires "start[ing] from scratch and try[ing] to rethink 'race' as a piece of political reality, inculcated soon enough, but as something that belongs to an entire ensemble of givens to be managed."[29] It requires the analytical "dissolution of the psychoanalytic object in the hiatus that yawns between this 'great black mirage' and 'great white error.'"[30] What is that object but the (rights bearing, self-possessed) individual, which emerges, Spillers argues, "not so much as the solution of a willful struggle against the mass but as the name of new relations of labor and sociality"?[31] Those relations, one wants to add, are differentially available across the color line. Without positing individuality as a goal to obtain—it is the smallest unit of legitimation within capitalist modernity and also the fantasy bribe that attaches us to our own exploitation—one could observe that one thing the color line does is parse out access to individuality as the prestige modality of social legibility. Under such conditions, the familiar terms of social analysis—race, class, gender, sexuality—all seem to fail and fall short of the phenomena and populations they describe. They must be analytically held in abeyance and reconstructed in order to avoid reproducing the erasures and silences one found at the outset. If one wanted, she could call that process love.

Love is not an unvexed issue within Black Studies, since it can often be a means by which people bind themselves to "the dominative mode of culture and its elaborate strategies of thought and expression."[32] And what might it look like or be as a mode of *reading*? The idea of paranoia—which pertains, for Sedgwick, to a style or performance of knowledge rather a judgment of the veracity or falseness of what's known—may apply with qualification to certain styles of self-confirming theorizing that does not fail to uncover the "antiblackness" it seeks. Spillers herself, in an earlier moment, refers to "our current state of cultural analysis" circa 1994, which "can only imagine, in large part, the life-world as the motion of *crisis*, as the urgent immediacy, overwhelmed by the 'real,'" and that "therefore, has no *theory* of the past, even though it brims over with the coercive, unreflected principle, or law, of our present."[33]

What I'm calling Black Reconstruction is not simply "optimism" (which, after all, is an affective and intellectual orientation to time and narrative rather than analysis). But it also may not be "weak" or reparative theory. It does, I think, have to do with love. In other words, Spillers's way of reading "the persistence of the effects of slavery in American culture and society" *is* reparative, but strictly in the sense that it creates new (theoretical) objects and directing attention to alternative accounts of the ways the residual effects of slavery as legal and social process invade and disrupt even those most intimate interpersonal affairs, including love itself.[34]

But what love? The subversive gift Richard Iton wrote about?[35] Spillers's attention to the interstitial nature of Africanity itself helps me read the ambivalence in that formulation, where what is most intimate and most *mine* still registers in the world. Ambivalence, born of deep incompatibilities between fantasy and need, may be inescapable, but it is not the end of the story. In a context adjacent to Spillers, Lauren Berlant writes of love as "motivating force": "the desire to induce change without trauma, to become revolutionized and open and yet more oneself."[36] Not, I take it, self-annihilating ascesis but abundance. To live, open to and with others, despite the fraying a modernity whose highest form of power—the power to refuse to let die that accompanied the power to confiscate even that surplus value embodied in unclaimed children—shrinks the domain of intimacy precisely by expanding it into multiple unavowable families.[37] Love, critical love, is no small thing even now, even after the stunning "success" of black culture which allows for fans but does not require deep commitment to the lives of the producers or intended listeners, the "community of texts and propositions" Spillers writes about.[38] Even after the promotion of a certain Black feminism that seems hitched exclusively to the project of resolving the contradictions of a nation state whose recent rightward lurch was a reaction to Black women (I'm thinking of the women who coined "Black Lives Matter," but also those women whose habits of voting are held to be salvific of a democracy they rarely experience outside their communities, if there). Such love, not necessarily for the nation or some abstraction but ultimately interfering with or holding in abeyance individualities and liberal freedoms marks the possibility of a substantive Black freedom, which is to say substantive human freedom.

One striking feature of Spillers's reading, as noted and enacted on the page, is its provisional nature. The postures and dispositions of reading gets somewhere other than repair, which for Berlant always threatens to collapse into narcissism or "smothering will" precisely because of the "overvaluation of a certain mode of virtuously intentional, self-reflective personhood" endemic to creative and intellectual labor. At stake, from my perspective, is the problem of misrecognition (*méconnaissance*), which for Lauren Berlant "describes the psychic process by which fantasy recalibrates what we encounter so that we can imagine that something or someone can fulfill our desire"?[39] Fantasy is not synonymous with "fancy," but names instead "what manages the ambivalence and itinerary of attachment," by generating "representations to make the subject appear intelligible to herself and to others throughout the career of desire's unruly attentiveness." Misrecognition as sustained fantasy—which I think includes the overconfidence Berlant describes—is one mechanism by which the dominated attach themselves to the dominant order whether because they misrecognize that order as key to their survival or because they believe themselves uniquely skilled to navigate it. "Part of the problem," Spillers argues, "is to grasp the whole issue as a feature of the human ecosystem that arises in the historical moment rather than in nature and divine force." An analysis that starts from Africanity may or may not be "reparative." But it is, I have been arguing, part of a reconstructive project insofar as it endeavors a new theoretical accounting of the social and psychic ensemble that can track fantasy within the very scene of subjection, extended into the production of socially legible subjectivity and agency. That this way of reading does not relinquish or disavow its attachment to the world or desire for transformations that will ultimately render obsolete, at least partially, current "protocols of reading" and "elaboration[s] and complication[s] of competing, overlapping, and complementary discourses."[40]

For the remainder of this essay, I want to draw attention to two recurrent themes, preoccupations, and questions that inform Spillers's early work: community and grammar. We can grasp these differently when we consider them in conjunction with the protocols of reading and/as critical love I have been developing. "Grammar" has firmly established itself within the contemporary Black Studies lexicon as something akin to "structure," or the law-like, semi-conscious ordering of structures of feeling, thought, and institutions. It has become common to discuss the "grammars" of violence or any other structuring of rules and order that allow for the arrangement and rearrangement of signs and tropes to produce meaning. (Spillers herself refers famously to "An American Grammar Book," as well as a "grammar of feeling" and, by way of Kenneth Burke, a "grammar of motives.") But grammar's relation to community—which may be a term for the infrastructure of the intramural rather than an idyll of harmonious living-together—is less commonly elaborated. "Community," with its air of outmoded political stances and precepts, usually appears shrouded by a certain amount of skepticism. It is not a synonym for the intramural, I think, but it belongs to the same universe of discourse. Citing every instance of these concepts would not be worthwhile. A few select citations, however, will give a sense of the dense conceptual weave that binds her thinking on the page. These words resonate, resound, modify, repeat, insist, as a kind of challenge, at least as much as insistence on slavery in the formation and bifurcation of a certain America does.

The term "community" and its cognates resound in the essay from which the title of the symposium ("embody and catalyze") organized at Vanderbilt University to celebrate Spillers's retirement from teaching derives, "Moving on Down the Line: Variations on the African-American Sermon." In context, Hortense writes, "the sermon, as the African-American prototypical public speaking locates the primary instrument of moral and political change within the community. But at crucial times, the sermon not only catalyzes movement, but *embodies* it, *is movement.*"[41] Allowing for differences of composition and reception, her statement strikes me as imminently true of her own writing: it catalyzes and embodies the movement it describes and demands. Demurring from the fantasy of a "master code" for the sermon, she offers "a 'community of texts and propositions'" as an alternative to "tradition," citing the former's evasion of "the dynastic, the hierarchical, and the prior."

The idea of community, for all the ways one might critique it, Spillers writes, "seems to hold out the possibility of intervention, of inclusion." More than that, "a 'community' of subject-positions is always a partial effect of some putative plenitude. Yet we *need* the fiction of 'community' in order to speak at all."[42] In another context, she refers to "The missing word—the interstice—both as that which allows us to speak about and that which enables us to speak at all—shares, in this case, a common border within another country of symbols—the iconographic."[43] If we take *"to be able to speak at all"* to mean to *"to make socially legible action/speech,"* we need the fiction of community because of the irresolvable movement between synecdoche and metonymy—or in language Spillers more often used in her early essays between the subject of the enunciation and the enunciated subject. This has as much to do with the conditions of possibility for any speech act (grammar as the contentless text that produces meaning without reference), but, ineluctably, with what counts as a socially meaningful statement. "In order to say the 'not-sayable,'" Spillers writes, "I must say—I must enter the chain of significant differences inscribed by the sentence."[44] At stake, again, is what it is to be Black and woman. The effect of the 'not-sayable,' of the missing words, is that the status of Black women oscillates between "nonbeing" and indistinction (from black men) on the one hand, and the iconic—for good and for ill—in popular discourse. "In order to supply the missing words in the discourse of sexuality," she writes, invoking Kenneth Burke, "we would try to encounter agent, agency, act, scene, and purpose in ways that the dominative mode certainly forbids."[45] "To dissipate its energies," she continues, "requires that the feminist investigator actively imagine women in their living and pluralistic conformation with experience." At stake is not a thin universality, the "mythic view," but attention to "the division of women's community along various fault lines [as] the superior talisman that has worked across the centuries."[46] At stake are failures of critical imagination and, thinking about some of the rhetoric surrounding Black women in the present we might say a faulty, transactional love that inadequately attends to the particularity of Black women's experience to the universality of women's experience under the dominative mode of hetero-patriarchal racial capitalism.

The relationship between the subject of enunciation, the grammatical "I," and the subject whose actions are socially legible and thus properly agential is at once metonymic—because attached to specific situations, genres, and discourses—and synecdochic insofar as being able to speak as part of a larger whole legitimates speech and action in the first place. Rather than "read 'community' as homogeneous memory and experience" Spillers invites us to "think of [community] as a content whose time and meaning are 'discovered' [and as yet] undecided." It is at least analogous to Kristeva's text, which "produces the subject rather than simply being produced by her." Community thus

> becomes *potentiality*; an unfolding to be attended. One might go on to say, then, that African-American community articulated in these documents

becomes, at times, a systematic elaboration of a particular historical order that one makes up as she or he goes along, with whatever comes to hand and is already in hand; at other times, an invention of the dominant culture (to the extent that the violence of captivity has been imposed on the subject).[47]

Following these lines of Spillers's thinking, one is unable to *innocently* begin speaking "*as a* black man / woman / gender nonconforming person" and so on without having to interrogate the assumptions underpinning that self-positioning, and the material difference between the speaker and those whose experience she claims to embody. One must avoid the privilege of the paranoid position that seems to speak from an enlightened vantage point on the other side of crisis.

Put differently, reading *liberates* us from that pseudo-innocence, which is to say attachment to the dominative "mythic view." I am thinking of another paradigmatic invocation of community in her "post-date" on Harold Cruse's "Crisis of the Negro Intellectual." There she notes (citing Michael Thelwell) that "black intellectuals as a social formation sprout teeth precisely because the liberal view, itself a political position, sutures power differences that conceal the moves it performs as a natural 'innocence'" and cautions that "the old 'community,'" stable supposed ground of analysis, "is neither what nor where it used to be." If we consider these coordinates of a larger project, as I do, we can read them together this way: if we see the figure of the Black intellectual as a "locus of crisis," then to persist as if the tacitly gendered "old 'community'" still exists somewhere or is the necessary ground of our analysis will be to obscure power differences that shape the very social terrain we would analyze. Tacitly gendered because in the reversal of a part-whole relationship the critic can sidestep the ways social relations produce and *re*produce race in favor of arguing that race—a generalized Blackness in the present critical vogue—produces or stalls social relations. And that generalized Blackness tends to be embodied most paradigmatically in relatively affluent black men.

I've been trying to show the ways starting with the question of community leads us to questions of grammar in the broadest, most dynamic sense. I often think of the ways Spillers's work navigates feminist and other theory, in ways analogous to her account of Ishmael Reed's relationship to Harriet Beecher Stowe: not granting it priority or positioning herself as apprentice to it, but as "elaborating [it as] a repertory of strategies that denote, that circumlocute, a particular cluster of discursive acts" signifiers and virtues whose claims to universality the reality of black women's positioning brings up short. In that instance, she analogizes this repertory to a set of traffic signals. Elsewhere she refers to "a category of alignment that establishes a perspective between prior statements and counter- and successive statements." Counterstatements as well as successive statements. Insofar as those encode social norms for licit and sensible movement through shared space, we could well understand those discourses to function rather like grammar, whose semi-visible ordering of words and propositions rely on and justify past ones. The aim is not to show simply that people break, ignore, or resist grammatical norms of this kind, but, citing her, to "encourage a counter-narrative in pursuit of the provenance and career of word- and image-structures in order that agent, agency, act, scene, and purpose regain their differentiated responsiveness." Word-and-images structures to read, to decode, by which to know the world, and perhaps to love.

Notes

1. Spillers, *Black, White, and in Color: Essays on American Literature and Culture* (Chicago: University of Chicago Press, 2003), 299. Spillers's recourse to architectural and spatial metaphors, especially in light of her topography of Africanity as interstitial, awaits elaboration in a future occasion.
2. Spillers, *Black, White, and in Color*, 283
3. Spillers, "Critical Theory in Times of Crisis," *South Atlantic Quarterly* 119, no. 4 (October 2020): 683.
4. Lauren Berlant, *Cruel Optimism* (Durham, NC: Duke University Press, 2011), 125.
5. Lest this version of the African diaspora once again exclude Africa, I want to pause here to note that the colonial legacies of sexual regulation persist throughout the African continent, organized around the articulation of chauvinistic forms of Christianity and popular nationalist views that homosexuality is not "native" to Africa rather than reading anxieties about African "deviance" as a justification for colonial rule in the first place.
6. Spillers, *Black, White, and in Color*, 155, 157.
7. Spillers, *Black, White, and in Color*, 14.

8. Spillers, *Black, White, and in Color*, 279.
9. Spillers, *Black, White, and in Color*, 168. Emphasis added.
10. Spillers, *Black, White, and in Color*, 168. Emphasis in original.
11. Spillers, *Black, White, and in Color*, 277.
12. Spillers, *Black, White, and in Color*, 169.
13. Spillers, *Black, White, and in Color*, 299.
14. Spillers, *Black, White, and in Color*, 299.
15. Ellison, *Invisible Man* (New York: Vintage, 1995), 13.
16. "The Politics of Intimacy: A Discussion," in *Sturdy Black Bridges: Visions of Black Women in Literature*, ed. Roseann P. Bell, Bettye J. Parker, and Beverly Guy-Sheftall (Garden City, NY: Anchor Books, 1979), 88.
17. Spillers, "Critical Theory in Times of Crisis," 683.
18. Roland Barthes, *The Rustle of Language*, trans. Richard Howard (New York: Farrar, Strauss, and Giroux 1986), 58.
19. Spillers, *Black, White and In Color*, 42.
20. Spillers, *Black, White, and in Color*, 262.
21. "Afropessimism and Its Others: A Discussion between Hortense J. Spillers and Lewis R. Gordon," YouTube, posted by Soka University of America, May 24, 2021, https://youtu.be/Z-s-Ltuo6NI.
22. Spillers, *Black, White, and in Color*, 382.
23. Spillers, *Black, White, and in Color*, 385.
24. Moten, "Blackness and Nothingness (Mysticism in the Flesh)," *South Atlantic Quarterly* 112, no. 4 (Fall 2013): 738–39.
25. Spillers, *Black, White, and in Color*, 277.
26. Eve Kosofsky Sedgwick, *Touching Feeling: Affect, Pedagogy, Performativity* (Durham, NC: Duke University Press, 2003), 128, Sedgwick's emphasis. Perhaps it goes without saying, but let me nonetheless clarify that the notion of positions does not commit one to saying Spillers or her work is "depressive," any more than identifying a "paranoid" structure or positionality governing some ways of thinking discredits them or denies the reality of their arguments. It's also the case that the same thinker—and Sedgwick identifies this in her own work—can move between depressive, paranoid, schizoid, or other positions.
27. Spillers, *Black, White, and in Color*, 382.
28. Spillers, *Black, White, and in Color*, 382. Emphasis in original.
29. Spillers, *Black, White, and in Color*, 394.
30. Spillers, *Black, White, and in Color*, 393.
31. Spillers, *Black, White, and in Color*, 389.
32. Spillers, *Black, White, and in Color*, 157.
33. Spillers, *Black, White, and in Color*, 461.
34. Spillers, *Black, White, and in Color*, 461.
35. Richard Iton, *In Search of the Black Fantastic: Politics and Popular Culture in the Post-Civil Rights Era* (Oxford: Oxford University Press, 2008), 8.

36. Lauren Berlant, "A Properly Political Concept of Love: Three Approaches in Ten Pages," *Cultural Anthropology* 26, no. 4 (2011): 685.
37. Adélékè Adéèkó argues by way of Hegel's dialectic of recognition that the master is defined not only by the will to live, but more precisely "by the will to prevent the defeated [the slave or bondsman in Hegel's allegory] from dying, either by suicide or through a rebellious mutiny" that would end in either the death of the slave or the master. *The Slave's Rebellion: Literature, History, Orature* (Bloomington: Indiana University Press, 2005), 19. Read back into the scene of slavery, it is also the power to make live, to facilitate the reproduction and expanse of children born of his loins or those of enslaved men compelled to "stud" or encouraged to have marriages whose sanctity would not be respected, born of women whose maternal status did little to change their social position irrespective of the child's parentage.
38. Spillers, *Black, White, and in Color*, 256.
39. Berlant, *Cruel Optimism*, 122.
40. Spillers, *Black, White, and in Color*, 279.
41. Spillers, *Black, White, and in Color*, 254.
42. Spillers, *Black, White, and in Color*, 257.
43. Spillers, *Black, White, and in Color*, 156.
44. Spillers, *Black, White, and in Color*, 288.
45. Spillers, *Black, White, and in Color*, 173.
46. Spillers, *Black, White, and in Color*, 173.
47. Spillers, *Black, White, and in Color*, 258.

Works Cited

Adéèkó, Adélékè. *The Slave's Rebellion: Literature, History, Orature*. Bloomington: Indiana University Press, 2005.

Barthes, Roland. *The Rustle of Language*. Translated by Richard Howard. New York: Farrar, Strauss, and Giroux, 1986.

Berlant, Lauren. *Cruel Optimism*. Durham, NC: Duke University Press, 2011.

———. "A Properly Political Concept of Love: Three Approaches in Ten Pages" *Cultural Anthropology* 26.4 (2011): 683–91.

Ellison, Ralph. *Invisible Man*. 1952. New York: Vintage, 1995.

Iton, Richard. *In Search of the Black Fantastic: Politics and Popular Culture in the Post-Civil Rights Era*. Oxford: Oxford University Press, 2008.

Moten, Fred. "Blackness and Nothingness (Mysticism in the Flesh)." *South Atlantic Quarterly* 112, no. 4 (2013): 737–80.

Sedgwick, Eve Kosofsky. *Touching Feeling: Affect, Pedagogy, Performativity*. Durham, NC: Duke University Press, 2003.

Spillers, Hortense J. "AfroPessimism and Its Others: A Discussion between Hortense J. Spillers and Lewis Gordon." YouTube, posted by Soka

University of America, May 24, 2021, YouTube. https://www.youtube.com/watch?v=Z-s-Ltuo6NI.

———. *Black, White, and In Color: Essays on American Literature and Culture.* Chicago: University of Chicago Press, 2003.

———. "Critical Theory in Times of Crisis." *South Atlantic Quarterly* (2020) 119 (4): 681–83.

———. "The Politics of Intimacy: A Discussion." In *Sturdy Black Bridges: Visions of Black Women in Literature*, edited by Roseann P. Bell, Bettye J. Parker, and Beverly Guy-Sheftall, 87–106. Garden City, NY: Anchor Books, 1979.

7 The Errant Protester

Tracing Black E/motion in the Visual Work of Hortense Spillers

AMARIS BROWN

> "I am my own historian from time to time."
> —Hortense J. Spillers

Scene I

In late November of 2015, local police broke into an administrative building on the campus of Brandeis University where approximately twenty-five graduate and undergraduate students lay sleeping. Aggravated by the murder of Michael Brown, the occupying students made demands that were straightforward and long overdue. Drawing a direct relation between the social discardability of black children by the state and the failure of higher-learning initiatives to "make black studies everyone's studies," the Concerned Students of 2015 challenged their institution by claiming *a right to an education that does not hate them*.[1]

As a non-member of the negotiations committee, I volunteered to document the occupation on my Canon D6. From the relative safety of a staircase overlooking the Bernstein Marcus lobby I cannot recall whether I took a photograph or a mental image of two Waltham police officers facing off with a small group of university students. After several days without showers, routine life, or fresh air outside the L-shaped corridor, the students stood their ground despite a rational fear of being invaded and arrested. While I pointed the camera at the police, who were addressing student leaders in words I could not make out but that carried the effect of "shut this shit down," my eye moved past the officers and landed upon a woman leaving the occupation.

As if prompted by the confrontation, the woman exited what had been, moments prior, a door locked and barricaded by protesters. Awakened by the boldness of her action and lack of hesitation to leave the scene of protest, I followed her. These were the first steps either of us had taken outside the Ford Hall 2015 Student Occupation since it began. What she did next grounds this chapter's exploration of political formations that stray from traditional sites of social protest. The young woman, with perfect form and agility, began to run in circles no bigger than a two-car parking lot. With tears streaming down her brown face, she created a perfect circuit of anger and sorrow. The errant protester guides this chapter's examination of black feelings that disappear under the weight of history and linger within and beyond the corridors of the American university.

In her own account of the Brandeis University Ford Hall takeover of 1969 as a doctoral student in the Department of English, African-American literary critic and black feminist scholar, Hortense Spillers, admits that upon hearing the National Guard could storm the building, she developed a mean case of hives. By focusing on this narrative detail against the dominant history of a national black studies movement overrepresented by masculinist leadership and Pan-Africanist solidarity, we redirect our attention to the figure of the errant protester whose immune system knows what the movement does not: that the reclaiming and renaming of the institutional space will not, with any guarantee, protect black lives inside or outside of it. This narrative pulls away from the center of historical accounts of protest and quite literally paints an image of Hortense Spillers as allergic to the formidable moment when "the protest become[s] a curricular object ... and in doing so, black studies [loses] its secrecy, its prohibitive and unspeakable characters."[2] Spillers's hives and the errant protester's exit are both momentary details that, in no metaphorical way, are symptomatic of an allergy to the conditions of containment occasioned by the massive demands of protest taking place inside the university.

The errant protester exhibits a politics of e/motion that cannot cohere within the grand scheme of The Occupation. Her action of running while weeping against the backdrop of mass protest might be considered inconsequential to or perhaps even undermining of the most "radical" forms of black collectivity and mass movement. Building on Therí Pickens's examination of the ableist discourses that "connive to constrain the socially acceptable emotional reactions from Black women," my theorization of errancy necessitates an engagement with Pickens's analysis of the social impermissibility underlying what she calls "black affective resistance." Black affective resistance extends an embodied theoretical space where emotions such as anger compel us to read black subjects on their own terms and not according to the institutional gains their anger (sometimes) makes possible. Following Spillers, Pickens reminds us that anger is one of "the gaps where black women disappear between two world events."[3]

As a black feminist creative practice, errancy describes the refusal to be fixed, stable, and knowable. It is the permission to find an exit—to occupy the gap—and is a tool for reading black affective resistance. By refusing to make sense of the world from the presumption of a stable position, errancy follows neuro/divergent conceptual pathways that embrace e/motion as a way of tapping into black singularity that is not bourgeois or socially numb to the masses, but an acceptance that not all modes of black being can be fully determined by the masses. This chapter asks: What happens when protest shakes performativity? When what we feel functions reliably as what we know? How then might we begin to describe the relationship between the errant protester and the debilitating infrastructures that seek to absorb their labor? Might we wander outside traditional sites of protest to embrace nondeterministic ways of reading black subjectivity, and, in doing so, refuse political projects of incorporation? In their refusal to be a normative intellectual subject, the errant protester demonstrates how the university functions as an ongoing site of racial/sexual enclosure that disappears forms of protest that are less observable.

In what follows, I trace the hand of the errant protester in the three-dimensional work of Hortense Spillers and Kameelah Janan Rasheed. Departing from literary engagements with Spillers's landmark writing, I focus on a recurring drawing that appears in her archive and was published in the essay, "*Chosen Place, Timeless People*: Some Figurations on the New World" (1985). I argue that Spillers's creative practice, and the drawing specifically, introduces a nondeterministic mode of reading the errant protester who has been anesthetized by history. Drawing upon Spillers's own strategic spatial experiences, I return to her theory of the "one" and argue that the errant protester cannot be mapped against available sociological models. This scene pivots on the figure of Sally Hemings, who appears as the errant protester in the work of both Spillers and Rasheed. Following Rasheed's imperative to question the knowability of the subject of her work, I read Spillers's drawing into Rasheed's installation *Worshipping at the Altar of Certainty* as a portal to liberate Hemings from the entombment of the Jeffersonian cannon. In search of black e/motions produced in and as the desire for exit, the scenes that follow examine the relationship between black subjects and the debilitating infrastructures that spit them out.

Scene II. The One (Who Matters)

> Maps introduce us to worlds not of our own—not of our own making and quite often, not of our own knowledge ... the eye simply cannot swallow the whole thing in a definitive act of intelligence.
>
> —Hortense J. Spillers, June 14, 1977[4]

Locating the errant protester requires that we look away from social momentousness. Although they may be allergic to the university, at times, they work inside of it. There is no judgment here. Many of us do things that are bad for our health. Errancy is not necessarily an abolitionist position; it is a way of doing our work that cannot be easily absorbed by the institution. It is about developing a creative practice that is indicative of a life outside and thus cannot be subsumed by university service or labor. It is forging new relationships with our hands, skin, and feet. It requires that we plan where and how and when we will make our exit. The errant protester is after a politics in motion—a refusal of stasis, capture, consumption. As Fred Moten puts it, "The university needs what she bears but cannot bear what she brings. And on top of all that, she disappears. She disappears into the underground, the downlow lowdown maroon community of the university, into the undercommons of enlightenment, where the work gets done, where the work gets subverted, where the revolution is still black, still strong."[5]

In her 1985 essay "*Chosen Place, Timeless People*: Some Figurations on the New World," Hortense Spillers describes her creative process of reading Paule Marshall's 1969 novel of the same name. Most of the essay focuses on Spillers's frustration at any attempt to summarize the novel because, in her own words, "single threads of it disappear into the whole, integrated fabric."[6] Instead, the critic reaches for a pencil to draw a simple pattern that might animate the novel's primary structural features. Myth, history, ritual, and ontology create a rich system of meaning and yet, the concentric circles sit above no key, no strategy for interpretation, no coherent subject to analyze. Fortified by the desire to sketch the nuances of the psychic geographies of Marshall's characters, the drawing depicts a "quantum of resistance" that experiments with the text beyond the protocols of traditional literary criticisms.[7]

Sometime during my second-to-last year of graduate school, I decided to frame this curious item of visual pleasure above my desk, anticipating that I would arrive at its meaning. I suppose I hoped that by looking into these ominous rings I would come to understand the drawing's spiritual import in my life, which at the time I desperately sought as an answer to all problems relational and doctoral. The drawing spoke to poet friends and visual artists who stumbled into our sun-soaked apartment on Tioga Street and who, upon asking to know more, faced what very little there was to say: that it illustrated Spillers's reading of Marshall's novel. It was Spillers's creative act that moved me. Her ability to simultaneously abstract and make intimate the colonial systems of domination staged by Marshall's novel while wholly making something that was not indexical of the novel itself. The drawing stood alone as an artwork, and I was determined to see it this way. The image challenged what I thought I knew about Hortense Spillers's work. She was a theorist. Wasn't she? Not an artist. Not a woman who in 1983 was thinking about black life in terms of shape and space.[8]

Spillers's drawing demonstrates the necessity of an embodied creative practice that cannot be fully absorbed by the university. In its intricacy and opacity, the drawing expands our engagement with the

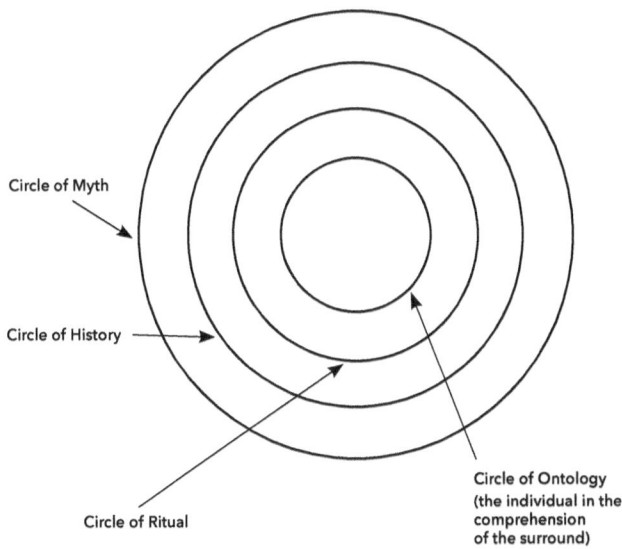

FIGURE 7.1. Spillers's conceptual map of ontology. Hortense J. Spillers, *Conjuring: Black Women, Fiction, and Literary Tradition* (Bloomington: Indiana University Press, 1985), 153.

theorist beyond the popular and the published, so that we might struggle with and through her creative practice in ways that newly animate and exceed her writing.[9] In its conceptual errancy, epistemic tools are of no use. We cannot think our way into or out of the drawing—*we must feel our way through*. In other words, to come to "know" the drawing, first, one must attempt to inhabit it—experience it as a portal and three-dimensional object where "theory" is not only something to be written or recited but sketched. Spillers's creative practice encourages us to approach three-dimensionality as an act of making matter felt.

Although the drawing refuses to convey straightforward meaning, it does extend a conceptual map. Spillers's map breaks from generations of sociological depictions of blackness. An attention to the circular shape of the drawing aesthetically registers the Du Boisian data portrait through what Margo Crawford describes as "the circular inseparability of the lived experience of blackness and the translation of that lived experience into the world opening possibilities of art."[10] Highlighting the entwinement of the social, infrastructural, and black artistic, Crawford evinces the material legacies of black sociological writing that Spillers must grapple with and potentially shake in order to break from Du Bois's data visualizations.[11] Depicted in swirls and circles, colorful shapes and mounds, maps and marks, W. E. B. Du Bois's data visualizations speak to an Afro-modern sociality that generally advances its status through legible forms of civic participation. The Du Boisian data portrait prioritizes the beauty of black collective movement; however, nowhere depicted in the sixty drawings commissioned for the Paris Exposition of 1900 are black Americans captured by the psychiatric system, the chain gang, or the reformatory. Nowhere depicted are the gender nonconforming, the disabled, the unemployed, the socially disqualified. They have been squeezed into or out of maps not of their own making. Where is the errant protester in the Du Boisian sociological map?

In her essay "'All the Things You Could Be by Now, If Sigmund Freud's Wife Was Your Mother': Psychoanalysis and Race," Spillers departs from her sociological forefather and a whole generation of thought responsible for shaping how we think about black social life. Spillers tells us, "What is missing in African American cultural analysis is a concept of the 'one.'" She writes:

> But if we can, we must maintain a distinction between the "one" and the "individual," even though the positions overlap. The individual of black culture exists strictly by virtue of the "masses," which is the only image of social formation that traditional analysis recognizes. . . . The individual of the lifeworld does not stand in opposition to the mass but at any given moment along the continuum might be taken as a supreme instance of its synecdochic representation. In other words, Every Black Man/Woman *is* the "race" as the logic of slave narratives amply demonstrates and the elements of the formula are reversible and commensurate.[12]

Distinguishing between the "individual" and the "one," Spillers liberates a position for the black subject in modernity who might have something to say about themselves.[13] Although the "one" is embedded in the social, Spillers suggests they cannot fully be represented by it. Like "cosmic Zora" who tells us she feels the subject of her race when thrown against a "sharp white background," the "one" cannot be brought under the universality of the subject even when that subject is asking: *How does it feel to be a problem?* The "one" or the "me" in "How It Feels to Be Colored Me" refuses grammatical attempts to trap the subject into place or time or social relation where she exists for someone else.[14]

Later in this essay, Spillers locates her own strategic spatial experience as exemplary of the "one" who is embedded in the social, in this case her congregation, but cannot be fully represented by the demands placed upon her participation within the social. She describes the experience of being young and "snaggle-toothed" sitting in the front pew, left of center. She recalls that when the choir was invited to perform at another church, her pastor invited the community (already full of worship and ready to take the afternoon off), to "send go." Spillers writes:

> The injunction always tickled me, as I took considerable pleasure in conjuring up the image of a snaggle-toothed replica of my seven-year-old self going off in my place. But the minister meant "send money" (i.e., pass the collection plate). Decades later, I decided that the "send go" of my childhood had an equivalent in the semiotic/philosophical discourse as the mark of substitution, the translated inflections of the self beyond the threshold of the fleshed natural girl. . . . One and one did not always make two but might well yield some indeterminate sum.[15]

The "send go" of Spillers's childhood flags our reading of the errant protester as the "one" who matters. By refusing to occupy her place in the social economy as the muted child, Spillers becomes an indeterminate subject—a subject whose e/motion cannot be mapped by available sociological models. In other words, where Du Bois gives us an image of black life inside the circle, dedicated to modernity's promises of black advancement through social inclusion, Spillers's drawing seeks to render black life within the circuit by imagining herself as both singular and indeterminate. Looking at Spillers's drawing, the "one" cannot be mapped because they are delighting in the possibility that they need not always show up! Theirs is a black life marked by errancy and that refuses stasis.

My reading of the errant protester is indebted to Spillers's conceptualization of the "one." As a theory of the subject in protest, the "one" distinguishes themself from within the masses through acts of both imagination and substitution. In turn, the errant protester takes one more step and makes an institutional exit. Although I have made a case for the "one's" unmappability, there is something to be gained in attempting to locate the "one" whose e/motions have been disappeared under the weight of history but nonetheless linger within and beyond the corridors of the American university. Where black affective resistance and affective labor are not only acquired to build institutions, but to stabilize them. Under these conditions, the errant protester resists the university's consumption of black e/motion through the refusal to be fixed, stable, and knowable. This appetite for consumption is one that Spillers extends from the university to the nation-state in her engagement with the figure of Sally Hemings.

In her lecture "Toward an Ontology: African American Women and the Republic," Spillers underscores the significance of African American women to the formation of new republics. Turning toward the textual and material traces of Sally Hemings as the "dirt [that must] be anesthetized" as a matter of historical propriety, she describes in no uncertain terms that the captured black child reveals "the boiling contradictions that moil around the center" of a democratic nation. In contrast to the innumerable historiographical accounts that pay tribute to Thomas Jefferson's centrality to the formation of the American nation-state, Hemings has no cannon. Spillers argues that without a body of writing to bring alongside Sally Hemings, works of fiction become the primary means through which to illuminate her experience as a preeminent national figure. As the muted subject of interracial sexual commerce, the historical fiction says little to nothing at all about her emotional world—she has no "official hearing."

> [We have] no way to easily form in the inner ear an aural image of the sound and grain of Sally Hemings's voice, the shape and meaning of her words, or how she might have felt as the quintessential instance of the conversion on her own body of the racial and sexual practices that define slavery as the perdurable social logic of the late colonial regime and beyond. In fact, we are not helped toward an act of capable imagination regarding the actual Sally Hemings at all. . . . The absence of intimate information

however mimics the very subject or thematics of non-subjectivity that slavery's social arrangements attempted to reinforce. On the one hand there are the modalities of being announced by discourse and in positions of discourse and on the other there are modes of being defined by their invisibility to this visibility and it is in the interworkings of these spheres of existence that the republic has its birth.[16]

In searching for the sound and grain of Hemings's voice, Spillers aches for an analytical opening into the lifeworld of the blackened subject. Hemings does not simply disappear, she is absorbed by Jefferson's legacy as an object among other objects belonging to his home. *She is the dirt that must be anesthetized*—deprived of feeling and awareness. Without a record of Hemings's sentience, we struggle to imagine what protest she may have put up—what door she might have broken down and attempted to exit. Spillers reminds us that, as the nation's most infamous concubine, Hemings has no rights to a story that she has authored. In the absence of intimate information regarding Hemings's life, Spillers encourages us to struggle with and through modes of being defined by their invisibility—modes of being that go beyond (or deep within) sociogenic discourses and that shift ground to reveal what Spillers describes as "a missing layer" of hermeneutic inquiry.

Spillers's drawing emerges within a discursive, ontological gap necessitated by black feminist theorizing to stage a more ethical encounter with Sally Hemings—the "one" who is silent, but not in silence.[17] As she disappears from the aural world, she takes with her modes of black affective resistance that go unheard. The final scene of this chapter reads Kameelah Janan Rasheed's installation as a three-dimensional rendering of Spillers's drawing. It functions as a portal to liberate Hemings from the entombment of the Jeffersonian cannon by making her practices of black affective resistance felt. My analysis finds that in Kameelah Janan Rasheed's installation, Hemings conspires with the artist to haunt the space of the rotunda, leaving her mark upon it. Guided by Spillers's drawing, which in its noticeable lack of a representative subject necessitates that we feel our way through, I fabricate Hemings's critique of the university as a site of racial/sexual enclosure through the material traces provided in Rasheed's verbal collages.

Scene III. Worshipping at the Altar of Certainty

In August 2021, African American visual artist and self-described learner Kameelah Janan Rasheed's site-specific installation *Worshipping at the Altar of Certainty* opened at the Williams College Museum of Art. Located in the college's first library, a neoclassical rotunda, Rasheed's installation forces our eye in the smooth pursuit of circular movement. The principal objects of Rasheed's work are shapes, marks, and archival clippings of words rendered in black and white. The only signs of corporeal involvement appear as xeroxed hands; all else is grainy, blackened, errant. A thin black piece of tape wraps around the circumference of the space above chair rail molding and we are reminded that we are not at the center of a circle, but a circuit. The installation stages a dimension—a plane of being, knowing, and experiencing that otherwise cannot be rendered by two-dimensional shape.

Worshipping at the Altar of Certainty simultaneously pursues Argentine writer Jorge Luis Borges's short story "The Library of Babel" (1941), a narrative about the infinite value that syntax, punctuation, and rhetoric place on ordering and disordering the world, alongside Ashon Crawley's conceptualization of centrifugitivity, which takes up modes of black being that are created in anticipation rather than arrival. In "Nothing Music: The Hammond B3 and the Centrifugitivity of Black Pentecostal Sound," Crawley imagines tonal responses to capture and confinement inspired by nineteenth-century maroon communities. Crawley defines centrifugitivity as those "tones that are not simply moving toward resolution but are on the way to varied directionality—not simply in a linear, forward progression but also vertically, down and up, askance and askew."[18] In the absence of what we can see, centrifugitivity permits us to hear black voices that draw our attention away from black collective movement. Noting the connection between black aurality and practices of errancy deepens our ability not only to look, but to listen for voices that have been cyphered out.

At the center of the rotunda, neoclassical roman columns reinforce the sense that we are in a hallowed space of monumentality and of worship to the social order. The columns also call to mind the architecture of the United States Capitol, showcasing the overlapping infrastructures

FIGURE 7.2. Kameelah Janan Rasheed, *Worshipping at the Altar of Certainty*, 2021. Archival inkjet prints, vellum, xerox paper, paint, pen, vinyl. Williams College Gallery, photograph by Bradley Wakoff.

of the university and the State. In 1822, Thomas Jefferson, architect and third president of the United States of America, began the construction of a rotunda on the campus of the University of Virginia. Modeled after the Pantheon in Rome, Jefferson's rotunda idolizes ancient Roman classical architecture as "a physical teaching tool"—a site of central knowledge.[19] Jefferson's use of slave labor to build his rotunda at the center of the University of Virginia's campus elucidates the contradictions of democratic idealism germane to the American university.

While Rasheed's installation does not explicitly engage with Jefferson, *Worshipping at the Altar of Certainty* confronts his legacy as an architect and gatekeeper of space, allowing us to draw a connection between the Confederacy, Christianity, Anglo-Saxon heritage, and the Roman Empire in the maintenance of anti-blackness to the social order.[20] The site-specific work adds another layer, or ring, of meaning to fabrications of liberal democracy. Critiquing what she describes as a "centered approach to knowledge," Rasheed forces us to look about the space for traces of a voice that might alter our experience of the room. Forcing our eye out—toward the perimeter—we are at a distance. The further we retreat into the circle's center, the more we lose our comprehension of the inkjet prints, the clipped words, the specificity of the annotations. Certainly, we miss the poem repeated along the baseboard:

> i eat the moist clumps of jealous hours and my mouth thickens around the sloppy horror of hero plots. the book wants to eat my imagination and sometimes I let it. and at times, i succumb to the canons i cannot banish.[21]

Unlike traditional line breaks on the page, the poem is severed by physical columns that distort our view. As the speaker's mouth becomes thick, thicker by the myth of mankind as savior, it is Sally Hemings we hear, Jefferson's slave and mother to all six of his children, who fixes her mouth in refusal. The poem registers the subject whose interior life is cannibalized by clamor. She is a voice at the periphery that does not need to be conjured, but already exists! Where she is not visible, she is nonetheless apparent. Like Phillis Wheatley who first wrote on the walls of her master's house before being sentenced to the page, Hemings hacks the circuit of myth by claiming the space of the line break. Her voice now circulates the room and anything she has to say will disrupt it, architecturally and otherwise.

More than a metaphysical connection, Hemings is an innate part of Rasheed's site-specific installation. Hemings exists as what Bernard Tchumi calls an "architectural paradox," shifting our experience of the installation through "the sensation that the materiality of the body coincides with the materiality of the space . . . unfolding against the projection of reason, against the Absolute Truth."[22] The architectural paradox of Hemings's body in the space disrupts and distorts any notion of a collective past, of a shared monument, of a communal site of worship to the social order. Within the rotunda, master and slave are once again brought under one roof. The immateriality of the body as it coincides with and contradicts the space challenges Enlightenment philosophies of reason and rationality that a body must appear where a body is wanted. Hemings exists *beyond the threshold of the fleshed natural girl*. Against a multilayered past, Hemings clings to the constitutional room as "undecidable—person or thing, or person-as-thing."[23] She symbolizes life that is not only disqualified but disposable. In struggling *with and through* Hemings as a paradoxical figure in the nation's founding, we must begin to imagine what her disappearance makes possible. We must imagine what Simone Brown argues as, "Black freedom practices ... [that] think about the productive possibilities of disappearance, not as being absented but claiming illegibility, or better, undetectability, when blackness confounds."[24]

Confronting realities lived at the perimeter of the circle, I cypher Hemings in where the historical record has deprived her of feeling and awareness. By confronting the material status of Sally Hemings in the fabrication of the site-specific installation, I place Rasheed and Hemings into a black feminist circuitous conversation by reclaiming the circle of ritual. I am attempting to tell a different story about the relationship between the body and the building that is both structural and affective so that there is no way to enter the room without the voice of Sally Hemings. While the tools of historiography suggest Hemings's

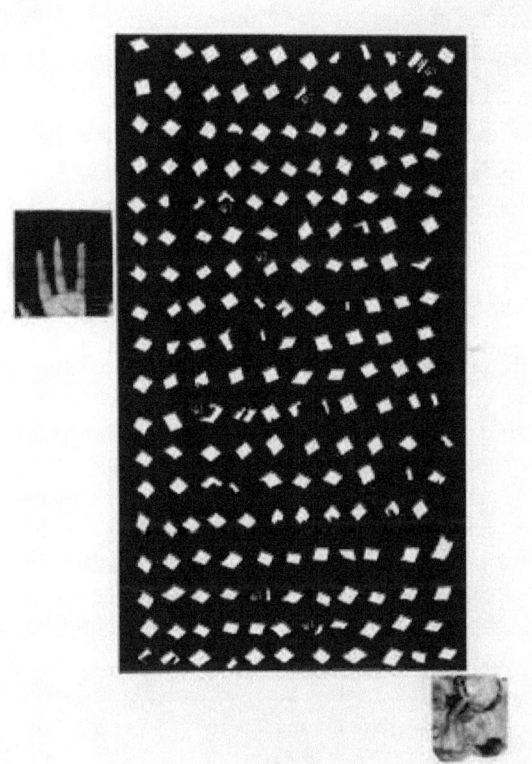

FIGURE 7.3. Detail from Kameelah Janan Rasheed, *Worshipping at the Altar of Certainty*, 2021. Williams College Gallery, photograph by Bradley Wakoff.

position as Jefferson's concubine, the mental effects of what would be legally determined rape are unknown. Claiming to *know* Hemings psychic or affective world *with certainty* is not the point. Guided by Spillers, I search for a methodological location where practices of black affective resistance belonging to the artist, the anesthetized black child, and the errant protester converge but are not collapsed.

The drawing gives us permission to follow the errant protester where their e/motion continues to be structurally denied. As a figure who loops back and forward, Hemings's imagined hands upon the wall appear through Rasheed's insertion of her own. They share in a current of black affective resistance. The "one" that is the artist and the "one" that is Hemings provide portals for one another and invite us to imagine what is invisible but nonetheless apparent: Sally Hemings's pliable presence, no longer disposable goods, she is *the one that counts*. When read together, Spillers and Rasheed demand that we break from traditional modes of social analysis and aesthetic consumption. The artist and the errant protester collide. This is not a place of hallowed institutionality; we are not in Du Bois's ring. We fall out of line. Here, the black woman is not a disposable good—every scrap in her notebook becomes useful. Her imprint is important. And although she has left her traces and defaced the walls, we are still left to wonder: what will she do outside?

Notes

The first iteration of this chapter was delivered as a symposium paper at "'Words Walking Without Masters': Conversations on the Creative Theoretical" organized by Shacoya Kidwell and Jehan Roberson at Cornell University April 21, 2022.

Epigraph. Box 1, Folder 23, Hortense J. Spillers Papers, Ms.2019.013, Pembroke Center Archives, John Hay Library, Brown University. Hereafter Spillers Papers.

1. On November 20, 2015, approximately one hundred Brandeis University undergraduate and graduate students gathered in front of the Bernstein Marcus administrative building. After issuing thirteen demands, including "the increase [of] the percentage of full-time Black faculty and staff to 10% across ALL departments and schools" and the appointment of "additional clinical staff of color within the Psychological Counseling Center in order to provide culturally relevant support to students of all backgrounds," the Concerned Students of 2015 aligned themselves with national student protesters refusing to turn their eyes from the brutal murder of eighteen-year-old Michael

Brown by Ferguson, Missouri, police and the debasement of his unalived body, which remained in the streets despite his mother's plea to collect him. For documentation on the Ford Hall 2015 Occupation and the list of demands please see "Concerned Students 2015 Email and Demands," Office of the President, Brandeis University, Nov 19, 2015, https://www.brandeis.edu/president/past/lynch-letters/2015-concerned-students-demands.html; and Phillip Martin, "Voices of #FordHall2015," *Brandeis Magazine*, Summer 2016, https://www.brandeis.edu/magazine/2016/summer/featured-stories/fordhall2015.html. Additionally, I would like to thank Jasmine E. Johnson for entering the occupation not only to hold class but also to teach us how to move within constraint. It is her language I borrow here.

2. In "The Black Studies Project: 50 Years and Counting," Rich Blint draws our attention to this overlooked detail in Spillers' experience within the occupation. Rich Blint, Bob O'Meally, Hortense J. Spillers, and Gayatri Chakravorty Spivak, "The Black Studies Project: 50 Years and Counting," posted by SOF-Heyman (Society of Fellows and Heyman Center for the Humanities), October 6, 2021, YouTube, https://youtu.be/RjZ-lGoDUQM. I underscore Spillers's point that black study existed before the institutionalization of black studies departments. As a graduate of the department of African and Afro-American studies at Brandeis University, I hope to join a conversation taking place between those committed to black studies and who are asking, what is the work of black studies *now*?

3. Pickens, "The Verb Is No," 15.
4. Box 2, Folder 5, Spillers papers.
5. Moton and Harney, *The Undercommons*, 26.
6. Spillers, "Chosen Place," 152.
7. Spillers, "Chosen Place," 173.
8. Although Spillers published the essay and the drawing in the 1985, she began working on drafts of the drawing as early as 1983. Early drafts of the essay and drawing are included in her papers at Brown University. Additionally, I would like to thank the members of the anthology for lending their interpretations of Spillers's drawing during our workshop. The group helped me to engage Spillers's drawing more thoughtfully by directing me to the paintings of Nell Painter and Alma Thomas.
9. Hortense J. Spillers's path-breaking essays include "Mama's Baby, Papa's Maybe: An American Grammar Book" (1987); "Interstices: A Small Drama of Words" (2003); and "'All the Things you Could Be by Now, If Sigmund Freud's Wife Was Your Mother': Psychoanalysis and Race" (1996); among many others.
10. Crawford, *Black Post-Blackness*, 2.
11. Battle-Baptiste and Rusert, *W. E. B. Du Bois's Data Portraits*. For a brilliant account of Du Bois's sociological drawings see the chapter "An Atlas of the Wayward" in Saidiya Hartman's *Wayward Lives, Beautiful Experiments*.

12. Spillers, "'All the Things You Could Be,'" 101.
13. Hortense Spillers describes this process in "'All the Things You Could Be By Now'" as "closing the distance one makes between herself and what she studies."
14. See Hurston, "How It Feels to Be Colored Me," 1928.
15. Spillers, "'All the Things You Could Be,'" 115.
16. Hortense J. Spillers, "Toward an Ontology: African American Women and the Republic," filmed March 5, 2009, at Rutgers University, posted by Rutgers University, June 23, 2009, YouTube, https://youtu.be/LXcYvugToIA.
17. Here I am referring to a clarification Maya Angelou makes in an interview with Welsh television host Mavis Nicholson where she describes how her child-self lived in the aftermath of the catastrophic event of her sexual violation by a trusted family member. Angelou explains that although she made silence her refuge, her mental life was not taking place in silence. The distinction is crucial. Angelou demonstrates how silence is undertaken as a practice of black affective resistance. "Maya Angelou interview | Civil Rights | Afternoon plus | 1984," broadcast Jan. 24, 1984, posted by ThamesTV, Oct. 9, 2018, YouTube, https://www.youtube.com/watch?v=90VWA-obyWA, 7:32.
18. Ashon Crawley, "Nothing Music: The Hammond B3 and the Centrifugitivity of Blackpentecostal Sound," *Ashon Crawley* (blog), Apr. 30, 2014, https://web.archive.org/web/20140816214431/http://ashoncrawley.com/2014/04/30/nothing-music-the-hammond-b3-and-the-centrifugitivity-of-blackpentecostal-sound.
19. "Thomas Jefferson, Architect: Palladian Models, Democratic Principles, and the Conflict of Ideals," Chrysler Museum of Art, October 19, 2019, https://chrysler.org/exhibition/thomas-jefferson-architect-palladianmodels-democratic-principles-and-the-conflict-of-ideals.
20. Maya Mackrandilal, "The Aesthetics of Empire: Neoclassical Art and White Supremacy," *Contemptorary* (blog), Nov. 17, 2017, https://contemptorary.org/the-aesthetics-of-empire-neoclassical-art.
21. "Kameelah Janan Rasheed: *Worshipping at the Altar of Certainty*," Williams College Museum of Art, Aug, 16, 2021, https://artmuseum.williams.edu/kameelah-janan-rasheed-worshipping-at-the-altar-of-certainty.
22. Tschumi, "Architectural Paradox," 40.
23. Spillers, "Toward an Ontology," 6, 30.
24. Brown and Abdur-Rahman, "Capture, Illegibility, Necessity," 68.

References

Battle-Baptiste, Whitney, and Britt Rusert, eds. *W. E. B. Du Bois's Data Portraits: Visualizing Black America: The Color Line at the Turn of the Twentieth Century*. Amherst: W. E. B. Du Bois Center at the University of Massachusetts, Princeton Architectural Press, 2018.

Brown, Simone, and Aliyyah Abdur-Rahman. "Capture, Illegibility, Necessity: A Conversation on Black Privacy" *Black Scholar* 51, no. 1 (2021): 67–72.

Crawford, Margo Natalie. *Black Post-Blackness: The Black Arts Movement and Twenty-First-Century Aesthetics*. Champaign: University of Illinois Press, 2017.

Hartman Saidiya. *Wayward Lives, Beautiful Experiments: Intimate Histories of Riotous Black Girls, Troublesome Women, and Queer Radicals*. New York: WW Norton, 2019.

Hurston, Zora Neale. "How It Feels to Be Colored Me." *The World Tomorrow*, no. 11 (May 1928): 215–16.

Moton, Fred, and Stephano Harney. *The Undercommons: Fugitive Planning & Black Study*. Wivenhoe, UK: Minor Compositions, 2013.

Pickens, Therí. "The Verb Is No: Towards a Grammar of Black Women's Anger," *CLA Journal* 60, no. 1 (Sept. 2016): 15–31.

Spillers, Hortense J. "*Chosen Place, Timeless People*: Some Figurations on the New World." In *Conjuring: Black Women, Fiction, and Literary Tradition*, edited by Marjorie Lee Pryse and Hortense J. Spillers, 151–75. Bloomington: Indiana University Press, 1985.

Spillers, Hortense J. "'All the Things You Could Be by Now, If Sigmund Freud's Wife Was Your Mother': Psychoanalysis and Race." *Boundary 2* 23, no. 3 (Oct. 1, 1996): 75–141.

Tschumi, Bernard. "The Architectural Paradox." In *Architecture and Disjunction*, 28–52. Cambridge, MA: MIT Press, 1994.

Wynter, Sylvia. "No Humans Involved: An Open Letter to My Colleagues." *Forum N.H.I: Knowledge for the 21st Century* 1, no. 1 (1994): 42–73. http://carmen-kynard.org/wp-content/uploads/2013/07/No-Humans-Involved-An-Open-Letter-to-My-Colleagues-by-SYLVIA-WYNTER.pdf.

8 "whatever marvels of my own inventiveness"

Black Feminist Archival Tradition in the Notebooks of Hortense Spillers

KIANA T. MURPHY

In an early typed draft of her seminal essay "Mama's Baby, Papa's Maybe: An American Grammar Book" (1987), Hortense Spillers adds a written addendum to the opening paragraph (Figure 8.1), now considered the essay's iconic opening: "My country needs me, and if I were not here, I would have to be invented."[1] The arrow in the margins prompts the turning of the page to an extended note, "invented from scratch," which she later deletes in a revision.[2] In another draft, she clarifies this note about invention, writing an additional marginal note on the back of one of the pages:

> As we contemplate this cultural subject, I wish to keep in mind a necessary distinction: "the black American woman" is not entirely coterminous with that population of African American women in the United States who carry on their individual and collective lives both consonant with and in contradiction to the fictions that have sprung up around their life histories. I am primarily concerned in this writing with the fictions—both official and "creative"—that intersect the "real thing" in the interest of helping

to provide a corrective and revisionary feature of cultural readings that [would] bear on our imagined and to-be-created-reality.³

Spillers's revisions in these 1985 drafts draw attention to the bifurcation between material reality and figuration, highlighting the symbolic weight of cultural fictions that endure. The echoes of personal invention, however, lingers here and enlivens Spillers's philosophical argument about the discursive figuration of Black women. The "I" in the first paragraph of "Mama's Baby" then functions doubly as fiction and as autobiographical metanarrative in an essay that situates itself between philosophical debates and feminist discourse. Reading this draft within the context of Spillers's notebooks (1966–1990), the relationship between the personal and the collective are magnified, rendering visible the act of seeing and bearing witness to a Black woman theorizing herself into existence.

The imperative outlined here in the drafts of Hortense Spillers's seminal essay "Mama's Baby" describes more broadly my readings of the late-twentieth-century archives of Black women writers and cultural workers as they straddle gap between the real and the fictional. In the opening of the published essay, Spillers considers a two-fold meaning of the term invention as a means to theorize against discursive

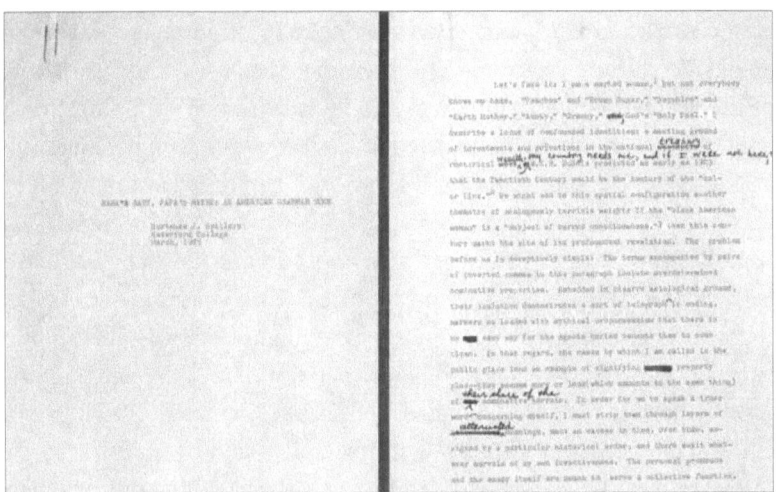

FIGURE 8.1. A typed draft of the title page and first page of "Mama's Baby, Papa's Maybe: An American Grammar Book," dated March 1985.

and symbolic orders that transfix Black women in material negation: (1) "My country needs me, and if I were not here, I would have to be invented" and (2) "In order for me to speak a truer word concerning myself, I must strip down through layers of attenuated meanings, made an excess in time, over time, assigned by a particular historical order, and there await whatever marvels of my own inventiveness. The personal pronouns are offered in service of a collective function."[4] In notes for a 1985 talk at Dartmouth College drawn from the essay, Spillers makes this conceptual paradox plain: "The historical subject of black women in the United States has been 'studied,' 'narrated,' 'criticized' and 'spoken for' from everybody's point of view, but their own."[5] Examining the Spillers archives, particularly the four boxes that hold more than forty notebooks—some bound and others not—I consider how these early writings stage a layering of this discursive order, emphasizing not only the inventive distortions of discursive systems but also the possibilities of invention that are made anew when these distortions are laid bare through the processes of drafting and revision. Expanding what Jennifer Nash calls a binaristic framework of injury and recovery that often defines the political grammars of Black feminist theorizing, Spillers's personal writings illustrate an entangled affect of what Joseph Winters calls "hope draped in black" that not only defines Black life but also the archives of other Black women writers in the 1970s and 1980s.[6] Situated alongside cultural historians and literary critics who read the history of the archive as part and parcel of an anti-Black world order, I read Spillers's notebooks as an instructive narrative re-figuring of Black life, and consider her self-writing as a contribution to contemporary renderings of Black women's archival methodology of writing through being, what Spillers extends in a note for her 1985 talk on "Mama's Baby," "A marked woman, her name a repetition of masks."[7]

As such, the archive offers another paradigm to read Spillers's published work: as luminously unfinished, actively in process, and building toward a future not yet here. I also read these complicated strivings as a cultural phenomenon specifically connected to late-twentieth-century Black archives, which marked a shift from redress, recovery, and repair to a consideration also of practices of refusal and embodiment that constituted the creation of archives by Black women cultural workers themselves. The late twentieth century marked the institutionalization of Black Studies and Women's and Gender Studies, the emergence of social and cultural movements in the 1970s and 1980s, efforts to preserve Black cultural institutions, and a major shift in the dominant discourses on race, gender, and sexuality toward an intersectional reckoning with difference.[8] As such, I place Spillers within a cadre of Black women writers, theorists, and cultural workers of this period—such as Toni Morrison, Gloria Naylor, Toni Cade Bambara, Ntozake Shange, Audre Lorde, Octavia Butler, Cheryl Wall, among many others—who diligently made collecting and preserving their papers an integral part of their writing practice.

Indeed, I find myself most drawn to Spillers's earliest notebooks dated 1966–1972. In them, Spillers takes note of her creative process, often writing marginal notes to herself to return to earlier musings. For example, in the cover of a notebook dated 1972, Spillers writes a minor note to herself inside the cover of the journal: "There's poetry here, come back to them."[9] In between handwritten essays and book reviews, copies of talks written out at length, class notes, annotated sermons, and other notated ephemera (such as grocery lists, phone numbers, and names), Spillers's writing occasionally ventures over into the poetic, often interceded by autobiographical musings of her own life. As such, more than ten years prior to her publication of iconic essays such as "Interstices" in 1984 and "Mama's Baby, Papa's Maybe: An American Grammar Book" in 1987, Spillers's notebooks stage their own intercession into what she herself calls the "missing word" of Black women in discourse. On another level, her papers also function as a Black feminist interruption of archival silence. This of course is not an argument that ignores the potential gaps and silences present—intentionally or unintentionally—within Spillers's archive, but one that considers how Spillers's collection functions as one of many counternarratives to archival loss and instead recalls the surplus of archives crafted by Black women writers and theorists in the late twentieth century.

In recent years, scholars have increasingly centered archives of slavery as critical indexes to reimagine the study of Black history, literature, and culture. Scholars such Saidiya Hartman, Marisa Fuentes, Christina Sharpe, Jennifer Morgan, among others have developed critical strategies to read against the violence of the archival record and read materials otherwise.[10] Other scholars have also considered these strategies in light of the significance of twentieth-century archives, particularly highlighting the importance of Black archives to our understanding of literary culture.[11] In a recent special issue of *The Black Scholar* on Black archives, editors Zakiya Collier and Tonia Sutherland continue this line of inquiry to examine the relationship between Black archives and Black archival practice, where they describe Black archival practice as "more than just the inclusion of narratives of Black life in the archival stacks and more than a diversification of the profession ... [but as a practice that is] marked by the transformative and iterative art of holding sacred space in our praxis for the memory of what makes Black life possible."[12] Indeed, the special issue centers methods and protocols of contemporary Black archives such as the essay by archivist Holly Smith who examines the practice of witnessing that is called forth in the archives of Toni Cade Bambara and Audre Lorde or Sasha Ann Panaram's essay that highlights how knowledge systems and archival protocols are already embedded within the archives of Black women writers such as Octavia Butler.[13] In this chapter, I extend the concerns of the special issue by placing emphasis on the archives of the late twentieth century, specifically those of Black women writers and theorists prominent in the development of Black women's writing and cultural criticism in the 1970s and 1980s. I read Spillers's archive—specifically her notebooks—as exhibiting another method of reading that I will call "archival abundance." By reading an archive abundantly, I mean that these archives not only provide a counternarrative to the often-violent protocols of institutionalized archiving, but also makes clear that the sheer excess of the archives call for multiplicitious, contradictory, and unlikely readings. Considering this protocol of reading for contemporary Black women writers' archives of the late twentieth century, I turn to Spillers's notebooks to not only trace the budding origins of her later critiques of discursive silence, but also center her turn to the twinned relationship between the poetic and the autobiographical as an early archival intervention in Black feminist study. A demonstration of her own inventiveness, Spillers's notebooks, I argue, perform the methodological work of archival abundance: full of their own plurality, contradictions, and gaps, the notebooks function as a call for collaborative witness and testimony on one hand and the marvels of Black woman inventiveness on the other.

Hortense Spillers's Notebooks and the Marvel of Invention

The Hortense J. Spillers archive comprises roughly thirty boxes of material dating from 1966 to 1995 and includes diaries, notebooks, writing drafts, professional correspondence, and conference and teaching materials. To read Hortense Spillers's archive in light of other Black women writers of the late twentieth century is to read her work as a theorist and creative writer, which Spillers herself deliberately reflects on and practices in her notebooks. One of her creative pieces, which started out as a series of notes in a notebook, would go on to be published in 1975 as the short story "Brother Isom" in *The Black Scholar*. Alongside short fiction, Spillers's turn to poetry is a reoccurring preoccupation in her notebooks—as a critical mode of thinking through philosophical questions of Black being as well as developing early meditations on Black feminist critique. The notebooks are the earliest dated items in the Spillers archive, making the late 1960s and early 1970s a critical intellectual influence.

Spillers received her bachelor's degree in 1964 and master's degree in 1966 from the University of Memphis, and later her doctoral degree in 1974 at Brandeis University. In her early notebooks, Spillers discusses the Memphis that shaped her consciousness—the city that saw some of the largest sociocultural and legal shifts in the United States such as the Civil Rights Act of 1964, the Voting Rights Act of 1965, and budding activism on college campuses to institute Black Studies. In a notebook dated between 1979 and 1980, more than a decade later, Spillers writes a talk for Mississippi Industrial College, now known as Rust College, reflecting on the significance of education a few years before the college closed due to the inability to compete with post-desegregation efforts. In it, Spillers reflects on her own upbringing in the 1950s, an hour away from the college, and remembers "when the memory of Pearl Harbor was still freshly etched on America's brain . . . [when] black was a curse word . . . [the time of] two mutually exclusive worlds, all the visible universe was stretched before me on either side of the great division of color."[14] Spillers describes the audience as being part of a post-1954 South, where the illusion of progress had superseded an awareness of the erosion of public education: "Look back at Reconstruction and its aftermath: Unless we are ever mindful in struggle we are doomed to repeat ourselves—start all over again—over and over again. You're working hard probably, but not hard enough. Learning is not a luxury; it might not even save you from pain, but I am sure that in it is the one systematic thing that stands between us and the lash. If we would love, we must know, and we will know because we love."[15]

The connection between knowledge and love for Spillers, as a weapon against the lash, is integral to some of her early notebook writings. In them, she labors through a creative stream of consciousness where she thinks capaciously about the project of education and what can be made possible outside of its violent machinations. In an early journal entry dated October 1966, Spillers meditates philosophically on the "The Quest for Permanence."[16] She begins with a question: "Why do men seek permanence—that quality in things and of people that will endure?"[17] The entry (Figure 8.2) then meanders into a consideration of "Man's nature" to discover and conquer the meaning of life, those inordinate aspects of living that eludes the conscious mind, that she later describes as faith. She continues:

> Whatever a man grounds or bases his faith upon—himself and the powers of his mind—his own indestructibility amidst the onslaught and on rush of madness—science and scientism—devils and angels—heaven and hell—god and satan—is fed and sustained by his faint suspicion that any day now meaning will stop eluding his grasp and he will uncover in at least one encounter, or thing, or person, endurance and permanence.[18]

This constant pursuit toward consciousness—moving through polarities of meaning—is sustained by the fear of mortality. As such, Spillers supplants the vexed signification of Man to think through both the corporeal and the existential dread of the end of the human that is predicated on the fact that "[Man] has not uncovered all the mysteries of the cosmos."[19] The universal then for Spillers becomes a material metaphor for what it means to know, and the ways the accumulation of

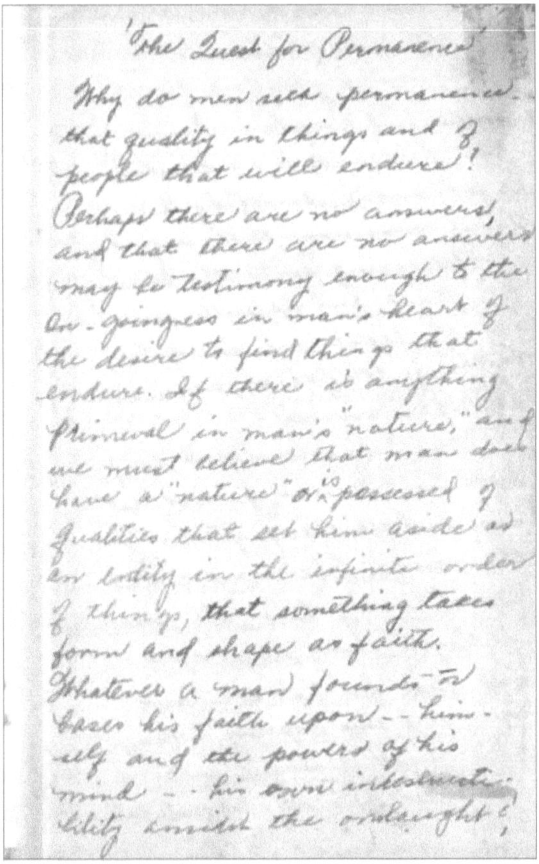

FIGURE 8.2. A page dated October 1966 from one of Spillers's early journals.

knowledge produces a fear of the unknown, a fear of seeing "through a 'glass darkly' . . . only in part."[20] Spillers reads this drive toward closure as a critical misreading of the longevity of the human, and feigned ignorance of the fact that "the trouble with life and finite being is that they do not stop long enough to be examined."[21] Even as the cosmos of life exceeds arm's reach, Spillers rearranges this notion to a mode of thinking with the cosmos—to read "beingness" as having a plenitude that eludes capture, even as human beings strive toward an understanding of this metaphysical reality. Spillers maintains this sentiment in her musings, now analogizing the deterioration of the human with the deterioration of meaning:

> By the time one experience is about to be made life and blood, another takes its place and another. The process goes on until man knows one thing— Few experiences are meaningful and few experiences "hang" together or meaningfully relate to ones before and after. By the time he realizes the remote and foreboding, the making it intelligible because of sharper focus, chaos enfolds again and he suffers almost irreparable set-back.[22]

Spillers describes beingness here as a series of displacements, a constant undermining of what has happened before, a sharpening into chaos. As such, Spillers adds another dimension to "Man," a word always already signifying a racializing project of humanism, and discloses the chaos of knowing as an impossibility of repair. Instead, the finitude of being becomes the nexus through which life can be lived and partially understood.

Against the backdrop of the 1960s, Spillers's focus on the cosmos as a site for being is an intuitive intellectual move that follows in the spirit of Black power and the call for rearranging the scenes of Blackness. She imagines this coming to consciousness as a tentative and ongoing overlap between reality and the dream, what she calls the "mecca of the mind":

> And what is faith? Faith is the compulsion to keep moving, knowing that total reality and complete comprehension are within the range of one's possibilities. As long as these remain within the range of possibility man is still eluded, not because he is a fool in his heart but because he grows forever toward and into his infinite possibilities, and only he has set the limits to what he can become. Only he knows that those limits are presently out of sight because that's how largely he can dream. But to unite the dream and the reality, the possible and the present, is to unite one's total being. Such unity is the culmination of faith. Such unity is arriving, at last, to the mecca of mind. Here faith and being are all the same because one has uncovered the essence of the other. Man has become what he has imagined.[23]

Extending her stream of consciousness here, Spillers meditates on the spirit of knowing and what it means to know in the gaps: know one's possibilities, understand the limits, and begin to bridge the unknown with the possible. Spillers's later writings on the Black sermon for her dissertation coupled with her own religious upbringing also functions as intellectual grounds for her thinking here. The capacity of "Man [becoming] what he has imagined" is an apt phrase to describe the becoming documented in Spillers's notebooks. The insights displayed here—the centering of the cosmos, the development of insurmountable faith coupled with the question of being, and the quest for knowledge—would later become foundational to Spillers's canonical feminist essays in the 1970s and '80s. Here, however, readers of her archive can witness the promise of this invention within Spillers herself, as she delves into the philosophical as a means of understanding her own place in the academy and her personal response to the call for Black power.

These questions of becoming verge into specific racial concerns at the closing decade, when in a later 1966 entry (Figure 8.3) of the same journal Spillers contemplates "The Dilemma of Being Black."[24] She muses first over what she calls the estrangement of history, which she clarifies later as the enduring impact of chattel slavery on the fracturing of Black communities across the diaspora. The doubled farce and material reality of "color" as difference becomes a mask for systemic violence, constelled now as a question of identification instead of power. Spillers's early consideration of "color" as symbolic code for being Black in America, or as she describes in her journal as being on the "verge of the abyss . . . to already have fallen into the abyss," echoes some of her later sentiments in "Mama's Baby":[25]

> These undecipherable markings on the captive body render a kind of hieroglyphics of the flesh whose severe disjunctures come to be hidden to the cultural seeings by skin color. We might well ask if this phenomenon of marking and branding actually "transfers" from one generation to another, finding its various symbolic substitutions in an efficacy of meanings that repeat initiating moments?[26]

With the 1960s marking an increased visibility firmly rooted in an effacement of power, Spillers continues to reflect in this journal entry on the new performances—which can be read also as those "severe disjunctures" that Spillers describes—required of Black male leaders, such as

Martin Luther King Jr. and Stockley Carmichael, who she argues are emerging from a long tradition of Black leadership, activism, and intellectual thought that spans back to the turn of the century with W. E. B. Du Bois. Mirroring the sonic inflections of Black power, Spillers muses over the tension between discourse and action, which she describes as "determining how to finish breaking the camel's back:"[27]

> Perhaps to sing "we shall overcome" or shout "burn baby burn" is to speak symbolically; we know now that the present human dialogue is outmoded, narrow and exclusive; what black men want today is what we've always wanted–to help structure the terms of the dialogue–to reveal to ourselves our own voice–beauty–authority–in short–to join the human race as a full participant with room to become whatever we will, even if that's nothing. To be uncommitted to the struggle is to be immoral, to shrink action is to be enslaved again. We must get on up, wherever we are, and move now.[28]

Spillers names this urgency as critically related to the Black man's dilemma in the revolution. However, it is instructive to note in these journal pages how Spillers fluctuates between the autobiographical and the universal. The use of the word *Man*, in the earlier journal mentioned before, for instance, becomes a substitute for Spillers's own voice, her critique of Black men in the movement, and the philosophically complicated "we" that is used to describe the human population. This slippage between racialized and gendered frames of positionality between the journals is key to Spillers's Black feminist praxis. Indeed, this collapsing of positionality to trouble the lines of the human is critical grounds for Spillers's indictment of Black political movements. For her, the common refrains of the Civil Rights Movement of the 1950s and the Black Power Movement of the 1960s threatens to linger too heavily in the symbolic, a narrowing out of what Spillers considers to be a much longer freedom struggle that predates the present tense of Black power. Spillers balances the complicated status of civil and political recognition with the opaqueness of resolution: the freedom to be, in whatever way this "beingness" manifests. As such, political action in Spillers's case is an urgency that feeds off her earlier musings on permanence, a releasing of the desire to know and leaning into the unknown. Citing

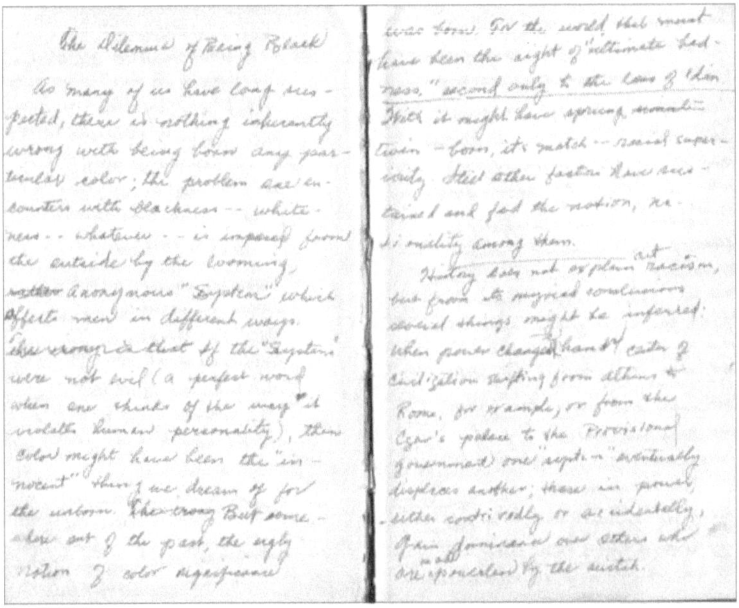

FIGURE 8.3. Two pages from 1966 or 1967 from Spillers's early journal.

a hyperawareness of the backdrop of political leaders being usurped into dominant structures of power, Spillers crafts a critical indictment of political movements that fail to consider an ongoing commitment and struggle to move toward discourse that affirms the beauty of the "whatever" of Black being.[29] Indeed, this porosity of subject positions, which doubles for Spillers as an elasticity of being, becomes the philosophical opening for her later critical essays.

Spillers's journal entry then moves into a more intersectional thinking, anticipating the energies of the decade to come, as she considers how a single-issue politics will inevitably falter to the sinister logics of power and domination. She not only encourages Black political leaders to view dissension as a critical praxis for political strategizing, but also consider these divergences as key to survival:

> What the "brothers" must do is listen to dissension and divergent views, because as we liberate ourselves we cannot assume nor insists that we're better than others or that one ism solves the worlds anguish; we must admit that Caliban is there when we look in the mirror some morning

and that just as the aims of the French Revolution got bogged down in personalities, egos, temperament so can the "Black Revolution." Because hate is legislated, etc. we need love now more than ever—love for ourselves—love for each other. If this persists, if we can keep a sharp eye on that light above the fog, if we can stare across the wide abyss at each other (age, viewpoints, goals) and still feel kinship. "We shall overcome" and by whatever means necessary.[30]

Personality and ego aside, Spillers reflects again on the usefulness of "love" as a political strategy, a feeling that has the possibility of not only superseding the insidious nature of structural hatred and violence but also moving toward new forms of kinship. Indeed, Spillers mirrors the political vision of the Combahee River Collective's 1974 statement: [we] "see as our particular task the development of integrated analysis and practice based upon the fact that the major systems of oppression are interlocking. The synthesis of these oppressions creates the conditions of our lives."[31] The chasm that marks the "abyss of Blackness" is transformed through intersectional knowledge, an exchange of egotistical leadership for nuanced communal relations the supersede the crux of representation and identity. At the close of the journal entry, the political sentiments of the '60s and '70s are also no longer separate sites of indictment but intermingled and connected to ongoing sites of resistance. This recalls the existential meditations demonstrated in the first entry as Spillers now drifts in and out of the personal toward the closing. This political strife (and striving) is never exempt from the psychological toll of "doing the work." In fact, the entry ends with a separate section, a personal reflection dated shortly after 1969, where Spillers displays a fleeting sentiment of the turmoil and weight of intellectual labor that occasionally moves in and out of the journal. She laments, briefly: "There is so much pain about me on this night. It is thick, heavy. Like another layer of skin. I should have been doing my work. There is salvation in work and a man must be about his business whatever it is."[32]

At the turn the decade, Spillers's notebooks begin to shift away from the existentialism of Black power rhetoric of the 1960s toward an explicit feminist critique that matched the development of Black feminist cultural shift in the 1970s. Alongside the extensive volume of archives collected

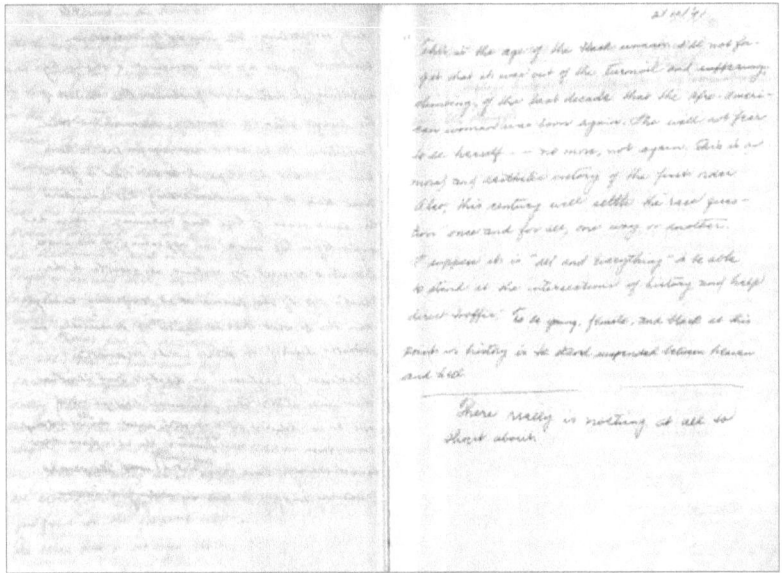

FIGURE 8.4. An entry from February 10, 1971, in one of Spillers's notebooks.

in the late twentieth century by Black women writers, Spillers's archive can also be read as a staging ground where published texts are given a plurality of textual speech—where a cadre of characters, personal narratives, imagined geographies, political commitments, and genres are revised while also making space throughout the drafting process for personal invention.[33] Her collection represents a possibility to read abundantly: examining how published works are undone by compilations of drafts and notes, how self-curation demands alternative reading practices, and how the sheer abundance of her papers makes space for plural and unfolding modes of thinking and interpretation across her writing.[34] In an adjacent fashion, Spillers early notebooks also document the intensive psychological labor of this cultural work (Figure 8.4). In the folds of a notebook dated 1971—words that also mirror Spillers own language in her writings during this decade—the positionality of Black women becomes both a moral and ethical prerogative. With the early proliferation of Black women's writing, the dilemma of Blackness and the existential dread of waning permanence that marked the call of the 1960s is inscribed in a new language:

> This is the age of the Black woman. I'll not forget that it was out of turmoil and ~~suffering~~ climbing of the last decade that the Afro-American woman was born again. She will not fear to be herself—no more, not again. This is a moral and aesthetic victory of the first order. Also, this century will settle the "race" question once and for all, one way or another. I suppose it is "all and everything" to be able to stand at the intersection of history and help direct traffic." To be young, female, and black at this point in history is to stand suspended between heaven and hell.[35]

Moving away from her indictment of Black male political leaders, Spillers writes a short journal entry that marks the energy of the 1970s as a new age, as Black women climb out of the shadows of Black Power. This becoming is a "first order" victory in which Black women now tackle the race question at the intersection of history and culture. Building on her earlier journal entry where she called on Black men to take up divergent views, Spillers here centers Black women's "suspension" as a critical site where this recognition of divergence can be made possible. Throughout her journals, Spillers also reflects on this "all and everything" standpoint as emblematic of her own relationship to academic institutions. This constant shuttling between the personal and the collective is a critical praxis in Spillers journals, but also another entry point into understanding her essays as well.

Two years later, in a journal entry dated 1973, Spillers's poetry deeply examines the concerns of the decade, in line with the tradition of Black women writers who were at the time experimenting with genre to bridge the silence around Black women's experiences.[36] In the cover of the journal, Spillers writes the minor note mentioned earlier: "There's poetry in here, come back to them."[37] Indeed, Spillers writes a number of poems that reflect some of the key themes that would later emerge in her essays, which together work as creative archive of in-process theoretical musings. One of those poems "Black Mother Who Will Mourn For You," shares some of the language of "Mama's Baby" that would be published years later (Figure 8.5). A more poetic approach to this "dilemma" of suspension as she describes in her early journals, the poem considers the ways the proverbial "Black mother"—discursively and symbolically invented—can be spoken. Recall the opening of "Mama's

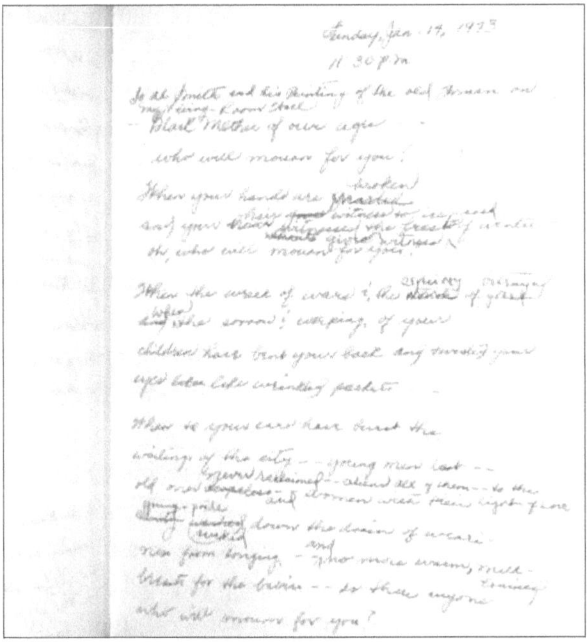

FIGURE 8.5. A page from Spillers's journal dated January 14, 1973.

Baby," now iconic in its nuanced simplicity, written almost ten years after this journal entry: "I am a marked woman, but not everybody knows my name. 'Peaches' and 'Brown Sugar,' 'Sapphire' and 'Earth Mother,' 'Aunty,' 'Granny,' God's 'Holy Fool,' a 'Miss Ebony First,' or 'Black Woman at the Podium.'"[38] Some of the names at the end of this list Spillers added on later in her revisions, an archival addition that insists on the ongoing nature of the "marked" naming that shifts only marginally through the decades. The poem elaborates on the connotations of a few of these names, beginning with a line that becomes a refrain: "Black mother of our ages / who will mourn for you?"[39] The speaker of the poem goes on to call for the witnesses to rise, those who will "say—yes, she was beautiful once, I knew her then, soft & warm like fur on camel, hair tender & yielding like the nap of kittens; strong as silk & as good to the touch as caramel cake. She was my lover."[40] The poem reorders the reader's sense of identification with an insistence on moving with the call of mourning, a grief that touches intimacy. A grief that remembers into the present and is unashamed of the claims of interrelation.

Spillers cycles back through the refrain of naming and the repetition starts to peel back the fictional layers of figuration. By the middle of the poem, a series of quotes appear that move from the echoes of the dark mundane register of the auction block, "a piece of chattel? ... can you name it in pounds, dollars, or pesos?," and later flow into an excerpt of a gospel hymn, "Nobody knows the trouble I've seen."[41] This calls the speaker to utter again the surplus of names at the beginning of "Mama's Baby," continued now in the cadence of persistent questioning: "What's the new price of female flesh when the blood of the lamb has been turned into kool-aid? Will we call her Ms. or Mrs. or Dr.? Welfare rights mother—black female intellectual! ... prostitute .... Can she get a witness?"[42] Here, the surplus is timeless, moving from the auction block to the family home to the professional realm, where even stature cannot bear the weight of bloody fictions. The poem then goes quietly into melancholic refrain, posing a scene of the possible: "Had she lived into a mellow old night / candle-rich song warmed by the blood, / who would have mourned? / Black mother of our ages—mother of time—the time of our lives—who will mourn for you?"[43]

These poetic writings that punctuate the notebooks illuminate the varying ways Spillers understood herself as a writer first and foremost. The poetic intervention coupled as melancholic remembrance follows a tradition and aligns Spillers with a cultural moment of Black women's writing that insisted on the need to create alternative fictions and assemble an archive that speaks back to the "missing word" of Black women's lives.[44] An attention to the labor of writing (and archiving) in this way is also reflected in a 1975 journal entry that engages the purpose of writing as both a matter of theoretical concern but also personal conviction:

> The one story I haven't attempted to look at is my own. There is so much about my past which I refuse to echo even ... say nothing of extended explanation. I must confront how much about myself I really know before I can project any other persons. To come to grips with my life right here in America is a beginning engagement which renders the African past no less significant in the long run, but a temporarily secondary emphasis. To believe that writing is therapeutic is, I believe, not to be a writer at all, but it seems certain that the ego must be sufficiently strong at rest to quiet one's

numerous fears—of exposure no less than the very self. The fear of writing is a distortion—one trembles for other reasons which writing as process only conceals. It may be that addressing the process which is an exercise of intelligence and imagination is one of several routes of redemption.[45]

To understand Spillers as a writer in the business of storytelling adds nuance to her theoretical essays. As suggested in this entry, Spillers is concerned with the intensive labor that comes with the process of writing one's own story at the same time that she queries the origin point of storytelling for the Black woman. In one sense, Spillers follows Sylvia Wynter's theorizing of the science of the word, especially as her work as a writer and critic stages imaginative arrangements of words that create new meanings and expose the latent anti-Black logics of Western thought.[46] In another, she queries how writing itself can toggle between exposure and concealment, or what Katherine McKittrick describes as the ways "black thinkers imagine and practice liberation as they are weighed down by [. . .] biocentrically induced accumulation and dispossession . . . the weight that bears down on all black people, inside and outside the academy, and puts pressure on their physiological and psychic and political well-being."[47] Indeed, as McKittrick continues, "black intellectual life is tied to corporeal and affective labor" although remaining still impossible to trace, track or capture.[48] Even so, Spillers's journals imperfectly document the traces of this intellectual labor, that labor most specifically tied to the livelihoods of Black women, and remind of the corporeal hinges of Black thought. Spillers's statement about the relationship between learning and the lash in her 1979 talk at Mississippi Industrial College also resonates here in the cruel toil of rendering clear one's own story against the backdrop of an anti-Black world. For Spillers, writing is not an easing of this burden but should foster a trembling that comes with tending to one's past. Rather than obscure the pain and fear of one's own life, writing should in fact mine the personal for its "intelligence and imagination" toward a redemption that is not wholly reparative but offers critical engagement with the vexed relationship between positionality and possibility.

It is not surprising, then, that Spillers also considers the possible affordances of the genre of autobiography in an early 1967 journal entry located in the same journal that she wrote "The Quest for Permanence" and "The Dilemma of Being Black."[49] She writes, yearning toward clarity:

> The capacity to tell a truth honestly is the genius I would wish for. I'm beginning here sketches which I trust will grow into a truth. What I want to portray is a young woman at the beginning of things. This is not an autobiography or even any such sketches, but an effort to find out where young women, like myself, are going, they haven't lived long enough to be content; they fight the urge to "face," and in their fight will, perhaps, become pure. Do they have faith? What do they have? Do they need God? What do they need? Are they fearful? Then what do they fear? Are they learned? Have they applied their learning to their living? Are they fools in their heart?[50]

What follows is a short list of the months of the year, from September to April, that charts out briefly what season each month would entail, each ending with the word "Love." For example, September would be "all novelty and excitement. Love?" while in December "the storm mounts. Love."[51] Spillers then goes on to chart two chapters of what this fictional Black woman's journey would look like and the accompanying cast of characters. The questions asked here—personal and not—share a similar tone to Spillers's previous journal entries in the notebooks: her descriptions of the cosmos, her questioning of being, her critiques of activism, and most importantly her continued meditations on the steady ordinariness of love. Here, there is a toying specifically with the autobiographical to consider the positionality of Black women and to document a truth about their particular order of living. Here, the "collective function" that Spillers announces at the beginning of "Mama's Baby" is given texture. Not distancing herself fully here from the significance of the "I," Spillers puts her positionality to work, where her personal narrative becomes the foundation to unraveling and complicating the meaning of broader philosophical questions. Much like the ongoing series of naming in her poems (also reiterated and clarified in "Mama's Baby"), the series of questions also work here to tell another origin story for Black women that includes the nuanced realities of their faith, fear, consciousness, and even foolishness. Indeed, Spillers's move toward fictional writing as an autobiographical hinge demonstrates her yearning to offer a loving, descriptive interior life of Black women, which to her is the heart of the written word.

Alongside the handwritten notes of lectures, drafts of essays, class notes, and bibliographies, the notebooks also show Spillers's written excerpts of scriptures and sermons, most of which were transcribed as she was finishing her dissertation on the sociocultural significance of Black preachers. In her 1973 notes, Spillers adds her own interpretations in the margins with a focus on tonality, cadence, and phrasing. Even amidst the research notes for her project, however, small mementos of Spillers musings of her own life abound between the pages. While flipping through the sermon notes, one item, a notecard that ends the journal's written pages, fell out:

> I did not know what I know now: my life to me is a mystery—a fluid equation suspended between two glowing poles of fire. The fire does not burn the water, but char broils it—fizzing sounds like beef in a hibachi, yet I survive. Where is he who will love me now despite myself, small, obscure, and afraid? A glowing mystery I am: Watching my reflections against the glossy side of the two-hot poles, I dance around them, flirt with them, draw near them, but never kiss, for I am fluid and changing, and in the center! This center does not hold, defying the physicist.[52]

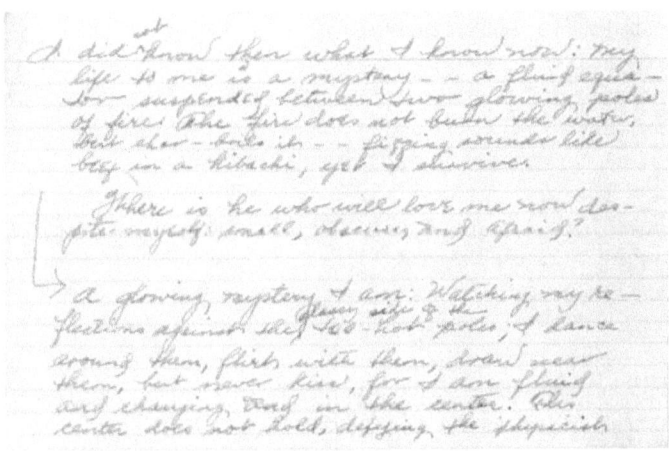

FIGURE 8.6. An undated notecard that had been tucked in Spillers's journal.

Undated and loosely inserted (Figure 8.6), the notecard works as a summation of the notebooks as a whole: describing the multiplicitous possibilities of self-invention that exceed Western epistemologies of being. Instead, Spillers's note-to-self toggles between the "I" and the figuration of the "African American woman," defying the physicist and remaining in the luminous liminality of suspension, or lingering in, as Katherine McKittrick describes, the rigorous Black methods of wonder and curiosity.[53] I did not know what I was searching for in the Spillers archives initially, but what I found was a Black woman—theorist, critic, writer—searching for meaning. To make meaning, not in ways to capture or dominate, but as an avenue toward the multitudes of Black living under the weight of overlapping systems of domination. Spillers's notebooks taught me how to understand reading and writing—especially her essays "Mama's Baby" and "Interstices"—as critical strategies for self-revision, a call for a reckoning with words and what it means to be. In other words, the notebooks taught me to read theory as both creative reworlding and a persistent documentation of a life in process, trying to be named—glowing, a mystery, a marvel.

Notes

1. Box 15, Folder 17. Ms.2019.013, Hortense J. Spillers papers, Black Feminist Theory Collections / Feminist Theory Archive, Brown University Library. Hereafter, Spillers papers.
2. Box 15, Folder 17, Spillers papers.
3. Box 15, Folder 17, Spillers papers.
4. Hortense J. Spillers, "Mama's Baby, Papa's Maybe: An American Grammar Book," in *Black, White, and in Color: Essays on American Literature and Culture* (Chicago: University of Chicago Press, 2003): 203–29.
5. Box 3, Spillers papers.
6. Jennifer Nash, *The Black Body in Ecstasy: Reading Race, Reading Pornography* (Durham, NC: Duke University Press, 2014); Joseph Winters. *Hope Draped in Black: Race, Melancholy, and the Agony of Process* (Durham, NC: Duke University Press, 2016).
7. Box 3, Spillers papers.
8. Mecca Jamillah Sullivan, *Poetics of Difference: Queer Feminist Forms in the African Diaspora* (Champaign: University of Illinois Press, 2021), 5–6.
9. Box 3, Folder 45, Spillers papers.
10. This includes a wide array of scholarly works across Black literary studies, visual culture, and history published in the past ten years, including Saidiya

Hartman's *Scenes of Subjection: Terror, Slavery, and Self-Making in Nineteenth-Century America* (Oxford: Oxford University Press, 1997), "Venus in Two Acts," *Small Axe* 12, no.2 (2008), and *Wayward Lives, Beautiful Experiments: Intimate Histories of Riotous Black Girls, Troublesome Women, and Queer Radicals* (New York: W.W. Norton, 2019); Marisa Fuentes's *Dispossessed Lives: Enslaved Women, Violence, and the Archive* (Philadelphia: University of Pennsylvania Press, 2016); Christina Sharpe's *In the Wake: On Blackness and Being* (Durham, NC: Duke University Press, 2016); and Jennifer Morgan's *Reckoning with Slavery: Gender, Kinship, and Capitalism in the Early Black Atlantic* (Durham, NC: Duke University Press, 2021). In conversation with these texts, I am also thinking of more recent experiments in Black archival study including Tiya Miles's *All That She Carried: The Journey of Ashley's Sack, A Black Family Keepsake* (New York: Random House, 2021); Alexis Pauline Gumbs's *M Archive: After the End of the World* (Durham, NC: Duke University Press, 2018); and Kimberly Drew and Jenna Wortham's anthology *Black Futures* (New York: One World, 2020).
11. I am thinking here about Brent Edwards's *The Practice of Diaspora: Literature Translation, and the Rise of Black Internationalism* (Boston: Harvard University Press, 2003) and Jean Christophe Cloutier's *Shadow Archives: The Lifecycles of African American Literature* (New York: Columbia University Press, 2019).
12. Tonia Sutherland and Zakiya Collier, "Introduction: The Promise and Possibility of Black Archival Practice." *The Black Scholar* 52, no. 2 (2022): 4.
13. See Holly A. Smith, "'Wholeness Is No Trifling Matter': Black Feminist Archival Practice and the Spelman College Archives." *The Black Scholar* 52, no. 2 (2022): 16–27; and Sasha Ann Panaram, "Bloom's Butler's Taxonomy," *The Black Scholar* 52, no. 2 (2022): 38–49.
14. Box 5, Folder 10, Spillers papers.
15. Box 5, Folder 10, Spillers papers.
16. Box 3, Folder 42, Spillers papers.
17. Box 3, Folder 42, Spillers papers.
18. Box 3, Folder 42, Spillers papers.
19. Box 3, Folder 42, Spillers papers.
20. Box 3, Folder 42, Spillers papers.
21. Box 3, Folder 42, Spillers papers.
22. Box 3, Folder 42, Spillers papers.
23. Box 3, Folder 42, Spillers papers.
24. Box 3, Folder 42, Spillers papers.
25. Box 3, Folder 42, Spillers papers.
26. Spillers, "Mama's Baby, Papa's Maybe," 207.
27. Box 3, Folder 42, Spillers papers.
28. Box 3, Folder 42, Spillers papers.
29. Here I am thinking with Rinaldo Walcott's use of "whatever" to describe the whatever of Black studies, contending with the field's discursive assumptions: "On the agenda here is to think simultaneously a number of over lapping

concerns—community, black queer positions, and what I call the 'whatever' of black studies. In terms of the 'whatever' of black studies, I draw on and develop Giorgio Agamben's formulation of the 'whatever' to suggest one way in which the uncertainties and commonalties of blacknesses might be formulated in the face of some room for surprise, disappointment, and pleasure without recourse to disciplinary and punishing measures. This is a whatever that can tolerate the whatever of blackness without knowing meaning—black meaning, that is—in advance of its various utterances." See Rinaldo Walcott, "Outside in Black Studies: Reading from a Queer Place in the Diaspora," *Black Queer Studies* (Durham, NC: Duke University Press, 2005), 95.
30. Walcott, "Outside in Black Studies," 95.
31. "The Combahee River Collective Statement." Combahee River Collective, 1977.
32. "The Combahee River Collective Statement."
33. Here, I am thinking about the collections of Toni Morrison, Gloria Naylor, Octavia Butler, June Jordan, Audre Lorde, bell hooks, Toni Cade Bambara, and Lucille Clifton, among others.
34. Thanks to Alexis Pauline Gumbs and Kevin Quashie for helping me clarify this point on abundance, with which I am referring here to both the size of the collections but also the kinds of alternative readings made possible by the items collected by the writers that supplement the published work.
35. Box 3, Folder 43, Spillers papers.
36. At this time, the 1970s saw the publication of now canonical texts: Toni Morrison's *The Bluest Eye* (1970) and *Sula* (1973); Alice Walker's *The Life of Grange Copeland* (1970); Maya Angelou's *I Know Why the Caged Bird Sings* (1970) and *Gather Together in My Name* (1974); Mari Evans's *I Am a Black Woman: Poems* (1970); Sonia Sanchez's *We a BaddDD People* (1970); Ntozake Shange's *For Colored Girls Who Considered Suicide / When the Rainbow Is Enuf* (1976); Audre Lorde's essay "The Uses of the Erotic" (1978) and poetry collection *The Black Unicorn* (1978); and Nikki Giovanni's *Black Feeling, Black Talk, Black Judgement* (1970), among many others.
37. Box 3, Folder 45, Spillers papers.
38. Spillers, "Mama's Baby, Papa's Maybe," 203.
39. Box 3, Folder 45, Spillers papers.
40. Box 3, Folder 45, Spillers papers.
41. Box 3, Folder 45, Spillers papers.
42. Box 3, Folder 45, Spillers papers.
43. Box 3, Folder 45, Spillers papers.
44. Spillers, "Interstices," 156.
45. Box 4, Spillers papers.
46. By this, I am interested in Spillers's use of "American grammar" as an index for the silent void of Black women's positionality in discourse and how her readings parallel some of Wynter's propositions of the relationship between words

and nature, a rethinking of the human species as thusly bios-mythois. To read a succinct analysis of Wynter's "science of the word," see Katherine McKittrick, Frances H. O'Shaughnessy, and Kendall Witaszek, "Rhythm, or, On Sylvia Wynter's Science of the Word," *American Quarterly* 70, no. 4 (2018): 867–74.
47. Katherine McKittrick, *Dear Science and Other Stories* (Durham, NC: Duke University Press, 2021), 3.
48. McKittrick, *Dear Science and Other Stories*, 3.
49. Box 3, Folder 42, Spillers papers.
50. Box 3, Folder 42, Spillers papers.
51. Box 3, Folder 42, Spillers papers.
52. Box 4, Spillers papers.
53. McKittrick, Dear Science and Other Stories, 5.

References

Cloutier, Jean-Christophe. *Shadow Archives: The Lifecycles of African American Literature*. New York: Columbia University Press, 2019.
Collier, Zakiya and Tonia Sutherland. "Black Archival Practice Vol. 1." *The Black Scholar* 52, no 2. (2022): 1-6.
Drew, Kimberly, and Jenna Wortham, eds. *Black Futures*. New York: One World, 2020.
Edwards, Brent Hayes. *The Practice of Diaspora: Literature, Translation, and the Rise of Black Internationalism*. Cambridge, MA: Harvard University Press, 2003.
Fuentes, Marissa. *Dispossessed Lives: Enslaved Women, Violence, and the Archive*. Philadelphia: University of Pennsylvania Press, 2016.
Gumbs, Alexis Pauline. *M Archive after the End of the World*. Durham, NC: Duke University Press, 2018.
Hartman, Saidiya. *Scenes of Subjection: Terror, Slavery, and Self-Making in Nineteenth-Century America*. Oxford: Oxford University Press, 1997.
———. "Venus in Two Acts." *Small Axe: A Caribbean Journal of Criticism* 12, no. 2 (2008): 1–14.
———. *Wayward Lives, Beautiful Experiments: Intimate Histories of Riotous Black Girls, Troublesome Women, and Queer Radicals*. New York: W.W. Norton, 2019.
McKittrick, Katherine. *Dear Science and Other Stories*. Durham, NC: Duke University Press, 2021.
McKittrick, Katherine, Frances H. O'Shaughnessy, and Kendall Witaszek. "Rhythm, or, On Sylvia Wynter's Science of the Word." *American Quarterly* 70, no. 4 (2018): 867–74.
Miles, Tiya. *All That She Carried: The Journey of Ashley's Sack, a Black Family Keepsake*. New York: Random House, 2021.
Morgan, Jennifer L. *Reckoning with Slavery: Gender, Kinship, and Capitalism in the Early Black Atlantic*. Durham, NC: Duke University Press, 2021.

Nash, Jennifer. *The Black Body in Ecstasy: Reading Race, Reading Pornography*. Durham, NC: Duke University Press, 2014.

Panaram, Sasha Ann. "Bloom's Butler's Taxonomy." *The Black Scholar* 52, no. 2 (2022): 38–49.

Sharpe, Christina. *In the Wake: On Blackness and Being*. Durham, NC: Duke University Press, 2016.

Smith, Holly A. "'Wholeness Is No Trifling Matter': Black Feminist Archival Practice and The Spelman College Archives." *The Black Scholar* 52, no. 2 (2022): 16–27.

Spillers, Hortense, J. "Mama's Baby, Papa's Maybe: An American Grammar Book." In *Black, White, and in Color: Essays on American Literature and Culture*, 203–29. Chicago: University of Chicago Press, 2003.

———. "Interstices: A Small Drama of Words." In *Black, White, and in Color: Essays on American Literature and Culture*, 152–75. Chicago: University of Chicago Press, 2003.

Sullivan, Mecca Jamillah. The *Poetics of Difference: Queer Feminist Forms in the African Diaspora*. Champaign: University of Illinois Press, 2021.

Winters, Joseph. *Hope Draped in Black: Race, Melancholy, and the Agony of Process*. Durham, NC: Duke University Press, 2016.

9 All the Things You Could Be by Now If Hortense Spillers was Your Mentor

NICOLE A. SPIGNER

We were in her lush living room. Rich brocades in golds and burgundies decorated the wide, plush sofa and chairs filled with down. The warm and deeply colored hardwood floor was broken only by a large and ornate wool Persian rug where my sweet pit-Shar Pei-something rescue dog, Neoma, found her comfy spot next to the sofa. The now-empty center seat cushion on the sofa held the soft imprint of its most frequent sitter who was busy moving from place to place in the room, sorting and organizing her mail, more than a few unread *New York Times* issues, and stacks of student papers that needed grading and feedback. The ceiling towered above us, and tall windows encouraged the afternoon light to stream in from three different directions.

The MSNBC talking heads yelled from the 65″ flatscreen mounted above a delicious, deep-red console whose stillness juxtaposed the chaotic movement on the television. We were talking about what we might do later that day, and for me, it included another attempt to work on my never-ending monograph draft. Regardless of my effort, the manuscript still felt stifled and stilted. I had trouble accessing the "flow" that "every" article on successful writing claimed was my reward for the countless days of chipping away at my project. I'd never experienced the bliss I'm *supposed* to feel while writing. I had not found that flow, bliss, or whatever the term du jour was—the disconnection from self-criticism that I felt during a good yoga practice or a long walk on one of the many Nashville greenways. I felt burdened by my sense of obligation to finish this project—one that I felt very attached to and upon which my career was dependent—and was frustrated with my experience of self-doubt and -disappointment that had risen to the surface since I began my graduate school writing practice.

"How do you become a better writer?" I asked her.

Standing in the middle of the room, she slowly turned to me. Her hand moved fluidly toward her face, and her thumb and forefinger rested gently against her chin. Her eyes moved from the corner of the room, where she seemed to be looking for the answer. She tilted her head ever so slightly as her eyes met and held mine fast.

"Write," she said.

The tv seemed to go silent. I revised her answer into a question.

"Write?"

"Write."

It seems like such a simple thing: write. I'd had conversations about writing with other senior colleagues, attended some writing retreats, explored coaching, yet the advice that echoes every time I worry that my work will never be enough is that of Hortense Jeanette Spillers, from that day in her living room. Like much of what I experienced with her as my graduate school advisor, the instructions were unadorned, clear, and action-oriented. Write.

This is an essay about Hortense J. Spillers and writing. It is also an essay about Spillers as mentor and teacher. Ultimately, this is an essay about Hortense J. Spillers and craft, her various but related methodologies that result in the exemplar writing, course development and execution, and student mentorship for which she is known. This essay considers three major categories where Spillers's craft comes to bear: mentorship, praxis, and writing. All three of these categories are interconnected in that Spillers's mentorship supports her praxis which supports her writing which supports her mentorship and praxis. More to this point, her writing betrays her investment in craft. Most of the explorations of Spillers's work concentrate on Spillers as Theorist, and rightfully so. However, this essay is doing something very different. Here, I am trying to demonstrate how Spillers's writing reflects the holistic scholar and person that she is.

There is equilibrium in Spillers's intellectual and material worlds, as they reflect one another. Just as you experience the attention to detail and linguistic ornamentation in her writing, her environment simultaneously suggests effortless talent and deeply measured study. Spillers's writing mixes a clear voice and accessible style (very much like "write") with densely layered words and images whose meanings evolve as the audience evolves. In a word, Spillers writes literature, perhaps especially when critical.[1] With a combination of intuitive and studied expertise, she arranges her rooms with solid, confident furnishings made of lovely and sometimes ornate materials, whimsical, comforting heirlooms, and aesthetically exciting artwork of various media. Her world is colorful and rich. The scholarship that readers experience comes from a place of wholeness and consistency. She surrounds herself with furnishings, art, and architecture that reflect not only her taste but can be seen as a reflection of the complexity of her thought and her position as perpetual student of art and culture.

Without question, Spillers is one of the most treasured and respected theorists of our time. She has influenced more scholars than can be counted. Traces of her work can be found in nearly all contemporary Black Studies scholarship—and largely outside of Black Studies, as well.[2] She changed the way we understand literary criticism and theory. Her published writing evidences some of the most layered and complex thinking, with a rigor and style that many younger scholars strive to imitate. However, she also gives us a model for doing this work with joy, creativity, care, and an unmatched thoughtfulness. This essay is about Spillers's praxis—the way that she teaches us to read and think, how to get our ideas down on paper, and how to move through this academic world with a Black Feminist ethic, practicing what she preaches and graciously encouraging us to lean into ourselves and our vulnerabilities as a matter of scholarly methodology. This is an essay about Spillers and craft.

Mentor

Hortense J. Spillers became my mentor long before I ever met her. In the fall of 1992, I was enrolled in University of Pennsylvania's College of Arts and Sciences. For my father, I tried to be pre-med; for my heart, I filled my schedule with literature classes. I loved research because I found solace in the darkness of the library, surrounded by the smell of yellowing paper and decaying bookbinding materials. One afternoon, I found myself in the stacks of Van Pelt Library, doing cursory research for a Black literature class that I have since forgotten. Journals were not yet electronic, and I sat down noisily on a round stepstool in the narrow space between shelves of books with the bound *Diacritics* on my lap. The red of the binding was somewhat worn for a text that was only five years old. The heaviness of the large volume took some time to adjust and balance on my perch.

In my typical fashion, I started to skim the first few paragraphs of the now extremely famous "Mama's Baby, Papa's Maybe," the title of which I recognized from cheeky conversations by older Black women in my family who told stories of our wayward menfolk, shaking their heads and laughing at all the "foolishness" that brought children precariously into the world. I felt welcomed by the title because of this familiarity and its promise to speak in a language I could understand. My eyes insouciantly scanned over the first few paragraphs until I realized I was not retaining anything I was "reading." I did not expect the density of language and images I would encounter through this reading experience. I returned to the beginning.[3]

"Listen, I am a marked woman..."[4]

I paused, realizing that skimming was not the way into this text—I could not glean meaning by quickly and casually passing my eyes over the words. This reading required my attention and forced me to slow down. This text demanded that I read outright. This reading demanded that I concentrate and surrender to the text: to "listen" to it, to hear and see the lessons it was trying to teach. Moreover, somehow, organically, and without even realizing what was happening, I wanted to give it all it required. So, I adjusted myself on the stool, wheels awkwardly squeaking below me, and I started to read.

And I read. And the space grew quiet and still.

And I read. And the narrow beams of light that barely cast a shadow on my refuge completely disappeared as the evening fell.

And I read. I do not know how long I sat there, but I remember a tingling sensation in one of my feet. I remember feeling my booty getting heavier and heavier on the textured top of the metal stepstool, but I do not remember adjusting myself.

When I was done, I looked up, and the darkness seemed illuminated. Colors were brighter than when I began. Sounds returned and I could hear the other students speaking in hushed tones and harsh whispers. I didn't understand everything I'd just heard and seen in the article, but I knew that I was changed. I knew that the world had changed. Who I understood myself to be was forever different. My Black Feminine experience had a historical context that I had never considered before. I'd heard about the veil; famous men's intellectual production largely populated my Black Studies education. However, I had never *felt* the veil lift before this moment. I had new eyes, parts of me reborn.

This is how I first met Dr. Hortense Jeanette Spillers—with this now celebrated gift that she has given us all. "Mama's Baby, Papa's Maybe" is currently so well-known, that it seems no Black Studies student will graduate without having read it multiple times. However, at the time, I felt it was only mine. Awestruck, I could have never imagined that the writer of this field-bending, personally transformative work would one day be a voice on the phone turned adviser turned friend turned godmother. However, at that moment in library, I understood Spillers was a mother of ideas that had permanently reshaped my sense of self and the world.

Years later, working with Spillers was a dream come manifest. I pursued Vanderbilt's program with a significant quantity of fervor because of the opportunity to work with her, the writer of that article that held me fast in Van Pelt Library in 1992. In addition to Spillers, I would also work with extraordinary Colin Dayan and remarkable Ifeoma Nwankwo, Caribbeanists who would challenge (well, everything, but particularly) my American-centered-ness. At the time, I did not know that the indomitable Lynn Enterline would join Spillers, Dayan, and Nwankwo to collaborate on my dissertation project and help me see what I had never seen. These incredible mentors patiently taught me how to navigate my research questions and helped to build my literary criticism toolbox. They all encouraged the intellectual curiosity and experimentation that moved me toward Black Classicism, although none of them identified specifically with that area (together, they were a dream team for my project). However, Spillers's mentorship was singular as she tapped into her affinity for languages and expertise on classical literature to guide me through the process.

In preparation for entrance into Vanderbilt's English graduate program, I requested Spillers as my first-year advisor. We met weekly in her sun-filled, high-ceilinged office with rich rosewood furniture. Every time I entered her office as a graduate student, I felt like I was sitting at the feet of my teacher—very much like I had when I first began studying yoga and Vedic philosophy with Dr. Vijayendra Pratap in Philly. In yoga class, we sat on our mats in front of Doctor (our nickname for Dr. Pratap), with him slightly elevated on a platform merely inches above the floor. The difference seemed small, but in those few inches lay a lifetime of knowledge, study, and experience from which we were fortunate to learn. Another set of lifetimes was mapped across the expanse of Spillers's desk, some of which I witnessed her sharing with myriad students who walked into that space. Not surprisingly, her lessons were multi-dimensional: sometimes as simple as "write," other times as dense as her thinking, but always deeply challenging and with the potential to transform. Always from the perspective and motivations of a Black Feminist.

Somewhat akin to the Black Feminist ethic also taught by bell hooks in *Teaching to Transgress*, Spillers is never shy about bringing her biography and family history into a conversation if it is useful. I have witnessed her break into a personal story in a Q&A (while asking a question and while answering) and during her office hours.[5] I would not say she always applies a personal anecdote; however, Spillers knows exactly when a personal reflection can impart the perfect lesson. For instance, when I asked her if she ever doubted herself when she wrote, she paused and considered the question, much like when she told me to "write." Her response may have surprised someone who did not know that an anecdote could contain all the answers.

"I grew up in segregated Memphis," she began slowly, thoughtfully.

She read the question on my face and continued with a smile in her voice.

"The smartest person that I knew was Black. The dumbest person that I knew was Black. The most beautiful person I knew was Black. The ugliest person I knew was Black. So, when they told me that I could write, I believed them."

Her voice, written or spoken, has a ring of its own. Years later, when I recited back this experience to her, I asked her if it sounded like her. She laughed and conceded that the response did, in fact, sound like something she would say. She knows her own voice and "story better than anyone—its ingoings and outcomings. Like the commas and semicolons of a convoluted, twisted sentence, they [are] intricately known to [her]."[6] Her writing confidence comes from her personal story and the ways that she was insulated from the racist machinations that arrest self-knowing and -belief for so many of us. Spillers's Black-centered upbringing fostered self-trust that would have otherwise been disabled by racist-inflected comparison.

Segregation provided Spillers a dimensional Black environment with the gamut of human example. Most of the history of segregation is taught through the lens of struggle: the histories of lynching, forced migration, and disenfranchisement. Of course, there was another side to that story—undoubtedly several sides. I'd only heard elders talk in hushed tones about what was lost through integration: Black economic independence and agency, safe spaces, and the Black social heyday during the early twentieth century. Spillers's experience highlighted what may have been lost on a more personal and psychological level. It feels worrisome, in our post-Civil Rights world, to toy with nostalgia for segregation. And yet, the origins of Spillers's writing confidence suggest that when Blackness is central, there is a broader set of possibilities for Black people.

I understood in Spillers's "segregated Memphis" story that much of my intellectual insecurity developed because I was compared to white people. Her story made me think of my upbringing in 1970s and 80s Harrisburg, a small, primarily Black and Brown capital town in Pennsylvania. There were only a few white students in my public schools, and most were in the high-achieving classes (as they were called at the time) and labeled "gifted and talented" and therefore deserving of unique educational privileges. I thought of the one white girl who always scored 100% on every test and that there were absolutely no white children in the special education hall of my elementary school. I remember the wildness of my experimental public middle school, which expected us to stay focused when there were only three walls in every classroom.

The open design of then Harrisburg Middle School separated the 2500-person student body into several "houses" with large common spaces visible to most classrooms. This configuration left us with countless distractions, including those from other noisy and unruly classrooms, of which there were many, as well as students and teachers walking in the common spaces. The common space was also often the stage upon which the majority-white teaching staff administered a variety of public humiliations, paddling and berating amongst others, to disruptive students who were mostly Black American, Puerto Rican, or Cuban. More often than not, it was a Black boy who was on deck to receive a flogging for some foolishness. These public punishments served as a warning to those who would rebel against this impossible system in which we were expected to learn. Famously in my family, my sister disenrolled herself and refused to return after only a short time in this middle school. We kids nicknamed it "the zoo" without understanding the full implications of this moniker.

What would it have been like to be taught by Black teachers from my community rather than mostly white teachers who lived outside of Harrisburg proper? It is rumored that the town was a testing ground for educational services as well as consumer products throughout my childhood. Kids discussed how we were the first to have Utz crab chips or other products that companies tested before national release. I was administered my first IQ test at age four, so the school could determine what grade I should enter because of my late birthday and if I should enter the "gifted and talented" program being developed at the time. I and a small handful of older students, again a disproportionate number of white students, were intermittently removed from our regular classrooms so that we could work on puzzles, art, and research projects unavailable to the wider school population. I remember the teasing I received because my classmates assumed I was being pulled from class because of some defect or disciplinary reason. Only bad kids must leave class. This meant social ostracization from many groups of children in my class. How might things be different if we were set up for success through the school's environmental configuration rather than being a testing ground for educational theorists who had likely never stepped foot in the classroom? What if my mostly Black school district had a racially representative set of teachers and staff? What if we were all treated as if we were "gifted and talented"? What if, during my childhood, "the smartest person" in my class was Black?

So, Spillers's answer to my question recontextualized my imposter syndrome and deepened my dedication to a Black-centered classroom.[7] While teaching at the PWIs where I studied and have been employed, I have never had an all-Black classroom; I try to make my syllabi as Black as possible. In Spillers-esque fashion, and as I will discuss later, it is not the amount of work on the syllabus that is key but rather how one enters the work, the time that one spends deepening analysis and therefore, much like the Invisible Man title character, embarking on an intellectual and political katabasis. In this world of anti-wokeness, anti-CRT, anti-Black Studies, and re-popularized overt anti-Blackness, it can be dangerous to carve out these much-needed spaces, especially in a PWI.[8]

This danger reminds us of the urgency of the Black Feminist liberation project and that we must take up as much space as possible, regardless of the outcome. More than that, Spillers reminds us that while writing is valued more in the profession, we [should] have an investment in teaching:

> Inasmuch as we have been socialized to think of teaching as a chore and of research and writing as the glory of the language games we play, it is little wonder that the vocation of the teacher in us is less well thought of than the publishing scholar in us and, most likely, less well rewarded. But it seems to me that we are missing half the scholarly commitment if we are not looking out for younger people and their intellectual aspirations.[9]

Our writing is important, certainly and as Spillers has demonstrated throughout her career. Her admission that we have been socialized to value our written scholarship over our scholarship-in-action is more of Spillers's Black Feminist ethic as an intervention. One of the tricks of this profession is that quite often, the priorities of the institution or field can eclipse our personal motivations.[10] Many of us entered this profession because of a passion for something: reading, a desire to help people, love of discovery, a romantic yearning for truth. Teaching is not just how to keep the lights on or one of the service components justifying our positions and paychecks.

Teaching is scholarship, at least "half of the scholarly commitment," and from Spillers I have learned that my writing is an extension of my classroom, rather than the reverse. Teaching is our scholarship in action. If we allow, our teaching practices can give rise to writing. Our classrooms and offices are the labs, the writing projects are the reports. Furthermore, while our current call to action will never force us to be as lonely as Spillers might have been—forging one's career while nearly always being the only Black Feminist in the room—we have returned to a time when the immediacy of the project is as legible as ever. We need this action, and we need to prioritize it as we do written scholarship.

Praxis

In her 2010 graduate class, "The Troika Plus One," we studied the famous trio of writers Richard Wright, Ralph Ellison, and James Baldwin. The "plus one" was David Bradley and his 1990 *The Chayensville Incident*, a novel Spillers placed in the legacy of the more famous and studied "troika" whose deeply entangled relationships have fascinated Blackademia for decades. Upon Spillers's introduction to the class, we all knew this would be something different.

We sat in the sterile Benson Hall classroom, the towering windows partially covered by aging mini blinds that let slats of tree-filtered light gently enter the room. The long conference tables sat end to end, creating a large rectangle so that all the people in the room faced one another throughout the three hours of class. There was no place to hide in this large plainly decorated room. Students sat in bold relief against unadorned walls and the semi-orderly furnishings, like a living art gallery or stage with minimalist design. Spillers explained: instead of the typical version of class that focused on one principal text each week, the class was meant to concentrate only on four works.

Four novels? This seemed impossible, indulgent, and unlike any other class I would take in my three years of graduate-level coursework. Of course, like with any graduate class, we were expected to do outside research and fill in the scholarly cracks, but Spillers intended for us to spend time with primary texts themselves. We were to explore the bounty of language and imagery that the novels gave to us, to excavate layers of meaning based on the words on the page, first and foremost. Before we could theorize the text, we had to understand the text. We had to understand that which we would abstract, or else from where would the theory come?[11]

To this end, on the first day of discussing *Invisible Man*, we spent the entire three-hour class on the first page of the prologue. I had previously known that an effective literary scholar could widely and deeply extend a close reading, but I'd never witnessed it in action at this level. Like I experienced with her writing, Spillers set the pace. The class began unhurriedly.

If you have taught, you know that the beginning of a class is often stilted and full of hesitation. Students presume that there are tricks in the tasks set by professors—because, quite frankly, often there *are* tricks. However, when Spillers asked us to turn to the first page of the prologue, for someone to read it out loud, and then for us to consider the specific text on that page, she was not setting any traps. Instead, she asked us to linger on the novel's language, these concepts of invisibility, haunting, and materiality that Ellison introduces in this opening page.

She invited our reactions, and the class stayed quiet. *She wanted us to read? And she wanted us to start at the very beginning?* We should not have been surprised that the writer of "A New American Grammar Book" wanted us to close read and do it with breadth, depth, and within grammatical and historiopolitical contexts. She pointed out that Ellison named Edgar Allen Poe in this introduction to his novel forty years before Toni Morrison proclaimed: "No early American writer is more important to the concept of American Africanism than Poe."[12] Spillers wanted us to thoughtfully consider what sideshows may have to do with Blackness and how hypervisibility, as experienced through the sideshow/circus/performance, relates to invisibility. She wanted us to contemplate and then offer our own understandings about how Blackness, Black bodies, and particularly Black male bodies could provide a "distorted" glimpse only into the "surroundings" in which Black people exist.[13] Perhaps even more importantly, she wanted us to understand what Ellison meant when his Invisible Man accused his white observers of seeing "themselves, or figments of their imaginations" rather than him as he sees himself.[14] She wanted us to read, *really* read.

She was asking us to lay down the typical grad-student classroom dueling jargon and spend time with the language and images crafted for us by Ellison. She was asking us to take the time and space to get to know a text—that which we rarely felt in the harried process that is graduate studies. She was asking us to raise questions as she might: "What is this thing called 'race'? . . . Our deadliest abstraction? Our most nonmaterial actuality? Not fact, but our deadliest fiction that gives the lie to doubt about ghosts? In a word, 'race' haunts the air where women and men in social organization are most reasonable."[15] However, she was not asking us to raise her questions.

Spillers is not interested in replicating herself or merely returning to thoughts she's already had. She encouraged us to raise our own questions, to tap into our unique contributions to discourse. She taught us that each time a text can be new and through it we can be renewed. She taught us that our scholarship is ours and only ours, that the point is to tap into what we uniquely offer. We were expected to navigate the extensive layers of that richly dense first page, the opening to one of the most well-known novels written by any Black person in the US. She wanted us—like in the writing she produced—to slow down and take our time. Lingering on the text lead to more developed analysis. By extension, we were to learn how to spend time with the language of *any* work of art. She wanted us to work together to build upon one another's ideas and be in real, evolving conversation. She was teaching us the value of slow work and thoughtful discourse in preparation and perhaps contrast to the graphomania encouraged by increasing demands for publication by the profession.[16]

As I now teach my undergrad and graduate classes, I understand that close reading, this fundamental literary analysis methodology, seems lost.

I, too, have experienced the worrisome silence when I ask students to express what they are reading in their own words, to apply their definitions along with or in contrast to those inferred by the author, the OED, and history. I struggle to get students to read texts closely—to engage with the words on the page at such a focused and minute level that they reveal not only the world but the genius of the text. Close reading is an art that we are losing at record speed. Spillers taught us that the only way to understand a text and how it might apply to our lives, politics, and environmental contexts is to spend time deeply considering the text itself. She taught us that the lessons given to us by the Black critic/author/thinker/ancestor are our intellectual and creative birthright if we decide to claim them.

Through this, Spillers expanded my understanding of a Black Feminist ethic with the importance of getting out of the way of a text and letting it instruct us. "What does the writer teach us, or illuminate in us, concerning situations for which we need a name . . . ? What does the writer take with her from experience to the transmuting work itself?"[17] Spillers places the writer before us as pedagogue who offers us a vocabulary to name and categorize our experiences. The writer comes literally and syntactically first: "the writer teach[es] us." We must privilege her experience, vocabulary, and constructions if we are to learn from them. The written word opens new worlds to us, often places we cannot access otherwise. We can access places that do not exist but reflect the world in which we live or the interiority of a character or writer we will never meet. Moreover, the relationship between scholar/student and text is a means of accessing new places in ourselves. To engage critically in the world of words, one must try to understand the material and be prepared to be *transformed* by it.

Spillers teaches us that while it is impossible to be impartial, we can step back from a text and see what *it has* to say before we engage with what *we want* to say. In this, we have the opportunity to be directed *by* the text and resist our instinctual desire to fit the text into the curves and corners of ourselves and our thinking. How do you make meaning from a text? First, you must read. Read, then write. You must be able to recognize where the text ends, and you begin: "The literary work describes, or carves out an arena of choices, and in doing so, the writer suspends definitive judgment. . . . The narrative which the writer offers for consideration operates according to the logic of literary form."[18] You must then use that recognition to bring yourself back into the text—or you can skip this last step if you are not interested in the practical application of or seeing your personal connection to the text. However and through her example, Spillers taught me that whether inside or outside the classroom, this last step is important to the Black Feminist project.

This literary analytical process of stepping back and reading a text on its own terms before applying it to your life inspires a connection to the text. This is how Spillers identifies "literary criticism, not the only, or even pre-eminent, instrument at our disposal, [that] gives us a clue to the text of our own experiences."[19] This is not an overly romantic view of this process. Of course, everyone enters into a text with biases and experiences that color their reading. However, deliberately stepping aside and privileging the text decenters the self, if only temporarily, and allows us to develop or apply an ethic to our reading practice. It is an honest way to do literary criticism in the classroom; it is how students can experience a common ground and gain greater understanding by working together.

Many of Spillers's generation privilege collaboration and connection as a Black Feminist practice.[20] In the classroom, this looks like students who bring what they have to bear into conversation. For literary classroom discussion, students discuss terms, images, etc. together to map the linguistic geography of a text. Each student brings their individual experience and expertise into the room, contributing their readings inflected by that individuality, thus providing a very dimensional understanding of the text. For instance, if I am familiar with Patrice Rankine's reading of *Invisible Man* as *The Odyssey*, I will see Ellison's title character's journey as one to consciousness and intellectual dimension previously unavailable to him, in much the same way as the heroic was transformed from brute action to intellectual strategy in Homer.[21] If I understand the connection between horror, slavery, and the sideshow, I will understand why Poe is in the *Invisible Man* prologue. However, the text must be central and foundational to any of this learning. In other words, the text must also be considered on its terms—as comfortable or uncomfortable as that might make a student feel. You must ethically, carefully, sincerely, fervently read. From there, all else will follow.

Write

One can look at Spillers's writing trajectory to understand the importance of reading and the art of literary criticism. Although we consider Spillers a theorist first and foremost, her work is primarily and fundamentally that of a literary critic. All of her work engages text, directly; and much of her writing concentrates on very specific authors: Harriet Jacobs, William Faulkner, Ralph Ellison, Gwendolyn Brooks, Martin Luther King, Toni Morrison, and more. The 1980s were a prolific time for Spillers, with her publishing no fewer than fourteen different pieces. It is during this time that there is a clear shift in Spillers's writing.

We receive "Interstices" while Spillers is deeply diving into Black women's literature, specifically. In truth, Spillers is always thinking about women's artistic production; however, it is in the 80s that she establishes herself as a scholar of Black women's lit. This shift truly begins in 1979 with "The Politics of Intimacy," where she thinks about existing, antiquated frameworks of intimacy that cannot represent "the intimate life of Afro-American women." Also in 1979, she published "Gwendolyn the Terrible," the first of two articles that concentrate on the work of Gwendolyn Brooks. I suggest that notions of intimacy, interiority, and poetics (particularly those of Gwendolyn Brooks, her favorite poet) drive Spillers's scholarship at this time and inspire her to dedicate a decade to women's work.[22] But, it is also during this time that we receive the first overtly theory-centered piece: none other than "Interstices" (1984). In other words, her literary methodologies, and particularly her immersion in Black women's letters, lead her to the theory for which she is most recognized. I'm claiming that without the extended study of Brooks, for instance, we may not get "Interstices" or "Mama's Baby" or "'All the Things You Could Be.'" More than that, it is this intimate knowledge and relationship to Black women's literature that yields Spillers's most powerful writing lesson: leaning into one's vulnerability.

The last time Spillers and I talked about writing, this piece you are reading was on my mind. This time, we sat in that beautifully brocaded room in the evening, the lamps had just been turned on, and the last of the daylight weakly eking in. The room seemed to wrap itself around and comfort us. I did not tell her I was enthusiastic *and* anxious about this writing assignment. What is it to write about someone that I respect, care about, and love so much? Instead, I opened a conversation by sharing my memory of her lesson on self-doubt and segregation that you just read. I never admitted to her that I was terrified that I couldn't write an essay worthy of my profound experience of her as my teacher. Still, she sensed what I needed.

"I think writing is always an anxiety-producing process," she generously offered.

Nearly too stunned to reply, I sat quietly in the plush wingback chair, hoping she would expand. This answer complicated what I'd learned before.

"Each time one begins a new project, she thinks about how others might and likely will respond. It always provokes a lot of worry. But you do it anyway, even though it has those implications. You keep going."

At first, I thought that this response contradicted the story of her upbringing that she'd shared before. I'd never imagined that Hortense Jeannette Spillers felt anxious about putting her ideas in the world. However, one can be confident, know what they are saying, and still fear bringing that thinking to light, especially when the entire profession thrives on and models competition and assessment. But, again, here she was modeling vulnerability so that her forever student/friend/goddaughter might have a chance of seeing her way around paralysis. Here she was demonstrating the dimensionality of her mentorship. I'd not considered that one must accept anxiety as a part of the process. Instead, I'd been desperately trying to find my way out of that anxiety.

"So, this is always how it's going to feel?" I asked, unsure if it was relief or concern I was feeling.

She turned to me from the middle of her luxurious couch. With a sympathetic smile halfway upon her lips, she gave me a small shrug and nodded.

"Yeah, I think so," she said with sympathy. "But you write, anyway."

Coda: Career Dreams

The purpose of this collection of essays about or influenced by Dr. Hortense Jeannette Spillers is to honor the scholar, teacher, and mentor she is and has been. Through this essay, I hope that I highlight how Spillers's tutelage, direction, and writing parallel the public-facing scholarship she produces. I also hope to demonstrate how she has shaped me as a thinker while never asking me to be like her (who ever could be?) and has helped me understand better the world in which I live, particularly the academic one. However, there is one last lesson that I want to share because it is about what might motivate Spillers's methodologies and projects. The short answer: she does it for love. She does it because of the Black people and particularly the Black women who raised and nurtured her. She does it for those who have touched her throughout her career. But perhaps most importantly, it is for a perhaps surprising and veritably lost reason: because of her love for a woman whom she may never meet (although, she has met many of us).

Many years ago, in 2016 and after attending the *Callaloo* meeting and conference, Spillers and I would sit in Brown's Hotel in London and she would give me an answer to a question that I will never forget. As with all Spillers's favorite environments, the beautifully appointed Brown's Hotel exudes luxury. Sitting off Piccadilly, on the very quiet street of Aberdeen, the hotel offers respite from the center of popular shopping in London. It is her London refuge, and entering the building reminds me of the warmth and comfort of her living room in the evening.

We shared a delicious meal which included a rich flourless chocolate cake covered by a shiny ganache that reminded Spillers of her favorite dessert made by her mother. She was shocked to see the cake and it immediately took her back to her childhood, the drama of the cake's shine, the sensory explosion when it hit her tongue. "A patent leather chocolate cake" she called it. Her eyes looked far away as she returned to Memphis, telling me stories of her youth and of her first model of womanhood. Her love for Mother was inextricable from her experience of the cake, the energy from which transformed my own bites of chocolate cake into a sublime experience.

Returning upstairs after dinner, we sat in her expansive quarters, at least five times the size of the graduate-student-budget garden room I'd ignorantly booked in the former red-light district. She sat on the king-sized, crisp sateen white duvet finished with gold satin rope, organizing her bags and preparing for her flight the next morning. We talked as we always did, with a cacophony of news reporter's voices in the background but focusing on one another. However, the stories of home and food and adoration for Mother opened the door to a question I thought I'd never ask.

"What do you ultimately want from your career?"

As usual, she paused and took the space and time to find her answer.

"Sometime in the future, perhaps, a woman will pick up something that I have written," she said, miming a person reading a book before continuing.

"She will read my work and it will help her."

I stayed silent, struck by the way this answer moved my spirit. I immediately thought, *It* has *helped her*.

I'm certain that I'm not the only one who can claim from her personal perspective that Spillers has achieved exactly what she wants from her career. Her career goal is parallel to her teaching motivation, how she is "looking out for younger people" including those she may never see or know. She reminds us why we are supposed to be doing this work: to help, to make this difficult existence somehow less difficult for those we touch. She has helped me. She continues to help me. Whether you have long read the work of Dr. Hortense Jeanette Spillers or have just made it to her, I truly hope that this essay helps you.[23]

Notes

1. I am suggesting, here, that Spillers's essays are literary not only because essays *are* literary production, but because of her dedication to and use of poetics in her writing. Her academic work is criticism, theory, and literature, simultaneously. Her critical work is joined by at least one unpublished novel, what Spillers has called her "juvenilia," currently held in her papers at Brown University, as well as the short fiction "A Lament" (1977) published in *The Black Scholar* and an award-winning short story featured in *Essence* (1974). There *may* also be one or two novels that have yet to make it to the archive. See also footnote 6.

2. During Spillers's retirement celebration, American Literature scholar Dana Nelson claimed that Spillers was the most cited contemporary Black scholar (of them all). According to Google Scholar, her most famous, "Mama's Baby, Papa's Maybe: An American Grammar Book," has been cited no fewer than 4,787 times.
3. Alternatively, in the words of Spillers, "We have now to do with beginnings." Hortense J. Spillers, "'All the Things You Could Be by Now, If Sigmund Freud's Wife Was Your Mother': Psychoanalysis and Race." *Boundary 2* 23, no. 3 (October 1, 1996): 75.
4. Hortense J. Spillers, "Mama's Baby, Papa's Maybe: An American Grammar Book," *Diacritics* 17, no. 2 (1987): 65.
5. See how she begins her 2020 speech delivered during the fiftieth-anniversary celebration of Brandeis University's Department of African and African American Studies. Hortense J. Spillers, "'A Moment of Protest Becomes a Curricular Object,'" *Souls* 22, no. 1 (January 2, 2020): 5–10. https://doi.org/10.1080/10999949.2020.1822725.
6. Hortense J. Spillers, "Isom," *Essence* 6, vol. 1, (May 1975): 42.
7. Spillers also gives us hope about personal power amid social limitations when she discusses Brooks's Maud Martha character: "The limitations that are imposed on her, however, in no way mitigate her own considerable abilities to shape and define the world as she encounters it." Spillers, "Order of Constancy," 231.
8. I use the term "woke" advisedly, and recognize that largely in the Black community, it has fallen out of fashion. The terminology of "wokeness" has been appropriated and denatured by right-wing extremist policy- and lawmakers to further white supremacist agendas that rely upon the suppression of Black anti-racist history, art, and criticism. I used "anti-wokeness" because of its current pervasiveness but also because within its linguistic implications is the admission that these anti-Black agents of oppression wish us all to stay "asleep" and therefore unable to continue the political, curricular, and psychological changes that come with anti-racist, anti-homophobic, anti-transphobic, anti-misogynistic, and anti-classist practices.
9. Hortense J. Spillers, "Reading the Future, Future Reading," *Women's Review of Books* 8, no. 5 (February 1991): 20. https://doi.org/10.2307/4020912.
10. When I had the fortunate experience of writing coaching with Michelle Boyd of Inkwell Writing Retreats, she had me reflect on this very thing. Through her guidance, I understood that tenure or recognition from the institution was not an effective motivation for me. My first assignment from Boyd was the following writing prompt: "What is my original motivation? What brought me to the work that I am doing, and why was I first interested in doing this research?" To this end, I also recommend Black Literature scholar Koritha Michell's 2021 *Time Magazine* article, "I'm a Black Woman Who's Met All the Standards for Promotion. I'm Not Waiting to Reward Myself."

11. I was first introduced to this concept by my mother, Kathleen Spigner (nèe Hughes), who studied art and was a painter of oils and acrylics before ever marrying and having children. While considering abstract art, and mostly of the pop art against which she was highly prejudiced, she would ask, "How can one make abstract art if they've never practiced realism? Of what, exactly, are they abstracting?"
12. Toni Morrison, *Playing in the Dark: Whiteness and the Literary Imagination* (New York: Random House, 1993), 32.
13. Ralph Ellison. *Invisible Man*. (New York: Knopf Doubleday, 1995), 3.
14. Ellison, *Invisible Man*, 3.
15. Spillers, "All the Things," 78.
16. The concept of graphomania was introduced to me by Justin Mann who applied this psychological term to identify the expectation of publication for, especially, newer scholars. In this, Mann taps into not only the *actual* demands of the profession, which are ever-increasing, but also the *mythology* of the mad genius academic: a manic, hermetic, usually male professor, toiling endlessly away in their writing space, pencils in their hair or behind ears, fueled by coffee and the voices in their head and producing masterpiece after masterpiece. Since earning my graduate degree in 2014, I have already witnessed increased expectations for "production" by graduate students and junior faculty. Once upon a time, no one expected a graduate student, so newly introduced to academic writing and thinking, to produce publishable works. What does it mean that students are being pressured to publish early thinking, in this way? Why require a book from *every* humanities junior scholar, flooding the market while overburdening university presses, when some of our most beloved teachers forged their careers on excellent articles? I heard at least one colleague, who shall remain nameless, say that they think of their first publications as "trash" and would rather never discuss them again. Why is volume the name of the game? Why do we insist that there are these singular, semi-codified paths through this profession, especially when we insist that humanities is the world of possibility?
17. Hortense J. Spillers, "'An Order of Constancy': Notes on Brooks and the Feminine," *Centennial Review* 29, no. 2 (1985): 223.
18. Hortense J. Spillers, "Formalism Comes to Harlem," In *Black, White, and in Color: Essays on American Literature and Culture* (Chicago: University of Chicago Press, 2003), 84.
19. Hortense J. Spillers, "The Politics of Intimacy," Roseann P. Bell, Bettye J. Parker, and Beverly Guy-Sheftall, eds. *Sturdy Black Bridges: Visions of Black Women in Literature* (Norwell, MA: Anchor Press/Doubleday, 1979).
20. Here I mean the work of Combahee River Collective (1977), Akasha (Gloria T.) Hull, Patricia Bell Scott and Barbara Smith (1982), Patricia Hill Collins (1990), Johnnetta B. Cole and Beverly Guy-Sheftall (2003), bell hooks (2003), Joy James (2013), and many other Black Feminist analyses of Black community

and connection as essential to liberation. In all of these works, some of which are co-edited collections of essays, collaboration is foundational to a Black Feminist praxis in part as a counter to patriarchal individualism and as a matter of collective activism and healing. In Audre Lorde's "The Master's Tools Will Not Dismantle the Master's House" (1984), she famously said: "without community, there is certainly no liberation, no future, only the most vulnerable and temporary armistice between me and my oppression." I would also like to include the work of Lynn Weber, Elizabeth Higginbotham, and Bonnie Thorton Dill to open the Center for Research on Women at the University of Memphis (see their 1997 essay).

21. Patrice D. Rankine, *Ulysses in Black: Ralph Ellison, Classicism, and African American Literature* (Madison: University of Wisconsin Press, 2008).
22. There is one exception: "When Formalism Comes to Harlem" (1982), where Spillers calls the field to consider formalism's impact on Black writers primarily from the Harlem Renaissance and their relationship to Toni Morrison who wrote in their legacy. "When Formalism" may also be considered Spillers first overt call to the field to vary and expand its foci through lenses rarely applied to Black literature, the stakes of which she raises throughout the rest of her career and particularly when she later asks scholars to engage with psychoanalytic theory in "'All the Things You Could Be'" (1996).
23. Considering the spirit of help, I must thank my very dear and absolutely brilliant colleague-friends Justin L. Mann, Petal K. Samuel, and Tracy Vaughn-Manley for their deep reading and thorough feedback. More than that, thank you Tracy for urging me to write *this* version of "my Spillers essay." Petal, thank you for the multiple reads. We are so fortunate to have found one another and to approach our working relationships and friendships with such compassion, empathy, and love.

ARCHIVAL FRAGMENT 4: Images of Hortense Spillers in her living room

10 The Black Living Room

SHONIQUA ROACH

While the Black home is frequently imagined as either a target of state violence or a space from which to flee, a broader Black queer feminist intellectual and cultural archive of Black dwelling spaces reveals the Black home as a paradigmatic site of resistance to state-sanctioned infringements on Black erotic life. This is to say, the Black home is a crucial site of both violence and resistance for Black women living within the heart of US empire. This essay maps a Black feminist intellectual and erotic history of one specific site within the Black home—the "Black living room"—engaging the erotic function of vernacular street art that adorns the living room walls of contemporary, working-class Black women. In the process, the essay contends that the "Black living room" constitutes a discursive and material space within which Black women use material culture and interior design to mount visual campaigns against anti-Black violence and to assert the value of Black erotic being and becoming. The Black home, though mired in anti-Black violence, remains rife with liberatory, insurgent, and erotic potential.

In her groundbreaking 1987 essay "Mama's Baby, Papa's Maybe," Black feminist literary artist and theorist Hortense Spillers elegantly examines the ways in which Black women's captivity and servitude in New World communities throws the "customary lexis" of gender and sexuality—e.g., reproduction, motherhood, pleasure, desire, domesticity, and so on—into "unrelieved crisis."[1] Spillers unpacks, for example, how "female gender for captive women's community is the tale writ between the lines and in the not-quite spaces of an American domesticity."[2] American domesticity, according to Spillers, is a "cultural fiction" that is grounded in the specificity of white heteropatriarchy.[3] By contrast, "the human cargo of a slave vessel—in the fundamental effacement and remission of African family and proper names—offers a *counter*-narrative to notions of the domestic."[4] Following Spillers, I am invested in theorizing the ways in which Black domesticity—specifically, the visual and material space of the Black living room—offers a *counter*-narrative to notions of American domesticity. Indeed, in what follows, I map out "the Black living room" as a paradigmatic site of Black feminine sovereignty under the press of contemporary US imperial power.

What might it mean to rethink Black domestic life not as a site of pathology but as a material, spatial, psychic, and erotic ground, rife with luscious possibility for and material evidence of Black care labor? What might it mean to rethink Black domestic space not as a paradigmatic site of state violence—the place where US police officers invaded the home of Breonna Taylor and killed her, for example—but as part of a genealogy and geography of anti-imperial insurgence? This essay engages a Black feminist intellectual and erotic history of the Black living room and uses a vernacular family photograph of a living room in globalizing Southern California as a portal through which to engage the art that adorns the walls of contemporary, working-class Black women. I do so to posit that the living room constitutes a space where Black women have used material culture and interior design within domestic geographies to undo the work of US empire. Practices of empire are not limited to certain state operations or "hermetically sealed" by the borders of the nation-state.[5] The social, political, and economic structures at the heart of US empire at home are inseparable from US empire's exercises abroad, and US empire's exercises abroad continue to rely on logics and practices of (white) domesticity and Black captivity. This essay thus works against empire's historical and ongoing mandates for the (hetero- or homonormative) domestic sphere to serve as a cornerstone for the ever-expanding nation-state, or for Black female sexuality, reproduction, and head-of-household-ing to always already be figured as a threat or boon (or both) to the neo-imperial body politic. Instead, I refigure and reimagine Black women's homes—specifically, a

Black living room in California—as visual and material meeting places where "our deepest yearnings for different kinds of freedom can take shape and find rest," that is, as brimming with erotic potential.[6]

California is indelibly marked by various US imperial histories, including the afterlives of transatlantic slavery and US imperial expansion in the West, the growth of military and carceral infrastructures, and ongoing imperial operations abroad. By empire, then, I mean multiple discursive and material operations of gendered and sexualized power that are racialized and classed yet not bound by (or to) state form. Throughout this essay, I invoke empire to capture anti-Black policies of sociopolitical repression / economic dispossession (such as Welfare retrenchment) and the anti-black discourses that facilitated and normalized these exploitative practices. Here, I read domestic spaces and phenomena as both resistant to and complicit in US empire. Domestic spaces and phenomena are thus inextricable from a broader, transnational history of empire. For example, increased spending on militarization during the Reagan era produced the heightened policing of immigrant communities of color at home, the domestic surveillance of Black-female-headed households by agencies like Child Protective Services (CPS), *as well as* the invasion of Grenada. I call our attention to the "domestic" reach of US empire to make visible alternative genealogies of Black women's domesticity that are rooted in, and framed by, imagery, politics, and practices of decoloniality.

Given what the American studies scholar Amy Kaplan calls "the imperial reach of domesticity," the relationship between empire and the realm of the domestic is particularly significant.[7] Across her flagship article, "Manifest Domesticity," and book, *The Anarchy of Empire*, Kaplan attunes us to the ways in which nineteenth-century separate-sphere ideology—the presumption of a division between the private and public, women's and men's spheres—facilitated American empire-building while obscuring the ways in which white women writers and activists mobilized narratives of domesticity to facilitate US territorial expansion.[8] As Spillers's oeuvre make clear, the formation of these nineteenth-century ideologies of domesticity relied on Black captivity, specifically, the sexual and reproductive exploitation of Black female captives. Indeed, as white women textually tended to hearth and home, their conceptions of the home were predicated on the violent exclusion of Black women from the discursive and material territory of womanhood and the domestic.[9] This is despite the fact that, as Spillers observes, the material "care of Anglo-American families . . . has largely been entrusted over time to black women."[10] Black female captivity was thus central to the production of, and interplay between, the white (female) home and the US frontier. Here, I take up Kaplan's invitation to examine the intimate entanglements between (notions) of home and the US frontier. Yet I depart from Kaplan by marking out a Black feminist, specifically a Spillersian, genealogy of domesticity under US empire, a genealogy in which Black women have insurgently dwelled and made Black dwelling insurgent.

This alternative genealogy can be traced back to the middle passage, wherein Black captives on slave vessels offered "counter-narratives to notions of the domestic."[11] This alternative genealogy can be traced back to transatlantic slavery, wherein enslaved Black women converted plantation slave quarters into radical sites of care, insurrection, and careful insurrection.[12] This genealogy extends to Black women's post-Reconstruction-era domestic novels, which aesthetically and textually intervened into a US imperial order that had constitutionally sanctioned, while socially prohibiting, Black civic participation.[13] This genealogy encompasses those early twentieth-century urban boardinghouses that wayward Black women transmuted into sensuous scenes of sexual experimentation in spite of a nation-state that had deemed Black women sexually dangerous.[14] This genealogy also holds a Black living room, my mother's Black living room, where we find the powerful visual reminder that Black erotic freedom begins in and with the intimate, interior conditions of our everyday lives under US empire. In the Black Living room, the erotic is not just a resource for self- and community-making; it is also an insurgent mode of power through which Black women might undo and unmake imperial worlds.

This essay dwells on two photographs of my mother in the living room of her Section 8 home in San Diego, California, where we—my mother, my three sisters, eventually, my mother's second husband, and I—lived for five years in the early 2000s.[15] The first photograph, which features my mother, Letisha, sitting on her living room couch, introduces one

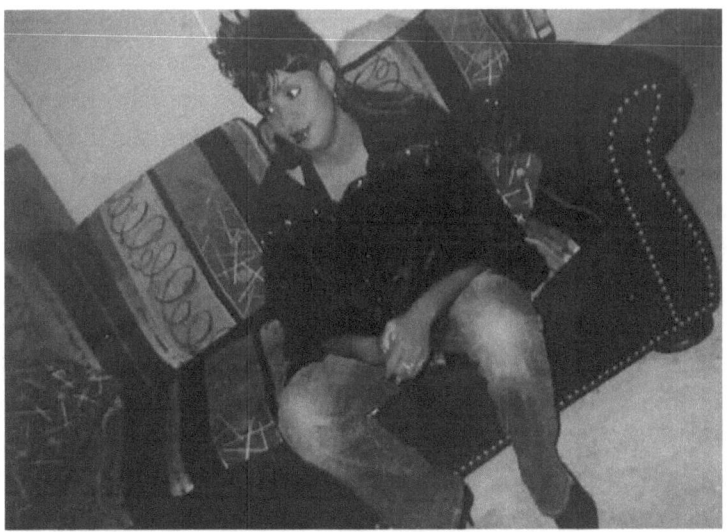

FIGURE 10.1. Letisha in her living room.

of the keenest Black feminists I have ever known: a caramel-colored, gray-eyed Black girl who rocked light-blue denim jeans on her shapely ass, Egyptian-styled French braids adorned with gold hair jewelry, and who frequently scoured the swap meet that flanked the Tijuana, Mexico, border for locally made Afrocentric art to display in the home she sustained for herself, for her four daughters, and for any other Black woman in need of support, boarding, and affirmation. I situate Letisha's life and domestic practices within a brief political and economic history of California as an instantiation of US empire. In so doing, I signal US Western expansionism as a critical component of the history of US empire. I elucidate how California's imperial motives have historically been enabled by domestic logics of race and gender that continue to inform the vulnerability of the nonwhite home to the incursions of state and capital. More specifically, I draw tight focus to the prism of California public policies that continue to structure the material availability of Black housing, as well as images of and ideas about (Black) domesticity.[16]

The second photo I examine features one such piece of Afrocentric art that my mother exhibited in our living room, a mass-produced canvas titled *The Motherland*. Dwelling on a photograph of *The Motherland* image, the first thing that visitors encountered upon entering Letisha's home, intimates the ways that Letisha labored domestically, which is to say both politically and aesthetically, to resist "the imperial reach of domesticity" by rejecting empire as an apparatus of (anti-Black) rule and disturbing state attempts to manage racialized gender difference.[17] As social workers, housing inspectors, police officers, and predatory businessmen frequently populated the doorstep of Letisha's hard-won home, this print represented one of the few ways Letisha was able to exercise a modicum of agency in the face of the anti-Black reality of what the sociologist of slavery Orlando Patterson has named "social death."[18] Letisha's story and aesthetic decisions in her living room, which I put into conversation with other Black feminist intellectual and cultural productions on Black living rooms by the Black feminist historian Stephanie Camp, the poets June Jordan and Elizabeth Alexander, and the Black queer feminist visual artist Mickalene Thomas, among others, reveal how the Black living room, in the Black feminist critical and creative imaginary, is one central "emancipatory project in which women can love themselves, love women, and transform the nation simultaneously."[19] As a conceptual frame, "The Black Living Room" illumines the ways in which images in and representations of Black women's living rooms reveal the domestic lives of Black women as sites of spatiopolitical struggle.[20] Indeed, the Black living room offers a space for Black life and living in excess of capture, generating Black beauty as a radical

FIGURE 10.2. Letisha's Black living room.

form of imperial surplus, of rejecting empire's capitalist and patriarchal visions of freedom in favor of Black erotic autonomy.[21]

Insurgent Dwelling: Some Notes on Method

I mobilize a range of methods, from intellectual, cultural, and family history to autoethnography. In so doing, I work within a long Black feminist writing tradition that works at the intersection of the personal, political, and theoretical, or what the Black lesbian feminist poet Audre Lorde would call "the erotic," to deeply and meaningfully engage the everyday, intimate lives of Black women, particularly working-class and workless poor Black women.[22] This tradition can be traced back to myriad Black feminist genealogies: Anna Julia Cooper's *A Voice from the South*; Barbara Smith's *Home Girls*; Lorde's *Sister Outsider*; Spillers's 1980s essays—"Mama's Baby, Papa's Maybe," "Interstices," and "An Order of Constancy"—Alexander's *Pedagogies of Crossing*.[23] Black feminist personal expository writing has been beautifully rendered in recent works, such as Terrion Williamson's *Scandalize My Name*, Christina Sharpe's *In the Wake*, and Saidiya Hartman's *Wayward Lives*. Working squarely within this Black feminist writing tradition, I draw on my mother's quotidian domestic labors and aesthetic choices to reveal not only the intricacies of imperial power dynamics but also the ways in which Black feminine "survival [is willed] through diverse acts of form, woven from the stuff of everyday life."[24]

Bringing together auto-ethnographic writing with an emphasis on the work of the vernacular family photograph, I draw on the insights of Black feminist visual culture studies theorists—Patricia Hill Collins, bell hooks, Leigh Raiford, Kara Keeling, Tina Campt, Nicole Fleetwood, Jasmine Cobb, Simone Browne, and Zakiyyah Iman Jackson, among others—who have brilliantly theorized anti-Blackness as a structuring logic for the dominant visual field, including the realms of mainstream news media, cinema and television, state-captured images, digital media, as well as ethnographic and studio photography. There is also a significant and evolving body of Black feminist literature that attends to the oppositional gazes, and artistic, performative, and affective strategies through which Black communities "trouble vision," as Fleetwood frames it, in the dominant visual field.[25] Raiford's and Campt's elegant examinations of the role of photography within spectacular and quotidian Black freedom struggles is particularly useful for my discussion of these two photographs.[26] I rely on these two vernacular images to render legible Letisha's domestic labor in and on the Black living room, while being careful to heed Campt's call not to equate vision with knowledge.[27]

Notwithstanding the complexities of representation, I dwell on these images, which reveal and conceal the Black living room as an interface for state power. Of course, I am not a reliable narrator, but I am also one of the most reliable narrators. In *Image Matters*, Campt heart-wrenchingly describes her "wounded relationship" to vernacular family photographs of her mother, who passed away earlier in Campt's life.[28] Her words moved me deeply, and powerfully described my own wounded relationship to photos of my own mother's vivid and powerful presence, as the photos simultaneously "image the presence of [her] loss [and the] loss of her presence."[29] The fact that these are my own mother's photographs does not negate the necessity of their inclusion into the photographic archives of the Black diaspora. Despite the imperial conditions under which these two photographs were taken—conditions that were, as I explicate, predicated on the regulation of Black women's erotic freedom—my mother was able to curate a Black living room rife with erotic potential.

While Black feminists often engage and define the erotic via public, spectacular, mediated performances of Black sexuality, I insist on a 1970s and 1980s Black (lesbian) feminist conception of the erotic that engages and defines the erotic (and its polymorphous manifestations and possibilities) in the private, quiet, interior lives of Black women.[30] My conception of the "erotic" here and in my broader intellectual project is thus indebted to Black feminists Lorde, Spillers and Alexander. In her 1978 speech-cum-essay, "Uses of the Erotic: The Erotic as Power," Lorde conceptualizes the erotic as a mode of counterintuitive power, feeling, and labor that women might wield to reshape and reconstruct the terms and conditions of life and living in an anti-Black, antiqueer, antiwoman, world. For Lorde, the erotic is a personal and communal project principally concerned with freeing up (Black) women's "various life endeavors" from heteropatriarchal state power and racial capitalism.³¹ In conversation with Lorde, Spillers's erotic project is invested in troubling the racialized and classed terrain of feminist theory to render the lived experiences of Black female social subjects as a fertile site for feminist claims-making about sexual pleasure and danger.³² In Spillers's hands, the (ungendered) Black female social subject becomes the site from which to consider anew the complexities of sexuality and erotic freedom without reifying essentialist assumptions about womanhood, femaleness, and gender. Alexander's erotic project is similarly concerned with discursive and material constraints on Black women's "various life endeavors," and works to unearth and undo the state-sanctioned sexual exploitation of Black women under neo-imperial tourism.³³ Much like Lorde and Spillers, Alexander reclaims the erotic as a mode of power, feeling, and labor that might undo state formations, and the imperial world, entirely.

A politics of the erotic must grapple simultaneously with Black intimate life; histories of colonialism, slavery, and racial formation; globalization; and sexual politics. What are, and what might be, the conditions of possibility for erotic freedom in the everyday lives of Black women, (socially) dead and dying, alive and living, claiming and curating home by the wayside of state power? By homing in on working-class Black women's domestic practices, I join Black feminist theorist Erica Edwards in studying the "full range of positions Black women occupied in the culture that justified and spread US imperialism throughout the late twentieth and early twenty-first centuries."³⁴ In the process, I argue that many Black women mobilize domestic space to chart out anarchic possibilities within US empire and fashion the Black home as a crucial locus of erotic freedom within a broader genealogy and geography of resistance to state-sanctioned infringements on Black erotic life.

The Black California Outdoors

In Figure 10.1, Letisha sits on a multicolored couch she had recently procured. She is settling into a new apartment in Barrio Logan, one of the racially segregated areas of San Diego, that Black, Mexican, and Filipino immigrants had been lured and relegated to under various articulations of US empire.³⁵ She dons early 2000s hip-hop couture, clad in a velvet and faux fur Baby Phat cape coat, matching gray-wash Baby Phat bell-bottom jeans, and black pointed toe booties from Aldo. Her hair is intentionally ghetto fabulous, the stylistic outcome of a Saturday trip to Hair Ballers, one of the few Black hair salons in San Diego where Black women gathered across socioeconomic, religious, spiritual, and sexuality differences to see a stylist who actually specialized in Black hair care, to exchange gossip and beauty tips, and to share political strategies for navigating the so-called military city's resources for low-income, Black residents.[36] Letisha's makeup is impeccable, her carefully arched eyebrows intimating the Black and Brown girlhood community formations she grew up in, and where she learned how to pencil chola eyebrows. Her painted-black lips are pursed as the look in her eyes appears all-knowing. She looks beyond the camera.

I start with the Black California *outdoors*—the political, economic, and intimate history that structures Letisha's living room and invites us to dwell here first—without letting such a structure overdetermine what then becomes possible *indoors*, in Letisha's living room. I dwell on this photograph to introduce you to Letisha and to locate her place within a brief history of California's imperial motives. Here, I want to emphasize the word *place* because I mean it in at least three senses of the term: geographic, archival, and epistemological. California, as a material, political, and social landscape, presumes and fundamentally requires that subaltern populations, such as Black women, have no relationship to the production of space. Indeed, from its historical gold rush to its warm, sunny beaches; from the indelible icon of the Hollywood sign emblazoned across public theater and domestic television screens to the pervasive iconography of its open highways, California has historically epitomized the American dream of economic, political, and social opportunity. This representation depends on the invisibility and explicit erasure of its imperial history of indigenous genocide and dispossession, US chattel slavery, racial exclusion and containment, anti-Blackness and the post–World War II management of Black dissent through misogynoir.

A brief imperial history: the antebellum United States acquired California—and what is now the US Southwest—in the Mexican-American War of 1846–48, as part of its late nineteenth-century US empire-building project. US colonizers in what had previously been part of Mexico, invited white settlement to California (and to the US West more broadly). White settlement of California (and the US West) was facilitated, in part, by state inducements of cheap or free land. For example, the Homestead Act of 1862 enabled "Americans" to submit a claim for up to 160 acres of federal land after living on, improving, and paying a small registration fee for it.[37] White settlers obtained (through recruitment and coercion) Asian, Mexican, Filipino, and other nonwhite laborers who performed work in the agricultural, fish canning, gold mining, farm, railroad, and defense industries.[38] Racial hierarchies and polymorphous forms of discrimination, from employment to housing sectors, pervaded the daily lives of nonwhite laborers and migrants.

In the early twentieth century, when most of the country was captivated by the failures of Reconstruction and World War I, various US senators suggested that Japan, rather than Europe, posed the "most immediate threat" to US democracy and empire-building.[39] This presumptive threat spurred the building of a West Coast military fleet to "protect" the nation from the "threat" of Japan. Of course, such anti-Asian discourse had a precedent in US anti-immigration policies such as the Chinese Exclusion Act of 1882, and the specific targeting of Japan and Japanese American communities precipitated Japanese Internment in (and around) California in 1942.[40] Put simply, California was (and is) a complex imperial landscape made possible—indeed, funded—by indigenous dispossession, transatlantic slavery, anti-immigration, anti-Asian, and anti-Mexican formations.

During World War II, federal money poured into California, and the availability of "lucrative defense jobs made the 'Golden State' a prime destination for Black southern migrants."[41] The communities of color who were first pushed and pulled to California by the promise of high-paid wage labor in California's post–World War II wartime industries were subsequently targeted for incarceration and removal by the end of the twentieth century, despite California's crime peak in 1980, and in tandem with what the Black feminist abolitionist Ruth Wilson Gilmore calls the "most ambitious prison-building project in the history of the world."[42] This counterhistory of California tracks with Letisha's life and experiences there, and opens space through which to chart some of the forms of anti-Black violence and decolonial resistance that Letisha encountered and would come to marshal in her life and living room in San Diego, California, in the early 2000s.

Letisha's parents, Adell and John, were part of the mid-twentieth-century Black migration to the West, structured by the wartime industry that Roger W. Lotchin, Wilson Gilmore, Donna Jean Murch, and others map. Adell "quit the South" in 1958, leaving an extended sharecropping family in New Boston, Texas, after surviving several instances of state-sanctioned violence, a history that Darlene Clark Hine maps in her foundational essay "Rape and the Inner Lives of Black Women."[43] In San Diego, Adell joined the household of an uncle, who had settled in one of the oldest working-class, Mexican American waterfront communities, Barrio Logan.[44] By this time, much of Barrio Logan had already been ceded to the US Navy to secure the city's urban development.[45] This transaction between early twentieth-century San Diego politicians and the US state transformed Barrio Logan into a residential/industrial zone to which nonwhite immigrants were restricted and where the 32nd Street Naval Station, the second-largest naval base in the US, was housed.[46] When Adell's mother, Classie Rose, joined her family in San Diego in the early 1960s, she challenged local race-restrictive covenants prohibiting the sale of property to Black individuals and acquired a small house in Barrio Logan. It was one of the few neighborhoods in San Diego where Black dwelling was permissible and affordable.[47]

In the mid-1960s, Adell met John, a young, Black naval officer, at the 32nd Street Naval Station. John remained in San Diego at the conclusion of his military term in the late 1960s to coparent his and Adell's three daughters—LaTanya, Letisha, and Lelisha—whom Adell raised in Section 8 housing in Barrio Logan. Letisha was born in 1968—a year, a decade—of revolution and counterrevolution. Citizenship and voting rights were codified into US law; civil rights and Black freedom struggle activists were assassinated, incarcerated, and deported. Black and women of color welfare rights activists struggled for housing, reproductive, and economic justice; the Fair Housing Act was passed. Opposition to the Vietnam War amplified; COINTELPRO attempted to squash radical Black (feminist) internationalisms.[48] Urban rebellions and student movements surged; the first Black studies department formed at

San Francisco State. The prison industrial complex expanded; Barrio Logan prepared for the spatial struggle that would yield Chicano Park.

The counterrevolution was well underway when Ronald Reagan began his two-term governorship of California. Reagan's governorship and subsequent presidency spanned the first few decades of Letisha's life. His infamous anti-Black-woman agenda, as exemplified by his anti-welfare reform measures as California governor, and rhetorical figuration of the welfare queen in the context of his US presidential campaign, would structure the conditions of possibility for Letisha's, and other women of color's, domestic lives.[49] From the start of his political career, Reagan banked on what Spillers calls the "national treasury of rhetorical wealth," that is, Black women, to further the postwar US imperial agenda of regulating both capital and decolonial resistance movements abroad and "at home."[50] Indeed, as defense industry jobs dwindled and disappeared, and California's multiracial population grew, Black women would become the discursive and material currency through which "the welfare-warfare state began the transformation . . . to the workfare-state, whose domestic militarism is concretely recapitulated in the landscapes of depopulated urban communities and rural prison towns."[51] Indeed, Reagan's gubernatorial campaign platform hinged on sending the proverbial "welfare bums back to work," and as the feminist historians Premilla Nadasen and Felicia Kornbluh note, Reagan, and other state actors, had already coded Black women as the proverbial "welfare bums" in question. His inaugural speech as California governor cited welfare dependence and fraud as one of the "major problems" that he would tackle as governor.[52] Reagan delivered on this promise via the passage of the California Welfare Reform Act of 1971.[53] This act, which Reagan hailed as the "the most comprehensive reform of welfare ever attempted, not only here in California but in the United States," spurred welfare retrenchment and sponsored (domestic) militarization.[54]

Militarization encompasses and finances wars abroad, the policing of domestic immigrant of color communities, such as Barrio Logan, and the surveillance of Black female-headed households, such as Adell's and Letisha's, by state agencies like CPS.[55] Nadasen and Kornbluh unpack, for example, how, in the wake of such welfare retrenchment and domestic surveillance efforts, Black women's domestic spaces in California became subjected to constant scrutiny. In Kern County, California state officials created a widely adopted program called "operation weekend" that authorized social workers and investigators to invade the homes of welfare recipients, particularly Black female recipients, during non-business hours. This was part of a statewide effort to locate and expose welfare fraud.[56] As a recipient of state services, Letisha was routinely subjected to at least one monthly home inspection performed by a state agent familiar with, if not influenced by, the popular portrayal of Black women as lazy, lascivious, and "domestically dysfunctional."[57] Letisha, like many Black and immigrant of color communities in Southern California, would come to be intimately familiar with the anti-Black police state. According to Wilson Gilmore, "By the early 1990s, everyday experience had come to include familiarity with the routines of police, arrests, lawyers, plea bargains, and trials."[58] This familiarity extends to the low-income housing and military industrial complexes, given that Barrio Logan was partially owned by the US Navy, and, there, police officers endeavored to enforce the "color line" that separated Barrio Logan from other (white and affluent) areas of the city.[59]

From the sexualized labor exploitation of enslaved Black collectivities to aid the nation-building project to Reagan's targeting of Black women in California for surveillance, punishment, and removal, the US empire's relationship to Black women has been characterized by fungibility—which I have elsewhere defined as "the material and discursive elasticity of Black women."[60] Reagan's ideologies and policies would come to serve as the conceptual blueprints for legislative enactments such as the Personal Responsibility and Work Opportunity Reconciliation Act of 1996 that would facilitate the massive socioeconomic transformation of the United States into a superpower on the global imperial stage. Such policies would also intimately touch and shape the contours of Black women's intimate lives. It certainly structured the conditions within which Letisha's home life was built, in low-income housing with Adell, and the ways in which she would build her own home life in low-income housing as an adult.

By the late 1990s, Letisha had relocated back to San Diego from Philadelphia after the end of her first marriage to a naval officer from a lower middle-class Black family in Philadelphia. Now deemed a "young," "poor," Black single mother of four girls, she acquired low-income housing under the Section 8 program and curated a shockingly beautiful home space in the center of Barrio Logan, where she raised her four girls, attended community college, and worked a full-time job, in addition to her full-time job as a Black mother constantly staving off the state violence that underwrote her home. If, as Keeanga-Yamahtta Taylor suggests, "black housing appeared to embody and reflect the deficiencies it had long been accused of harboring," then Letisha was tasked with curating a home space that both reflected and responded to racialized gendered inequities in the public sphere, as well as to the racism that surrounded and penetrated her intimate, interior life.[61] Letisha frequently advised her daughters that it "does not matter where you live, but, rather, what you make of it," and she put this ethos to work each weekend when she drove thirteen miles south of El Barrio Logan to the Tijuana, Mexico, swap meet to acquire beautiful, inexpensive prints of Black women and children to hang on the living room walls, and Mary J. Blige and SWV albums to put on full blast while she cleaned on the weekends and prepared Sunday community dinners.

I offer this brief imperial history of Black California to contextualize the ways in which empire continues to shape and inform the structures within which Black women, particularly working-class and workless poor Black women, live without suggesting that empire overdetermines when, where, and how Black collectivities dwell and freedom dream.[62] It was in and through this imperial geography that Letisha forged a home and curated a living room that visualized and imagined alternatives to the fungibility of Black women under US empire. Interior design and material culture were essential for both ensuring housing security and for Letisha's work in the register of the erotic—for making seen, *felt*, and known the innate value and preciousness of Black life and Black future possibilities in a sociopolitical context in which Black people, particularly Black women, were routinely positioned as parasitic, valueless, and socially dead.

Next, I dwell on a second photo of Letisha, one of her and her second husband, Malcolm, in front of the primary print that adorned her living room wall. I analyze the print, situating, remembering, and speculating about its meaning in the process. That is, I engage in an erotic reading of the photo, one in tune with my own memory of my mother's feelings about the living room. In so doing, I argue for Black women's living rooms as literal and metaphysical interfaces through which Black women challenge state authorities whose imperial plans rest on Black women's dispossession. Black women's discursive and material negotiations of Black living rooms visually and epistemologically generate space through which, to quote Camp, "whole other worlds, free worlds [might be] imagined and, ultimately made."[63] Letisha's Section 8 home was both *public and private*, subject to the whims, violence, and curiosity of the white state agents and non-Black subjects consistently surveilling or violating her home.

My engagement with Letisha's living room spills over into a broader Black feminist critical and creative genealogy of Black living rooms. Through this genealogy, which begins with the slave cabin, I dwell on the ways in which Black women's homemaking in the midst of anti-Black confinement and violence provides the grounds from which to navigate social and corporeal death, and the constant threat of it. Black homemaking is not reducible to easy understandings of aesthetics as resistance, if a failed home inspection or police check gone awry could result in an eviction, a reduction in Welfare benefits, premature death,[64] or all of the above. Black homemaking, then, is labor—hard labor.

The Black Indoors: Letisha's Living Room

I no longer have access to the twenty-by-twenty-inch canvas print with which my mother decorated our Barrio Logan home. I do not have access to any of the images and accoutrements with which my mother adorned our living room walls. Due, at least in part, to shifts in housing policies—including the material disparities between housing costs and Section 8 vouchers; the structural disempowerment of Section 8 recipients who could be evicted at the whims of the program itself or by the homeowners who retained and acted on the "right" to file complaints against the collectivities who rented—my family would move to at least three more houses in San Diego, leaving behind furniture and acquiring new furniture and decorations in the process.[65]

I possess one Instamatic photograph of Letisha's living room in Barrio Logan (see fig. 10.2), and the photo reveals as much as it conceals:

my then-vibrant thirty-two-year-old mother at a particular phase in her life and second marriage to Malcolm, a debonair, young Black naval officer from Norfolk, Virginia; she and Malcolm in formal attire, on their way to a holiday party. She dons a slinky black halter dress and luminous costume jewelry. His face is clean-shaven, and he looks both tentative and rooted, with his arms partially wrapped around his new wife. A golden lamp stands behind them, its post and bulbs exceeding the frame of the photograph. Behind the lamp is a partially visible twenty-by-twenty-inch image of a young, brown-skinned, curly-haired, elegantly posed Black mother, standing on imagined burnt orange, green, and red African desert land, against a brilliant sunset, camels, and passersby. This exquisite brown-skinned woman wears a shoulder-baring, colorful, geometrically patterned chitenge wrap, which secures her chunky, sleeping, beautiful, brown baby against her nimble, muscular back. Her orange lapa, securely fastened around her ample hips, blends with the landscape, flowing down to the bottom of the print. The bottom of the print bears the emboldened and emblazoned phrase: *The Motherland*. Inscribed on the back of the photograph itself is the date the image was captured: December 14, 2000.

This canvas was one of many mass-produced pieces of "African" art, including prints and figurines, that Letisha purchased from the Tijuana, Mexico, swap meet. The print complemented the peach-colored leather couch that sat beneath it. The peach leather couches in Letisha's living room hugged the bodies of Black women and girls who gathered there to eat, play, fight, cry, argue, dance, and defend her household from US empire. In this way, the vernacular image above is important not only for what it depicts but also for the insurgent social practices of Black maternal and communal care it references—that is, Black women's critical labor to curate Black erotic life in the face of state violence.

Black American consumption of (representations of) Africa is not unproblematic. Kaplan notes, for example, how W. E. B. Du Bois's corpus patriarchally reimagines Africa as a maternal empire for Black American women.[66] Likewise, the Black feminist performance studies scholar Stephanie Leigh Batiste roots Black American consumption and performance of Africa within a longer genealogy of what she terms "representations of imperialism."[67] According to Batiste, "representations of imperialism" both mark Black American complicity in US imperialism and attest to the ways in which such representations indicate Black struggles for "freedom, dignity, and nationhood" in an anti-Black world.[68] The duality of such representations gestures to the afterlife of slavery as the backdrop against which Black women's domestic lives unfurled along the edges of California's military installation and defense plants.[69] In the context of postwar California, Letisha's Black living room functioned as a spatiopolitical project of "self-love" and as a "communal" endeavor to challenge the dispossession of Black women.

Letisha's living room thus exists in relationship to those of the Black art consumers that the sociologist Patricia A. Banks examines in her ethnography of upper-middle-class Black art collectors in Atlanta, Georgia, and New York City.[70] In *Represent*, Banks elucidates how Black communities forge and retain a sense of racial identity through the consumption and display of "African" art, which, for her, signifies a longing for a connection to a home from which Black ancestors were forcibly taken.[71] Though Letisha did not have the resources to purchase art by Romare Bearden, Ellis Wilson, or Brenda Joy Smith, her consumption of mass-produced images of Blackness did constitute an erotic freedom practice, one that enabled Letisha to design and inhabit a Black living room that, to paraphrase Lorde, asserted the "lifeforce of [Black] women" and reflected Letisha's "creative energy empowered."[72] Letisha's design choices worked on the inhabitants of the home both affectively (being able to sense—visually and otherwise—a relationship to Blackness that is celebratory, rather than stigmatizing) and epistemologically (signaling a system of meaning-making within which Blackness is centered, and not relegated to negative epistemological space—as in the negative inverse of that which is proper, acceptable, alive, worthy of protection, etc.).

In this way, Letisha's Black living room might be thought in terms of what the American studies scholar Sylvia Chan-Malik terms "insurgent domesticity."[73] In her discussion of images and representations of Black Muslim women's domesticity in the post–World War II period, Chan-Malik develops the concept of insurgent domesticity to reflect how domestic spaces and practices of US Muslim women signified alternative, and insurgent, forms of nation-building, as well as notions of transnational encounter and global citizenship. In the face of anti-Black-woman public policies, Letisha reclaimed an iconic colonial image of a Black woman with baby slung across her back—think here of the Black feminist historian Jennifer L. Morgan's "Some Could Suckle over Their Shoulder: Male Travelers, Female Bodies, and the Gendering of Racial Ideology, 1500–1770" transmuting the foundational logic of *partus sequitur ventrem* from a social death sentence into a social life lesson. The image on the canvas also affirmed her commitment to iterating the beauty and worthiness of her deepest-complexioned daughter, whom she lovingly insisted on calling her "chocolate star." Here, within a domestic space in Barrio Logan where Black girls and women were never meant to survive, Black mothers and their children were beautiful, elegant, and worthy.[74] Their bodies and (maternal) labors were acknowledged with reverence. And they had luscious and capacious Black erotic freedom dreams to share with and impart to their communities.

The print was the first thing one noticed when entering Letisha's home: this was true not only for those who showed up with invitations to her home, most of whom were Black women or shared a love for the Black women living there, but also for social workers, housing inspectors, police officers, and predatory businessmen who arrived with the purposes of regulating and surveilling Letisha. In this instance, Black erotic freedom was a viewing practice. The print cited and rejected the sociopolitical degradation of Black women and emphasized the value of Black being and becoming. It echoed Letisha's efforts to unsettle what the Black feminist Christina Sharpe calls "the overriding engine of US racism that cut through [her own family's] living room," and her desire to consistently "[work] at joy . . . and [make] livable moments, spaces and places in the midst of all that was unlivable there."[75] Letisha's Black living room disturbed the quotidian grammar of violence that shaped her domestic space, and invited household residents and visitors to imagine a Black future beyond slavery and its afterlife in the Americas.

Letisha's use of this print, and the work of and in her living room, can be placed within a broader genealogy of the Black living room. Such a genealogy begins after the Middle Passage, in one of the first grounded New World locations where Black women were forced to innovate new conceptions of home: the slave quarters. In *Closer to Freedom*, Camp invites historiographies of slavery to reconceptualize what resistance is and where it takes place. She notes that most historiographies of slavery inscribe resistance as a public, masculine endeavor. Think: the slave revolt; Frederick Douglass's physical and public confrontation with a white male captor; a triumphant, if terrifying, solo flight from the plantation. Each of these scenes paints a familiar picture of Black resistance in and to slavery. Understudied, however, as Camp and other historians such as Sarah Haley remind us, are the actions, registers of labor, and affective attachments that structured the private and intimate spaces—the slave cabins—where Black female captives developed and encouraged a collective political consciousness that stoked fresh imaginaries of Black freedom and polymorphous forms of resistance to slavery and anti-Black subjugation.

Within the slave cabins to which they were relegated, captives constructed living rooms out of spaces that lacked material divisions. Camp's archival work excavates an enslaved Black woman (uncannily) named California, who, in 1842, lived on a Waverly, Mississippi, plantation with her husband and some of their children.[76] California was consistently described by slaveholders in the official record as difficult to manage, in part because she thought and acted as if she were "free." As a talented laundress, California hired out her own labor and somewhere in her travels acquired abolitionist print material, which she "stuck up in her cabin."[77] Camp contends that the prints that California owned and displayed were an important part of her imaginary landscape wherein she could be free, and where she could encourage her children to freedom dream. This abolitionist material, as displayed, allowed California's children and others who visited to "imagine and plot a future beyond slavery." If we understand California's interior design efforts as a conscious attempt to invest her home with "antislavery political meaning," as Camp would have it, then we must relocate the Black home, and the living room therein, as a crucial locus of political meaning-making where Black women might claim and use space to articulate and provoke their erotic desires, or Black (freedom) dreams. California reminds us that the Black living room is necessarily a Black feminist site for historical and theoretical investigation.

Though we did not encounter California and the abolitionist prints stuck up in her cabin until 2004, there exist glimpses of the erotic possibility of Black living rooms in the Black feminist creative and critical archive. There is Lutie Johnson and the Harlem street that itself transformed into "an outdoor living room" during blazing hot summers that propelled Black people to gather outdoors.[78] There is Black feminist poet June Jordan's 1985 poetry collection, *Living Room*, in which Jordan protests the reproduction of US imperialism via the desensitized and intrusive stuff of television news: a gang-raped Black woman, a nuclear war, US imperial exploits in Nicaragua, the Atlanta murders, Soweto, the Lebanese struggle, environmental destruction, global poverty, and starvation.[79] There is the cadre of Black television sitcoms, organized around Black families whose life-worlds unfold and shape-shift around a singular green couch or paisley furniture set. It is the iconic image of *Waiting to Exhale*'s protagonists Savannah, Bernie, Robin, and Gloria, synchronously rolling their asses and two-stepping to TLC's "Creep" in Gloria's warm, sumptuous, plant-filled, candle-lit Arizona living room that holds, and spills over with, thirty-something-year-old Black women's met and unmet desires for love, romance, friendship, and validation. It is Mickalene Thomas's mixed-media visual corpus, wherein bedazzled Black flesh, limbs, breasts, and lips come together in tender erotic embrace.

Black Living Room, Black Freedom

In 2004, the Black feminist poet Elizabeth Alexander published *The Black Interior*, an essay collection united by the metaphoric notion and material space of the "black interior." Alexander defines the Black interior as a politically dire Black metaphysical space that exists "beyond the black public everyday toward power and wild imagination that black people ourselves know we possess but need to be reminded of."[80] Exploring such topics as her mother's interior design choices in their living room, Alexander conceptualizes the Black living room as an instantiation of the Black interior, an alternative Black imaginary of Black freedom and insurgent possibility. Alexander defines the material Black living room as a simultaneously private and public space. Typically, Alexander argues, the living room is not boundaried by a door, yet it possesses structural integrity. It is also often "consciously arranged and presented" for public viewing and engagement.[81] Alexander engages the definitional parameters of the living room—it is not a space with a specific function in mind (like the kitchen or the bedroom): the living room can be, like her mother's living room, a space for "an aesthetic made collective ... to announce that this is our home, sacred and beautiful."[82] The Black living room, then, is a site for making the self and the collective—for crafting and curating a space to be sacred and beautiful, even and especially in the face of anti-Black violence. The Black living room offers a glimpse into the ways in which Black women's domestic practices continuously incite the realignment of global politics.

The Black living room is neither neutral nor self-evident. It is a counternarrative and a collective erotic offering. A discursive and material site of struggle for Black erotic possibilities. For California, the Black living room functioned as a material space through which to hang prints that depicted and offered the possibility of interpreting and imagining Black futures beyond slavery. For Alexander, the Black living room is a politicized "presentation space" and an intentional site of Black self-making. And for Letisha, the living room was all of these things, and more: the living room allowed Letisha to curate an imaginary for herself, for her daughters, and for her community. The artwork that Letisha displayed in her living room said to visitors, wanted and unwanted, loving and unloving: this home is *sacred* and *beautiful*, and there are Black girls and women here. And here, even with the impending threat of social and corporeal death, which is to say, everyday threats of material violence, inspection, eviction, and housing insecurity, we can dwell. Here, *we can imagine ourselves to be free.*

Notes

Writing—like home-making, writing as a form of home-making—is a collective erotic endeavor. I thank Erica R. Edwards, Christina Sharpe, Tina Campt, Faith Smith, Aliyyah Abdur-Rahman, V Varun Chaudhry, Emily A. Owens, Kimberly Bain, Michelle McKinley, Terrion Williamson, Christen Smith, Petal Samuel, Christopher Lee, and Melani McAlister for their critical labor and feedback.

1. Hortense J. Spillers, "Mama's Baby, Papa's Maybe: An American Grammar Book," *Diacritics* 17, no. 2 (1987): 76.
2. Spillers, "Mama's Baby, Papa's Maybe," 77.
3. Spillers, "Mama's Baby, Papa's Maybe," 72.
4. Spillers, "Mama's Baby, Papa's Maybe," 72.

5. M. Jacqui Alexander, *Pedagogies of Crossing: Meditations on Feminism, Sexual Politics, Memory, and the Sacred* (Durham, NC: Duke University Press, 2006), 4.
6. Alexander, *Pedagogies of Crossing*, 65.
7. Amy Kaplan, "Manifest Domesticity," *American Literature* 70, no. 3 (1998): 600.
8. Kaplan, "Manifest Domesticity"; and Amy Kaplan, *The Anarchy of Empire in the Making of US Culture* (Cambridge, MA: Harvard University Press, 2005).
9. Angela Y. Davis, *Women, Race & Class* (New York: Knopf Doubleday, 1983).
10. Hortense J. Spillers, "Interstices: A Small Drama of Words," in *Pleasure and Danger: Exploring Female Sexuality*, ed. Carole Vance (Boston: Routledge & Kegan Paul Books, 1984), 91.
11. Spillers, "Mama's Baby, Papa's Maybe," 72.
12. Angela Y. Davis, "Reflections on the Black Woman's Role in the Community of Slaves," *Black Scholar* 3, no. 4 (1971): 2–15; Sarah Haley, Shoniqua Roach, Emily Owens, and Keeanga-Yamahtta Taylor, "Confinement, Interiority, Black Feminist Study," *Black Scholar* 51, no. 1 (2021): 3–19.
13. See Lora Romero, *Home Fronts: Domesticity and Its Critics in the Antebellum United States* (Durham, NC: Duke University Press, 1997); and Claudia Tate, *Domestic Allegories of Political Desire: The Black Heroine's Text at the Turn of the Century* (Oxford: Oxford University Press, 1996).
14. Saidiya Hartman, *Wayward Lives, Beautiful Experiments: Intimate Histories of Social Upheaval* (New York: W. W. Norton, 2019).
15. Section 8, otherwise known at the Housing Choice Vouchers program, is the US government's primary vehicle for assisting low-income families with "decent, safe, and affordable housing in the private market." It offers housing vouchers, administered locally by public housing agencies who receive federal funds from the US Department of Housing and Urban Development (HUD), to subsidize the cost of housing for individuals and families who meet the requirements of the programs. Critical housing studies scholars such as Keeanga-Yamahtta Taylor and Eva Rosen have illuminated the ways in which HUD-administered programs, such as FHA loans and Section 8, have been detrimental to low-income Black women, as these programs either financially exploit Black women or increase the surveillance and policing of Black dwelling spaces. See Taylor, *Race for Profit: How Banks and the Real Estate Industry Undermined Black Homeownership* (Chapel Hill: University of North Carolina Press, 2019); and Rosen, *The Voucher Promise: "Section 8" and the Fate of an American Neighborhood* (Princeton, NJ: Princeton University Press, 2020).
16. For a discussion of contemporary struggles for Black housing justice, see Moms4Housing, https://moms4housing.org. Moms4Housing is an activist collective of Black mothers based in Oakland and the broader Bay area. They endeavor to "reclaim housing for the Oakland community from the big banks and real estate speculators."
17. Kaplan, "Manifest Domesticity," 600.

18. By social death I mean the structural and quotidian fungibility and disposability of Black individuals and communities during and after transatlantic slavery. In Slavery and Social Death, Orlando Patterson offers a comparative history of slavery to make conceptual sense of the specificity of transatlantic slavery and its continued impact on notions of Black personhood and kinship formations. Patterson finds that enslaved Black collectivities lacked natality, honor, and publicly recognized repute, which allowed enslaved Blacks to "be used in ways not possible with even the most dominated of nonslave subordinates." Patterson, *Slavery and Social Death: A Comparative Study* (Cambridge, MA: Harvard University Press, 1982), 32.
19. Alexander, *Pedagogies of Crossing*, 65.
20. For a vibrant discussion of Black feminist geographies and Black women's place-making practices throughout the diaspora, see Katherine McKittrick, *Demonic Grounds: Black Women and the Cartographies of Struggle* (Minneapolis: University of Minnesota Press, 2006).
21. See Kevin Quashie, *Black Aliveness, or a Poetics of Being* (Durham, NC: Duke University Press, 2021).
22. See Audre Lorde, *Sister Outsider: Essays and Speeches* (Trumansburg, NY: Crossing Press, 1984).
23. Anna Julia Cooper, *A Voice from the South* (1892; repr., Oxford: Oxford University Press, 1990); Barbara Smith, *Home Girls: A Black Feminist Anthology* (New Brunswick, NJ: Rutgers University Press, 2000); Lorde, *Sister Outsider*; Alexander, *Pedagogies of Crossing*. For an engaging discussion of contemporary Black feminist writing aesthetics, see Jennifer C. Nash, "Writing Black Beauty," *Signs: Journal of Women in Culture and Society* 45, no. 1 (2019): 101–22.
24. Hortense J. Spillers, "'An Order of Constancy': Notes on Brooks and the Feminine," *Centennial Review* 29, no. 2 (1985): 234.
25. Nicole Fleetwood, *Troubling Vision: Performance, Visuality, and Blackness* (Chicago: University of Chicago Press, 2011).
26. See Leigh Raiford, *Imprisoned in a Luminous Glare: Photography and the African American Freedom Struggle* (Chapel Hill: University of North Carolina Press, 2011); Tina Campt, *Image Matters: Archive, Photography, and the African Diaspora in Europe* (Durham, NC: Duke University Press, 2012); and Campt, *Listening to Images* (Durham, NC: Duke University Press, 2017).
27. See Campt, *Listening to Images*, 6.
28. See Campt, *Image Matters*, 202–3.
29. Campt, *Image Matters*, 202.
30. See Shoniqua Roach, "Black Sex in the Quiet," *differences* 30, no. 1 (2019): 126–47.
31. For a robust discussion of heteropatriarchy and racial capitalism, see Lorde, *Sister Outsider: Essays and Speeches*.
32. Spillers, "Interstices."
33. Alexander, *Pedagogies of Crossing*, 22.

34. Erica Edwards, *The Other Side of Terror: Black Women and the Culture of US Empire* (New York: New York University Press, 2021), 2.
35. In *Living for the City*, the historian Donna Jean Murch argues that Black and nonwhite migrant communities were drawn to California by "lucrative defense jobs." Murch, *Living for the City: Migration, Education, and the Rise of the Black Panther Party in Oakland, California* (Chapel Hill: University of North Carolina, 2010), 15.
36. For a history of San Diego's formation as a "military city" that boasts one of the US's largest naval bases, see Roger W. Lotchin, *Fortress California, 1910–1961: From Warfare to Welfare* (Champaign: University of Illinois Press, 2002).
37. The US government granted more than 270 million acres of land while the law was in effect. For a discussion of the racial politics of the Homestead Act, see the Black cultural geographer Carolyn Finney's *Black Faces, White Spaces: Reimagining the Relationship of African Americans to the Great Outdoors* (Chapel Hill: University of North Carolina Press, 2014). Finney notes, for example, the Homestead Act's connection to the Indian Removal Act of 1830, chattel slavery, emancipation, and the state-sanctioned rescindment of Black land titles given under the Homestead Act in 1866.
38. For rich histories of racial formation in California, see C. L. R. James, *Fighting Racism in World War II* (New York: Monad, 1980); Ruth Wilson Gilmore, *Golden Gulag: Prisons, Surplus, Crisis, and Opposition in Globalizing California* (Berkeley: University of California Press, 2007); Rudy P. Guevarra Jr., *Becoming Mexipino: Multiethnic Identities and Communities in San Diego* (New Brunswick, NJ: Rutgers University Press, 2012); and Yến Lê Espiritu, *Home Bound: Filipino American Lives across Cultures, Communities, and Countries* (Berkeley: University of California Press, 2003).
39. Lotchin, *Fortress California*, 24.
40. After the attack on Pearl Harbor in 1942, 110,000 Japanese Americans were deemed a threat to national security, forcibly evacuated from their homes, and detained in concentration camps in California, Oregon, Washington, Arizona, and Hawai'i. See Michi Weglyn, *Years of Infamy: The Untold Story of America's Concentration Camps* (Seattle: University of Washington Press, 1996), 36. For more on Japanese Internment, see Commission on Wartime Relocation and Internment of Civilians, *Personal Justice Denied* (Seattle: University of Washington Press, 1997); and Gary Y. Okihiro, *Encyclopedia of Japanese American Internment* (Westport, CT: Greenwood, 2013), among others.
41. Murch, *Living for the City*, 15.
42. Gilmore, *Golden Gulag*, 14.
43. Adell Juanita Scott's obituary, California Cremation and Burial Chapel, January 3, 2007. See Darlene Clark Hine, "Rape and the Inner Lives of Black Women in the Middle West," *Signs* 14, no. 4 (1989): 912–20; Shoniqua Roach, "(Re)turning

to 'Rape and the Inner Lives of Black Women': A Black Feminist Forum on the Culture of Dissemblance," *Signs* 45, no. 3 (2020): 515–19.
44. See El Barrio Logan Community Plan, the City of San Diego, Dec. 2021, https://www.sandiego.gov/planning/community-plans/barrio-logan/planning-studies-reports.
45. Lotchin, *Fortress California*.
46. Lotchin argues that "by the time of the bombing of Pearl Harbor, California cities had created a well-entrenched pattern of pursuing military wealth in order to create urban greatness. San Diego had already acquired the foundation for its present status as one of the two largest American naval bases. Its assets included the Eleventh District naval headquarters, a naval training station, a marine base at nearby Camp Pendleton, the Naval Radio Station, North Island Naval Air Station, the destroyer fleet, and assorted repair facilities." *Fortress California*, 1.
47. Housing discrimination against people of color was commonplace in California, and race-restrictive covenants were explicitly enforced until the passage of the Rumford Fair Housing Act of 1963.
48. See Judy Tzu-Chun Wu, *Radicals on the Road: Internationalism, Orientalism, and Feminism during the Vietnam Era* (Ithaca, NY: Cornell University Press, 2013); and Sean Malloy, *Out of Oakland: Black Panther Party Internationalism during the Cold War* (Ithaca, NY: Cornell University Press, 2017).
49. For rich discussions of the history of US welfare, welfare reform, and women of color's welfare rights activism, see Premilla Nadasen, *Welfare Warriors: The Welfare Rights Movement in the United States* (Abingdon-on-Thames, UK: Routledge, 2004); and Felicia Ann Kornbluh, *The Battle for Welfare Rights: Politics and Poverty in Modern America* (Philadelphia: University of Pennsylvania Press, 2007).
50. Hortense Spillers, "Mama's Baby, Papa's Maybe," 65.
51. Gilmore, *Golden Gulag*, 86.
52. See "Ronald Reagan: Second Inaugural Address," delivered Jan. 4, 1971, The Governors' Gallery, California State Library, https://governors.library.ca.gov/addresses/33-Reagan02.html.
53. With this act, the California legislature cut welfare expenditures, attempted to put antifraud measures in place, instituted a one-year residency requirement for welfare recipients, and placed additional limitations on money that welfare recipients received from outside sources.
54. See "California Legislature Approves Welfare Reform Bill after Compromise with Reagan," *New York Times*, August 12, 1971, https://www.nytimes.com/1971/08/12/archives/california-legislature-approves-welfare-reform-bill-after.html.
55. See Dorothy Roberts, *Shattered Bonds: The Color of Child Welfare* (New York: Basic Civitas Books, 2002).

56. Kornbluh, *Battle for Welfare Rights*, 29. Operation weekend was declared unconstitutional in 1968.
57. See Taylor, *Race for Profit*, 168.
58. Wilson Gilmore, *Golden Gulag*, 6.
59. Guevarra, *Becoming Mexipino*, 61.
60. Shoniqua Roach, "Black Sex in the Quiet," *differences: A Journal of Feminist Cultural Studies* 30, no. 1 (2019): 134. My characterization of fungibility in "Black Sex in the Quiet" builds on the critical labor of Saidiya Hartman in *Scenes of Subjection: Terror, Slavery, and Self-Making in Nineteenth-Century America* (New York: Oxford University Press, 1997), and Erica R. Edwards, "Sex after the Black Normal," *differences: A Journal of Feminist Cultural Studies* 26, no. 1 (2015): 141–67.
61. Taylor, *Race for Profit*, 112.
62. I borrow the term *freedom dream* from the title of Robin D. G. Kelley, *Freedom Dreams: The Black Radical Imagination* (Boston: Beacon Press, 2003).
63. Stephanie Camp, *Closer to Freedom: Enslaved Women and Everyday Resistance in the Plantation South* (Chapel Hill: University of North Carolina Press, 2004), 116.
64. For riveting examinations of Black women's domestic spaces as sites of death and police terror, see Christen Smith, "Impossible Privacy: Black Women and Police Terror," *Black Scholar* 51, no. 1 (2021): 20–29; and Marisa J. Fuentes, "'Attending to Black Death:' Black Women's Bodies in the Archive and the Afterlife of Captivity," *Diacritics* 48, no. 3 (2020): 116–29.
65. For a discussion of the Section 8 program, see Rosen, *Voucher Promise*.
66. Kaplan, *Anarchy of Empire*, 206.
67. Stephanie Leigh Batiste, *Darkening Mirrors: Imperial Representation in Depression-Era African American Performance* (Durham, NC: Duke University Press, 2012).
68. Batiste, 2.
69. In *Lose Your Mother: A Journey along the Atlantic Slave Route*, Saidiya Hartman traces the legacies and impact of the Atlantic Slave trade on Black subject and kinship formation, as well as on Black senses of home and belonging, in the African diaspora. She argues that "slavery persists as an issue in the political life of black America because . . . black lives are still imperiled and devalued by a racial calculus and a political arithmetic that were entrenched centuries ago." The "afterlife of slavery" names postslavery conditions of Black imperilment and devaluation, and is characterized by "skewed life chances, limited access to health and education, premature death, incarceration, and impoverishment." Hartman, *Lose Your Mother: A Journey along the Atlantic Slave Route* (New York: Farrar, Straus and Giroux, 2008), 6.
70. Patricia A. Banks, *Represent* (Abingdon-on-Thames, UK: Routledge, 2012).
71. Banks, *Represent*, 40.
72. Lorde, *Sister Outsider*, 43.
73. Sylvia Chan-Malik, *Being Muslim: A Cultural History of Women of Color in American Islam* (New York: New York University Press, 2018), 77.

74. See Lorde's poem "A Litany for Survival," *The Black Unicorn: Poems* (New York: Norton, 1978), 31–32.
75. Christina Sharpe, *In the Wake: On Blackness and Being* (Durham, NC: Duke University Press, 2016), 3–4.
76. Camp, *Closer to Freedom*, 152–97.
77. Camp, *Closer to Freedom*, 161.
78. Ann Petry, *The Street* (Boston: Houghton Mifflin, 1946).
79. June Jordan, *Living Room: New Poems* (New York: Thunder's Mouth, 1985).
80. Elizabeth Alexander, *The Black Interior: Essays* (Saint Paul, MN: Graywolf, 2004), x.
81. Alexander, *The Black Interior*, 9.
82. Alexander, *The Black Interior*, 4.

Journal #2   Nov. '70
[Writing Backwards, no Less!]

This would be the perfect spot for a poem or a versed inscription, or a picture, but I don't write poems, nor do I draw pictures. This spot, then, except for the one line above and this one, will be blank until I can say something that makes sense for a beginning — — one thing, though, the idea across the page about writing to die in bed is quite true! I can think of no more pleasant way to go, especially if your man is beside you. What is more, your man being with you — (in bed, & out) is perhaps a dynamite way to live too! We sexy folk stay in trouble because we want love like some people want money. The truth is that the "love depression" never ended, and the banks of love are still insolvent. After the "Revolution" gets here, I'm going to ask the Generals to set up at an FDIC of love so that "broke" niggers like myself can be sure that their few checks won't bounce. I'll dedicate this to Aphrodite!

ARCHIVAL FRAGMENT 5. Journal entry from 1970

bless march 9, 1971
I'm a big-foot, mississippi-delta
nigger, and I'a been coming a   November 4, 1970
long time, it will go on.
The cry of the human heart is plaintive and
remote. but listen! For it is one's own.

The heart is ripe in dark soft and open places, mellow
all over, these can let blood two ways: as the
vital juices of our loving, or as the dark, violated
blood of war. When I die, let me die in bed.

                              enroute.
                    Written from London to
                    Boston, Dec., 1968
How does one feel after a long journey?
I suppose that it all depends on how much
has been relieved. London came unexpectedly;
the circumstances of the moment were simply incredible — no one was prepared. but, for sure,
I had to make the journey. What I found there
was a vibrant, black humanity, trembling often with all the dangerous impulse of this revolutionary hour. I loved the people, though they often
spoke in what was for me a strange accent.

ARCHIVAL FRAGMENT 5. Journal entry from 1970

11 Mama's Marvelous Tar Baby

Black Feminist Experiments in Spillersian Ecdysis

RA MALIKA IMHOTEP

Centered before you on stage/page
I carry a chorus of [ungendered] black femme genius.
The names marked into my flesh are inescapable.
So I dance with them. Leave nothing left behind.
each wag of my tongue / move of my pen / sway of my hips /
    steals my stories back / offers up a truer word.

Lil Cotton Flower Is . . . The Marvelous Tar Baby

Blackness. A light shines on an empty play space. A glass bowl filled with strips of paper is centered between two bottles of molasses. Mic'd offstage, I am reading a found poem putting Hortense Spillers into dialogue with Lucille Clifton, Toni Morrison, and Ntozake Shange.

Let's face it.
I am a marked woman
But not everybody knows my name
Let's face it.
My country needs me and if I were not here I would have to be invented
Let's face it.

In order to speak a truer word concerning my self, I must strip down through layers of attenuated meanings, made in excess in time over time, assigned by a particular historical order
Let's face it.
there await whatever marvels of my own inventiveness.
Let's face it.
I must strip down.
In the service of a collective function.
Let's face it.
Being alive and being a woman and being colored is a metaphysical dilemma
I haven't yet conquered.
Let's face it
The names by which I am called in the public place
Do not exhaust me
Let's face it.
Everyday something has tried to kill me
And has failed.

Then there is music. Black lesbian composer and vocalist X'ene Sky's piano cover of Nina Simone's "Wild as The Wind" plays. I enter stage right, barefoot wearing a white cotton nightgown and a black chiffon apron. My waist-length yarn braids are pulled back into a high ponytail. I am wearing red lipstick. My movements are a slow and deliberate series of gestures I arrived at in conversation with Bajan dancer and performance-maker Valencia James. I caress my face, grab my neck with both hands, clench the sides of my stomach, spread my legs. This cycle carries me to each corner of the stage before I find center. At some point I am crawling. Rolling around, giving my best "afro-modern contemporary" bodywork.

I walk into the play space. Centerstage with my back to the audience, hands undoing the apron. It falls in front of me.
Grinning and feeling all accomplished he surrendered to this muse, mistaking my tenor for that of his own greed. You see, the morning i

came to him Brer Fox was out to get the best of that ol' Brer Rabbi—
the quick moving trickster always pullin' the wool over Brer Fox,
Brer Bear and even Ol'Massa.

Payin' them no mind, i made use of Brer Fox's ol' hands and fix'd myself
up real nice and round in all the right places: two pearls through
which to see, a wood button for a nose, a thick red slash of lip—all
set into the soft blackness of my face.

My hands slow waft up to my sides then bend at the elbows casting an eerie "hands up don't shoot" silhouette against the white screen before me. They fall down to find the buttons on the front of my gown. It falls as I bend forward. (The crowd doesn't know whether to cheer or remain silent in witness.)

i whisper'd into that ol' Fox's ear to dress me up nice and alluring, and
he fetch a few spools of yarn to weave atop my head and set me
down right at the lip of the river where as i can watch the water
glitter. little did he know, this here water is my Ma Dear. She the
only one i answer too.

While i settle into my prettiness, Brer Fox look on and commence to
singing to himself about the rabbit he finna catch on my account and
what a nice dinner that meat'll make once it meet his eatin' plate.

And so's i just sit there, lookin' out at the water, havin' deep conversations his ears ain't pitched to catch. Thanking Ma Dear for letting
me take form this evening. Not paying much mind to the Fox but
thanking him for his hands all the same.

I turn to face the audience. Rhinestoned pasties catching the light. My body a smooth length of even brown. My face carries no distinct emotion but a focused gaze out. I drop to my knees and let my weight fall stage-left as I start to remove the strips of paper from the glass bowl. I arrange them on the ground in front of the bowl before reaching for the bottles of molasses. One is a deep-ebony-almost-black, the other lightened with copper mica pigments.

Then trot up that ol' Brer Rabbit—moving so fast he almost missed this lil' ol' black thing sitting at the river's edge.

At the sight of that Rabbit, Brer Fox jump under the bush cross the road and hide

Then Brer Rabbit pause, double back and give me a deep glance over—lookin' real close with some secret heat behind his eyes. First Brer Rabbit get to talm'bout how i'm is a "sassy ol' Jay bird."

I smile as I raise the lighter bottle mixing the pigment with each flip of my wrist. After a little struggle with the cap I pick up both bottles and empty them into the glass bowl. Making the two sticky streams dance around each other as the pool at the bottom of the bowl.

and I'm almost flattered 'cept for that flame in his eye tell me to keep to myself.

Brer Rabbit commence to getting awfully familiar. He say "hey there, brown sugar how 'bout you let me have a lick at yo sweetness!" and my Tar Baby self just sits there, ain't sayin' nothin'—Brer Fox still tucked away under the bush, softly humming his eatin' song as he watch.

When satisfied, I put down the bottles and place my hands into the bowl. Mixing the molasses, then raising my hands and watching with delight as gravity pulls the sticky mess down to coat my fingertips.

Brer Rabbit say "okay now! *Earth Mama* why don't you bend over and carry my load?" Tar Baby ain't sayin' nothin' and Brer Fox, he lay low.

I begin to coat my arms. My eyes following the molasses with sustained attention. I coat my right leg then reach for a strip of paper that reads "BROWN SUGAR." I coat my thigh in the molasses mixture then stick on the paper. REPEAT ON LEFT LEG.

Brer Rabbit keep searching for a name I'm primed to respond to, he
seem to speak from a list that start off calm but then grow indignant: alright then *peaches*? He grumbles ... how 'bout it *sapphire*?, oh you must think you *god's holy fool*?—

I dip my hands back in the bowl and smile as I lift them to my face. I coat my cheeks in the molasses mixture then slide both hands around my neck recalling the cycle of gestures from the beginning of the performance. I affix a strip of paper that reads "SAPPHIRE" to the center of my chest.

"How you come on, den?" Brer Rabbit, ask ... gettin' big mad.
Tar Baby stay still, en Brer Fox, he lay low.
Brer Rabbit fix his mouth to say, "black as I is, my nose up so high I caint even smell my own breath."

Then "EARTH MAMA" across my belly and right shin. "JEZEBEL" along the side of my left knee cap. "PEACHES" on my chest atop of "SAPPHIRE." "MISS EBONY FIRST" on my belly. "EARTH MAMA" moves to my right shoulder.

Say he got something to fix me. And I'm just there, ain't sayin' nothin' as the sun heat me up into softness.
Brer Rabbit puff up his chest and says: "I'mma learn you how to talk to a respectable man like me if it's the last act of this here show." And I don't know who he think he talkin' to but being the Tar Baby I am, I keep my mouth shut. Sitting pretty. Getting soft in all the right places.
Brer Rabbit yelling now. He say, *"Cain't you hear me calling you, miss honey? Or is you as dumb as you is black? If you don't fix yo' face and greet me imma bus' you wiiiiiide open"*
& Ain't much of nothing for me to do in the face of no madrabbitnigga so I just stay still. Wondering if Brer Fox still watching, i can't hear him humming no more ...

Hands dip back into the bowl of molasses then raise to cover my face. My eyes are closed. Now covered in the molasses mixture. I caress my face, grab hold of my neck, my belly, then slide my hands down my open legs.

Brer Rabbit keep on yelling . . .
Tar Baby, keep on sayin' nothin' . . .
Then that niggarabbit draw back his fist and it land right upside my head where the sun been kissin' and he get stuck. He try to grab at my neck and that hand get stuck too. He kick his legs up right at the *di space between* my legs. He yanking and pulling and twisting just gettin' more tied up in my sticky mess of a body.

Hands dip back into the bowl. I bring my arms before my face and caress them. My left hand sliding down my right forearm as my finger curls softly toward my face. REPEAT. Right hand over left arm.

In the struggle I commence to melt 'round myself and it look like we dancing in a pool of molasses.
& I aint never say nothin'
"If you don't let me loose," he shout "I'mma kick the natal stuffing outta you." I don't say nothin' but I think deep about where I was befo all dis. In the dark wet warmth of Ma Dear's belly. The natal stuff I used to swim in. that which this here rabbit is tryna beat out of me.
& I ain't say nothin'

I brace my shoulders and fold my legs underneath me. My forearms fall toward my knees. I assume a meditative posture and take a series of visibly deep breaths as molasses drips from my face.

Then here come that ol' fox talm' bout "Howdy Brer Rabbit . . . you look sorta stuck up this mawnin'"
Brer Fox laugh and laugh and laugh. Laugh like he done forgot how I moved through his hands this morning. What a pretty thing I made myself before he trotted me out for some Rabbit meat.

With my eyes closed i turn to the side and lay down with my knees raised.

Right as the turpentine start to drip out the round of button hole of my eyes, Ma Dear, the river, rear up real big flooding the marsh. She grab me from off the log and start to mixing her sweet waters all around that rabbit and I.
Soon I am loosed from him. Loosed from the slug of flesh that held him and I together.
Soon I give up my self in a dark warmth, the color of tar.
And Ma Dear say, "Baby, I tried to told bout messing with these skin-folks. They don't know how to hold something soft and black as you. Next time be sure to fix yourself with teeth to smile and a tongue sharp enough to cut."

I caress myself as I gather all the strips of paper from my sticky brown body and pull them into a ball that I hold prayerfully at my chest. Laying there I take another series of visibly deep breaths. FADE TO BLACK.

II. "... I must strip down ..."

When Black feminist philosopher and literary critic Hortense Spillers says "my country needs me, and if I were not here I would have to be invented," I see Brer Fox grabbing hold of some turpentine and tar to make him up an alluring and adorned object that will entrap his adversary, Brer Rabbit. In this folkloric association, the Tar Baby becomes another figuration of Spillers's assertion that her distinctly Black and feminine form represents a plasticized subjectivity essential to the well-being of the nation that hails her. In the time of slavery and into its afterlife, representations of Black femininity have been sources of both contention and empowerment. Black feminine figures in art, archives, and political discourse embody the rhetorical needs of the communities that conjure and claim them. Scholars of antebellum history and political economy have illuminated the ways Black women's reproductive capacity functioned as the principal site of their value, fundamentally shaping their experience of slavery and their expressions of sociality and resistance.[1] Over time, the Black feminine figure was reduced to a function, a performance of labor, often but not exclusively mobilized against its own interests. The foundational process through which the Black feminine figure was made instrument shrouds the "flesh-and-blood entit[ies]" that exist at various positions within the locus of Blackness and femininity.[2] Thus, grappling with the sticky matter of Black femininity elicits new forms of exuviation and interpretation.

One performative method of the strategic revelation necessary to "speak a truer word," is burlesque. Burlesque is a word of multiple significations. With regards to genre, it is a literary, dramatic or musical work intended to cause laughter "by caricature of the manner or spirit of serious works, or by ludicrous treatment of their subjects."[3] In contemporary parlance and practice it is most associated with staged striptease performance. Robert Allen begins his historiography of American burlesque with Briton Lydia Thompson's 1868 debut in New York. Thompson's blonde beauty, charismatic sexuality, and crass disregard for propriety made her comedic performances of cross-dressed European masculinities a praised spectacle that provoked "hysterical antiburlesque discourse" which consequently inspired larger crowds.[4] One white theater critic of the era described the monstrosity of burlesque as that which defies the natural and the conventional by forcing "the conventional and the natural together just at the points where they are most remote."[5] Allen extends this to characterize burlesque as "one of several nineteenth-century entertainment forms that is grounded in the aesthetics of transgression, inversion, and the grotesque."[6] In her transgression of convention, the burlesque performer, he continues, represents a construction of the "low other."

Defined by Peter Stallybrass and Allon White, the low other is that which is "despised and denied at the level of political organization and social being whilst it is instrumentally constitutive of the shared imaginary repertoires of the dominant culture."[7] Here "the low other" resounds as a synonym for Spiller's configuration of the "pornotrope" wherein the material history of the United States (and by extension the modern world) the "Black woman" is constructed as the irresistible yet destructive low other against which proper "morality," "sexuality," "femininity," and "womanhood" are defined. In a sense, the "Black woman" is the archetypal burlesque but as indicted by the histories of segregation that I return to later in my discussion of the 'Chitlin Circuit,' the dark-skinned feminine figure was often barred from the most celebrated burlesque establishments. But as performance historian Jayna Brown points out, the gestural vocabularies of Black femininity (shimmy dances, snake hips, and other "primitive" movements) as first appropriated through the form of female minstrelsy would go on to shape the performance repertoire of American burlesque.[8]

The moves I make through the conceptualization and performance of theoretically charged Black feminist burlesque acts considers the Black folkloric figure of the Tar Baby a useful heuristic for understanding the "irresistible, destructive sensuality" Spiller's attributes to the captive body in the context of US chattel slavery.[9] In this same gesture Spiller writes against the presumed masculinity of the captive body and presents a critical engagement with the ways an agender captive body is both masculinized by its abjection through undifferentiated labor and feminized by its availability for violation and abjection through reproduction.

Tar is black and sticky—its material both performs and signifies its blackness, and in its blackness it demands engagement. In the folktale, it is the voiceless glamour of the Tar Baby that entraps Brer Rabbit. The tar of her body draws him in and holds him as prey. Most readings of the Tar Baby folktale center Brer Rabbit as the archetypal trickster figure. In Black literary and cultural discourse, identification with Brer Rabbit has been understood as a central component of the trickster tale's importance to the Black folk tradition and by extension the Black world.[10] Read for their depictions of masculinist cunning, these trickster tales give Black folk's space to envision themselves as *smarter than ol' massa*. The briar patch has been hailed as the field / the ancestral lands / the ghetto / the hood—and all the other unlivable geographies in which black folks make and sustain life. While these readings are warranted, I'm stuck on the femininized Blackness of the Tar Baby and what seeing (and refusing to discard) this black femininized figure as more than just a means to an end might open up for critical inquiry into the ways we conceptualize Black femininity outside binary constructions of gender, gendered aesthetics, and gendered performance. In what follows I explore examples from Black feminist performance history to offer what I am calling a Black trickster genealogy of American burlesque. Starting my analysis with the mid-century erotic fire dances of Lawanda Page, and ultimately reaching back even further to Ida Forsyne's early twentieth-century European tour as "Topsy," then back up through the contemporary spacetime of my own hyper-referential Black feminist performance interventions on the neoburlesque stage, this cyclical, anachronistic genealogy refuses to discard the central roles that Black feminine figures have played in establishing the sexual cultures dramatized in contemporary American burlesque, and modernity writ-large.

In what some might consider a counterintuitive application of the Tar Baby folktale's meaning, L. H. Stalling asserts that a revisionist Tar Baby, like that fictionalized by Toni Morrison in her novel of the same name, works as "an active being, less constructed by other individuals or beings but still caught in between roles and representations and one's own self," to exemplify the queer aesthetics and rhetorical strategies that enliven the work of Black feminine figures in performance. Specifically, Stallings reads the Tar Baby trope in the "chitlinfyin(g) drag," (a mode of low-class Black vernacular camp) employed by twentieth-century Black female comediennes, namely LaWanda Page.[11]

Page's entertainment career began as a dancer and burlesque performer in the 1930s billed as "The Bronze Goddess of Fire" traveling a circuit of performance venues and social establishments that catered to Black audiences in the eras of de jure and de facto racial segregation in the United States. This informal conglomerate of Black entertainment venues was colloquially referred to as the "Chitlin Circuit." While the Chitlin Circuit was not an explicitly queer space, its function, as described by Stallings, "did address the needs of Black people consistently ascribed to the realms of [non-normative sexualities]."[12] While white burlesque performers were navigating censure in the mainstream theater scenes of New York and LA, Black exotic dancers, and burlesque performers, who were often already marginalized within those venues, were able to perform more covertly within the anti-normative Black spaces of the Chitlin' Circuit. Touring the Chitlin Circuit, "The Bronze Goddess of Fire" met the comedian Redd Foxx and years later Redd Foxx would cast Lawanda Page as the unforgettable "antiwoman," Aunt Esther on his sitcom *Sanford & Son*.[13] For Stallings, Page's appearance as both the exotic "othered woman," a bronze goddess lighting cigarettes with her fingertips, and the slick mouthed elder aunt, refusing to perform femininity in ways that the male trickster/comedian demands, symbolically connect Page's performance work to the figure of the Tar Baby.[14]

When positioned as the Tar Baby (Aunt Esther) to Redd Foxx's Brer Rabbit (Fred Sanford), Page appears to lose the game of dozens, but her cultural significance as a voice of queered excessive Black femininities point us toward other modes of survival.[15] In my own scholarly work, I refer to these shapeshifting aesthetic and performance strategies employed by Black women (of various gender presentations) and gender non-conforming Black femmes in response to the threats of patriarchal violence, and other masculinist interruptions, as the condition of *being-in-blackfeminineflesh*.[16] Thus, I engage the Tar Baby through critical analysis, creative writing, and performance as an emblem of the sticky trickster technologies that enable anti-normative Black survivals. By bringing the Tar Baby into the performance lexicon of American burlesque, I broaden the scope of the Black vernacular tradition and use that tradition to expose the racial fault lines of contemporary erotic entertainment.

American lexographer and cultural critic, H. L. Mencken coined the term "ecdysiast" (ec-deze-e-ast) to taunt mid-century white female burlesque performers who were struggling to defend their craft and careers from Depression-era moral panics.[17] Mencken's neologism was taken from the Greek ekdysis meaning "a stripping or casting off" which had been used scientifically since the mid-nineteenth century in reference to animals like snakes and birds that shed and molt respectively. This antiquated term strikes me as relevant to contemporary neoburlesque for several reasons. The term's contested history and political utility seem to anticipate contemporary discourse on the classist and often racialized distinctions made between neoburlesque, stripping, and other variants of sex work.[18] I am also drawn to *ecdysiast* for its other-than-human referent to the act of stripping off layers of one's own skin. While Mencken may have initially meant it as a pejorative association, it calls to mind the fleshy ante-human erotics I always heard in *Spiller's* declaration that "In order for me to speak a truer word concerning myself, I must strip down."[19]

My work as Lil Cotton Flower performs an embodied citation of this Spillersian declaration. Thus, I mark myself a *Spillersian Ecdysiast*, one who self-consciously utilizes choreographies of the erotic, public economies of desire, and Black feminist rhetoric to court my own marvels through acts of bodily exposure. This embodied citation of Black feminist critical theory brings the scriptive gestures of the text to the body, my body.

III. Confessions of a Spillersian Ecdysiast

> Let's face it. I am a marked woman, but not everybody knows my name. "Peaches" and "Brown Sugar," "Sapphire" and "Earth Mother," "Aunty," "Granny," God's "Holy Fool," a "Miss Ebony First," or "Black Woman at the Podium": I describe a locus of confounded identities, a meeting ground of investments and privations in the national treasury of rhetorical wealth. My country needs me, and if I were not here, I would have to be invented.
>
> Hortense Spillers "Mama's Baby, Papa's Maybe: An American Grammar Book"

I think a lot about what it means for my "petite dark-skinned Black femme body" to take up space on the neo-burlesque stage. I am aware that my flesh is always, already imbued with a litany of tropes "topsy," "jezebel," "sapphire," "brown sugar," to "chocolate drop." As I performatively redress myself with these labels as they are articulated by Spillers in the opening of "Mama's Baby, Papa's Maybe," staining them sticky with molasses, I am acknowledging with Spillers that though they were not of my invention, I do have some responsibility or intimate relation to them.[20] In my theorizing practice which includes staged performance, I decide how I want to relate to them. As the Tar Baby, I engage them as an anointing then ultimately pull them together into a ball I hold prayerfully above the center of my chest. I interrupt the straightforward line of consumption between the spectacular body and audience that most burlesque relies upon by adding voice rooted in Black feminist literature and shaped by distinctly Southern histories and oral tradition. Beginning a body-focused performance with an off-stage recitation where my body is concealed, makes the presence of my body, the

FIGURE 11.1. Lil Cotton Flower's Debut Performance of "Topsy Cotton Belt" from San Francisco in 2019.

link between my body and voice, the first in the series of "reveals" that make the work burlesque. I preface my staged-presence, my body, with voice so that even if I "don't say nothin" while I strip down there is still the lingering trace of story left in the audience's mind.

Through an interplay between Black feminist citation, embodied silence, vernacular orality, and staged presence, my work performs what L.H. Stalling terms "trickster-troping," utilizing "desire [as] a primary tool in self-invention and the reading [and staging] of difference."[21] I see this as another manifestation of what Saidiya Hartman has termed "deconstructive performance," revolt staged at the sight of enjoyment.[22] There is a Black queer feminist genealogy of the trickster figure that is largely rooted in the work of Audre Lorde. In poetry and prose, Lorde referenced a pantheon of West African trickster figures namely Eshu, Legba, and her own syncretic formulation, Afrekete.[23] These tricksters of the Fon, Yoruba, and Dahomey peoples preside over the crossroads, serve as messengers between the gods, and betray gendered binaries through performances of brazen sexual fluidity. Afrekete is brought into further relief in the short story "Tar Beach," which also appears as chapter 31 of Lorde's biomythography, *Zami*. As ethereal Black lover-goddess, Afrekete strips a heartbroken Lorde down to her most erotic dimensions. In scenes of sensual play between their bodies and various fruits of the earth, Lorde enfleshes a trickster-goddess who takes a multiplicity of forms: "Kitty," a consummate Black lesbian lover, a night club singer, a market clerk, a mother, and a party-goer. Afrekete teaches "roots, new definitions of our women's bodies," Afrekete bears the scars of wars waged "in the enemies stronghold," Afrekete is "too tough and crazy not to" survive.[24]

Kara Provost reads Lorde's identification with the trickster as part of her insistence on language and voice as a tool for the transformation of self and society. Describing Lorde's need to translate herself across various planes of racial, sexual, social, and religious difference, Provost asked "How can she find a viable self, a viable voice, in the face of these contradictory expectations?"[25] To which the Tar Baby as trickster answers: *the most viable voice might be no voice at all*. The Tar Baby-trickster plays on and departs from the Legba/Eshu/Afrekete tradition by invoking what Ianna Hawkins Owen describes as "declarative silence."[26] While silence is typically understood as a space evacuated of agency, Owen's investigation of declarative silence as a black rhetorical strategy argues that "even in conditions of unfreedom, defeat and resistance can coexist in the same gesture."[27]

The Marvelous Tar Baby act further troubles the distinction between silence and agency by utilizing an *interior* voice to interrupt discursive silence. The Tar Baby, a folkloric character who canonically "says nothing," remains silent in the world of the story while audiences privy to Lil Cotton Flower's performance get to hear Tar Baby-trickster's withheld perspective. Staging the Tar Baby's internal dialogue does not interrupt the external drama and violence of their hailing in the scene of the folktale. They continue to "say nothin" to the host of character's that surround and instrumentalize them; even as their internal dialogue reimagines the terms of these relationships ("Brer Fox grabbed some tar and turpentine and *let me make myself* through his hands").

Rewriting the Tar Baby's silence as an external choice that does not foreclose the potential of internal reflection and depth, is a performative invocation of what Kevin Quashie has termed the "interior self-measure" of Black expressive quiet.[28] The performance genre of neoburlesque is particularly suited for this kind of public presentation of Black feminine interiority. As explicated by Mecca Jamilah Sullivan, black queer performers within the neoburlesque industry often stage "a black queer feminist intersectional critique of and through the erotic" that brings us into dialogue with a tradition of Black feminist performance that branches out from Ntozake Shange's 1974 invention of the "choreopoem."[29] Using what Sullivan diacritically terms "body/language," the choreopoem and its queer progeny proffer an "expressivity defined by embodiment" in which voicing and silence coexist in tandem and in tension.[30]

Sullivan's invitation to consider the sensual storytelling that shapes Black feminist burlesque as a form of "queer choreopoetic performance," helps me make sense of the contradiction I feel in connecting the Tar Baby's declarative silence to my act of embodied voicing. The quiet erotic expressions of my black femme body merge with the poetic interiority of the Tar Baby to invoke what Spiller's terms "the nuantial"—a space of nuance that the black life-world at-large, and the black woman's sexual-world in particular, have been disallowed.[31] Shange's innovation of the choreopoem—a form where multiplicities of distinctly Black feminine body and voice are interdependent and staged publicly—intervenes against this structural refusal to see the nuance laden in Black feminine subjectivity. In 1975, the year before Shange's *for colored girls who have considered suicide / when the rainbow is enuf* was adapted as a book and produced on Broadway, Spillers wrote and produced *Sparebone: A Drama in Three Acts with Music and Dance* as part of the Wellesley College Centennial. The fusion of drama, music, and dance in Spillers's *Sparebone* brings the work into relation with the form of the choreopoem. This relation is explicitly illustrated in the opening scene of the play titled "The Dance of Josephine." Wordlessly, Josephine [Baker] performs "a feline, seductive dance of fertility and black magic ... in dazzling costume and mask."[32] This staged performance mobilizes an erotic construction of Black femininity to establish the play's context in 1920s Paris and gives specific attention to the presence and experiences of Black American expats.

Within this black magic tradition of Black feminist embodied expression, I am brought back to the way of Afrekete, trickster-goddess of the tongue and the erotic. Refusing easy comprehension, layers of vernacular orality and embodied silence within The Marvelous Tar Baby act, voiced and embodied by Lil Cotton Flower (an avatar of Ra Malika Imhotep), portray a history of black femininity as publicly hailed (into the scene of racialized and gendered violence) and internally understood (as a figure that experiences yet transcends that violence through its own erotic self-fashioning and connection to the natural world).[33] This history produces modes of performance as intricate and at times contradictory as the unresolved "metaphysical dilemma" from which they spring.[34]

My first ever burlesque act, titled "Topsy's Cotton Belt," was danced in tribute to Ida Forsyne, Black Patti, and the long legacy of Black women vaudeville performers and chorus girls that laughed, twisted, shouted and smiled as they laid the foundation for contemporary neoburlesque. I was first inspired to experiment with burlesque as a medium for Black feminist storytelling by a line in Jayna Brown's book *Babylon Girls: Black Women Performers and the Shaping of Modernity*. In the chapter "Letting The Flesh Fly: Topsy, Time, Torture, and Transfiguration," Brown writes:

> Female minstrelsy has its own history, shaped by notions of the black female body's abilities, availability, and utility. In the mid-nineteenth century, "female minstrelsy" was an official stage circuit term. It evolved into and was renamed "burlesque" in the 1880s but carried forward the practices of racial mimicry from earlier stage conventions. Early burlesque was female-dominated popular stage work that was often satirical and always about dance, presaging the later chorus line dancers.[35]

And suddenly I was overwhelmed by the thought of lithe white-bodied ingenues in their glittery tasseled pasties feasting on Topsy's remains. As elucidated by Brown, the untamable young Black slave girl, Topsy from Harriet Beecher-Stowe's *Uncle Tom's Cabin*, embodies the "childlike simplicity" projected on to Black folks in the late eighteenth and nineteenth centuries. In staged adaptations of Uncle Tom's Cabin, Topsy was a character designed to be played by a white woman in blackface. As such Topsy existed as a "therapeutic opportunity [for white female performers] to access realms of freedom [proper] womanhood was otherwise constructed against."[36] As Topsy, and in other female minstrel derivatives, including burlesque, white women got to act out and disregard the stoic purity they had been culturally ascribed to. In these performances of freedom they dramatized their presumed power over and access to the Black female body.³⁷ But when Black female performers like Ida Forsyne "played Topsy," Brown argues, the character's movements register a spiritual reclamation of the Black body. Free from the respectability politics of the New Negro and seemingly immune to the violence of chattel slavery, Topsy embodied "the disruptive creativity of the black female child," whose acts of transcendence reflect that of Black performers from the nineteenth century to present times.³⁸ This was also an assertion of the nuantial, allowing Black femininity to occupy the space between celebratory race-forward performance and unruly corporeal freedoms. Brown's provocative argument is supported by Forsyne's own articulations of her body in performance. Though she did not have access to the kinds of literacy utilized by contemporary Black feminist performance artists to document their own relationships to their work, Forsyne was written *about* throughout the early twentieth century and left behind at least one trace of her own perspective in an interview conducted by Marshall and Jean Stearns between 1960 and 1966 for their critical account of the evolution of American vernacular dance.³⁹

Forsyne never performed as the character Topsy in staged renditions of *Uncle Tom's Cabin*, but due to the ubiquity of *Uncle Tom's Cabin* and the archetypal caricatures it gave life to, Forsyne was billed as "Topsy, The Famous Negro Dancer" when she toured London in 1906 with The Tennessee Students.⁴⁰ Naturally "little, black and cute," Forsyne could not escape her archetypal semblance as "Topsy" on stage. The bodily comportment she was born into rendered her an unnatural sight, "the little lady who 'was not born but just grew.'"⁴¹ Topsy is an imagined object, Forsyne was a Black female performance artist, the conflation of the two anticipates what has been discussed in recent works in Black performance studies as object performance.⁴² Black feminist object performance makes use of this fungibility between living Black female performer and unreal racialized gendered performance trope. As Topsy, Forsyne performed her own burlesque, emerging from a potato sack center-stage backed by a line of white ballet dancers who were paid extra to perform in blackface. Described by Brown, Forsyne as Topsy would reveal herself "limb by limb, then danced wildly until a shot rang out and she fell to the floor." Forsyne herself articulates this fall as rolling "over and over and up." But when the Stearns wrote of the act in the book project for which Forsyne was interviewed, they described her movement as "over and over and dead." In this discrepancy, Brown sees the interplay between the tropes of inescapable suffering and inhuman resilience that overwrite Black performance in the popular imagination.[43]

Understanding Forsyne's "Topsy Sack Dance" (1906) as a burlesque act is a needed intervention in the historization of both Black performance and burlesque performance in the US. In its originary sense, minstrelsy was always a burlesque. On the minstrel stage, the exaggerated subject was Black life but because white supremacy was the popular sensibility of the time the performances were presumed to be representative, and even more heinous, accurate. Wriggling herself out of a potato sack, limb by limb, dancing wildly across the stage until a shot rang out and then falling to the ground rolling over and over and *up*, Forsyne referenced "the historical memory of living as a commodity, as well as the black child's [and black woman's] familiar proximity to violence, cruelty, and death."[44] She made a burlesque of the quotidian suffering she had momentarily escaped as a Black child born in Chicago in the wake of Reconstruction.[45] And she also performed a dramatic reveal inside a physical theater narrative that resonates with the performance structures of much contemporary burlesque.

I make the decision to consciously stage these histories in my burlesque because their erasure bolsters oppressive patterns of consumption that make the space of the stage unsafe for the low other. When first performing "Topsy's Cotton Belt" in San Francisco I knew I needed to end the act by spinning over and over and falling "up." I repeated the phrase "over and over and up" in my head as Nina Simone's rendition of "Save Me" built to its rhythmic conclusion. I spun my body as Nina scatted out "save save save" and fell to the ground with the song's last note. A friend in the audience said I looked possessed as I caressed my out of breath body before hurriedly rising to clear the stage for the next performer. Based on audience applause I won that first showcase. As I walked through the crowd a white male from the audience tapped me on the shoulder and told me that my act was "well-played"; another commented on my smile. They had gotten something I didn't intend to give. Something felt incomplete.

In retrospect I understand "The Marvelous Tar Baby" as a sequel to "Topsy's Cotton Belt," an attempt to correct for the things my first act missed. It didn't start that way. It started with me sitting in my room feeling unsafe in the world (maybe another Black girl had been murdered, I can't be sure). I wanted to write a folktale and didn't know where to start so I read the one most familiar to me: Joel Chandler Harris's 1880 rendition of "the Wonderful Tar Baby Story."[46] The story, the treatment of the Tar Baby was so violent. Having heard my father tell the story innumerous times during my childhood, I didn't remember it that way. But in this reading the violence registered deeply, and I decided to write something from the perspective I most identified with—that of the dark, sticky, embattled Tar Baby.

I turn to acts of Spillersian Ecdysis, to claim my inheritance as Topsy *and* Forsyne's progeny. This is also a provocation toward the present longed for in Lorraine O'Grady's 1994 essay "Olympia's Maid: Reclaiming Black Female Subjectivity." O'Grady writes:

> When, I ask, do we start to see images of the black female body by black women made as acts of autoexpression, the discrete stage that must immediately precede or occur simultaneously with acts of auto-critique? When, in other words, does the present begin? . . . now seems a paradigm for the willingness to look, to get past embarrassment and retrieve the mutilated body, as Spillers warns we must if we are to gain the clear-sightedness needed to overthrow hierarchical binaries: "Neither the shameface of the embarrassed, nor the not-looking-back of the self-assured is of much interest to us," Spillers writes, "and will not help at all if rigor is our dream."[47]

I'm struck by the rhetorical ease with which O'Grady "tags" Spillers into her own ruminations. It models a practice of citation that is enabled by the conversational lilt that undergirds most of Spillers's prose. She is talking to us and with us. Handing us language to help choreograph the ways we think about and feel into ourselves. Perhaps most famously this occurs in the opening to 1987's "Mama's Baby, Papa's Maybe." I have already demonstrated the way Spillers's undeniably poetic direct address sticks to the reader. With this rhetorical gesture, Spillers summons up an internal amen corner before she overturns everything we thought we knew about slavery and its hold on us. But this same command of vernacular appears instructively in other moments throughout her oeuvre (i would even say it happens in every essay if you read with an ear trained on a certain kind of southern slick talkin' genius).

In the essay "An Order of Constancy: Notes on Brooks and the Feminine," Spillers uses Gwendolyn Brooks's novel *Maud Martha* (1953) as the basis for a critique of the gynocritical anxieties of her feminist scholar contemporaries. The novel, she argues, presents a necessary interdependence between femininity and masculinity in the body and life experiences of a Black woman. Another space of critical nuance, in this case overwritten by a biocentric race for feminist theory. As a scholar pursuing the non-binary edge of Black feminist ontological possibility, I feel seen and anticipated in the ways Spillers names the anxieties that attend the project of "defining the 'feminine' in ways that do not offend its primary subject."[48] As explored by Spillers, Brooks's dark-skinned, working-class, female-born protagonist, Maud Martha represents a "feminine [that] is neither cause for particular celebration nor certain despair but near to the 'incandescence,' it is analogous to that 'wedged-shaped core of darkness' through which vision we see things in their fluid passage between dream and waking reality, as multiple meanings impinge on a central event."[49] The word that pulled me into this quote is "incandescence." The dictionary defines incandescent as "emitting light as a result of being heated." And in this passage, "incandescent" is a direct reference to Virginia Woolf's "A Room of One's Own" (1929). The quote from Woolf cited in Spillers's footnote says, "Perhaps a mind that is fully masculine cannot create, any more than a mind that is purely feminine. . . . Coleridge . . . meant, perhaps that the androgynous mind is resonant and porous; that it transmits emotion without impediment; that it is naturally creative, incandescent, and undivided." So perhaps the sum of these definitions, following Spillers's statements about the mutual co-constitution of masculine and feminine in Brooks' work (and maybe by extension in the distinctly Black feminine poetic order of things) is that the Black feminine is constructed and enacted as an "androgynous mind/lens" that allows for a different illumination/sighting of things. Here "things" are material, experiential, and epistemological. Spillers's critique of feminist "gynocritical" theorizations of the feminine is that they too often engage the feminine as merely an "object of the attention of another."[50] Spillers seeks to engage the feminine and "the subject with feminine attributes" on their own terms. "Shadowy and ubiquitous on the world's body," Spillers's construction of the [Black] feminine is an immensely powerful entity that reproduces sameness and difference at once.[51]

Tracing the feminine through Brooks' literary ingenuity, Spillers concludes that the Black feminine (distinct from but related to the "flesh-and-blood entity" of the female body and still tethered to the tropes of social and physical reproduction) locates and creates from the convergence of antithetically destined properties—"female," "male," "mind," "body," "same," "other," "past," future," "beholder," "beheld."[52] This convergence shapes the Black feminine as an androgynous *all-and-nothing* sort of figure. A self that is plural. In the tradition of Black feminist solo-performance that I evoke through Ida Forsyne, LaWanda Page, Lorraine O'Grady, and Lil Cotton Flower, the singular figure of a Black feminine performer embodies Spillers's assertion that "the personal pronouns serve a collective function."[53]

I am wondering now if it is all an attempt at sublimation. Me interpreting critical theory as a choreographic invitation, asserting my perspective on to a "minor figure" of a well-worn folktale, learning something new about my own ability to survive through the repetition of this act. As I coat myself in molasses, I imagine ablution. Baptizing myself in the fragrant sticky blackness, I become at once edible and medicinal (traits that are always, already read on to my black femme body). This cleansing is hauntingly entangled with the history latent in blackstrap molasses, a byproduct of the global sugar economy as heavy with black sweat and suffering as the cotton plant. I think about Karen Finely in "We Keep Our Victims Ready" (1990), covering herself chocolate in a provocation about sexual violence, degradation, and consumption. I think about Yoko Ono in "Cut Piece" (1964), sitting still allowing the audience to approach her with scissors and do as they will. I think of Rhodessa Jones in "The Legend of Lily Overstreet" (1986), donning mask and denuding her body to tell the story of an embattled yet vibrant exotic dancer. These are the referents my performance conjured in the minds of witnesses, peers, and mentors. Through the lens of feminist performance art, I offer a contemplation of racialized femininity, consumption, survivorship, and vulnerability. To my own mind, I am principally engaging in a call-and-response dialogue with the folkloric traditions I was born into.

I am still afraid that those who see me, my performances, or still images of my flesh-work, will dismiss it all as frivolous nudity or worse, self-exploitation.[54] I have learned that neither the work itself nor the arts institutions that seek to display it, will protect me from harm.[55] I wonder if those who bear witness to these experiments will grant me the benefit of my own depths or even dare to face the histories revealed as I strip down. I wonder if they will even take the time to hear me, or if they rather I just didn't say nothin . . .

But true to my trickster lineage, I remember, in the face of death and violation: my silence will not protect me.[56] These are all my stories, my power. My Tar Baby–trickster sensibilities are both bait *and* switch. They attract, they disgust, they stain, they cleanse. In this genealogy of dark and messy provocation, I am but one figure in a long line of inescapable shadows. Without me, there is no light.

[**Fade to Black**]

Dedication

This essay is dedicated to the memory of my father, Akbar Imhotep; mathematician, actor, poet, storyteller, puppeteer, puppet-maker. Father to Akilah Walton, Garvey Imhotep, and Malika Saramaat Imhotep (me!). Husband to my phenomenal mother, D. Makeda Johnson. It is dedicated to his sister, Ira Dean Davis-Ridley, who would share her cotton-picking with him so that he wouldn't come up short at the weigh in. It is dedicated to the unnamed court of ancestors unafraid of the erotic who guided me back into my body and come with me on stage. It is dedicated to the memory of my niece, Iyana Walton, walking into my father's hospice room and proclaiming "DID YOU KNOW YOUR DAUGHTER IS A STRIPPER?" To which my father responded, "I know she is an artist."

Notes

The first section of this essay is a transcript of a live performance conceptualized by Ra Malika Imhotep, performed by Lil Cotton Flower, at The Body Political Variety Show October 2019, Chicago, IL.

1. Lindon Barrett, *Blackness and Value: Seeing Double* (Cambridge: Cambridge University Press, 1998); Saidiya V. Hartman, *Scenes of Subjection: Terror, Slavery, and Self-Making in Nineteenth-Century America* (New York: Oxford University Press, 1997); Stephanie M. H. Camp, *Closer to Freedom: Enslaved Women and Everyday Resistance in the Plantation South* (Chapel Hill: University of North Carolina Press, 2005); Kimberly Juanita Brown, *The Repeating Body: Slavery's Visual Resonance in the Contemporary* (Durham, NC: Duke University Press Books, 2015); Adrienne D. Davis, *"Don't Let Nobody Bother Yo' Principle": The Sexual Economy of American Slavery, Black Sexual Economies* (Champaign: University of Illinois Press, 2019), https://www.universitypressscholarship.com/view/10.5622/illinois/9780252042645.001.0001/upso-9780252042645-chapter-002.
2. Hortense J. Spillers, "'An Order of Constancy': Notes on Brooks and the Feminine," *Centennial Review* 29, no. 2 (1985): 245.
3. *Oxford English Dictionary*, "burlesque (n.), sense 1" March 2024, https://doi.org/10.1093/OED/6948822370.
4. Robert Clyde Allen, *Horrible Prettiness: Burlesque and American Culture* (Chapel Hill: University of North Carolina Press, 1991), 16.
5. Allen, *Horrible Prettiness*, 25.
6. Allen, *Horrible Prettiness*, 26.
7. Peter Stallybrass and Allon White, *The Politics and Poetics of Transgression* (Ithaca, NY: Cornell University Press, 1986), 5.
8. Jayna Brown, *Babylon Girls: Black Women Performers and the Shaping of the Modern* (Durham, NC: Duke University Press, 2008).
9. Spillers, "Mama's Baby, Papa's Maybe," 67.
10. Lawrence W. Levine, *Black Culture and Black Consciousness: Afro-American Folk Thought from Slavery to Freedom* (Oxford: Oxford University Press, 1978).
11. L. H. Stallings, *Mutha Is Half a Word: Intersections of Folklore, Vernacular, Myth, and Queerness in Black Female Culture* (Columbus: Ohio State University Press, 2007), 124.
12. Stallings, *Mutha Is Half a Word*, 127.
13. Stallings, *Mutha Is Half a Word*, 129.
14. Stallings, *Mutha Is Half a Word*, 129.
15. "Dozens" denotes the Black vernacular tradition of social banter that is somewhere between "playful" and "violent." The game of dozen is played on school yards, street corners, and living rooms and one could convincingly argue you that within the Black queer community this practice has been rearticulated as "reading" and "throwing shade." In scripted comedic battles with Red Foxx,

Lawanda Page's character is always made a punch line through the denial of her femininity and desirability. Stallings, 29.

16. "being-in-blackfeminineflesh: Towards an Embodied Veneration of BeTTy BuTT's Inexhaustible Pleasures," *TDR: The Drama Review* 67, no. 3 (Sept. 2023): 15–31.

17. In 1940 burlesque performer Georgia Sothern wrote to H. L Mencken and several other American lexographers pleading for a new word that might interrupt the stigmas associated with "strip tease" performance: "It happens that I am a practitioner of the fine art of strip-teasing. Strip-teasing is a formal and rhythmic disrobing of the body in public. In recent years there has been a great deal of uninformed criticism levelled against my profession." H. L. Mencken, *The American Language Supplement 1: The American Language: An Inquiry Into the Development of English in the United States*, 4th edition (New York: Alfred A. Knopf, 1945); Andrea Friedman, "'The Habitats of Sex-Crazed Perverts': Campaigns against Burlesque in Depression-Era New York City," *Journal of the History of Sexuality* 7, no. 2 (1996): 203–38.

18. While many sex workers and sex worker organizers rightfully make hard distinctions between the labor of full-time and or survival sex worker my experience as a Black burlesque performer and the conversations between burlesque performers of color I have witnessed and participated in muddy those distinctions. Many burlesque performers have at one point,\ or another participated in the formal and/or underground sex industries. And further, regardless of the setting in which I take off my clothes my particular body is always read in relationship to the bodies of Black femme and female erotic laborers. In my work organizing in the campaign to decriminalize sex work in Louisiana, I have personally identified my work in burlesque as recreational sex work. For me "recreation" indicates that staged erotic performance is not my main source of income. *21st Century Burlesque Magazine*, "Burlesque Performer: You Are Not a Sex Worker," February 24, 2016, https://21stcenturyburlesque.com/burlesque-performer-you-are-not-a-sex-worker.

19. Thinking here about recent trends in Black Studies that critique western humanism through critical engagements with Blackness and animality. Spillers and Sylvia Wynter are forebears of this theoretical tendency. Spillers taught us how Black flesh had never been permitted to be a properly regarded body in the Western sense. Wynter taught us the political constructions of Western Man1 and Man2 were imperial aberrations of human beings. Spillers, Hortense J. "Mama's Baby, Papa's Maybe," 65–81; Sylvia Wynter, "Unsettling the Coloniality of Being/Power/Truth/Freedom: Towards the Human, after Man, Its Overrepresentation—An Argument," *CR: The New Centennial Review* 3, no. 3 (2003): 257–337; Zakiyyah Iman Jackson, *Becoming Human: Matter and Meaning in an Antiblack World* (New York: NYU Press, 2020); Alexander G. Weheliye, *Habeas Viscus: Racializing Assemblages, Biopolitics, and Black Feminist Theories of the Human* (Durham, NC: Duke University Press, 2014).

20. In a 2018 conversation with Gail Lewis at the ICA in London, Hortense Spillers offered the following: "I would not like to see a reification, or a reading of [the ungendering formulation] back into my historical subjectivity or subjecthood as though it exhausted my possibility because it does not. It certainly defines how I am situated in the world that calls me by my name—or whatever other name it's calling me. and I have to answer to all of them whether I like them or not, and try to be responsible to them. But *I am not exhausted by them, I'm that plus*. And it's the *'plus'* that I'm trying to get to . . ." [italics mine], Hortense Spillers and Gail Lewis at the Institute of Contemporary Arts. Institute of Contemporary Arts, 2018. https://www.youtube.com/watch?v=tQoORQqSaWU.
21. Stallings, *Mutha Is Half a Word*, 35.
22. Hartman, *Scenes of Subjection*, 42.
23. Kara Provost, "Becoming Afrekete: The Trickster in the Work of Audre Lorde," *MELUS* 20, no. 4, (Winter 1995): 45–59.
24. Audre Lorde, *Zami* (New York: Crossing Press, 1982), 250.
25. Provost, "Becoming Afrekete," 48.
26. Ianna Hawkins-Owen, "still, nothing: Mammy and Black asexual possibility" *Feminist Review* 120, no. 1 (2018): 70–84. https://doi.org/10.1057/s41305-018-0140-9.
27. Hawkins-Owen, "still, nothing," 77.
28. Kevin Quashie, *The Sovereignty of Quiet: Beyond Resistance in Black Culture* (New Brunswick, NJ: Rutgers University Press, 2012): 45.
29. Mecca Jamilah Sullivan, *The Poetics of Difference: Queer Feminist Forms in the African Diaspora* (Champaign: University of Illinois Press, 2021), 101.
30. Sullivan, *The Poetics of Difference*, 94–95.
31. Spillers, *Black, White, and In Color*, 14.
32. "Play: *Sparebone*: typed draft," 1975 (Ms.2019.013) Box 18, Folder 11, Hortense J. Spillers papers, Feminist Theory Archive, Brown University.
33. The designation "avatar" here connotes both the words etymological root as relating to the descent of a spiritual deity to the earth and it's redefinition in the context of Black feminist performance as a "simulated [being]" forged from a process of "self-objectification . . . that provides the possibility for (though never the guarantee of) and emancipated subjectivity." Uri McMillan, *Embodied Avatars: Genealogies of Black Feminist Art and Performance* (New York: NYU Press, 2015), 7–8.
34. In the "No More Love Poems 1–4" Section of the original choreopoem *for colored girls who have considered suicide / when the rainbow is enuf* (1973), Shange writes: "but bein alive & bein a woman & bein colored is a metaphysical dilemma/ i havent conquered yet/ do you see the point/my spirit is too ancient to understand the separation of soul & gender." Shange, *for colored girls who have considered suicide / when the rainbow is enuf* (Chicago: Shameless Hussy Press, 1973).
35. Brown, *Babylon Girls*, 57.
36. Brown, *Babylon Girls*, 71.

37. Brown, *Babylon Girls*, 72; Spillers, "Mama's Baby, Papa's Maybe," 77.
38. Brown, *Babylon Girls*, 58.
39. Marshall and Jean Stearns, *Jazz Dance: The Story Of American Vernacular Dance* (New York: Hachette Books, 1994).
40. Stearns and Stearns, *Jazz Dance*, 252.
41. Stearns and Stearns, *Jazz Dance*, 252.
42. See McMillan, *Embodied Avatars*; and Amber Jamilla Musser, *Sensual Excess: Queer Femininity and Brown Jouissance* (New York: NYU Press, 2018).
43. Brown, *Babylon Girls*, 62.
44. Brown, *Babylon Girls*, 62.
45. In the cyclical nature of black time that same suffering would meet her upon her return to the US in 1914 as she struggled to find work that suited her prowess and credentials as a performer. Forsyne felt discriminated against by her own people on account of her dark skin and after failing to book shows in Harlem's most noted theater she "gave up any idea of doing what [she] wanted to do" and took a gig coon-shouting on Coney Island. Stearns and Stearns, *Jazz Dance*, 254. Eventually she did land off-and-on work through the infamous Theater Owners Booking Association (T.O.B.A), the premiere vaudeville circuit for black performers in the 1920s, but because of her artistic affinity for Russian dance (for which she had achieved much acclaim in Europe) she was woefully unappreciated by Black audiences. From 1920 to1922, she worked as a maid and dancer for white female Vaudeville icon Sophie Tucker. In 1926 she toured the South with The Smart Set and had her first encounters with the horrors of the Jim Crow South. The experience marred her so that despite achieving relative success performing with Bessie Smith from 1927 to1928, Forsyne quit dancing all-together when Smith was asked to embark on a Southern tour. After the conclusion of her performing career Forsyne worked as a domestic and spent her last working years as an elevator operator. Stearns and Stearns, *Jazz Dance*, 254.
46. I was introduced the folktale "Brer Rabbit and the Tar Baby," along with the rest of the Uncle Remus Tales and a near exhaustive oeuvre of Afro-diasporic folklore by my father Akbar Imhotep (1951–2022) who performed as resident storyteller at the Wren's Nest, the home of Joel Chandler Harris, located in Atlanta's West End neighborhood for thirty-five years. My decision to describe the Tar Baby as "Marvelous" as opposed to "Wonderful" comes out of study and practice of Black feminist surrealism I was initiated into by kai lumumba barrow. As I understand "the Marvelous" is the beautiful expansive otherwise that ruptures and defies the "common-sense" of empire's culture of domination.
47. Lorraine O'Grady, "Olympia's Maid: Reclaiming Black Female Subjectivity," in *Writing in Space, 1973–2019* (Durham, NC: Duke University Press, 2020), 98.
48. Spillers, "An Order of Constancy," 224.

49. Spillers, "An Order of Constancy," 228.
50. Spillers, "An Order of Constancy," 224.
51. Spillers, "An Order of Constancy," 226–27.
52. Spillers, "An Order of Constancy," 245.
53. Spillers, "Mama's Baby, Papa's Maybe," 67.
54. In the performance memoir *Swallow the Fish*, Black feminist performance artist Gabrielle Civil recounts the ways her piece "Displays (after Venus)" was received by Black women in the audience during a residency at Mt. Holyoke. In their Black and feminine bodyminds, Civil's invocation of Saartjie Baartman ("The Hottentot Venus") evoked personal and collective feelings of shame and genuine concern for Civil's well-being. In response, Civil concludes, "To Venus and back: at the end of the orbit, when we round our way home, all we have left is this: this body, word and flesh, a corpus of writing, a birthday suit." Gabrielle Civil, *Swallow the Fish* (Virginia: Civil Coping Mechanisms, 2017), 181
55. In July of 2022, at the opening of my first solo-exhibition titled "... marvels of my own inventiveness ..." I was sexually assaulted by an attendee I did not know. After the tussle, in which only one person in the gallery intervened, it was discovered that the assailant had taken suggestive photos of "The Marvelous Tar Baby" performance, which was being projected onto a wall toward the back of the gallery. At the time of writing there has been no redress.
56. This silence is distinct from the declarative silence discussed earlier. This reference to Audre Lorde's 1978 essay "The Transformation of Silence into Language and Action" understands the queer choreopoetic play between the silence and the voice of The Marvelous Tar Baby act as "an act of self-realization" despite its quiet expressivity. Lorde, Audre "The Transformation of Silence into Language and Action," *Sinister Wisdom*, no. 6 (1978).

Works Cited

Allen, Robert Clyde. *Horrible Prettiness: Burlesque and American Culture*. Chapel Hill: University of North Carolina Press, 1991.

Barrett, Lindon. *Blackness and Value: Seeing Double*. Cambridge: Cambridge University Press, 1998.

Brown, Jayna. *Babylon Girls: Black Women Performers and the Shaping of the Modern*. Durham, NC: Duke University Press, 2008.

Brown, Kimberly Juanita. *The Repeating Body: Slavery's Visual Resonance in the Contemporary*. Durham, NC: Duke University Press, 2015.

"Burlesque Performer: You Are Not a Sex Worker." *21st Century Burlesque Magazine*, February 24, 2016. https://21stcenturyburlesque.com/burlesque-performer-you-are-not-a-sex-worker.

Camp, Stephanie M. H. *Closer to Freedom: Enslaved Women and Everyday Resistance in the Plantation South.* Chapel Hill: University of North Carolina Press, 2005.

Civil, Gabrielle. *Swallow the Fish.* Virginia: Civil Coping Mechanisms, 2017.

Davis, Adrienne D. "'Don't Let Nobody Bother Yo' Principle': The Sexual Economy of American Slavery." In *Black Sexual Economies*, edited by Adrienne D. Davis and the BSE Collective. Champaign: University of Illinois Press, 2019.

Friedman, Andrea. "'The Habitats of Sex-Crazed Perverts': Campaigns against Burlesque in Depression-Era New York City." *Journal of the History of Sexuality* 7, no. 2 (1996): 203–38.

Hartman, Saidiya V. *Scenes of Subjection: Terror, Slavery, and Self-Making in Nineteenth-Century America.* New York: Oxford University Press, 1997.

"Hortense Spillers and Gail Lewis at the Institute of Contemporary Arts." YouTube. Posted by Institute of Contemporary Arts, June 5, 2018. https://www.youtube.com/watch?v=tQoORQqSaWU.

Jackson, Zakiyyah Iman. *Becoming Human: Matter and Meaning in an Antiblack World.* New York: NYU Press, 2020.

Levine, Lawrence W. *Black Culture and Black Consciousness: Afro-American Folk Thought from Slavery to Freedom.* Oxford: Oxford University Press, 1978.

Lorde, Audre. "The Transformation of Silence into Language and Action." *Sinister Wisdom*, no. 6 (1978).

———. *Zami.* New York: Crossing Press. 1982.

McMillan, Uri. *Embodied Avatars: Genealogies of Black Feminist Art and Performance.* New York: NYU Press, 2015.

Mencken, H. L. *The American Language Supplement 1: The American Language: An Inquiry into the Development of English in the United States*, 4th ed. New York: Alfred A. Knopf, 1945.

Musser, Amber Jamilla. *Sensual Excess: Queer Femininity and Brown Jouissance.* New York: New York University Press, 2018.

O'Grady, Lorraine. *Writing in Space, 1973–2019.* Durham, NC: Duke University Press, 2020.

Owen, Ianna Hawkins. "Still, Nothing: Mammy and Black Asexual Possibility." *Feminist Review* 120, no. 1 (November 1, 2018): 70–84. https://doi.org/10.1057/s41305-018-0140-9.

Provost, Kara, and Audre Lorde. "Becoming Afrekete: The Trickster in the Work of Audre Lorde." *MELUS* 20, no. 4 (1995): 45–59. https://doi.org/10.2307/467889.

Quashie, Kevin. *The Sovereignty of Quiet: Beyond Resistance in Black Culture.* New Brunswick, NJ: Rutgers University Press, 2012.

Spillers, Hortense J. "Mama's Baby, Papa's Maybe: An American Grammar Book." *Diacritics* 17, no. 2 (1987): 65–81. https://doi.org/10.2307/464747.

———. "'An Order of Constancy': Notes on Brooks and the Feminine." *Centennial Review* 29, no. 2 (1985): 223–48.

———. "Play: *Sparebone*: Typed Draft," 1975. (Ms.2019.013) Box 18, Folder 11. Hortense J. Spillers papers, Brown University, Feminist Theory Archive.

Stallings, L. H. *Mutha Is Half a Word: Intersections of Folklore, Vernacular, Myth, and Queerness in Black Female Culture*. Columbus: Ohio State University Press, 2007. http://www.jstor.org/stable/j.ctt1kgqw94.

Stallybrass, Peter, and Allon White. *The Politics and Poetics of Transgression*. Ithaca, NY: Cornell University Press, 1986.

Stearns, Marshall, and Jean Stearns. *Jazz Dance: The Story of American Vernacular Dance*. New York: Hachette Books, 1994.

Sullivan, Mecca Jamilah. *The Poetics of Difference: Queer Feminist Forms in the African Diaspora*. Urbana: University of Illinois Press, 2021.

Weheliye, Alexander G. *Habeas Viscus: Racializing Assemblages, Biopolitics, and Black Feminist Theories of the Human*. Durham, NC: Duke University Press Books, 2014.

Wynter, Sylvia. "Unsettling the Coloniality of Being/Power/Truth/Freedom: Towards the Human, After Man, Its Overrepresentation—An Argument." *CR: The New Centennial Review* 3, no. 3 (2003): 257–337. https://doi.org/10.1353/ncr.2004.0015.

ARCHIVAL FRAGMENT 6. *Sparebone* program, 1970

November 17, 1992

Professor Hortense Spillers
Department of English
Emory University
Atlanta, Georgia

Dear Professor Spillers:

    I am writing on behalf of the Women's Studies program at Johns Hopkins Univerity to invite you to give a lecture for a one-day conference, "New Directions in Black Feminist Criticism", on Friday, April 2, 1993. We plan a small conference which will feature three distinguished scholars in the field: yourself, Deborah McDowell, and Cheryl Wall. We can, of course, cover your expenses, travel and accomodation, and offer you an honorarium of $500.00. We would be pleased to hear from you on any aspect of you work, and would like to ask you to speak for 45-50 minutes.

    I also wanted to thank you again for the trouble you took to come all the way out to California and to participate in the conference. I was sorry that my own health kept me from hanging out more, but I would love the chance to talk with you more about the kind of work you are doing. I very much appreciated your talk and have enormous respect for your contributions to literary theory. What is the chance that I can persuade you to accept this invitation? There are many of us here who are strong admirers of your work, and we would consider ourselves quite fortunate were you to accept our invitation.
    You can reach me at ███████████

                    Sincerely,

                    Judith Butler
                    Professor of Humanities

ARCHIVAL FRAGMENT 7. Letter to Hortense Spillers from Judith Butler, 1992

12 Grammars and Impression Points

Appreciating Hortense Spillers

DEBORAH E. MCDOWELL

In the opening paragraph of Spillers's 1977 essay "Ellison's 'Usable Past': Toward a Theory of Myth," she recounts the afternoon her instructor of American Literature at Memphis State University returned one of her essays with this comment: "Why be content with the lightning bug when you can have the lightning." I might adapt Professor Elizabeth Phillips's comment to her young college student and ask instead, "Why be content to be the lightning bug when you can be the lightning?" In the roughly four decades that I have known Hortense Spillers and avidly read (and learned from) her work, she has indeed been the lightning, producing a luminescent body of work of intellectual force and power, work that has energized, influenced, and transformed, a variety of critical conversations, foremost among them, Black Studies, feminist theory, gender and sexuality, and cultural studies, broadly speaking. In case you haven't detected it already, this short piece is an unabashed encomium for Hortense Spillers and her immense contributions to academic scholarship.

I actually knew of Hortense Spillers long before I ever met her. In that proverbial phrasing, her reputation had preceded her. Her name was summoned inevitably in any conversation in which African American women scholars gathered to discuss the state and fate of literary studies, Black studies, but more specifically, to consider our fate and future in the often-unwelcoming space of the US academy. Hortense was held up to those of us who entered the profession a few years after she did, as one who set the standards to which we should all aspire. Of course, no one told us that emulating Hortense Spillers was a bar few of us could ever reach, even if we worked all day every day and twice on Sunday. Those of us who knew that decided that we could, at best, aspire to learn from her. And learn from her, we did.

In that 1977 essay, published but three years after she received her PhD from Brandeis, we see Spillers's intellectual signature: her habits of mind, her expansiveness of vision, her consistent investments, her theoretical amplitude, the depth and breadth of reading, evident in the astonishing range of reference in literally everything she writes. Here, in "Ellison's 'Usable Past'" she is thinking with Jorge Luis Borges, Roland Barthes, Dante, Ortega y Gasset, Northrup Frye, Ferdinand Saussure, Joseph Campbell, the King James Bible. In reading this piece, I am reminded of that famous passage from *The Souls of Black Folk*, in which Du Bois claims as his intellectual province any thinker in the broader pantheon of world literature:

> I sit with Shakespeare, and he winces not. Across the color line, I move arm and arm with Balzac and Dumas, where smiling men and welcoming women glide in gilded halls. From out of the caves of evening that swing between the strong-limbed Earth and the tracery of stars, I summon Aristotle and Aurelius and what soul I will, and they come all graciously with no scorn nor condescension. . . . Is this the life you grudge us, O knightly America? Is this the life you long to change into the dull red hideousness of Georgia? Are you so afraid lest peering from this high Pisgah, between Philistine and Amalekite, we sight the Promised Land?

Importantly the references in Spillers's work are in no wise merely ornamental, "show-offy," pedantic, or self-indulgent; rather, they are evidence of a mind at work, thinking and engaging deeply with other minds across the span of centuries, just as many of her most ardent fans and readers have aspired to think and engage with Spillers, to grapple with the often-demanding force of her writing, as well as the stakes—at times uncomfortable stakes—it always announces.

In his introduction to "W. E. B. Du Bois and the Questions of Another World," a special issue of *The New Centennial Review*, in which Spillers also has an essay, Nahum Chandler describes Du Bois's "indefatigable commitment to the labor of thought" and his "respect of justice."[1] This description applies with equal aptness to Hortense. Diffused throughout everything she writes is evidence of a thinker discontent with intellectual simplicities and complacencies, a thinker with fine-grained critical insights and discriminations. But these insights and discriminations, to borrow Spillers's own words, have always been in the interest of making a "contribution to a larger project" that might move us toward some semblance of justice or what she termed in "Chosen Place, Timeless People," an essay on Paule Marshall, "our best hopes for a New World humanity."

Something is always at stake for Spillers. In the essays she published in the 1980s, for which she is perhaps best known—"Mama's Baby, Papa's Maybe," "Interstices, A Small Drama of Words," for example—she situates herself within the larger project of feminist and Black feminist studies. As she notes in "Whatcha Gonna Do?': Revisiting "Mama's Baby, Papa's Maybe: An American Grammar Book," a conversation with Saidhya Hartman and others:

> What I was trying to do when I wrote [that essay] was to find a vocabulary that would make it possible, and not all by myself, to make a contribution to a larger project. I was looking for my generation of black women who were so active in other ways, to open a conversation with feminists. Because my idea about where we found ourselves in the late 1970s and the mid-1980s, was that we were really out of the conversation that we had, in some ways, historically initiated. In other words, the women's movement and the black movement have always been in tandem, but what I saw happening was black people being treated as a kind of raw material. That the history of black people was something you could use as a note of inspiration but it was never anything that had anything to do with you? You could never use it to explain something in theoretical terms. There was no discourse that it generated, in terms of the mainstream academy that gave it a kind of recognition. And so my idea was to try to generate a

discourse, or a vocabulary that would not just make it desirable but would necessitate that black women be in the conversation.[2]

Thanks to Spillers, and many others, of course, Black women were "in the conversation," changing it, quarreling with it, insisting that their work not just be recognized, but also engaged. Just as important, Black women were in conversation with each other in the mid-80s, united in the understanding captured in the title of that iconic anthology, *All the Women Are White, All the Blacks Are Men, but Some of Us are Brave*. As Spillers notes, "editors Gloria T. Hull, Patricia Bell Scott, and Barbara Smith realize[d] that public discourse—certainly its most radical critical statements included—lapses into a cul-de-sac when it approaches this community of [Black] women and their writers."[3]

While Spillers's intellectual contributions range across a vast territory of scholarly inquiry, I have personally felt her greatest impact over the interrelated fields of scholarly inquiry commanding my own academic foci and occupations for the past forty years: 1) the writings of African American women / feminist criticism and 2) the origins and development of Black Studies as an institutional/bureaucratic entity within the mainstream academy of the United States. Allow me to take these topics up, albeit briefly, with specific reference to the following Spillers essays, discussed in no particular order, nor in any thoroughgoing way. Typically, far less engaged than the canonical "Mama's Baby, Papa's Maybe," these essays—"A Hateful Passion, A Lost Love" (1983), "Cross-Currents, Discontinuities: Black Women's Fiction" (1985), "*The Crisis of the Negro Intellectual*: A Post-Date" (1994) and "The Idea of Black Culture" (2006)—establish, with equal intellectual force and rigor, the "impression points" (a recursive term for Spillers) of her entire corpus. Because of the sheer elegance and aesthetics of her prose, as often as possible, I will allow Spillers to speak in her own words, words that have changed so many of mine/ours.

The Community of Black Women Writing

Throughout my writing and teaching on African American women writers, I have relied upon Spillers as a guidepost and lodestone, most especially in the units focusing on the 1980s, that watershed decade in their broader literary history, when to borrow Spillers's often-quoted line, "the community of Black women writing in the United States" came to be "regarded as a vivid new fact of national life."[4] Her 1983 essay "A Hateful Passion" focuses on what she terms "changes in black female characterization" as represented in three novels by Black women—Toni Morrison's *Sula*, Margaret Walker's *Jubilee*, and Zora Neale Hurston's *Their Eyes Were Watching God*—but the overarching investments of that piece concern "laying to rest ... the formulation of the critical postulates that govern our various epistemologies," especially regarding "the black female personality." As she notes, "when the black female personality exists at all in the vocabulary of public symbols," it is through the "limited repertoire of powerless virtue and sentimental pathos."[5] Spillers argues that, with her novel *Sula*, Toni Morrison broke that calcified mold, introducing a "rebel idea" and a new structure of feeling that inscribed a new dimension of Black female being. Trapped historically in political and ideological struggles, this "black female being" necessitated from the artist new figurations, and from the audience of readers, especially academics, new theories and interpretations. Such interpretations had long been mired in reflexive interpretive arrangements that center "an 'oppressor,' a 'whitey,' a male, a dominant and dominating being outside the self." Spillers goes on to say, "No Manichean analysis demanding a polarity of interest—black/white, male/female, good/bad—will work here," for in the end, what ails Sula is traceable to "the absence of a discursive, imaginative project."[6] While I and classes of students have often wrestled with just how much we want to accept this reading, as we ponder how/if a "self" can be so easily abstracted from structures of domination, we also know that Spillers's reading can't simply be dismissed. Indeed, that Sula lacks a "discursive, imaginative project" must be owing, at least in part, to the structures of domination within which she must live and move up there in oppressive landscape of "The Bottom." It is not at all surprising to me that Spillers places such faith in the power of Black women's discursive projects, faith in the transformative power of their work as creative intellectuals, for her career-long "passion" has existed in this very thing: making and mapping the world/s of discourse, while refusing to see Black women consigned to their outposts and peripheries. Never inclined to read simplistically or to homogenize complexities, in "Hateful" Spillers is prepared to concede that "Black women writers likely agree on a single point: whatever the portrayal of female character yields, it will be rendered from the point of view of one whose eyes are not alien to the humanity in front of them."[7]

To reinforce the arguments she makes about Sula as rebel woman-for-self, Spillers reads Morrison's "breakthrough" character in relation to Walker's Vyree (*Jubilee*) and Hurston's Janie (*Their Eyes*). Collectively, they constitute "peak points in a cultural and historical configuration of literary issues," that function to challenge the very idea of "literary tradition," an idea predicated all too often on unexamined assumptions about "movement" "development," and on misunderstandings of chronology. Admittedly, having already deployed in my own work, and introduced to my students, an uncritical understanding of "tradition," Spillers served as corrective, not simply in "A Hateful Passion," but also in "Cross-Currents, Discontinuities: Black Women's Fiction," her afterword to *Conjuring: Black Women, Fiction, and Literary Tradition*, co-edited with Marjorie Pryse. There, she reminds us, as have multiple theorists before her, that "Traditions are not born. They are made. We would add that they are not, like objects of nature, here to stay, but survive as *created social events* only to the extent that an audience cares to intersect them."[8]

Spillers credits the "work of black women's writing community" with contributing to an ongoing, and necessary, redefinition of "tradition," especially by "suggesting that the term itself is a critical fable intended to encode and circumscribe an inner and licit circle of empowered texts."[9] She understands, needless to say, that historically Black women have not been inside that magic circle, no matter who happened to be drawing it. But lest that statement be misread as a bid for "inclusion," Spillers makes a bold move, one empowering herself and other members of Black women's writing communities to "stand outside that circle and, in fact, to try to *choose* this standing-apart-from as the locus of a radical dissent and critique that the collective and individual 'I' must keep alive for the duration."[10]

The imperative of "aliveness" for Spillers explains, not just her critique of "tradition," but also her critique of the accepted and taken-for-granted nominative "Black women writers." Throughout "Crosscurrents" she refers to "the community of black women *writing*" (emphasis mine). As she explains in the very opening sentence of that afterword, "I deliberately substitute the participle for the noun to suggest not only the palpable and continuing urgency of black women writing themselves into history, but also to convey the variety of aims that accompany that project."[11] Spillers's deliberate choice of "writing" instead of "writers" works to reinforce the arguments she makes above about the fictions and fables of tradition along with their circumscribing effects. The aliveness of the participle, "writing," proffers an invitation to construct a new "grammar" for literary and cultural studies, even a new "grammar of motives" for such study, to borrow the title of one of Spillers's constant interlocutors, Kenneth Burke. In re-reading the essays selected for this encomium, it became even clearer to me that Spillers's clarion calls for and invitations to construct new grammars, vocabularies, and epistemologies, extend far beyond the realm of literary studies / feminist theory. Her essays on the origins and development of Black/Africana Studies in the US academy give those calls a particular urgency, never more so than at this moment in the history of US higher education.

The Mission/s of Black Study

In *"The Crisis of the Negro Intellectual:* A Post-Date," Spillers takes as her point of departure Harold Cruse's classic and controversial text *The Crisis of the Negro Intellectual* (1967). When she published this essay in 1994, the twenty-fifth anniversary of Cruse's text had passed without notice, although the critiques and urgencies Cruse's book raised at the time of its publication remained no less urgent in 1994. Spillers sets herself the task of exploring, among others, three vitally urgent and interrelated questions: 1) "what is the work of the black creative intellectual?" 2) what constitutes a "crisis" for the African American creative intellectual at the moment? 3) "can we begin to map the [intellectual] terrain anew?"[12]

In an earlier essay, Spillers had conceded that "certain ideas . . . can only be approached with a very wide-angled lens."[13] and she takes that wide-angled approach in this roughly fifty-page essay. This piece must be read and re-read, for the following brief summary could never capture the layered and complex arrangements that generally define Spillers's interrogations, and those arrangements are evident in this essay, in particular. Here, while we find Spillers acknowledging, as ever, her "restlessness to change and inform [her] own conceptual language," the essay captures her equal restlessness to change the conceptual language and terms, along with the reflexive questions that have led to the very "crisis" (if not "crises") confronting the Black creative intellectuals intergenerationally.[14]

While considering a range of concepts and vocabularies circulating throughout discourses of Black Studies, at least since its belated arrival in predominantly white mainstream academic institutions in the late 1960s and early '70s, Spillers reserves her most trenchant insights for the concept of "community." As she notes, "Perhaps the 'purest' object that black creative intellectual always imagines as the unmediated 'thereness' is situated in his/her concept of natal community."[15] And after exploring in expansive detail what that concept has meant historically to a diverse group of Black intellectuals, including W. E. B. Du Bois and Harold Cruse, Spillers concludes unapologetically, that "the time has come for us to rethink community." The "Black intellectual's current view of community is not only fictional," she argues, but it also "describes an inadequate fiction."[16] She continues, "for both Du Bois and Cruse, community stood in for a preeminent stability." Although "both writers left its borders [of 'community'] open to expansion," the cultural analyses of that concept, notes Spillers, "has not moved beyond the benchmarks left by" these two intellectuals.[17] And perhaps that stagnation helps to explain, at least in part, the reflexive questions the "community" concept has provoked perennially for Black scholars, at least since the 1960s. For the intellectuals of that decade and since, "community became . . . an obsessive feature of speech, underscored by a certain anxiety." That anxiety manifested itself variously, but most repetitively in versions of the question: "What responsibility does the Black intellectual have to the Black community?" or, more bluntly, "What will you do to save your people?" have persisted.

In *"Crisis"* Spillers plops herself right down in the middle of these questions and debates, focusing on perhaps one of their most lamentable iterations: "The Special Responsibility of the Black Intellectual in the

Age of Crack," a public forum held in Boston in 1994, the year Spillers published this essay. Permit me a minor detour here to call attention to Spillers's wit and humor, which any reading of her essays will already have revealed. In response to the question, Spillers asks "Isn't it also the 'age' of email?"[18] She then asks the essential question: "what does it mean to sum up the age under the rubric of crack ... and who said that the black creative intellectual could even begin to know how to fix it?" Spillers then provocatively turns this tiresome question regarding "social responsibility" on its head by asking, "What is the obligation of white intellectuals to *their* people?"[19] The unstated assumption, of course, is that white intellectuals bear a primary "responsibility"—and have earned a right—to pursue their intellectual projects freely, fully, and without regard for "the community," narrowly defined. Spillers claims that right—as well as that responsibility—for herself as well as other Black creative intellectuals. But if she relieves Black creative intellectuals of the "responsibility" of "saving" their communities, she does not relieve them of the responsibility to rethink the idea of community, to see it as an "object of knowledge," a site of inquiry, a "position in discourse," as a "layering of negotiable differences" that cannot be contained within the "palm of the hand."[20]

To those who would argue that academic "intellectuals must go back to community," Spillers rejoins, the intellectuals inevitably bring the community with them, bearing it "between [their] ears." Spillers challenges "black creative intellectuals" to see "the academy as their laboratory, to "get busy where they are," fulfilling a responsibility to "reading, writing, and teaching."[21] Black intellectuals are not in the "salvation 'business,'" she argues, and can only "save" via the only way they know how: as "reader[s]/writer[s]/thinker[s]/teacher[s]."[22]

Buried in a lengthy footnote (Spillers's footnotes are often essays unto themselves), deep into this wide-ranging and erudite essay on *The Crisis of the Negro Intellectual*, Spillers suggests, perhaps in anticipation of the controversy her own essay might elicit, "the work of the intellectual is to make her reader/hearer discomfited, unoriented and, therefore, self-critical. She is not, in fact, a "Dr. Feelgood," or "Mr. Goodbar."[23]

In essays and interviews that followed upon the *"The Crisis of the Negro Intellectual,"* Spillers continues her work of discomfiting and disorienting, of challenging the conceptual complacencies that have tended to define Black Studies. Asked by Keith Leonard to comment on whether there "could be and should be a direct connection between what goes on in the discipline in the university and what goes on in the community on the streets," Spillers answered,

> I always thought that the community was never located just in a particular place but that the community was wherever I was. If I was in a university, that was fine because the community was there with me by implication. Therefore, I didn't see any reason why any black person in the academy should feel apologetic about being out of the community because the community was there. So, that's what I thought. I still tend to think so even though that is probably the most difficult plane to maintain or to hold up because in some ways it's patently obvious that, demographically, there is a difference. But I always thought that perhaps one of the problems with certain Black Studies formulations was deciding that you could draw boundaries or limits to what community was and what it meant by confining it within certain square feet. You know, Roxbury, Harlem, all of those and communities like them all across the United States, I always thought that they extended or expanded their borders as people who belonged to them, people who were natally or natively born to them, ended up someplace else. . . . But I have also thought that one of the ways to define community is to expand it, to embrace what people do in the community so that you expand the definition of community.[24]

Ultimately, Spillers's insights about "community" in academic disciplines and discourse compels an inward look at the workings, protocols, and arrangements of the increasingly corporatized university, particularly as they relate to Black Studies. Like other interdisciplinary fields of study, the "value" of Black Studies remains contested and subject to arbitrary measuring rods. In the interview with Keith Leonard, Spillers stresses the importance of scholarship for the sake of scholarship and not "simply for the sake of the polls and for the ratings game." Black Studies, she goes on to say, must "become a critique of that style of procedure and operation and to reward scholarship because scholarship teaches us something. That it has a value that you can assign a place to that is not just an aspect of GNP, you know that it has a place in the spiritual GNP. And that's what I would like to see Black Studies help universities do, to come back to a recognition of the actual place of scholarship in the world."[25]

The trajectory of Hortense Spillers's distinguished fifty-year career demonstrates that she has recognized the place of that scholarship in the world. "Acting in and on behalf of community" from her perch in multiple academic institutions, she has understood, as she put in a recent interview with Denise Ferreira da Silva, "thinking is not a luxury. It's not about leisure. It's not fun and games." I agree with da Silva that Spillers's texts "exemplify methods, they are . . . instances of ways to think critically. Her words, whether delivered in recollections or reflections, host, drag, and brush against your thinking, demanding that it go further into and through the complexities it must address."[26] Indeed, what Spillers observes of Paule Marshall's novel *The Chosen Place, The Timeless People* (1969) can be said of her own work: "although the work does not confront the reader with an opacity or impenetrability of surface, it demands . . . as much care of the detail from the reader as the detail has received from the writer."[27] Such care is demanded of Hortense Spillers's own work and the returns on that care and investment are infinitely rewarding.

Notes

1. Nahum D. Chandler, introduction to "W. E. B. Du Bois and the Questions of Another World," special issue, *CR: The New Centennial Review* 6. no. 3, (Winter 2006), 1–5, 2.
2. "'Whatcha Gonna Do?': Revisiting 'Mama's Baby, Papa's Maybe: An American Grammar Book': A Conversation with Hortense Spillers, Saidiya Hartman, Farah Jasmine Griffin, Shelly Eversley, and Jennifer L. Morgan," *Women's Studies Quarterly* 35, no. 1/2, (Spring-Summer 2007), 299–309, 300.
3. Hortense J. Spillers, "A Hateful Passion, A Lost Love: Three Women's Fiction." In *Black, White, and in Color: Essays on American Literature and Culture*, 93–118 (Chicago: University of Chicago Press, 2003), 321.
4. Hortense J. Spillers, "Cross-Currents, Discontinuities: Black Women's Fiction," In *Conjuring: Black Women, Fiction, and Literary Tradition*, edited by Marjorie Lee Pryse and Hortense J. Spillers, 249–61. (Bloomington: Indiana University Press, 1985), 249.
5. Spillers, "A Hateful Passion," 297.

6. Spillers, "A Hateful Passion," 296.
7. Spillers, "A Hateful Passion," 297.
8. Spillers, "Cross-Currents," 250.
9. Spillers, "Cross-Currents," 251.
10. Spillers, "Cross-Currents," 251.
11. Spillers, "Cross-Currents," 249.
12. Hortense J. Spillers, *"The Crisis of the Negro Intellectual*: A Post-Date," *boundary 2* 21, no. 3 (1994): 65–116, 73, 67.
13. Hortense J. Spillers, "'The Permanent Obliquity of an In(pha)llibly Straight': In the Time of the Daughters and the Fathers," in *Changing Our Own Words: Essays on Criticism, Theory, and Writing by Black Women*, ed. Cheryl A. Wall, 127–49 (New Brunswick: Rutgers University Press, 1989), 128.
14. Spillers, *"The Crisis of the Negro Intellectual,"* 89.
15. Spillers, *"The Crisis of the Negro Intellectual,"* 102.
16. Spillers, *"The Crisis of the Negro Intellectual,"* 102.
17. Spillers, *"The Crisis of the Negro Intellectual,"* 103.
18. Spillers, *"The Crisis of the Negro Intellectual,"* 101.
19. Spillers, *"The Crisis of the Negro Intellectual,"* 101.
20. Spillers, *"The Crisis of the Negro Intellectual,"* 104.
21. Spillers, *"The Crisis of the Negro Intellectual,"* 92–93.
22. Spillers, *"The Crisis of the Negro Intellectual,"* 102.
23. Spillers, *"The Crisis of the Negro Intellectual,"* 83.
24. Keith D. Leonard and Hortense Spillers, "First Questions: The Mission of Africana Studies: An Interview with Hortense Spillers," *Callaloo* 30, no. 4 (Fall 2007): 1,057.
25. Leonard and Spillers, "First Questions," 1,064.
26. "Sending Language into Battle: Interview with Hortense Spillers," *boundary 2* 51, no. 1 (2024): 3.
27. Hortense J. Spillers, "*Chosen Place, Timeless People*: Some Figurations on the New World," in *Conjuring: Black Women, Fiction, and Literary Tradition*, ed. Marjorie Lee Pryse and Hortense J. Spillers, 151–75 (Bloomington: Indiana University Press, 1985).

13 Bridging Figurations
Hortense J. Spillers, Essayist

THADIOUS M. DAVIS

I have a particularly deep fondness for *Conjuring: Black Women, Fiction, and Literary Tradition*, the 1985 collection edited by Marjorie Pryse and Hortense Spillers that goes way back to before it was published. No, this is not a backstory about times spent discussing the proposed edition of essays or long conversations about the inclusions. Instead it is something quite different, which speaks to a very different time for so many Black Women academics during the 1980s who started out in the 1970s, and the silences and opacity in our lives then but also now. Hortense and Marjorie invited me to submit an essay, but unknown to them I was struggling as the caregiver for my terminally ill grandmother who had come to live with me, supposedly temporarily, in Chapel Hill after what was diagnosed as a case of heat exhaustion in New Orleans. Indeed struggling, I was barely able to maintain my three-class teaching schedule and other departmental duties, even though the transparent view was only that I had achieved tenure and promotion to full professor. A highwire balancing act of struggle! But Hortense and Marjorie had no idea. That invitation was a bright spot in a dismal period. Even though I could not manage to submit a piece, I loved that I was asked, and still imagine what it would have meant had I been able to muster time and energy, "elbow room" à la Georgia Douglas Johnson, to send them a feminist essay on Nella Larsen. This is a brief bridging backstory that Hortense has never heard. But it's why I treasure *Conjuring* and know its essay landscape intimately from teaching its terrain.

This affection for *Conjuring* together with recognition of opacity in the blues-inflected lives of Black women in academia leads me to meditate on the significance of the essay form for Black women scholars, critics, theorists, and creative writers, especially for Hortense emerging in the 1980s. When *Conjuring* appeared in 1985 with Hortense's essay, "*Chosen Place, Timeless People*: Some Figurations on the New World," and her "Afterword: Cross-Currents, Discontinuities: Black Women's Fiction" who could have imagined the theoretical and historical impact on the critical turn to Black theoretical writing, feminist critical thinking, and African diasporic reading. It was a time when the New Critics still held sway and when Marshall McLuhan's message was not quite resonating. Above all, it was a time when to evoke culture in writing about Black literature was deemed sociology. Telescoping, Hortense wrote of Paule Marshall's novel that it was "a staged dialectics of human involvement that will reinvoke . . . our best hopes for a New World Humanity."[1] But she also observed "the individual and converging dramas unfold[ing] on a historical background that articulates the urgencies of *difference* primarily by way of the dynamics and psychodynamics of ritual."[2] What I find especially compelling is the language specifically related to grammar and writing itself. Spillers acknowledges the work of rhetoric and Kenneth Burke's *Grammar of Motives* in her analysis of *Chosen Place, Timeless People*.[3] She writes, for instance, that "figurative alliances within the delegated narrative," situate "contrastive degrees of mimetic experience side by side," "allow[ing] interpretation to range freely within the borders of related grammars."[4] Such language points to the meticulous inner workings of the critical essay for the accomplished essayist.

In the first iteration of this essay, for a panel celebrating Hortense's retirement, I observed that sitting together for that occasion were Hortense J. Spillers and Deborah E. McDowell, whose "The Neglected Dimension of Jessie Redmon Fauset" also appeared in *Conjuring*.[5] The two are the incomparable essayists from their generation of Black women feminist critics. Both were consummate essayists from the very start of their careers. Academia is the richer not only for their pioneering work but also for their perseverance in writing stellar, ambitious, brilliant, and luminous essays.[6] Not surprisingly, when Cheryl Wall's edited collection *Changing Our Own Words: Essays on Criticism, Theory, and Writing by Black Women* appeared in 1989, a few years after *Conjuring*, it contained three essays that would soon become iconic: Hortense's "'The Permanent Obliquity of an In(pha)llibly Straight': In the Time of the Daughters and the Fathers" and Deborah's "Reading Family Matters," along with Mae G. Henderson's "Speaking in Tongues: Dialogics, Dialectics, and the Black Woman Writer's Literary Tradition."[7] These three essays, as Cheryl would point out years later, also formed the theoretical and critical seeds that inspired her own monograph *Worrying the Line: Black Women Writers, Lineage, and Literary Tradition* (2005). Furthermore, I suspect that had Cheryl Wall extended her 2018 book, *On Freedom and the Will to Adorn: The Art of the African American Essay*, beyond creative writers, she would have turned to the Black women essayists issuing from the 1980s.[8]

The very genius of these essayists, scholar-critics may not have been valued then, but it is now. In Hortense's case, in particular, her capacious work has ignited a generation of followers and admirers. That is one of the amazing stories to be celebrated and acknowledged as tradition, which Hortense had already forecast in *Conjuring* as "an active verb, rather than a retired nominative.... Quite correctly 'tradition' under the head of a polyvalent grammar—the language of learning woven into the tongue of the mother—is the rare union of bliss toward which African-American experience has compelled us all along."[9] There, Hortense with "the language of learning woven into the tongue of the mother" is at once speaking about the creative writing of African American women and speaking to the critical essay writing by African American women, comprising the larger "Black America women's writing community."

Hortense ended her afterword to *Conjuring* with the awareness that "emergent communities" are demanding "that we now consider our shared symbolic economies in light of patriarchist *and* heterosexual hegemony," and foreshadowing, she wrote, "the literatures of the American classroom changes."[10] "The day will come," she dared to predict, "when the Black America women's writing community will reflect the currents both of the new critical procedures and the various literatures concurrent with them."[11] "If that happens, [she speculated] the academy meets life, and life the academy, in a situation of emphases neither of whose resonance and value we can afford to deny in our own small strivings."[12]

Conjuring and those 1980s collections of Black women's essays are intricately connected to teaching and making new ideas accessible for classrooms and teacher practitioners. What these scholars understood perhaps intuitively was that the essay, not the larger book, was the wave of the future. Without that teaching laboratory access and dissemination, the much-vaunted scholarly book that for so long had been and continues to be the academic standard for tenure and promotion could not yield the portability and impact of the essay in the classroom or subsequent longevity in actual lives. As Hortense also mused in the afterword: "Students become adult readers sometimes who expect their learned values to be flattened and, in turn, valorize (and buy) that literature which they have been taught to value as 'hard' and 'really good.' (It might be interesting to study, though, to what extent the *permissible* culture is undermined among undergraduate populations by 'soap opera' forms, or Every Intelligent Person's 'Nancy Drew' fiction that she/he hides between the covers of the infamous brown paper bag.)"[13]

Prescient remarks on an eventual transformation in pedagogy! One of the unmarked aspects of the power of the essay is its ability to reshape intellectual thought and spark critical dialog particularly in the classroom. Extracted from the edited collection or large tome, the essay basically becomes a teachable object and subject that has a life of its own, independent of the scholarly book. Pushing the theoretical inventory, catalyzing the field, and exploding old notions of how to be impactful in a discipline while turning that very discipline into something new can now be witnessed in the legacy today in popular culture, televisual forms, graphic novels, digital media, blogs, podcasts, op eds, and articles in the once and future holy grail of periodical publications, magazines and newspapers, that was the work issuing from Hortense and the essayists of the 1980s. Inevitably they gave birth to a new generation of racial scholars with a journalistic bent seeded in popular discourse and culturally specific discursive often restorative acts. Portability of Black women's intellectual thought by the 1990s meant that many comers began to glean from the new syllabi and to read the transcripts of Black feminist intellectuality, just as Hortense predicted. A visionary thinker, she well understood that the signs of the body and of the mind were not inseparable in labor, living, and loving.

Reading the "hieroglyphics of the flesh" and mapping history in writing on and in the flesh, Hortense has indeed survived all that Audre Lorde broached in "Who Said It Would Be Simple," and Hortense has become the single most quoted and modeled essayist of that generation, not simply a theoretician of Black American life with a feminist or womanist stance, but a cultural seer surveying the literary and historical landscape from the vestige point of her own Black body and mindset.[14] Often outrageously adventuresome, she has defined the process and practice by which to capture her own intellectual and aesthetic vision; that is, by contemplating her own female body and flesh and determining that what she beheld was a continent, not an island, a body politic that could be extrapolated to message and interrogate whole entire arenas of thought, desire, and need. That work makes the racial gendered body the subject field for scholarly inquiry but effectively it draws a map to signpost a known yet unexplored and overlooked body, at once historical and philosophical. What brazen thought! It is exactly what Ralph Ellison identified in a Black cultural rebuttal to a misguided charge of Black absence in "Change the Joke, Slip the Yoke."[15] That is why it is important and significant to recognize a woman who understood the manifold jokes and ubiquitous yokes, and who commandeered and commanded in ways that only now all these many years later may be read in the essays, the trenchant malleable works of an inimitable process and practice.

All eyes are on Hortense now, some with understanding, many in imitation, others clueless and along for the high ride though the slippage. But some, quietly working though the undeniably Black woman's witty and wise navel gazing, sly, playfulness in the space of a few words, an extended title, or an entire essay while designing, building, and elevating the tactile particles of Black women's intellectual thought in the 1980s to a new standard evident to some by the 1990s and apparent to many in the new millennium. Hortense managed to break through to that other realm imagined in Octavia Butler's *Parable of the Sower*.[16]

Standing joyfully in the space with those who were brave and wrote out of their capacious knowledge and bodily convictions, she demanded space, announced presence, and modeled belonging. Hortense kept on pushing through storms and fog, and through bad times of noticed or unremarked tolls on Black living in these Americas, but heralding the good times of light and power, joy and grace to be and showing how to be empowered and to comprehend the meanings of power. With full-throated laughter, a mischievous ambiance, elegant demeanor, and unmistakable voice, all grounded in intellectual rigor and figured in folk ethics, that pathbreaking Hortense is here, her whole self here, standing in her own light, radiating and narrativizing outward to all who now see so that they and we too can continue in sightedness and rejoice in grace and the word.

Notes

1. Hortense J. Spillers, "*Chosen Place, Timeless People*: Some Figurations on the New World," in *Conjuring: Black Women, Fiction, and Literary Tradition*, ed. Marjorie Pryse and Hortense J. Spillers (Bloomington: Indiana University Press, 1985), 152.
2. Spillers, "*Chosen Place, Timeless People*," 160.
3. Spillers points out that she adopts the pentad of terms from Burke's "Introduction: The Five Key Terms of Dramatism," in *Grammar of Motives* (New York: Prentice-Hall, 1945), x–xvi.
4. Spillers, "*Chosen Place, Timeless People*," 170–71.
5. Deborah E. McDowell, "The Neglected Dimension of Jessie Redmon Fauset," in Pryse and Spillers, *Conjuring*, 86–104.
6. See, for example, Deborah E. McDowell, "*The Changing Same*": *Black Women's Literature, Criticism, Theory* (Bloomington: Indiana University Press, 1995).
7. See Hortense J. Spillers, "'The Permanent Obliquity of an In(pha)llibly Straight': In the Time of the Daughters and the Fathers," in *Changing Our Own Words: Essays on Criticism, Theory, and Writing by Black Women*, ed. Cheryl A. Wall, 127–49 (New Brunswick: Rutgers University Press, 1989); Deborah E. McDowell, "Reading Family Matters," in Wall, *Changing Our Own Words*, 75–97; and Mae G. Henderson, "Speaking in Tongues: Dialogics, Dialectics, and the Black Woman Writer's Literary Tradition," in Wall, *Changing Our Own Words*, 16–57.
8. See Cheryl A. Wall, *On Freedom and the Will to Adorn: The Art of the African American Essay* (Chapel Hill: University of North Carolina Press, 2018).
9. Hortense J. Spillers, "Afterword: Cross-Currents, Discontinuities: Black Women's Fiction," in Pryse and Spillers, *Conjuring*, 260.

10. Spillers, "Afterword," 259.
11. Spillers, "Afterword," 259.
12. Spillers, "Afterword," 260.
13. Spillers, "Afterword," 259.
14. See Hortense J. Spillers on the "hieroglyphics of the flesh" in "Mama's Baby, Papa's Maybe: An American Grammar Book." *Diacritics* 17, no. 2 (1987): 65–81. See also Audre Lorde, "Who Said It Was Simple," in *A Land Where Other People Live* (Detroit: Broadside Press, 1973); reprinted in *The Collected Poems of Audre Lorde* (New York: Norton, 1997).
15. See Ralph Ellison, "Change the Joke, Slip the Yoke," in *The Collected Essays of Ralph Ellison*, ed. James F. Callahan (1995; New York: The Modern Library, 2003), 100–112. Ellison's essay first appeared in *Partisan Review* (Spring 1958) and subsequently in *Shadow and Act* (1964), his first collection of essays. He concludes his 1958 response to Edgar Stanley Hyman's essay "on the relationship between Negro American literature and Negro American folklore" by stating: "for the novelist of any culture or racial identity, his form is his greatest freedom, and his insights are where he finds them." Ellison, "Change the Joke," 112.
16. See Octavia Butler, *Parable of the Sower* (1993; New York: Grand Central Publishing, 2000).

3)

[In the Flesh: a Situation for Feminist Inquiry] as a cultural construct, that repeats and reflects the dominative is that "gender" is nothing more or less than a rift in the global community of women that divides this world between the ~~West and the rest of us~~. To my mind, "gender" might be problematized at least two ways:
3. "Gender" does not only differentiate the cultural project along "men" from "women," "male"/"female," but it also separated "women-in-culture," who have "gender" from women-vestibular-to-line culture, who, according to the historic privileges of motherhood, stand <u>outside</u> the prerogatives of female gender, or the situations of gender. My special- Reasons for: sex-ized use of this term as a ~~nominal~~ political wea- ual pon will become obvious. this category differ-
4. I am identifying within the category of ence historic subjects African-American women, who, in their <u>historic situatedness</u>, pose a dramatic problem to the ways and means of feminist investigation; that community of women, <u>unprecedented</u> in theoretical narrative, which gives one a body, or layers of discursive clothing that protects the flesh from assault; layers of <u>naming</u>, <u>iconography</u>, <u>symbolization</u> (which, even if they add up to "unrepresentability,") pose a subject that cannot be said in the first place — — a contradiction in terms, if the sheer quantity of works on, about, for women in the last 15 years of life on either side of the Atlantic is taken into consideration.
5. Communities of women who have "body" — — on an analogy with communities of men who have the

ARCHIVAL FRAGMENT 8. "In the Flesh," handwritten talk

14 "All the Things You Could Be and All the Things You Are"

SHARON P. HOLLAND

> "race" is destiny in the world we have made.
> —Hortense Spillers

I. New York, October 20, 1961

Charles Mingus fashioned the beginnings of a tune called "All the Things You Could Be by Now, If Sigmund Freud's Wife Was Your Mother" sometime in the 1940s. It wasn't pressed into vinyl until 1961 as a Candid Records release on an album called "Charles Mingus Presents Charles Mingus." Introducing the "composition," to his audience, Mingus says that it is "dedicated to all mothers, and it's titled, 'All the Things You Could Be by Now, If Sigmund Freud's Wife Was Your Mother,' which means if Sigmund Freud's wife was your mother, all the things you could be by now, which means . . . nothing." It is no small irony that in psychoanalytic thought, Lacan (active since the 1920s in the discipline) began to forge his own direction as distinct from Freud in the early to mid-1960s.

The original 1961 liner notes, written by Nat Hentoff and replicated on the 2012 180-gram pressing by WaxTime Records, indicate that Mingus believed the title of the song stemmed from "the way the audience was reacting one night." In *I Know What I Know: The Music of Charles Mingus*, Todd S. Jenkins takes more license with Mingus's take on the audience, stating that they "got out of hand during a concert."[1] The difference here—one of interpretation—is slight, but worth noting. Those who "get out of hand" invite discipline or rebuke. And if the substance of the rebuke is to be reminded of "all the things you could be by now, if Sigmund Freud's wife was your mother," then we might think upon this proposition, this imaginary of a scene that produces both a wife and a mother in the context of Freud's own family, then a child is certainly being beaten. The staging here brings to the listener and the literary a range of possibilities, and we know from at least Freud's work that "the child being beaten is never the one producing the phantasy but is invariably another child, most often a brother or a sister if there is any."[2] The scene of rebuke—the dis here—opens up a kaleidoscopic affective life for human being, all in the service of solidifying that thing called "family" or at least demarcating filial bonds while simultaneously producing the specific qualities of one's pleasure. All the things . . . is all about our collective ph/fantasy as a community, and of course, dedicated to all mothers. {It also references, not too subtly, the pleasure we take in the violence among us.}

What interests me in Jenkins's take on Mingus's music, is a note at the beginning of his book from Sue Graham Mingus about illegal releases, record piracy and general malfeasance in the record industry. Her critique is blistering: "While it is understandable that reviewers call attention to formerly out-of-print or rare recordings for the buying public when they are released legitimately, they would do well to examine the shoddy behavior of entrepreneurs masquerading as collectors. I bring this to the reader's attention, because some of the Mingus material discussed in this book falls within that category."[3] Oh snap. Who's your Mama now? Cuz, Mr. Jenkins, it looks like Sigmund Freud's wife is truly your mother.

Both the original liner notes and music scholars report that Mingus instructs the musicians to keep "All the Things You Are" in mind—a Kern and Hammerstein song written for the 1939 musical *Very Warm for May*. The show was directed by Liza Minnelli's father, Vincente Minnelli and had a run from November 17, 1939, to January 6, 1940.[4] The short run in New York had much to do with changes that producer Max Gordon made for the show's New York debut. The original musical comedy had a plot that involved the lead character (May) coming home from school to find her father being shaken down by gangsters for gambling debts. When they attempt to kidnap her, she flees to the nearby estate of a "wealthy matron" whose children are rehearsing a play written by their "eccentric friend Ogden Quiller." {Please note that there are now three "wealthy matrons"—Sigmund Freud's wife, Mingus's wife, and now the neighbor's wife—in this mix, and we have yet to come across the fourth.} May's brother, a "big time Broadway director," arrives to help the show along and romance the matron's daughter. Gordon's changes included omitting what seemed like the implausible gangster plot and "the material for the flaming Ogden Quiller was toned down." I am curious about what makes the gangster plot "implausible," and of course, always worried about the disciplining of queer subjects.

The '39 tune made its way across the strings, keys, and vocal cords of many of the jazz greats, and in Mingus's genius, the standard becomes something other than itself. I start this contemplation of Spillers's most challenging essay (at least for me) with a bit of shade, no small amount of theft, and some queer possibilities. What exactly are "all the things you could be" aside from or inside of "all the things you are"? Somewhere in this swirl of meaning is the work of psychoanalysis that both Mingus and then Spillers, though more pointedly, allude to. And then there are the mothers. But we will get to that. I wish to start first with what Spillers imagines is the heart of the matter. The title of Mingus's song and Spillers's instrumentalization of psychoanalysis and its critique, sits in the thin air filled with smoke and particulate matter from a collective microbiome. "All the Things You Could Be by Now," references always "All the Things You Are," thus citing a dual temporality, a condition that Spillers would later remark upon as "the processional—the traversal of time and space" which is both conditional and actualized. But both Mingus in his statement and Spillers in her rejoinder, cut off the possibility of the conditional's realization by referring to a time anterior to its becoming. It is potentiality forestalled—the condition of "all mothers," perhaps. This being in two places at once, feeling more than one historical arc—the things you could be and the things you are—establishes a kind of praxis where Mingus and Spillers, one a player and the other a lover of jazz, meet.[5]

II. Memphis, April 1942 & {much later} May 2022

> We have now to do with beginnings.
>
> —Spillers, "'All the Things You Could Be'" (1996)

i. the analysand

Spillers reminds us first that where we begin is, of course, where we will end, which is precisely, the terrain of psychoanalysis. The provocation here is the (uneasy) relationship between psychoanalysis and race. This beginning is staged in *"intramural* engagements." Between the 1996 publication of "'All the Things You Could Be by Now'" and her return to this "intramural," in 2018 in an essay entitled, "Time and Crisis: Questions for Psychoanalysis and Race" for the *Journal of French and Francophone Philosophy*, the landscape changes from the stakes of Black Study and its engagements to the time/space continuum under which such Study exists. In the newer iteration of an older inquiry, Spillers reminds us that she is "searching for a protocol through intramural space."[6] While it is difficult to grasp what this "protocol" is in its entirety in such a brief rejoinder to an earlier essay, it is necessary to mark that Spillers seeks to make some *psychoanalytic* sense of the here and there of Black temporalities, both historical and embodied, though the more contemporary piece does eschew the body as an adequate location for inquiry. What indeed is the scene brought forward by the parsing of words like "Black" and "body" with concepts like the "one who counts" and "the individual"?[7] For Spillers, the "Lacanian notion" of "the one" rather than "the individual" breaks open the hold that "property and ownership" have on the individual; "the one" references the potential for being "in relation to others."[8] We now have several qualities of relationship, rather than one centrally defined by capital. This slight, but profound shift references, therefore, the "all the things you could be" of the earlier essay as it simultaneously brings psychoanalysis to bear upon scenes of Black living in the *everyday* that keep in mind "a psychoanalytic protocol, which has the advantage of positing an occasion for the recognition of a putative collective."[9]

The when-and-where-I-enter of psychoanalysis, for Spillers, is not that it has "wholesale application," but that it traverses the same terrain that she notes Frank Wilderson does, seeing that "there is no steady ground or disposition that black personality inhabits." Spillers understands that the social death of the subject as constituted in their being as thus barred from language requires the critic to travel to the central inquiry of a psychoanalysis whose quest is to discover that unconscious, which for Lacanians, "is 'structured like a language'"—it is *that* language that Spillers argues "must be revealed."[10] Therefore, the encounter of race and psychoanalysis, staged in the *after*life of the essay that brings us to my analysis, is one in which this subject, say an African-descended one, can be revealed to us as the steady murmur of the language of the unconscious. We must also remember that the 2018 essay for the *Journal of French and Francophone Philosophy* cuts into the aftermath of "Ferguson, Missouri, Flint, Michigan, Staten Island, New York, and Sanford, Florida."[11] It is Spillers's attempt to reckon with the afterlives of these crises, while also thinking through, at least in this essay's end, the "after-life of the Middle Passage" in a "trans-African world" where "the transgenerational transfer of guilt and trauma that traverses Africanity across time and space" must also find its reckoning.[12] This is the *intramural* space that signifies in the opening to my essay and that I will engage in the third section.

Since to begin in psychoanalysis is to always start with the child, in a kind of primal scene, might this language that Spillers refers to be pre-Oedipal, following upon those French feminists like Monique Wittig; or might this language be "phatic"—the getting-to-know-you work of discovering others, something that Spillers refers to, following Robert Scholes as having the desire of "contact itself"?[13] In other words, is the African-descended being, barred from language, kept from all discourse itself, or is this being, rather, engaged in a kind of "contact" or introductory language, something vestibular to the discursive, that requires call *and* response, an invitation to converse that therefore presages, language itself?[14] So that, we are not barred, but held suspended at its very threshold? These may or may not be fruitful queries or even psychoanalytic ones, so apologies for breaking the frame here, but I am in the business, like Derrida . . . of following through on the natural disposition of thought, as it inclines its head toward something other than that which can be seen, though it can be noticed, surely.

Interestingly enough, her first pages of the 2018 piece for *French and Francophone Philosophy* engage Ta-Nehesi Coates's *Between the World and Me* and the epistolary tradition he mirrors from Baldwin's "My Dungeon Shook," the former a letter to a son, the latter a letter to a nephew. As she tracks "from father to son, from uncle to nephew," Spillers notes the crisis of *time* stretched across *events* that galvanize around slavery. She quotes from Coates's inventory of ordinary musings about slavery:

> [It] is not an indefinable mass of flesh. It is a particular, specific enslaved woman, whose mind is active as your own, whose range of feeling is as vast as your own; who prefers the way the light falls in one particular spot in the woods, who enjoys fishing where the water eddies in a nearby stream, *who loves her mother in her own complicated way*, thinks her sister talks too loud, has a favorite cousin, a favorite season, who excels at dress-making and knows inside herself, that she is as intelligent and capable as anyone.[15]

The specificity of this "enslaved woman" who Coates is careful to be *particular* about, collapses in Spillers, ever curious and cautious about *gender*, to become just "the enslaved" or an "enslaved person." The *she*—like a ship or a house—is not remarked upon in her analysis and it is curious and one way in which we lose (y)our *mother*, or at least our dedication to her, all over again. But again, this is the genius of her critique of gender—the finding is always in its loss.

Spillers takes issue in Coates's text with its centering of the body, as she believes that the entirety of "black humanity cannot be reduced to its body" and this might be why she pays no attention to the "enslaved woman," whose capacities for pleasure in living are enumerated in a series of what Spillers terms "pastoral flavors" in scenes of living.[16] And yet, at the very end of this consideration of the *policed*-unto-death body of Black subjects and re-consideration of her earlier musings concerning psychoanalysis and race, she credits Coates with "at least [being] headed in the right direction, and that is to say, words that travel between fathers and sons and mothers and daughters on the vertical axis of the transfer of power and authority."[17] What *she*—Spillers that is—lands upon in this rethinking of her work on psychoanalysis and race is a suspicion of Fanon's sense that the *Oedipal* does not land in the Black self. Fanon's negation of this central psychoanalytic concern has its origin in his contention that, as Spillers explains, "life bears in on him/her with such ferocity that their responses are always drawn to the moment of his/her black body in a white world."[18] Spillers hopes this isn't the case and she notes that if this were our constitutive makeup, the consequences would be profound and amount to "the transfer of authority along vertical and horizontal axes, which trammeled passage engenders intramural violence at unfathomable levels of repetition and mindlessness."[19] I include this repetition in Spillers to mark the intramural across two contexts—the real reproductive work of family, the transfer of "authority" that without the psychoanalytic scene devolves into that other *intramural*, somewhat messier, and more violent than the one that rests upon Coates's vertical axis. While both Spillers and Coates require that "vertical axis" and its generational hierarchies, Spillers introduces us to the pernicious chaos of a more "horizontal" relationality, that menaces the kinds of relationships we hope for. The "all that you could be" of her unsettling inquiry. Even in the end, I still worry about what happened to that "enslaved woman" who *embodies* "black life under slavery's regimen."[20]

Moving back in time to that earlier query about psychoanalysis and race, Spillers offers something speculative. Noting changes across the map of psychoanalysis from Freud to Lacan, and landing on Lacan's sense of the subject, its object, and desire, Spillers proffers the following: "movement across an interior space demarcates the discipline of self-reflection, or the content of a self-interrogation that 'race' always covers over as an already-answered. But for oneself, another question is posed: What might I become, insofar as . . ." (408)? Hortense is masterful with an ellipsis. The echo chamber of *all the things you could be* and *what I might become* join Patsey in Solomon Northup's narrative— she also asks "what's to become of me?" as Platt leaves her on the Louisiana plantation they inhabited together to reunite with his biological family.[21] Something in the psychoanalytic is interstitial in this work; something provokes us to take a longer look at this (female) subject lost to us, and the failure (how rude!) of the respondent to bring forward the favor of a reply. Is it also impolite to ask questions that we already know the answer to?

ii. the intramural

> How do we take misogyny seriously within the Black intramural?
> —Tiffany L. King query for Frank Wilderson, interview

{And a question remains outstanding: what *do* we do when confronted with what we do to one another?}

I want to stop here and reflect upon what generally circulates across Spillers's essays—we have the steady problem of gender and its misalignments; the strange corporeal essence of the body; the temporal drag of time and space, always; and of course, the ways in which becoming "the emptiness and abstraction of a 'thing'" haunts the interpretive limit(s) of Black thought, writ large.[22] Rather than provide another interpretive framework for my musings about Spillers's work across at least four of her essays, I want to read *with* Spillers, going to the territories that she maps, thinking about some of her most pressing questions for Black feminist praxis and how we as the next generation, though now getting long in the tooth, might attempt, have attempted, to answer them.

Recently, I was reminded of how readings of Spillers vary across generations of scholars—from the women who were her contemporaries—like Claudia Tate, Thadious Davis, and Deborah McDowell, to a new generation of scholars like Marquis Bey or Shoniqua Roach. In a 2023 presentation before Jennifer Nash's convening of scholars in the Black Feminist Theory Summer Institute (August 2023), Marquis Bey expressed their frustration with the focus upon a few quotes from key pages in Spillers's most oft-quoted essay, "Mama's Baby, Papa's Maybe." Their critique seemed to stem from the number of white scholars who attempt to practice a kind of woke-ness by citing Spillers, but it also worried the uniflow of our collective citational practice as their remarks sought to move us beyond a single publication. But, generationally speaking, it was Spillers's early work in Faulkner Studies and Psychoanalysis that brought "Mama's Baby" to our attention. Black feminism had much to say about psychoanalysis in the '90s and her work was central in the saying. I would like to argue that, at the time it dropped in 1987, nobody knew yet what to do with the ways in which "Mama's Baby" ripped off the neat discursive dressing that sutured one kind of Black thought to another. In the wake of Bey's remarks, I also wondered a bit about how certain quotes tend to circulate, and I have always chalked it up to the fact that, like certain sections of Derrida or Levinas, or Marable or Douglass, some genius needs to be chewed and argued over, passed around like a good plate of food. I must admit I bristled at being told what to read and thought to myself: I was on the ground in graduate school when that essay dropped and it was a game changer, it worked its way into my intellectual life like a bad dream that sits at the edges of (y)our unconscious life, reminding us of its inevitable return and the necessity to keep on figuring out its meaning, lest you get consumed by its promised hold on (y)our waking life. As such, I thought, I'll read it as often as I like, whenever and wherever I choose to because it pleases me to do so. It was only days after that I understood my salty interiority—the object doesn't matter so much as the shifting interpretive practices that undermine it, to good effect.

I linger here for a bit on interpretive practices, or Spillers's penchant for deconstructing them into a pile of ash, thick and still-hot—because the practice of *reading* without settling upon one interpretive value is endemic to her work. This is part of that complex "intramural" that she undertakes to understand—that has its beginnings perhaps in her 1993 essay, "Black, White, and in Color, or Learning How to Paint: Toward an Intramural Protocol of Reading" extends through "'All the Things You Could Be,'" (1996) and has its reflective moment in Spillers's remarks in "Time and Crisis" (2018).[23] The intramural lands us in this particular nexus of bodies, thin air, and modes of reading.

Spillers's psychoanalytic essays ground themselves in literary readings, and the first essay to speak to the "intramural" ("Black, White, and in Color"), is no exception. Giving us one of the most perceptive readings of Marshall's *The Chosen Place, the Timeless People* (1969), a novel that breaks into the literary world on the cusp of the feminist and Pan Africanist movements in the Americas and, through its main character Merle, attempts to walk the tightrope of revolution, political and personal.

It is important to note that the grounding for the intramural comes from her *first* assessment of Marshall's novel and I would argue her work on the *interstitial* ("Interstices: A Small Drama of Words") in the groundbreaking collection *Pleasure and Danger* (1984) published out of that field-changing Barnard conference.[24] Her critical approach to the novel in 1985 ("*Chosen Place, Timeless People*: Some Figurations on the New World") observes that Marshall's third work of fiction is "[a] study of politics and society in an English-speaking Caribbean community and the turbulence that is stirred when representatives of corporate America are introduced to it . . . the novel is now available again in Vintage paperback after having been out of print for several years. The plausible reasons why the novel was, for all intents and purposes, 'lost' until the fall of 1984 will not occupy my attention beyond this note . . ."[25] Black feminist praxis is forever looking for what is lost, seeking pleasure in the finding, knowing that what we seek most likely cannot be found. This is the grounding of the intramural across some thirty years of Spillers's work—it is the fraught space between us, the (her) story we seek, and the struggle to affirm that what is lost is knowable to us in other ways. Moreover, the *subject* of our inquiry in black feminist praxis, or put more concisely, the *text*(s) laid open for our consideration, for Spillers at least, shifts and proliferates: as the novel itself, as the legible body of a character or African-descended person, or as the was/is of contested (her)story, within and without. In essence, the work of the *text* here is wielded both through psychoanalysis *and* deconstruction. Even if psychoanalysis returns the text to us, the deconstructive mind will render it as incomplete and circumspect as the established histories that make it *other*.

Black feminists like Saidiya Hartman and Christina Sharpe have worried the contours of loss, of what cannot be found, beautifully and eloquently. But very few have approached the parasympathetic predicament of a kind of unrecoverability in loss that at the site of the African-descended in the new world refutes normative temporal schemes because time cannot *accrue*. By using psychoanalytic tools and following upon French feminists like Julia Kristeva who sought to open up the territory of psychoanalysis for gender, Spillers and her contemporaries (Claudia Tate, for example) both changed the nature of psychoanalytic inquiry, and produced the grounding upon which the centrality of the white subject could be interrogated further.

Given the myriad temporal levels at which what can be called *civil society* functions in a *Chosen Place*, it is no wonder that Spillers chooses it to ground her discussion about the substance of the "[Black] intramural." On the island, a fictional place that recalls Marshall's "ancestral origins" in Barbados, we have American anthropologists, a ruling class of Black overseers indebted to an absentee class of stock and landholders, and the everyday people themselves, all producing a web of interstitial funk. While I do not have time to rehearse the novel's complex plot or to offer a reading of my own, it is more than curious that the focus of Spillers's first reading of the intramural that concerns me here, is decidedly *literary*. And that when she returns to consider the novel some eight years later, the focus of her reading is *psychoanalytic* and centers upon a scene in the late evening before the Carnival parade. In the first chapter of Part III ("Carnival"), one of the characters named Vereson "Vere" Walkes beats an unfaithful lover who Spillers names in her second critical assessment of the novel, the "Canterbury woman." In this instant, I am reminded of Platt's nee Northup's beating of Patsey in *Twelve Years a Slave* (1853) and its twenty-first century reenactment in Steve McQueen's *12 Years a Slave* (2013).[26]

But that *intra*mural is what we can and cannot see, or more precisely, it is what we can see all around us, but cannot *un*see, cannot account for with any regularity approaching habit. And if we are taking the *intra* in "intramural" seriously, then we need to pay attention to the footnotes. What this analysis of the intramural *scene* in Marshall's novel conjures for us too is a critical contestation that Spillers alludes to in the essay's opening sentence, and then resolves (at least somewhat) in a footnote. There, she reminds us of an accusation of homophobia in Marshall's novel and cautions critics: "That our various readings replicate today's fractured political scene will not come as news, but as *citizens* who are also *critics*, I think we owe it to the 'business' of our work to do more than simply impose our particular prejudice on forms of art."[27] She begins these cautionary remarks with a reference to yet another footnote (number 6) in a previous essay—nestling one text and its controversy inside another—bringing that first reading forward to us as a different kind of curiosity.

What could be more intramural than the notes section of a black feminist text? I am thinking specifically of Spillers's 1985 ("Some Figurations") footnote number 6 that gives us the details of her exchange with literary scholar Judith Fetterley who felt that "the work [*Chosen Place*] is homophobic." In her rejoinder to Fetterley in the notes, Spillers does not attempt to explain away Fetterley's contention, rather she opens up the possibility that Merle, having had a relationship with a white, "powerful Englishwoman" {here is our fourth woman of substance and power} and as a result lost her East African husband and her daughter, who return to Kenya, expresses ambivalence about the nature of her intimate relationship with a woman for a host of reasons. One of them is that "Merle is decidedly confused in her feelings for the mother culture."[28] I love it when a critic really *reads*, and this footnote sends up Fetterley's complaint as ill-informed, at the same time that it points up a common *feminist* concern for the negative bounty of procreation's force. I'd like to hold this *homosexual drag* in not-so-subtle relationship to the unfolding of the intramural as it moves from essay to essay, and perhaps sets us up for the work among us that gives way to my subsequent reading of what is lost, to what I believe is missing in Ryan Coogler's *Black Panther* (2018).

As noted earlier, Spillers's first approach to *Chosen Place* is decidedly *literary*, concerning itself with diachronic and synchronic time, and the extent to which histories of colonization and the rituals of revolution, all focused upon Carnival in the fictional Bournehills, produce a collapse of "agents" in the novel. In this regard Marshall's creative critique is a rejoinder to Jean Genet's play *The Balcony* (1956), where both the generals in the prevailing regime and the revolutionaries find themselves patrons of the same brothel. In her second pass at the novel, Spillers opens up the psychoanalytic frame because it lends itself, as noted earlier, to creating another text, a narrative that positions itself in that interstitial space. When I return to my copy of *The Chosen Place* (the 1984 reprint), I see that I have circled the same passages leading up to Vere's assault on "the girl," and the mirror she sits before as he comes into the house, walks into her room without knocking and they see one another through the vanity mirror: "she saw Vere suddenly well up in the mirror to the makeshift vanity table at which she was sitting."[29] The mirror might give us the classic psychoanalytic moment, but the sight of the girl, made up in white greasepaint and dressed in the same "lavish gown" in a room filled with boudoir dolls and Marshall's description of the "Canterbury girl" as having the eyes of "a sullen, intractable child" or of Vere as beating her "in the same puritanical manner a father might a child, to chasten and reform" bring us ever closer to its doorstep.[30] This coupled with the child he believes she denies him, with her statement that his return to her is about "the damn child I had for you" brings us back to the scene of abandonment and loss, to the wreckage of *family* that doesn't quite cohere.[31] In fact, this intramural is the one that haunts Spillers, as she attempts "to consider the place, for example, of fantasy, desire, and the 'unconscious,' of conflict, envy, aggression, and ambivalence in the repertoire of elements that are perceived to fashion the lifeworld."[32] The primal scene of the psychoanalytic beckons us and falls open for *display* like a Kara Walker silhouette.

In thinking first about this "intramural" and the scene between Vere and the Canterbury woman, mediated by mirror images in "Black, White, and in Color," Spillers moves through Faulkner criticism and lands on John T. Irwin's interpretation of Faulkner's use of doubling through the masculine brother/shadow. Spillers unmakes the gendering of such play by noting that "we might conclude, after Irwin, that the sister and the double, or the woman in the mirror, are not as well known; in this case, the subject identifies with the object thrown before her, at the same time that she recognizes that she is not one with it . . . no amount of recognition forestalls the peculiar and unique pleasure that the looker derives from seeing *in*, if not *through*, the glass."[33] Spillers's allusion to Irigaray's "This Sex Which Is Not One" (1977) is not subtle, and brings sexuality—*female* sexuality—front and center in this scene; but again, like the charge of homophobia leveled at *Chosen Place* or the somewhat muted flame of Minelli's Ogden Quiller, we see the drag here as Derrida's *trace*. We have to remember the *pleasure* in reading and being read, a queer or quare {thank you, E. Patrick Johnson} way of seeing that is also part of the drag of this scene—reading and being read are part of the *disciplinary order of things*. We might also remember that bizarre turn in southern histories, plantation histories, by extension, where a brother's love and longing for his half/sister—a trope that turns up across Faulkner's fiction—was an ever-present fact of the sexual lives of its inhabitants. The psychoanalytic scene makes itself known to the landscape of racial difference and "truth and illusion" begin to vacillate wildly, and Spillers offers that in the brief and haunting mirror scene "both characters . . . discover each other as the realized aspect of a self-alienation."[34] The interpretive schema is upended at every juncture because we cannot possibly know whose desire, what desire is being centered in these myriad scenes of (mis)recognition. In this house of mirrors, with no settled reflection of or for the self, we are left to disciplinary structures in order to bring order to chaos.

What pulls apart *interpretation*, what makes it somewhat disingenuous as a production of a whole self or the concerted and organized utterance of a kind of wholeness, is its relationship and/or reliance upon *integration*. We are never whole cloth, but pieced out, in sections, needing to be sutured and stitched into that fabric called *life*. Spillers takes this seriously by thinking through both the theory and the practice of psychoanalysis, something she comes to through her own translations of psychoanalyst work by Marie-Cécile and Edmond Ortigues (*Oedipe Africain*) in "'All the Things You Could Be by Now.'" We are reminded of feminist praxis at every juncture. And thinking of psychoanalytic practice, she reminds us that its purpose is to put forward for "the analysand a narrative, a text in the 'place' of a dropped-out content, or a content that was never there." She continues by linking this practice among texts: "what [then] is the relationship between a fictional text and the historical, or the community in history, both *inventing* and *invented* by its texts?"[35] This perhaps is the precursor to the meaning embedded in the question "All the Things You Could Be . . ." The settled answer is elusive, but it does speak to a practice, a kind of enumeration ("enumeration is not the point, though *repetition* is") that reverberates, shattering time/space, and if "Mama's Baby" is our core reading of that shattering, it opens up the question of gender, at least female gender, if there is such a thing, for a radical re-articulation.[36] *She* might be the matter that is the "dropped-out content," the invented entity, also inventing its signal *text*. A bold simultaneity.

But, what is the "text" that we can or must settle upon in our tale of psychoanalysis and race? What "text" (the one that needs to be *read*) produces the most fertile ground of meeting between psychoanalysis and race? While my prowess as a critic does not extend to psychoanalysis and its epistemological registers, I have some experience with *reading* of the literary sort. I am captivated by Spillers's movement across two decades, a de facto generation, of work on psychoanalysis and race. We begin in 1993 with thick literary readings ("Black, White, and in Color"), then we move to the density of the scene of psychoanalysis itself ("All the Things") in 1996, and in 2018, we find ourselves contemplating a set of questions around race and psychoanalysis in the time of Black Lives Matter and the particularities of state violence ("Time and Crisis"). My observation is a simple one, the "scene" of blackness that gives us a "text" in Spillers is ever-evolving. In this regard, she is at her most capacious and speculative. What comes forward is also the author's own sense of loss and even alienation in relation to the "old community, which . . . is no longer a space I would swear I know."[37] The tension is not about psychoanalysis and its tools or frameworks, though some discord is always noted; the predicament seems to be in the relationship between what I would call a black feminist examination of a (gendered) interiority—painted for us by our fiction writers, and the moment where that imaginary world which has fleshed out the experiential terrain of blackness, comes into contact with the "Real, where I would situate the politics and reality of 'race.'"[38] That politics is shifting, *gendered* ground, made all the more complicated by proliferating *texts*.

So, a curious thing happens in the last pages of "Black, White, and in Color," where we as readers engage the founding order of blackness and its intramural. Still reading Marshall's *Chosen Place, Timeless People* at the level of deep rhetoric, utilizing all parts and figures of speech, various grammars, lexicons and known and unknown syntaxes, Spillers moves us to that aspect of the intramural that must be forestalled: the query of the Black self that substantiates the erasure of the self's instantiation: "*Who* is the 'European' in me that the 'African' in me need fear?"[39] The grammar that gets us to the answer to this question is undoubtedly psychoanalytic, and the order of things, the *symbolic* order of things requires a turn and a confrontation, a kind of ethical (Levinas) order that cannot be resolved by *looking*. Working the scene across numerous psychoanalytic registers, we come to know these two characters and the enormity of the work before them. The confrontation between the two—"the girl" {also the mother} and Vere—in the glass leads not to seeing one another but to a realization of the other's "self-alienation." In many ways they are called to a moment where *recognition* is an impossibility, but yet is fully operable, if recognition is not of the self, but one's own *abandonment*. It constitutes loss without a history and psychoanalytic tools just might help us recover, not/never the *thing* itself, but a version (a text?) we can live with.

III. Oakland, 1992

> a mother-woman is rather a strange "fold" (*pli*) which turns nature into culture, and the "speaking subject" (*le parlant*) into biology.
> —Julia Kristeva, "Stabat Mater," qtd. in Spillers, "Black, White, and in Color"

In the opening scenes of *Black Panther* (2018), Erik Stevens (N'Jadaka) appears on the blacktop of an Oakland basketball court, sandwiched at least temporally or in the Real, capital "R," between the Crack Cocaine and HIV/AIDS epidemics, between this world {and me} and the world of his ancestral kin. His layup completed, Stevens's play is interrupted by lights in the sky. The "ship" as literal and figurative spacecraft arrives to steal his future, but it creates a bridge for his return, years later, as Killmonger, cousin to T'Challa. T'Challa, newly king, is the chosen son of the continent's fictious place and he rules, we find out without father-right, a bastard before the discourse of sovereign inheritance that can claim him. Stevens grows up to be Annapolis and MIT educated, and as fathers go, his seems to be at once articulated in two *bodies*: N'Jobu, uncle to T'Challa, and the US Military Industrial Complex.

Now, I am not a fellow traveler in Marvel or its multiverse, though I am quite positive that we might be living in some other one right now, so I am sure there are many corrections, emendations, and general arguments to be lodged in this story I am telling, but I stick with what comes to us in the digital film print, rather than what we can know from our deep dive into the multiverse's origin narratives. In many ways, *Black Panther* plays out the encounter of the Continent with its US brethren, word properly chosen. It sets the psychoanalytic scene of racial encounter between us, two pasts meet two presents, converging. The defining difference between Erik (née N'Jadaka) and T'Challa is that the former has no mother to speak of, she is simply "an American Woman," while

T'Challa is firmly rooted in a mythical world of mother-love and matrilineal might. What indeed are "all the things you could be" or "all the things you are" in this contest between biologically entwined issue, one of whom has certainly not only *lost* his mother, but has no mother we can find beyond an imaginary?

As we witness the contestation between men, one scripted as African, the other decidedly American, as their trips to the ancestral plane are geographically marked, we come more to agree with Spillers's understanding that—though he could not name it given his particular polemic—in *Black Skins, White Masks*, Fanon indeed points out "the extent to which the psychoanalytic hermeneutic has the least relevance to African diasporic lifeworlds."[40] This same opinion is repeated differently in her 2018 essay "Time and Crisis." For the purposes of the dance of continents that *Black Panther* enacts, a return to "All the Things You Could Be by Now," demonstrates the predicament of a decidedly diasporic *intramural*. Spillers reminds us "even though diasporic African and continental African communities share 'race,' they pointedly differ in cultural ways and means; the contrary view, which flattens out black into the same thing despite time, weather, geography, and the entire range of complicating factors that go into the fashioning of persons, is difficult to put to rest, given, especially, what seems to be the unchanging face of racism."[41] For Spillers, "racism" seems to be that connective tissue, the stuff of experience in ontologically driven cultures, that "flattens out black" and she intends, through the *praxis* of psychoanalysis, rather than through psychoanalytic critique, to get to those differences in another intramural that stretches between us, for sure.

I am interested in the motherless Stevens's representation of the evolved pathology of an American psyche bent on destroying the perceived figure of its abandonment—"We left him. We had to maintain the lie." What can you become without your mother, proper? Stevens is father-lacking—though his journey with the special heart-shaped herb produces a father who is very much present in his life—but the insurgent female, not "Black" but "American," who cannot exist in the new world order that is referenced as a particular place and time in African American experience in the film's storyboard needs to be reckoned with, perhaps like that language, that *call* with no response in the earlier section of my inquiry here. What we know of her is that Erik's father, brother of the King, falls in love with an "an American woman"—what does it mean to be an American woman, and does she *track* for us as a Black woman at all? What I am offering here is that his mother's biography is so incomplete that I cannot, even with the help of the best of psychoanalytic tools, *find* her *as I would wish to*. The one who has a hand in, "handles" ("Mama's Baby") and even "radicalized" Erik's father—who stays to fight this new world revolution, rather than return to what is ostensibly, paradise—cannot be known to us. And it does not escape me that this battle between continents and worlds is class-defined.

The doubly "lost" mother, who, given things on the ground, it appears has absconded with not only her life, but the revolution, at least in *Black Panther*, is decidedly American. When Stevens crosses the pond for that second time, at least genetically speaking, his focus is on his father, not his mother, and the psychic life of the Ancestral plane, what functions as a kind of (pre)consciousness features mostly fathers for both protagonists. Erik Stevens (née N'Jadaka) is a product of that new world into whose Black (W)hole—think Evelyn Hammonds here—our mother has disappeared. And apparently, so have all of the Black females/women with her, as not one of the Black adult persons depicted in the place of Erik's *living* is representationally cis-gendered *female*. In this instance, it is clear to me that she is not only *gone* (girl), but also deprived of being what we could call *mother*.

I circle back to that diasporic "lifeworld" that comprises the stuff of the ethical, as early in her contemplations of race and psychoanalysis, Spillers's conceptualization of this lifeworld recalls, with a bit of force, that question in Frank B. Wilderson's introduction to *Red, White, and Black*, "What are we to make of a world that responds to the most lucid enunciation of ethics with violence?"[42] The answer to Wilderson's question would be the destruction of the world {as we know it}, which exists in a narrowly defined ontology, but does not begin to encompass what this lifeworld might or can be. Spillers ever reminds us that "the ethical ... [is] the relational dimension of the lifeworld."[43] My reading of *Black Panther* is pointedly and necessarily brief, as I am unable to find that *mother* upon whom the axis of an encounter between psychoanalysis and race might surely? depend. Who can you be, what are all the things you can become, if you have no (Black) mother to speak of? Might your mother then become Sigmund Freud's wife; might you then become the quintessential *subject* of psychoanalysis? The *gendered* scene and/or text of Eric Stevens's becoming is decidedly *male*—and sets the stage for different encounters: one in which your father mothers you, one in which the male issue is unhanded by the mother, but whose revolutionary vision is handed over to the children (T'Challa and Shuri) of Wakanda and reframed for commerce and colonialism. In the end, the cousins return to Oakland, having bought several buildings, one in which Killmonger's father was killed by his brother. The *mission* is to create a "Wakandan International Outreach Center." Right before this closing visitation, during the scene of Eric's demise from a mortal wound T'Challa has inflicted, T'Challa says that perhaps they can heal him. Killmonger assumes that this healing will only lead to his incarceration, so requests that T'Challa "Just bury me in the ocean with my ancestors that jumped from the ships. 'Cause they knew death was better than bondage." Psychoanalysis is always already the scene of encounter between the continent and its issue. Killmonger's place is with the unknown dead and mother or no, he claims his status as issue, not progenitor, at least in this first iteration of the *Black Panther* series.

IV. "'All the Things You Could Be by Now . . .'" 2023

Spillers's investigation is two pronged, to get to the matter of the appropriateness of the psychoanalytic schema—its origin story perhaps—and the matter of Black lives. The other concern here is to throw some shade on other encounters, ones situated in the community of African-descended intellectuals for whom these questions proliferate rather than resolve.[44] Hortense Spillers opens this gorgeous provocation with the following question: "how might psychoanalytic theories speak about 'race' as a self-consciously assertive reflexivity, and how might 'race' expose the gaps that psychoanalytic theories awaken?"[45] She plots the terrain of this awakening, this exposure as "fantasy, desire, the 'unconscious,'" and as "conflict, envy, aggression and ambivalence."[46] I take this terrain seriously and suggest we might be able to plot our course—to find our mother, to lose her, perhaps, but most certainly to engage the discursive tension among us to better effect. This essay perhaps plots that loss purposefully, tracking the stories of three men who stage the struggle to find their mothers. In the end, what does it mean to be some other mother's son? And I'll end with Mingus, "It means nothing. You got it? Thank you."

Notes

My original remarks at the Vanderbilt conference included the following: Thank you to Dana Nelson, friend, and fellow traveler, for this invitation to honor Hortense Spillers, whose mind I've attempted to travel with since 1988, when Michael Awkward revised his syllabus in our AFAM Literature class at the University of Michigan and put "Mama's Baby, Papa's Maybe" in our mailboxes, and then invited you to campus. I have never looked back, though I miss the occasional Nat Sherman MCD between panels and the intake of smoke to make the mind more agile. I want to thank Tiffany Lethabo King for reminding me of the intramural in Spillers and to look for it again.

1. Jenkins, *I Know What I Know*, 78.
2. Freud, "A Child Is Being Beaten," 376.
3. Jenkins, *I Know What I Know*, xvi.
4. See Jackson Upperco, "V Is for . . . VERY WARM FOR MAY (1939)," *That's Entertainment* (blog), Oct. 27, 2014, https://jacksonupperco.com/2014/10/27/v--is-for-very-warm-for-may-1939.
5. Spillers's love of jazz is well known among friends and colleagues.
6. Hortense Spillers, "Time and Crisis," 26. Christina Sharpe skirts at the edges of Spillers' intramural, noting across two chapters of *In the Wake* (Durham, NC: Duke University Press, 2016), "How are we beholden to and beholders of each other in ways that change across time and place and space and yet remain" (101), and then, "so much of Black intramural life and social and political work is redacted, made invisible to the present and future, subtended by plantation logics, detached optics, and brutal architectures" (114). Sharpe is spot on about the temporality of the intramural, though I might want to quibble with the hidden nature of its invisibility to time's particular stamp.
7. Spillers, "Time and Crisis," 29.
8. Spillers, "Time and Crisis," 29.
9. Spillers, "Time and Crisis," 28.
10. Spillers, "Time and Crisis," 28.
11. Spillers, "Time and Crisis," 28.
12. Spillers, "Time and Crisis," 29.
13. Spillers, *Black, White and in Color*, 294.
14. I am well aware of the differences between language and discourse in critical thought, but I also want to muddy this ground a bit because I believe that understanding Black subjectivity, at least through the lens of what we have

understood as "Black Thought" can only be approached if language and discourse interact, at least for the time being.

15. Quoted in Spillers, "Time and Crisis," 26.
16. Spillers, "Time and Crisis," 27.
17. Spillers, "Time and Crisis," 30.
18. Spillers, "Time and Crisis," 30.
19. Spillers, "Time and Crisis," 30.
20. Spillers, "Time and Crisis," 26.
21. In *an other: a black feminist consideration of animal life* (Durham, NC: Duke University Press, 2023), I try to unravel the meaning of Patsey's abandonment. See, "vocabularies: possibilities," 16–50.
22. Spillers, *Black, White and in Color*, 282.
23. Spillers often returned to her earlier readings, recasting them in different configurations, pairing them with other texts she wished to explore. Her earlier piece, "*Chosen Place, Timeless People*: Some Figurations on the New World," appeared in Marjorie Pryse and Hortense Spillers, eds., *Conjuring: Black Women, Fiction, and Literary Tradition* (Bloomington: Indiana University Press, 1985) 151–75.
24. See Carole Vance, ed. *Pleasure & Danger: Exploring Female Sexuality* (Boston: Routledge & Kegan Paul Books, 1984). Spillers published "Interstices: A Small Drama of Words" in this collection that includes Cherrie Moraga, Sharon Olds, Alice Echols, and Gayle Rubin, among others.
25. Spillers, "*Chosen Place, Timeless People*," 151.
26. See my discussion of the narrative and the film in Holland, *an other*.
27. Spillers, "Black, White, and in Color," 500n2.
28. Spillers, "Some Figurations," 173n6.
29. Marshall, *The Chosen Place*, 272.
30. Marshall, *The Chosen Place*, 273, 272, 275.
31. Marshall, *The Chosen Place*, 274.
32. Spillers, "'All the Things,'" 377.
33. Spillers, "Black, White, and in Color," 283; emphasis in original.
34. Spillers, "Black, White, and in Color," 287.
35. Spillers, "Black, White, and in Color," 283
36. Spillers, "'All the Things,'" 294; emphasis in original.
37. Spillers, "Psychoanalysis and Race," 384.
38. Spillers, "'All the Things,'" 407.
39. Spillers, "Black, White, and in Color," 297.
40. Spillers, "'All the Things,'" 409.
41. Spillers, "'All the Things,'" 410.
42. Wilderson, *Red, White and Black*, 2.
43. Spillers, "'All the Things,'" 383.
44. Spillers, "'All the Things,'" 395.

45. Spillers, "'All the Things,'" 376.
46. Spillers, "'All the Things,'" 377.

Works Cited

Coogler, Ryan. dir. *Black Panther*. Marvel Studios, 2018.

Holland, Sharon P. *an other: a black feminist consideration of animal life*. Durham, NC: Duke University Press, 2023.

Jenkins, Todd S. *I Know What I Know: The Music of Charles Mingus*. New York: Praeger, 2006.

Sharpe, Christina. *In the Wake: On Blackness and Being*. Durham, NC: Duke University Press, 2016.

Spillers, Hortense J. *Black, White, and in Color: Essays on American Literature and Culture*. Chicago: University of Chicago Press, 2003.

———. "Time and Crisis: Questions for Psychoanalysis and Race." *Journal of French and Francophone Philosophy* 26, no. 2 (2018): 25–31.

Wilderson, Frank B., III. *Red, White and Black: Cinema and the Structure of U.S. Antagonisms*. Durham, NC: Duke University Press, 2010.

Albums:

"Songs in the Key of Life"
  Stevie Wonder — two records.

"Respect Yourself"
  The Staple Singers

"Reunited"
  Peaches and Herb

"The Best of Gladys Knight
  and the Pips"

Marvin Gaye "Live at the
  London Palladium"
  Marvin Gaye

ARCHIVAL FRAGMENT 9: Handwritten album list in Spiller's journal

Afterword

HORTENSE J. SPILLERS

(I)

This book, though not unique in this regard, was made possible by the untiring generosity of others, starting with the exemplary commitment of its editors, Margo Natalie Crawford and C. Riley Snorton. Even if academics are slow to admit it, we must recognize, finally, that our entire calling—perhaps we could name it "individual talent" or "genius"—is predicated on the outstretched hand and willing disposition of our colleagues. *The Flesh of the Matter*, then, takes prideful place in my career as the first post-retirement tribute in my behalf to a field of work both young and old—African American Literary and Cultural Studies. Based on what was called when I was a child, more than seven decades ago, "Negro History," Black Studies celebrated its fiftieth birthday at Brandeis University, for example, during the month of February, in 2019; I can attest that those years escaped as noiselessly as the batting of an eye, but not without enormous consequences—as far as I can tell, it has reconfigured humanistic study in the United States for sure. In short, trying to remember what the academy was like before the instauration of Black Studies is not so different from an attempt to re-ignite a dream that is fled forever. How often has one tried to "get back" into the dream, but not in this case. Only the conservative wing of the United States Supreme Court and handfuls of reactionary cranks, phatt-heads, and panjandrums across the country are unaware of the blessings of a widened and an enriched study of the human and its "geographies of reason," circa 1968–70. Who will tell them?

The pleasures afforded me in reaching across the generational aisle, the honor I feel, really, are immeasurable in gratitude for these powerful messengers and witnesses who allude to this enhanced orbit of scholarship and conceptualization in *The Flesh of the Matter*: Alexis Pauline Gumbs, Kevin Quashie, Fred Moten, Anthony Reed, Amaris Brown, Kiana T. Murphy, Nicole Adeyinka Spigner, Shoniqua Roach, Ra Malika Imhotep, Deborah E. McDowell, Thadious M. Davis, and Sharon P. Holland, all, join the editors in bringing to stand a volume of essays that demonstrate both the fruitful arrival and continuity of a relatively new curricular object that reaches American campuses some twenty years after the close of the most devastating war in human history, but that also marks a critical nodal point in the centuries-long struggle by subjects of the African Diaspora to realize definitively the claims and privileges of a global and national citizen-belonging. The work elaborated here traverses a repertoire of aims that are implicitly focused on this horizon.

(II)

When I was a child, I understood and spoke as a child and did nutty, childish things—like wearing my mother's pots and pans as if they were hats and helmets—but I also read newspapers, in imitation of my father, and one of the newspapers crossed the threshold weekly. Little by little, I came to realize that *The Pittsburgh Courier*—with its beautiful sepia tones and a center fold that featured full-torso close-ups of famous Black Americans, from Mary McLeod Bethune, Ralph Bunch, Jackie Robinson, and Thurgood Marshall, to Benjamin E. Mays, Horace Mann Bond, Phillipa Duke Schuyler, Mattwilda Dobbs, and Hazel Scott, among them—was not alone in belonging to a genre of newspapers distinctly different from the Memphis dailies, in our case, *The Commercial Appeal* in the morning and the *Press Scimitar* in the evening. Without nudging, but dawning on me as though my awareness of it came in with the oxygen I breathed, I began to sense that the weekly paper had been designed for me, while the dailies were not only not concocted with me in mind (except by negation), but were determinedly hostile to folk like me and our collective interests, yet we felt obligated, somehow, to pay real money to read these locals and stay abreast of events occurring across the city, the state, and the nation. I also grasped, eventually, the extent of the informal fraternity of black weeklies that aligned with *The Pittsburgh Courier*—*The Tri-State Defender*, *The Baltimore Afro-American*, *The Amsterdam News*, to name some of them—and that they were all trained on tracking the achievements and aspirations of Black America. The mind and imagination of a black child of my generation likely sprouted a split screen of contradictions quite early: on the one hand, the growing pride that comes with gazing at the stern, handsome, exquisite faces that graced the center fold of the *Courier*, and on the other, the hot resentment that suddenly bubbled up to the surface on seeing "Negro" spelled with a small n, or black women denied the honorific appellations "Mrs." and "Miss" (as the latter remained in use until Gloria Steinem's feminist activism of the 1970s brought us "Ms," both the magazine and the title). To this very day, that movie reel and its insistent contrariety are seared into my brain.

What I am attempting to sketch here are not only what could be called symptoms of a "sentimental education," but also the latter as a paradigmatic moment of habitation for the *arousal*, let's say, of what was already "Black Studies" when I was born. We are reminded that these weekly newspapers stood alongside black radio, the "race" record and the early days of recorded sound, the early movie industry, the black church, and the colleges and universities of the United Negro College Fund (UNCF). But if we add to these institutional and technological arrangements and innovations the apparently sempiternal "mystic chord" of black life that is absolutely elusive (if we try to define it), but utterly present, when, for instance, hundreds of black folk, strangers to each other, arrayed on either side of a football stadium and on either side of a highly competitive football match underway that afternoon all dance, in place, at halftime, (to "Move On Up and shock it to 'em!") in absolute sync, as though the two sides had been instructed and tutored by a single choreographer, then an observer has before her an instance of the very puzzle that black thinking has wrestled with for quite a long time. I am suggesting, then, that "Black Studies" are, therefore, existential to black life, whose origins disappear into the mists of human time. But what we can account for, by historiographical record, are the protoformations of the eighteenth- and nineteenth-century worlds induced by black personality's infernal hatred of domination and cruelty. Formally speaking, such activity culminates in revolutionary movement that gives birth to the nation-state of Haiti, on the one hand, and on the other, the contemplative gestures of freedom and abolition that engender scholarship as a revolutionary ruse, the turning one's back momentarily on the clock and consequences. The generation of African Americans, born, miraculously, just after Appomattox (W. E. B. Du Bois, 1868; Carter G. Woodson, 1875) caught the fret and fever of abolition democracy and ushered us into the precincts of history's seductive embrace. Before this, if free, we were preachers and poets, teachers and griots, healers and organizers, farmers and laborers, child-care givers and domestics, but it seems to me that with the generation of Ida Bell Wells, W. E. B. Du Bois, Anna Julia Cooper, and other distinguished black men and women of Reconstruction and post-Reconstruction, the power of the alienable that makes it possible to operate by surrogacy and substitution, by analogy and mimesis, abrupts on the horizon of black personality. "I" might now appear by way of signature and affect, rather than *in the suffering person of my body*, which marked enslavement. All modern work seems to be backed up by the logics of social distance most remarkably demonstrated by today's Zoom, for example, but before Zoom, there were photography and movies, sound technology and the telephone.

These engagements and appointments with freedness and freedom, ironically conducted when black life was threatened and imperiled by new dangers, opened the professions to black people and the protocols that accompanied them in whatever unevenly ongoing distribution of access such prerogatives might fall. The fifty-year sequence, then, in which Black Studies fits therefore signals a moment of maturation in civil and human rights struggle afoot for decades, and it makes a good deal of *poetic* sense that this particular manifestation of maturity appears at the heart of the academy—in this place where the Humanities unfold, inasmuch as it was *here* that the casting of the doubtful humanity of Blackness, in the quiet hush and dignity of its varied and enviable loci, found systematic favor, rationalization, and the most elegant of "proof." In other words, as far as I can see, the most violent expression of racist hatred, of race ideology, is embodied and embedded in *intellectual* motions and commotions, and it is still *here*, on this ground, that battle must be waged; at least my generation of students and intellectuals thought so, as did Du Bois's. But more than that, our intellectual heirs have caught the spirit of struggle and today drive an offensive more sure and powerful than we could ever have imagined. *The Flesh of the Matter* inscribes a fabulous case in point.

Hortense J. Spillers

Appendix

Transcriptions of Archival Documents

FIGURE I.1. *Excerpt of typed first page of "Interstices: A Small Drama of Words." Hortense J. Spillers papers, Ms.2019.013, Box 15, Folder 10, Pembroke Center Archives, John Hay Library, Brown University.*

Who Said It Was Simple?
There are so many roots to the tree of anger / that sometimes the branches shatter / Before they bear.

Sitting in Nedicks / the women rally before they march / discussing the problematic girls / they hire to make them free. / An almost white counterman passes / a waiting brother to serve them first / and the ladies neither notice nor reject / the slighter pleasures of their slavery. / But I who am bound by my mirror / as well as my bed / see causes in Colour / as well as sex

and sit here wondering / which me will survive / all these liberations.
Audre Lorde[1]

When I told a friend of mine that I was going to address the issue of sexuality as discourse during a spring conference at Barnard she laughed: "Is that what you talk about when you make love?" Silence. "Well?" Well, I hadn't thought of that, but now that she had broached the question, what about it? There probably

307

FRAGMENT 1. *Calendar entry for April 23–24, 1982, The Scholar and the Feminist IX Conference. Hortense J. Spillers papers, Ms.2019.013, Box 1, Folder 9, pg. 5, Pembroke Center Archives, John Hay Library, Brown University.*

April

23 / Friday   24 / Saturday

Birthday: Number 40. "Feminism and Scholar IX (Conference) Sexuality" "Interstices"

Barnard Gymnasium, N.Y.

FRAGMENT 2. *A letter from Toni Morrison to Hortense Spillers, 1984. Hortense J. Spillers papers, Ms.2019.013, Box 10, Folder 3, Pembroke Center Archives, John Hay Library, Brown University.*

224 River Road
Grand View-on-Hudson, NY 10960

9 July 1984

Hortense J. Spillers
5 College Circle
Haverford, PA 19041

Dear Hortense,

I suppose you're in Italy now, but I wanted to thank you for sending me your article. I was very much engaged by it, which is a heart-felt compliment, because generally when I read most criticism of Black women's literature, it seems so thin. You are quite a thinker.

Please keep in touch, so we can finish the conversations we always begin when we meet.

Regards,
[handwritten signature]
Toni Morrison
TM/jp

FRAGMENT 3. *Journal entry on Gwendolyn Brooks. Hortense J. Spillers papers, Ms.2019.013, Box 2, Folder 1, Pembroke Center Archives, John Hay Library, Brown University.*

Sunday, March 4, 1973
10:30 p.m.

I met Gwen Brooks tonight. She is a person of great humility—no pretense or sham polish. Though the Wellesley setting was hospitable enough, it would have been good too, to have talked to her in a more informal atmosphere; everybody was so much on his P's & Q's tonite that a good deal of the talk was "cocktail" repartee. I would like for her to read one of my stories.

I talked to Gwen Brooks about her interpretation of her poem "Mother" (the act of abortion and a woman's reflections concerning it); as she read the poem, there was nothing particularly striking or earth-shaking about the event. Her reading seemed to me very light, almost whimsical. I asked her if she felt that way, and she said no—that the poem was very serious. I thought so too. At the times when I've read the poem in various classes, I've given it a very solemn, really sorrowful emphasis. Her own reading was an articulate one, but a very different register prevailed. She is a very gentle person—not at all worried about anything apparently.

She said that it didn't matter at what age a person started writing. That's good! I told her about my "ten year" old novel—the one I launched ten years ago. I still have the carcass lying about. It's funny but it's there for the record.

I asked her where she thought black people were going; she laughed. Well, she said, she'd like to think that we're steadily moving toward some dynamic liberation but that we're not moving *steadily*—rather limpingly, falteringly, a few backward steps now and again. Then in her own quick way, she asked, "Are you worried?" I assured her that I was and wanted to go on about *how* worried, but she had to autograph some more anthologies and say "goodbye" to some people etc., since we were all getting ready to leave then. I'm glad I know her.

> Gentle Lady—Large-eyed and seeing
> Very quick, sudden, with her sudden questions
> Who's afraid of Gwen Brooks? I am!

FIGURE 8.1. *A typed draft of the title page and first page of "Mama's Baby, Papa's Maybe." Hortense J. Spillers papers, Ms.2019.013, Box 15, Folder 17, Pembroke Center Archives, John Hay Library, Brown University.*

[Title page]

MAMA'S BABY, PAPA'S MAYBE:
AN AMERICAN GRAMMAR BOOK
Hortense J. Spillers
Haverford College
March, 1985

[First page]

Let's face it: I am a marked woman,[1] but not everybody knows my name. "Peaches" and "Brown Sugar," "Sapphire" and "Earth Mother," "Aunty," "Granny," God's "Holy Fool," I describe a locus of confounded identities; a meeting ground of investments and privations in the national ~~stockpile~~ treasury of rhetorical ~~will~~ wealth; my country needs me, and if I were not here, W.E.B. DuBois predicted as early as 1903 that the Twentieth Century would be the century of the "color line."[2] We might add to this spatial configuration another thematic of analogously terrible weight: If the "black American woman" is a "subject of barred consciousness,"[3] then this century marks the site of its profoundest revelation. The problem before us is deceptively simple: The terms accompanied by pairs of inverted commas in this paragraph isolate overdetermined nominative properties. Embedded in bizarre axiological ground, their isolation demonstrates a sort of telegraphic coding, markers so loaded with mythical prepossession that there is no easy way for the agents buried beneath them to come clean. In that regard, the names by which I am called in the public place lend an example of signifying property plus—they assume more or less (which amounts to the same thing) of their share of the nominative terrain. In order for me to speak a truer word concerning myself, I must strip down through layers of attenuated meanings, made an excess in time, over time, assigned by a particular historical order, and there await whatever marvels of my own inventiveness. The personal pronouns and the essay itself are meant to serve a collective function. (1)

FIGURE 8.2. *A page dated October 1966 from one of Spillers's early journals. Hortense J. Spillers papers, Ms.2019.013, Box 3, Folder 42, Pembroke Center Archives, John Hay Library, Brown University.*

Oct. 1966

'The Quest for Permanence'

Why do men seek permanence—that quality in things and of people that will endure? Perhaps there are no answers, and that there are no answers may be testimony enough to the on-goingness in man's heart of the desire to find things that endure. If there is anything primeval in man's "nature," and we must believe that man does have a "nature" or is possessed of qualities that set him aside as an entity in the infinite order of things, that something takes form and shape as faith. Whatever a man founds—or bases his faith upon—himself and the powers of his mind—his own indestructability amidst the onslaught.

FIGURE 8.3. *Two pages from 1966 or 1967 from Spillers's early journal. Hortense J. Spillers papers, Ms.2019.013, Box 3, Folder 42, Pembroke Center Archives, John Hay Library, Brown University.*

[Page 1]

The Dilemma of Being Black

As many of us have long suspected, there is nothing inherently wrong with being born any particular color; the problem one encounters with blackness—whiteness—whatever—is imposed by the outside by the looming, anonymous "System" which affects men in different ways. If the "System" were not evil (a perfect word when one thinks of the way it violates human personality), then color might have been the "innocent" thing we dream of for the unborn. But somewhere out of the past, the ugly notion of color significance

[page 2]

was born. For the world, this must have been the night of "ultimate badness," second only to the loss of Eden.

With it might have sprung, twin-born, its match—social superiority. Still other factors have sustained and fed the nation, nationality among them.

———————————cut

History does not explain racism, but from its myriad conclusions several things might be inferred: When power changes hands (center of civilization shifting from Athens to Rome, for example, or from the Czar's palace to the provisional government) one "septem" eventually displaces another; those in power, either contrivedly or accidentally, gain dominance over others who are made powerless by the switch.

FIGURE 8.4. *An entry from February 10, 1971, in one of Spillers's notebooks. Hortense J. Spillers papers, Ms.2019.013, Box 3, Folder 43, Pembroke Center Archives, John Hay Library, Brown University.*

2/10/'71

"... This is the age of the black woman. I'll not forget that it was out of the turmoil and ~~suffering~~ climbing of the last decade that the Afro-American woman was born again. She will not fear to be herself—no more, not again. This is a moral and aesthetic victory of the first order. Also, this century will settle the "race question" once and for all, one way or another. I suppose it is "all and everything" to be able to stand at the intersections of history and help divert traffic." To be young, female, and black at this point in history is to stand suspended between heaven and hell.

There really is nothing at all to shout about.

FIGURE 8.5. *A page from Spillers's journal. Hortense J. Spillers papers, Ms.2019.013, Box 3, Folder 35, Pembroke Center Archives, John Hay Library, Brown University.*

Sunday, Jan. 14, 1973
11:30 p.m.

To Al Smith and his painting of the old woman on my living room wall.

Black Mother of our ages—
who will mourn for you?

When your hands are broken
and your hair gives witness to the ice-cold of winter—
oh, who will mourn for you.
When the wreck of wars & the certainty of betrayal
when the sorrow & weeping of your
children have bent your back and twisted your
eyes like wrinkled packets—
when to your ears have burst the
wailings of the city—young men lost—
never reclaimed—aliens all of them—to the
old ones and—women with their light of love
young-pride sucked down the drain of weari-
ness from longing—and no more warm, milk-strained
breasts for the babies—is there anyone
who will mourn for you?

FIGURE 8.6. *An undated notecard that had been tucked in Spillers's journal. Hortense J. Spillers papers, Ms.2019.013, Box 4, Pembroke Center Archives, John Hay Library, Brown University.*

I did not know then what I know now: my life to me is a mystery—a fluid equator suspended between two glowing poles of fire. The fire does not burn the water, but war—boils in—fizzing sounds like beef in a hibachi, yet I survive.

Where is he who will love me now despite myself: small, obscure, and afraid? A glowing mystery I am: watching my reflections against the glassy side of the too-hot poles; I dance around them, flirt with them, draw near them, but never kiss, for I am fluid and changing and in the center. This center does not hold, defying the [unintelligible]

FRAGMENT 4. *Images of Hortense Spillers in her living room. Hortense J. Spillers papers, Ms.2019.013, Box 6, Folder 22, pl. 1, pgs. 30–31, Pembroke Center Archives, John Hay Library, Brown University.*

FRAGMENT 5. *Journal entry from 1970. Hortense J. Spillers papers, Ms.2019.013, Box 1, Folder 22, Pembroke Center Archives, John Hay Library, Brown University.*

Hortense J. Spillers
Nov. '70
Journal #2
[Writing Backwards, No Less!]

This would be the perfect spot for a poem or a versed inscription or a picture, but I don't write poems nor do I draw pictures. This spot then, except for the one line above and this one, will be blank until I can say something that makes sense for a beginning—one thing, though, the idea across the page about wanting to die in bed is quite true! I can think of no more pleasant way to go, especially if your man is beside you. What is more, your man being with you (in bed & out) is perhaps a dynamite way to <u>live</u> too! We sexy folk stay in trouble because we want love like some people want money. The truth is that the "love depression" never ended and the banks of love are still insolvent. After the "Revolution" gets here, I'm going to ask the Generals to set up at an FDIC of love so that "broke" niggers like myself can be sure that their few checks won't bounce. I'll dedicate this to Aphrodite! HJS

FRAGMENT 6. Sparebone *program from 1970. Hortense J. Spillers papers, Ms.2019.013, Box 18, Folder 9, Pembroke Center Archives, John Hay Library, Brown University.*

[Page 1]

The Wellesley College Centennial presents:
SPAREBONE
A Drama in Three Acts with Music and Dance
by
Hortense Spillers

(Sparebone is that part of the living body which no other part can do without. Though the term may not be found in any of the biological sciences, we needn't despair because every biologist himself has one.)

Company
　　Master of Ceremonies; M. Governor . . . Nicholas Linfield

Jim Branch; Willie Beasley . . . Jame The Ellis
Jaky Navarre; "Club" Jessee Jonniken . . . Philip Kilbourne
Flotilde Palmer; Letha Han; Student . . . Wendy Urquhart
Nedra Thompson; Student . . . Susan B. Smyth
Virginia Hoskins; Student . . . Anne-Sojourner Wendell
Elizabeth Degas; Nanette; Student . . . Deborah Blackmore
Tall Unidentified Woman; Frieda Aikens . . . Debra Chasnoff
Dessie Hoskins . . . Jefrina Berry
May Degas . . . Heather Snow

[Page 2]

Gertha
Jenny
Other Children
Mama Han; Addie Mashola's Model . . . Barbara Toppin
Pete "Birdsong"; student . . . Cliff Weaver
Thomas Haverhill . . . James Butterfield
Nat of Turner's rebellion; O.K. Cole . . . Tim Davis
Mashola Beasley . . . Loretta Devine
Linny Beasley . . . Karen McPherson
John Beasley . . . Daniel Windham
Josephine Baker . . . Jeannine Otis Johnson
Messenger . . . Danny L. Scarborough

Dancers

Rhonda Babb	Heidi Iacurto
Alexander Brouwer	Elham Jezab
Karen Bell	Cheryl Nelson
Joan Ashley	Paul Schneider
Brenda Darrell	Sharon Scott
Tim Davis	Anne Spader
Elizabeth Dell	Joanne Wingood
Sarah Reynolds	Sandy Brown
Jackie Holloway	

ACT ONE

Paris, France, 1925
    Le Grand Due, A Nightclub
    Jim's Hotel Room

Intermission
(10 Minute)

[Page 3]

ACT TWO
Richmond, Virginia, 1833
>Degas Plantation House
>Slave Quarters of the Degas Estate
>Nat Turner's Cabin

Intermission
(10 Minutes)

ACT THREE
Louisville, Kentucky, April, 1968
>Mashola's Hat Shoppe
>Frankfort College

STAFF
Musical Director and Composer ... Daniel Windham
Director ... James Butterfield
Choreographer ... Danny L. Scarborough
Production Staff
Producer ... Susan B. Smyth
Set Design ... Eric Levenson
Lighting Design ... Evelyn C. White
Costume Design ... Jame Stoiko
Stage Manager ... Becky Strehlow
Technical Director ... Joseph Moreau
Assistant Technical Director ... Leslie Taylor

[Page 4]

Mask Design ... Marcia Duff
Roses ... Sarah Faulkner
Props Mistress ... Amy Fawcett
Sound ... Melinda Stewart
Poster Design ... Michelle Davis
Program Design ... Leslie Taylor
House Manager ... Diane Datcher
Set Crew
Rheba, Karen Bell, Kim Sammis,
Cliff Weaver, Bonnie Friedman,

Irene Mackum, Peggy Plympton
Lighting Crew
Rheba, Leslie Taylor, Kim Sammis,
Susan Costa, Mary Jess Wilson,
Amy Broaddus
Sound Crew
Ilona Pelzig
Beth Hadley
Seamstresses
Beth Wetch, Ellen Ryder, Germaine Nicoll,
Anne Wendell, Gail Chormley, Special thanks to B. Odom
Ushers
Members of Black Drama and Langston
Hughes Seminar.

Special thanks to: Margaret Lafferty,
Paul Bartsow, and the staff of Harambee House

FRAGMENT 7. *Letter to Hortense Spillers from Judith Butler, 1992. Hortense J. Spillers papers, Ms.2019.013, Box 9, Folder 28, Pembroke Center Archives, John Hay Library, Brown University.*

November 17, 1992

Professor Hortense Spillers
Department of English
Emory University
Atlanta, Georgia

Dear Professor Spillers:
I am writing on behalf of the Women's Studies program at Johns Hopkins University to invite you to give a lecture for a one-day conference, "New Directions in Black Feminist Criticism," on Friday, April 2, 1993. We plan a small conference which will feature three distinguished scholars in the field: yourself, Deborah McDowell, and Cheryl Wall. We can, of course, cover your expenses, travel and accommodation, and offer you an honorarium of $500.00. We would be pleased to hear from you on any aspect of you [*sic*] work, and would like to ask you to speak for 45–50 minutes.

I also wanted to thank you again for the trouble you took to come all the way out to California and to participate in the conference. I was sorry that my own health kept me from hanging out more, but I would love the chance to talk with you more about the kind of work you are doing. I very much appreciated your talk and have enormous respect for your contributions to literary theory. What is the chance that I can persuade you to accept this invitation? There are many of us here who are strong admirers of your work, and we would consider ourselves quite fortunate were you to accept our invitation.

You can reach me at xxx-xxx-xxxx.

Sincerely,
[handwritten signature]
Judith Butler
Professor of Humanities

FRAGMENT 8. *"In the Flesh," handwritten talk. Hortense J. Spillers papers, Ms.2019.013, Box 14, Folders 2 & 7, Pembroke Center Archives, John Hay Library, Brown University.*

Georgetown University
Friday Morning
June 20, 1986

[vertical note:] Re-translating it into an exteriority
I. Think of something <u>funny</u> to say. <u>Win</u> your audience.

But auditories of Conferences in Criticism and theory are not easily tickle. And I should know . . . and the topic that I want to invite your attention to over the next few minutes might be considered very much (and urgently)
[several lines of crossed out text]

a work in progress that addresses:

What is the topic? I. Aspects of relationships between African Am. Women's community

II. Even though my talk is entitled "In the Flesh," it is fair to say that
   I have been reading up

FRAGMENT 9. *Handwritten album list from Spillers's journal. Hortense J. Spillers papers, Ms.2019.013, Box 5, Folder 16, Pembroke Center Archives, John Hay Library, Brown University.*

Albums:
—"Songs in the Key of Life"
    Stevie Wonder—two records.
—"Respect Yourself"
    The Staple Singers
—"Reunited"
    Peaches and Herb
—"The Best of Gladys Knight and the Pips"
—Marvin Gaye "Live at the London Paladium"
    Marvin Gaye

Contributors

AMARIS DIANA BROWN is the John Holmes Assistant Professor in the Humanities in the Department of English at Tufts University. Amaris's work examines the politics of black affect in African diasporic literature and art. Her scholarship and teaching are situated at the intersections of twentieth- and twenty-first-century African American literature, black gender and sexuality, and black disability studies.

MARGO NATALIE CRAWFORD is the Edmund J. and Louise W. Kahn Professor for Faculty Excellence in the Department of English at the University of Pennsylvania. She is the chair of the Department of English. Her latest book, *What Is African American Literature?*, was published in 2021. Crawford is the author of *Black Post-Blackness: The Black Arts Movement and Twenty-First-Century Aesthetics* (2017) and *Dilution Anxiety and the Black Phallus* (2008). She is the co-editor of *New Thoughts on the Black Arts Movement* as well as *Global Black Consciousness*. Her essays appear in a wide range of books and journals, including *The Cambridge Companion to Contemporary African American Literature*, *American Literary History*, *South Atlantic Quarterly*, *Modern Drama*, *American Literature*, *The Psychic Hold of Slavery*, *The Trouble with Post-Blackness*, *The Modernist Party*, *Publishing Blackness: Textual Constructions of Race since 1850*, *The Cambridge Companion to American Poetry Post-1945*, *Want to Start a Revolution?: Radical Women in Black Freedom Struggle*, *Callaloo*, *Black Renaissance Noire*, and *Black Camera*.

THADIOUS M. DAVIS, a native of New Orleans, is the author of *Faulkner's "Negro": Art and the Southern Context* (1983), *Nella Larsen, Novelist of the Harlem Renaissance: A Woman's Life Unveiled* (1994), *Games of Property: Law, Race, Gender and Faulkner's "Go Down, Moses"* (2003), *Southscapes: Geographies of Race, Region, and Literature* (2011), and *Understanding Alice Walker* (2021). Her recent journal articles and book chapters include "Spaces of Remembering and Forgetting: On Antiracism"; "Going to Ground in Home: Toni Morrison's Mid-Century Political Modernism"; "To Breathe a Collective Air: On Edwidge Danticat"; "Imagining History: Brenda Marie Osbey and the Poetics of Imagination"; "Southern Geographies and New Negro Modernism"; "Richard Wright's Triangulated South: Formation as Preface and Prelude"; and "Writing 'the inaudible voice of it all': John Lowe's Crosscurrents."

ALEXIS PAULINE GUMBS is a queer black feminist independent scholar and an aspirational favorite cousin to everyone. Alexis is the author of several books including *Spill: Scenes of Black Feminist Fugitivity* and the biography *Survival Is a Promise: The Eternal Life of Audre Lorde*. Her book *Undrowned: Black Feminist Lessons from Marine Mammals* won the Whiting Award in Nonfiction and she is the recipient of the 2023 Windham-Campbell Prize in Poetry.

SHARON P. HOLLAND is Townsend Ludington Distinguished Professor of American Studies in the Department of American Studies at UNC Chapel Hill. She is author of *an other: a black feminist consideration of animal life* (2023). She is currently the president of the American Studies Association.

RA MALIKA IMHOTEP is a Black feminist writer, performance artist, and cultural worker from Atlanta, Georgia. They received their PhD in African diaspora studies and new media studies from the University of California Berkeley and are currently an assistant professor of International/Global African Diaspora studies at Spelman College. Their work looks at the ways Black feminine figures across the African diaspora subvert preconceived notions about black womanhood, black femininity, and labor through aesthetic practice.

DEBORAH E. MCDOWELL, a scholar of African American/American literature, is the Alice Griffin Professor of Literary Studies at the University of Virginia. In addition to her numerous pathbreaking essays, she is the author of *Leaving Pipe Shop* (1998) and *"The Changing Same": Black Women's Literature, Criticism, and Theory* (1995), and the editor of *The Punitive Turn: New Approaches to Race and Incarceration* (2013). She currently directs the Julian Bond Papers Project.

FRED MOTEN's recent projects include a poetry collection, *Perennial Fashion Presence Falling*; musical recordings and performances with bandmates Brandon López and Gerald Cleaver; collaborative research and writing of Moved by the Motion's staging of *Carmen* at the Schauspielhaus Zürich; and an essay collection, *All Incomplete*, written with longtime friend and writing partner Stefano Harney. Moten lives in New York with his comrade, Laura Harris, and their children, Lorenzo and Julian. He works in the departments of performance studies and comparative literature at New York University.

KIANA T. MURPHY is an assistant professor of American studies at Brown University. Her creative and scholarly work centers Black speculative aesthetics, Black girlhood studies, and Black women writers' archives. She is writing a monograph that centers Black women, queer, and nonbinary creators' techniques of world-building across genres. Her work is published or forthcoming in *The Black Scholar*, *American Quarterly*, and elsewhere, and has been supported by the Huntington Library; the NEH Institutes; the Center for Black, Brown, and Queer Studies (BBQ+); and The Institute for Citizens and Scholars.

KEVIN QUASHIE is Royce Family Professor of Teaching Excellence in English at Brown University. Primarily, his teaching focuses on black feminism, queer studies, and aesthetics, especially poetics. He is the author or editor of four books, most recently *The Sovereignty of Quiet: Beyond Resistance in Black Culture* (2012) and *Black Aliveness, or A Poetics of Being* (2021). *Black Aliveness* has been awarded two prizes: the James Russell Lowell Prize from the Modern Language Association (2022) and the Pegasus Award for Poetry Criticism from the Poetry Foundation (2022).

ANTHONY REED is The Norman L. and Roselea J. Goldberg Professor of Fine Arts and Professor of English at Vanderbilt University. In addition to many articles and book chapters on poetry and politics in the African diaspora, his publications include *Freedom Time: The Poetics and Politics of Black Experimental Writing*, *Soundworks: Race, Sound, and Poetry in Production*, and *Langston Hughes in Context*, co-edited with Vera M. Kutzinski.

SHONIQUA ROACH is an assistant professor of Black feminist theory and queer studies at Brandeis University. Her peer-reviewed work appears in *American Quarterly*, *boundary 2*, *differences*, *Feminist Theory*, and *Signs*, among other venues. Roach's forthcoming book, *Black Dwelling: Home-Making and Erotic Freedom*, offers an intellectual and cultural history of black domestic spaces as tragic sites of state invasion and Black feminist enactments of erotic freedom. Roach has been the recipient of a number of awards, fellowships, and grants, including those from the American Council of Learned Societies, the American Studies Association, and the Ford Foundation.

C. RILEY SNORTON is a visiting professor at Columbia University and the Mary R. Morton professor of English Language and Literature with appointments in the Department of Race, Diaspora and Indigeneity and the Center for the Study of Gender and Sexuality at the University of Chicago. He is the author of *Nobody Is Supposed to Know: Black Sexuality on the Down Low* (2014) and *Black on Both Sides: A Racial History of Trans Identity* (2017). He is currently the co-editor of *GLQ: A Journal of Gay and Lesbian Studies*.

NICOLE A. SPIGNER is an assistant professor in Black studies and English at Northwestern University. She is currently a Kaplan Humanities Center Fellow and a former Woodrow Wilson Institute Fellow (now called the Institute for Citizens & Scholars) and completed her PhD at Vanderbilt University. Her manuscript in development, tentatively entitled *Niobe Redux: Black New Women and Ovidian Transformation*, examines, through a Black Feminist lens, feminine transformation and motherhood in the works of Black New Women classicists.

www.ingramcontent.com/pod-product-compliance
Lightning Source LLC
Chambersburg PA
CBHW051208300426
44116CB00006B/474